Post-Jungian Criticism

SUNY series in Psychoanalysis and Culture

Henry Sussman, editor

Post-Jungian Criticism

Theory and Practice

⤳⤳

edited by

James S. Baumlin
Tita French Baumlin
George H. Jensen

foreword by
Andrew Samuels

STATE UNIVERSITY OF NEW YORK PRESS

Acknowledgments

Cover design by Eric Pervuhkin, whose oil painting, *Jacob Dreaming*, is reproduced courtesy of the artist. Two chapters have appeared previously in an earlier form: Sophia Andres's essay (chapter 5) elaborates upon her previous work, "Pre-Raphaelite Paintings and Jungian Images in Wilkie Collins' *The Woman in White*" (*Victorian Newsletter* 88 [1995]: 26–31), and Tita French Baumlin and James S. Baumlin's essay (chapter 6) revises their earlier piece, "'Reader, I Married Him': Archetypes of the Feminine in *Jane Eyre*" (CEA *Critic* 60 [1998]: 14–34). Also in chapter 6, William Holman Hunt's *The Light of the World* and *The Awakening Conscience* are reproduced courtesy of Foto Marburg/Art Resource and the Tate Gallery/Art Resource, respectively. In chapter 10, Eric Pervukhin's "Beat Hermit Tarot Card" is reproduced with permission of the artist, and three frames portraying Jack Kerouac's Shrouded Traveler from the documentary movie *Go Moan for Man* are reproduced with permission of Doug and Judi Sharples (© 2000 Real Films). Excerpts from Jane Hirshfield's interviews and poetry that appear in Andrew Elkins's essay (chapter 11) are reprinted with the permission of Jane Hirshfield and Wesleyan University Press (for excerpts from *Of Gravity and Angels*).

Published by
State University of New York Press, Albany

© 2004 State University of New York

All rights reserved

Printed in the United States of America

For information, address State University of New York Press,
90 State Street, Suite 700, Albany, NY 12207

Production by Christine L. Hamel
Marketing by Jennifer Giovani

Library of Congress Cataloging-in-Publication Data

Post-Jungian criticism : theory and practice / edited by James S. Baumlin, Tita French Baumlin, George H. Jensen ; foreword by Andrew Samuels.
    p. cm. — (SUNY series in psychoanalysis and culture)
Includes bibliographical references and index.
    ISBN 0-7914-5957-8 (alk. paper) — ISBN 0-7914-5958-6 (pbk. : alk. paper)
    1. Criticism. 2. Psychology and literature. I. Baumlin, James S. II. Baumlin, Tita French. III. Jensen, George H. IV. Series.

PN98.P75P64 2003
801'.95—dc21

2003052816

10 9 8 7 6 5 4 3 2 1

CONTENTS

FOREWORD

ANDREW SAMUELS

I am honored to have been asked to write this foreword, grateful to have been given a completely free hand, and responsive to the editors' invitation to range widely. I would like to focus on four specific issues, in the spirit of encouraging debate between the community of professional Jungian analysts and the academic world, and also in the hope of stirring up some disagreements and controversies among the authors of this historically significant and groundbreaking collection that seeks to establish a Jungian "track" of literary criticism on as firm a basis as other tracks, such as the many varieties of psychoanalytically derived literary criticism. It is clear that the time has come for those who have opposed the entry (or re-entry) of C. G. Jung into our universities to consider whether their opposition might be more the result of prejudice than of anything else. I write as a practicing post-Jungian analyst, in a spirit of congratulation for (and celebration of) this book, though with some mischievous intent.

I introduced the term "post-Jungian" (Samuels, *Jung and the Post-Jungians*) as a conscious imitation of the term "post-Freudian" (Brown). I was not aping terms like "postmodern" or "postcolonial," though— such is the telos of intellectual activity—those connections soon became manifest. By post-Jungian, I meant both a connection to and a critical distance from Jungian thought and practice. The idea was to create a permeable boundary around a discipline, allowing analysts and scholars to go freely on hunting expeditions to distant parts without having to worry about the gates being barred when they returned home. This present volume of essays is manifestly "post-Jungian" in this respect, and not only in its title.

My issues here are: (i) the reception of Jung and his ideas in the Western academy; (ii) the hidden and not-so-hidden politics of the evolving relationship between Jungian analysis and Jungian studies in universities; (iii) the manifold ways in which the clinical practice of analytical psychology can be enhanced by contact with academia; and (iv) the special problem of what I am going to call "the conservative academic Jungian" in relation to literary criticism.

There continues to be massive ambivalence towards Jung and his ideas in most disciplines in most universities. Many scholars report that they have to keep their Jungian proclivities secret, taking care to give camouflaged titles to lecture series and so on. In a way, universities could be seen as performing a useful function in their resistance to Jung, given the massive popular success of Jungian ideas. The cultural penetration of Jungian ideas, on the back of bestsellers such as Thomas Moore's "soul" books or Clarissa Pinkola Estes's *Women Who Run with the Wolves,* far exceeds that achieved by popularized psychoanalysis in its heyday from 1950–1970 (Tacey)

At the same time, there are equally popular (that is, in the sense of "less significant" from a scholarly point of view) criticisms. Richard Noll's *The Jung Cult* (1994), though academically slight, achieved notoriety with its claims that Jung was just a guru who achieved success by promising his followers godlike status. Similarly, those angry over Jung's intimate relationships with some female patients ignore the fact that contemporary ideas about sexual misconduct by psychotherapists had not crystallized by the first decade of the twentieth century.

But this is not to say that all criticisms of Jung are ill-founded from an intellectual standpoint. Far from it. In my travels around the world, lecturing to students of psychoanalysis and psychoanalytic studies (that is, not to students of Jung in any comprehensive sense), I ask them to join in a simple word-association experiment by associating as spontaneously as possible to the stimulus word "Jung." I have now had nine hundred individual responses to this request. By far the most common response to "Jung" is "Freud." Then there follows associations of anti-Semitism, Nazism, Germany, World War II, the 1930s. The third most common association is "mystic" (and, when unpacked, it is clear that these respondents mean "mystic" in the sense of woolly thinking, religious mania, or even psychosis). The fourth association is "archetypes." The results of this little experiment bear difficult tidings for Jungians. Imagine trying to sell a product when the main association in people's minds is to the rival product. Anti-Semitism is a matter of particular sensitivity in universities, conscious (as most academicians are) of twentieth-century history and how the Shoah and its consequences have impacted upon the world's universities. The charge of near-psychotic mysticism is not going to endear Jung to skeptical and rational academicians, either.

Now, I don't know how conscious it has been, but it is as if these seemingly intractable problems preventing the (re-)entrance of Jung into Western universities have stimulated research in precisely these areas where the case for Jung's inclusion seems weakest. We saw that "Jung" led to "Freud." In response, perhaps, there has been a growth of what has been called "the new Jung scholarship," based on the recovery of a "non-Freudocentric" reading (Taylor), which proceeds from the assumption that most of the ideas and approaches we now understand as quintessentially Jungian owe nothing at all to Freud and to Jung's relationship with him. Other influences (Theodore Flournoy and William James, for example) receive more careful consideration than hitherto and Jung's pre-Freud texts—for example, his student fraternity Zofingia Lectures of 1895 (*CW* Supplementary Vol. A)—are given greater prominence than in the perspective that sees Jung primarily as Freud's gifted critic and his most important dissident or schismatic.

Regarding Jung's anti-Semitism, my own work (*Political Psyche*; see also Maidenbaum and Martin) was written in response to the fact that senior members of the Jungian community had signally failed to take the lead in mounting an open, empathic, and scholarly response to such well-founded allegations. Succinctly, I believe that Jung's work was indeed anti-Semitic but that, if one tries to understand what he was attempting (albeit with disastrous results), other evaluations become possible. Jung was trying to create a culturally sensitive "psychology of difference," in which there would be no totalizing or universal discourse about how humans operate psychologically. Rather, Jung thought that Freud was trying to level out all psychological differences among groups by producing just such a discourse with a claim for universal and time-less applicability. Now, if Jung had gone on with this in a more sober manner, basing his claim on differences of culture and experience (rather than on something more literal, sometimes even on "blood"), he might well be hailed today as the pioneer of current attempts to create a tran-scultural or intercultural psychology and psychotherapy, something much needed in a world torn by ethnic, religious, and national strife.

Unhappily, instead, Jung based his approach on an assemblage of paired complementary qualities arranged in lists organized on the basis of "opposites." So, if Germans are earthy and emotional, Jews have to be presented as urban and rationalistic. If Germans have all the advan-tages of a young culture, then Jews have all the disadvantages of an old culture. If Germans have physical strength (like men), then Jews have to be devious to gain power over them (like women). When people adopt Jung's approach to "opposites," they should recall where that way of thinking can lead. And the main intellectual (as opposed to cultural or political) objection to Jung's theorizing about gender is also that it is much too dependent on "opposites" (Samuels, *Plural Psyche; Political Psyche; Politics on the Couch*).

So, Jung opened something up and then blew the opportunity to make something constructive and humane out of it, leading to the quite understandable charge of anti-Semitism. The task for contemporary Jungian analysts and scholars is to engage openly in debates about such matters and to work out a firm ethical foundation for Jung's "psychology of difference," so that we shall no longer feel the need to throw the baby out with the bath water.

The third association is that Jung was a mystic, with nothing nice being meant by that. The response has been an enormous body of work by Jungians on the psychology of religion in general and on mysticism and gnosticism in particular. I think that this work has been underpinned and informed by what Jung wrote in 1911 to 1912 on "two kinds of thinking" (*CW* 5, 7–33). There he said that, in addition to "directed thinking" (meaning thinking in words), there was something to be called "undirected thinking," meaning thinking in images, fantasy thinking, intuitive thinking. It is noteworthy that Jung called both "thinking," thereby anticipating the British psychoanalyst Wilfred Bion by many years. The relevance for our discussion of "mysticism" is that Jung can be reframed as a pioneer in a huge epistemological shift that has taken place in the West in the past hundred years. It is a shift with which universities are slowly coming to terms. Knowledge used to be legitimized from two distinct sources: information claims and authority. The third leg that has been added in the past fifty years or so is *experience*. This is why so many academic discourses now use notions of "story"—because notions of narrative truth (as opposed to historical truth) require a repositioning of "subjectivity," not as a handicap to be pruned or eliminated but as a new fount of knowledge. This is not the place to go further into developments in such areas as "tacit knowledge" or "soft knowledge" or (an unfortunate phrase) the "feminization of science," but they feed off the same shift in consciousness that Jung was pioneering with his "undirected thinking." Hence, what a mystic has to say can be taken more seriously these days by those whose mind-set remains strictly that of the Enlightenment.

The fourth association was to archetypes, and there has been a huge growth in the ways the theoretical concept of the archetype can be understood. We could begin with brain research, since current neuroscientific research on linkages between emotional experience and brain development cries out for a psychsomatic construct like the archetype. Then there are child developmental studies showing how there is a self in the baby that unfolds or unpacks over time (Fordham). This primary or original self contains "everything" (except the environment!) that the baby needs to grow and, in its organismic wholeness, bears a morphological similarity to the later and more archetypal version of the self that Jung developed—which includes everything (physical, mental, spiritual, social) to do with the subject. Finally, there is a total rethinking of archetypal theory in terms of affects that is gathering momentum (which I will discuss below).

Perhaps the main problem for academicians in the humanities has been their perception of Jung's (and hence Jungians') essentialism, foundationalism, and even fundamentalism. Often this comes up in relation to gender, though that is not the only topic so criticized. Jungians and post-Jungians are perceived as over-formalized, with our neat little quartets of archetypes and our oh so carefully balanced structures of the psyche, too definitional given the misuse of the theory of "opposites" that I described earlier, too backward-looking and even reactionary when treating of cultural values and politics. It is said (rightly) that there is a massive Eurocentrism in Jungian explorations of non-Western cultures, including the demeaning idealization of traditional cultures as "primitive." Some scholars would argue that an interest in mythology and the possession of right-wing political viewpoints often seem to go together (see Ellwood).

I turn now to the hidden and not-so-hidden politics of the relationship between Jungian analysis and Jungian studies in universities. I know from personal contact with several contributors to the present collection that this is by no means an irrelevant or peripheral issue. There would be little point in working on the relations between Jungian-oriented academicians and the wider intellectual world if we do not also consider relations within the Jungian communities. Let me begin by saying that the psychological leitmotif of this working-out of a new set of relations between clinicians and scholars is, of course, a massive and mutual projection. There are no prizes for such an obvious and global analysis. If the problem is projection, the prize is legitimacy. By legitimacy, I mean something quite precise: authority, power, influence (with their economic sequelae), and the whole paraphernalia of a top-dog/bottom-dog dynamic. In any struggle over legitimacy, each side will seek to characterize the other side in ways that enhance its own strengths.

Sometimes, certain analysts say that academicians cannot really feel or suffer complex emotions because of their precocious intellectual development, which vitiates empathy and sensitivity. As this character assassination of the typical academician continues, she or he cannot really understand most of the concepts derived from Jungian psychology, because their provenance, and certainly their utility, are matters on which only practicing clinicians can rule. No matter how subtle the theorizing of academic research may be as a therapeutic or analytical activity involving transference and countertransference, to rip all these ideas from their clinical setting is to do violence to them, and their subsequent deployment is likely to be misguided at best. Some analysts say that, because these are not really concepts but psychic images, they only respond to a certain kind of knowing or gnosis that is not usually found in universities.

So pervasive is this contemporary continuation of Jung's oft-repeated distrust of intellectuals that it creeps in even where unintended. Consider this extract from an intelligent and positive review of Christopher Hauke's *Jung and the Postmodern*. The reviewer is not intending anything nasty by what she says; it simply follows from her immersion within the political intricacies of the relationship between the Jungian analysts and the Jungian scholars.

> Hauke's intention to find a broad-market readership can make the text seem at times a bit too wide-ranging in content for my taste and it loses its focus because of this. I preferred the chapters that had more relevance to my work in the consulting room, aware that, for me, analysis is more about "affairs of the heart" than "affairs of the head." His book will, I feel sure, find a secure place as a standard text in many academic courses, and not just Jungian and psychoanalytic studies. As he makes no reference in his personal biography to his clinical training at the Society of Analytical Psychology, I imagine that Hauke considers himself first and foremost a scholar and an academician, rather than a clinician. Indeed, his book is a testament to his considerable intellectual abilities. (Wiener 120–21)

I said that the projections were two-way, and they are. Sometimes, certain academicians point out that many analysts do not think systematically or even rationally. Academicians tend to assert things rather than argue them through, and they have no grasp at all of the need for methodology. The analysts misuse their authority as the keepers of Jung's flame to exclude the great unwashed, and they show every sign of attempting either to control or to disparage the growth of Jungian studies (and the application of Jungian concepts to other disciplines in universities) so as to preserve their privileged position. The main research tool of the analysts—the case study—just does not pass muster. When Jungian analysts attempt to enter other fields, their lack of up-to-date knowledge is quite startling; so, what they have to say—about literature, anthropology, politics, popular culture, and so on—is intellectually second-rate. Some academicians who have had close encounters with the world of Jungian analysis point to its abuses of power, both in terms of how its organizations and institutions function and in the treatment situation itself. There is a good deal of anecdotal evidence that analytical admissions committees make life extremely difficult for professors who seek to train as analysts.

What can be done about this state of affairs? To a certain extent, there is nothing much that can be done, except to acknowledge the existence of struggles over legitimacy and publicly commit to do whatever is possible to diminish their intensity and prevalence. Still, as a proactive attempt to heal such divisions, those who teach Jungian ideas in universities might try to introduce experientially driven approaches to learning. For example, in the Master's program in Jungian and Post-Jungian Studies that I direct at the University of Essex, the students write a learning journal that brings an affective/experiential dimension into their research. The students write self-reflexively about what it has been like to study such-and-such a concept, topic, or theme. Similar moves include the use of arts-based approaches in conceptual learning, bringing the imagination in as a support for, and not in opposition to, cognitive learning.

The last section of this foreword raises a ticklish problem—that of the conservative Jungian academician who, it could be argued, has not kept up with developments in analytical psychology or (so it can seem) uses these ideas in mechanical, desiccated, or plainly wrong-headed ways, ignoring problems with the ideas that have been known about for a long time. From this depiction, it can be seen that, by "conservative," I mean dyed-in-the-wool, traditional, and old-fashioned, rather than committed to preserving something good from thoughtless change. Now, these remarks are not aimed at essays in this collection; this is not a review. Nevertheless, I would not feel comfortable if I did not mention the problem. Please note that I am not saying that new thinking, "post-Jungian" thinking if you like, comes only from the analysts. Quite the opposite. But the problem then becomes why some Jungian-oriented academicians are ignorant of the revisionary and post-Jungian work done by others of their number.

This conservatism can lead to the embarrassingly simplistic deployment of ideas. In a novel or play, any woman important to a man at a deep level is his anima. Any piece of controlled self-presentation to the world is the persona. Opposites abound, mandalas are sought for, tricksters found out, heroes and heroines spotted on their journeys. Now it might seem churlish to mention this, but something has to be done about it or these incredibly promising developments in many areas, not just literary studies, will diminish, and without really fulfilling their potential. The way the concepts are utilized is often in too stately or static a manner, laid over and across the (literary) material. Violence is done to Jungian context and literary text alike.

Let me give one illustration of what I am talking about, taken from a conference that I recently attended, which included a marvelous panel on film studies. The panelists referred to "archetypal figures" or to characters in films as being "archetypal." These were usually larger-than-life or stereotypical characters. Everyone could see why they were being called "archetypal," but it was more difficult to discern what was gained by the designation. It might have been that the character was regarded as a timeless and placeless expression of something universal, hence capable of exciting a universal response (an argument undermined by the dominance of Hollywood in many film vocabularies). But is this all there is to the archetypal dimension of experience—something more or less synonymous with stereotype? In post-Jungian analytical psychology, the view is gaining ground that what is archetypal is not to be found in any particular image or list of images that can be tagged as anima, trickster, hero, shadow, and so on. Rather, it is in the *intensity of affective response* to any given image or situation that we find what is archetypal. This can be something very *small scale*, not coming in a pre-packaged archetypal or mythic form. What stirs you at an archetypal level depends on you and where you sit and how you look at things and on your personal history. The archetypal can therefore be *relative, contextual, and personal*. This reframing of archetypal theory as a theory of affects is something that has not yet reached conservative academic Jungians.

When concluding salutary pieces like this, it is customary to end with a quote from Jung, usually done to improve the writer's chances of winning his or her audience. Hence the writer chooses a bit of Jung that he or she likes. Perversely, perhaps, but also (as can be seen) necessarily, I want to end with a bit of Jung that I do not like and that I see as a spur to all of us involved with taking Jungian ideas into our academic fields. In his memorial piece for Richard Wilhelm, written in 1930, Jung wrote:

> As a doctor who deals with ordinary people, I know that universities have ceased to act as disseminators of light. People are weary of scientific specialisation and rationalism and intellectualism. They want to hear truths that broaden rather than restrict, that do not obscure but enlighten, that do not run off them like water but penetrate them to the marrow. (CW 15: 58)

A book like this one can establish something quite the opposite: that academic literary studies, in an alliance with analytical psychology, can broaden, enlighten, and penetrate people to the marrow. In short, a book like this proves Professor Jung wrong.

LONDON, JULY 2002

WORKS CITED

Brown, J. A. C. *Freud and the Post-Freudians.* Harmondsworth: Penguin, 1961.

Ellwood, Robert S. *The Politics of Myth: A Study of C. G. Jung, Mircea Eliade and Joseph Campbell.* Albany: State U of New York P, 1999.

Fordham, Michael. *Children as Individuals.* London: Hodder, 1969.

Hauke, Christopher. *Jung and the Postmodern: The Interpretation of Realities.* London: Routledge, 2000.

Jung, C. G. *The Collected Works of C. G. Jung.* Ed. Sir Herbert Read, Michael Fordham, and Gerhard Adler. Trans. R. F. C. Hull. 20 vols. Princeton: Princeton UP, 1953–91.

Maidenbaum, Aryeh, and Stephen H. Martin, eds. *Lingering Shadows: Jungians, Freudians and Anti-Semitism.* Boston: Shambhala, 1991.

Noll, Richard. *The Jung Cult: Origins of a Charismatic Movement.* Princeton: Princeton UP, 1994.

Samuels, Andrew. *Jung and the Post-Jungians.* London: Routledge, 1985.

——— . *The Plural Psyche: Personality, Morality, and the Father.* London: Routledge, 1989.

——— . *The Political Psyche.* London: Routledge, 1993.

——— . *Politics on the Couch: Citizenship and the Internal Life.* New York: Other, 2001.

Taylor, E. "The New Jung Scholarship." *Psychoanalytic Review* 83.4 (1996): 547–68.

Tacey, David J. *Jung and the New Age.* London: Routledge, 2001.

Wiener, J. Review of Christopher Hauke's *Jung and the Postmodern. Psychoanalysis and History* 3.1 (2001): 117–21.

Introduction

Situating Jung in Contemporary Critical Theory

GEORGE H. JENSEN

> In all areas of production, from the Middle Ages until the
> beginning of the nineteenth century, the development of tech-
> nology proceeded at a much slower rate than the develop-
> ment of art. Art could take its time in variously assimilating
> the technological modes of operation. But the transformation
> of things that set in around 1800 dictated the tempo to art,
> and the more breathtaking this tempo became, the more read-
> ily the dominion of fashion overspread all fields.
> —Walter Benjamin, *The Arcades Project*

The present place of Jungian theory and archetypal criticism in the
academy can hardly be sketched without mention of fad and fashion.
From the introduction of Jung's theory of the collective unconscious
and archetypes, authors were drawn to its rich, varied symbolism and
critics to the power of its hermeneutics. From the publication of Frye's
Anatomy of Criticism in 1957 to the first murmurs of postmodernism
and poststructuralism in the early 1970s, archetypal criticism was one
of the most frequently discussed theories in literature classes.[1] While
failing to eclipse New Criticism, it certainly rivaled psychoanalytic and
Marxist criticism. In the current state of critical theory, a terrain where
undergraduates typically learn more theory than graduate students of a

generation past, theorists rise to superstardom and then are attacked from all sides, and new theories emerge at what seems to be a dizzying tempo; it is difficult to appreciate Frye's prominence and the one-time stamina of archetypal criticism. And yet, now, Frye is rarely read and archetypal criticism seems to have lost its glitter.

Perhaps so. It is out of fashion, yet still present. While archetypal criticism might not appear on the pages of *Diacritics* or *New Criterion*, might not announce itself in the subtitles of recent studies of prominent authors, an enormous volume of work appears each year. Intriguingly, even works that do not claim to practice archetypal criticism still employ Jungian terminology (archetype, persona, anima, animus, shadow) or a transparent paraphrase (recurrent patterns, mythic motifs, the evil twin, or the feminine side of a male). How can we explain this apparent contradiction, where archetypal criticism is passe *and* unavoidable?

WAYS OF READING, MISREADING, AND NOT READING JUNG

A partial answer is to understand how Jung is read and not read. We might begin with a comparison to readings of Freud. Most scholars would agree that the inclusion of a traditional reading of Freud's work in the current climate of poststructuralism and postmodernism is problematic: He embraced positivism (for example, see Freud *Standard Edition* 1: 283–346). His model might be described as intra-personal, rationalist, and even mechanistic (Volosinov 80). His focus on sexuality is often considered reductive, aspects of his work are sexist (Jacoby 62), and his abandoning of the seduction theory raises questions about his character (see Crews, Masson, and Mahony). Yet, scholars like Lacan, Kristeva, and Rorty still read Freud with a hermeneutic of faith, selecting passages or themes and reworking them into robust theories. In contrast, too many academics read only segments of Jung's works, find a few passages they cannot accept and dismiss his entire model of the psyche, which is arguably far more comprehensive than Freud's.[2]

Those who have read about Jung in a psychology textbook, sampled *The Portable Jung*, or know of Jung only through the academic equivalent of gossip, might describe him in a number of unflattering ways. He was the cognitivist who studied memory,[3] the structuralist who wrote about transcultural archetypes or developed a taxonomy of types (Baird 45), the liberal humanist who studied alchemy (Rowland 4), the Kantian phenomenologist who studied categories of mind, or the modernist who attempted to establish the mind as a foundation for knowledge (Rowland 5). When we look to the man, and not to his *Collected*

Works,[4] we find him described as a cult leader among the theosophists, a follower of the "volkisch" movement in Germany, or the flake who wrote about parapsychology and presaged the New Age movement (Noll passim). We even find charges of sexism and anti-Semitism.[5]

We could add other views of Jung, those frequently cited by scholars who read deeper into his works. He was a skeptic—open-minded yet not naive—who felt that there might be a psychological truth in occultism, alchemy, or UFOs. He was an early critic of positivism[6] who felt that psychology must address the spiritual (Eliade 14). He was the first psychologist to conceptualize development throughout all the stages of life, a process he called individuation (Homans 24). He was a fluid thinker who discussed the importance of moving beyond the limitations of gender roles and developed a taxonomy of type differences that unravels and reforms.[7] He understood social constructionism.[8] He made contributions to feminism.[9] He was a poststructuralist who wrote under erasure (Rowland 19, 21, 190; see also Rowland in this volume).[10] He developed an interpersonal psychology that accounts for the Other (Rowland 23). He was a hermeneut who worked out striking interpretations of texts (Rowland 22; Jensen, *Identities*). He was a political theorist who analyzed propaganda and mass psychology. He was a postmodernist who wrote of the multiplicity of self.[11] He might even be viewed as a post-postmodernist who anticipated postmodernism and moved beyond it by giving "equal weight to the multiplicity *and* to the unity of personality" (A. Samuels, *Plural Psyche* 22).[12]

We might never be able to find the real Jung or agree upon the definitive texts or reduce the heterogenous interpretations of his texts, but we can certainly discuss how Jung is read and misread and how Jung might be read. Certainly, one purpose of this volume is to present other ways of reading Jung.

Those who have thoroughly and intently read Jung will want to argue with passages. They will also, no doubt, find enormous potential that needs to be reworked and updated, as long as they approach Jung's texts with an open mind. Pratt, in her feminist rereading of Jung, Frye, and Lévi-Strauss, calls this "spinning among fields." She explains:

> I once watched with puzzlement as a group of French feminists happily debated the use of Freudian thought for feminist literary theory. I wondered how could they justify themselves as feminists? "We just play upon the two meanings of the verb *voler*," they reassured me. "In French it means both to steal—as in rob, fleece, plunder—and to fly away, take wing, to soar. We intend to fly away with those Freudian methods useful to our feminist purposes, and to leave the rest behind."
> ("Spinning among Fields" 94)

Readers will see something like Pratt's method at work in this volume, as authors avoid falling "into the trap of 'methodolatry'" (Pratt, "Spinning among Fields" 93) and rework or deconstruct Jung's theory, often by drawing in other theorists. Authors will take what they find "useful" and "leave the rest behind," an advisable strategy when approaching any modernist theory, given that the unconscious foundation of modernism is arguably racism, colonialism, and anti-Semitism.[13] While the theories of both Freud and Jung are certainly flawed by what modernism—our historical conscious—has repressed, their theories would also suggest that the conscious can be transformed by entering into a dialogue with the unconscious. This, too, is one of the purposes of this volume.

THE UNCONSCIOUS

Certainly, the most important concept to any form of depth psychology is the realm of the unconscious and its relation to the conscious. Although the unconscious is widely accepted, even in mass media, many of the cognitivists who currently dominate psychology departments in the United States believe that the unconscious does not exist. If the unconscious is viewed from a reductive Freudian model (as opposed to the Freudian model reworked by Lacan or Kristeva), the position of cognitivists is understandable.

Early in his career, Freud's descriptions of the unconscious and how it functioned seem mechanistic. He wrote of a monitor that (or should we use "who" here?) sorted thoughts or memories into two basic categories: those that might mesh with the individual's conscious life and those that must be repressed into the unconscious. In *Freudianism,* a Marxist critique of Freud's theory that is surprisingly (maybe disturbingly) similar to critiques offered by American cognitivists, Volosinov argues that Freud's concept of the unconscious does not really describe an unconscious because it is as rational as his concept of the conscious (85). More recently, the unconscious has been questioned because of its role in "recovered memories." The "accuracy" of memories that are recovered during therapy, some of which then become testimony in court cases, has rightly been questioned, especially when one considers that these memories emerge during a therapeutic dialogue.

To accept any "recovered" memory, we seem forced to move through a series of contradictions relating to the act of repression. How can an individual remember and forget at the same time? How can a boundary exist between the conscious and unconscious that is not really a boundary? In "The Transcendent Function," we find a hint of how Jung might answer these questions: "Consciousness, because of its directed functions, exercises an inhibition (which Freud calls censorship) on all incompatible material, with the result that it sinks into the unconscious" (*CW* 8: 69). Directed thinking, for Jung, is thinking in language, and so thinking in a culture and its ideology. Jung calls it an adaptive form of thinking, but it is also how we remember/forget. We "remember" (hold our past life together) by rehearsing it in language, by telling stories to ourselves and others. Stories, however, can cause us to "forget": "That didn't really happen," "I had a wonderful childhood," or, "I was a perfect parent." Individuals might also construct a story of silence. These stories are part of and sustained by larger narratives, the stories of our family or the stories of our culture. This is how we use language to "forget."

Despite our forgetting in stories, our prohibitions against speaking, our body may still react as if it remembers everything. A victim of physical abuse, who does not "consciously" remember the event, who does not, that is, speak of the event, may still cringe when somebody nearby scratches his or her head. Persons who have "repressed" painful events have feelings, physical reactions, visual flashes (bodily kinds of memory) that do not fit easily into their personal narratives or the narratives they hear spoken by those around them. When analysands begin to "remember" the "repressed," they may abreact, re-experience the event, perhaps triggered by dialogue with an analyst or a complex of signs in the environment. But to process the bodily remembering, work through it emotionally, analysands must translate it into language. Once we begin to bring these bodily forms of memory into language, we are constructing a narrative, transforming an identity, interpreting the body, often in dialogue with another. So there is some reason to be cautious about equating the narrative of a recovered memory with the historical event, even as we acknowledge that the analysand never completely forgot (see MacCurdy).

For Jung, we are somewhat aware of the material in the unconscious as the "boundary" between the conscious and the unconscious often dissolves in the disjunctions and gaps of our narratives. Because we live in language (as social constructionists argue) *and* beyond language (a point social constructionists rarely address), it is possible simultaneously to remember and forget. The very stories that we tell, our denials that anything actually happened, would not even be told if we did not remember, at some level, the event that we are trying to erase. The unconscious, in Jung's system, is not a location and repression is not a mechanism carried out by a censor somewhere (who

6 George H. Jensen

knows where?) in the psyche. Typical of the fluidity of Jung's thought, the unconscious is separated from the conscious only by a thin "boundary" of language and repression is ultimately a social act.

THE COLLECTIVE UNCONSCIOUS AND ARCHETYPES

It is interesting that even those who accept a rather mechanistic version of the unconscious often question the idea of a *collective* unconscious. To understand why so many find the collective unconscious and archetypes problematic, we should begin with what they believe Jung wrote. The common (mis)understanding of Jung's theory is that archetypes are universal images that are passed on genetically and stored in an area of the brain called the collective unconscious. A host of questions arise at this point that, even in the asking, indicate the categories of archetype and collective unconscious have already been reified: Can any image be universal? Can images be passed on genetically? Is there an area of the brain that could serve as the collective unconscious? Another reaction to this (mis)understanding of Jung's theory is to dismiss it without any thought at all, a gut response that this theory conflicts with fundamental—perhaps, even unspoken—beliefs: *Animal behavior is ruled by instincts and drives, but humans learn and change. Animals do not really feel. Animals do not solve problems. Humans are the products of language, history, culture.* When we bring these beliefs to the surface, when we reflect on how our language, history, and culture have shaped our thoughts, we might consider these questions and these beliefs to be an odd endorsement of a Cartesian split between mind and body or animals and humans.

Of course, we could avoid such problems by bracketing the collective unconscious. In *Anatomy of Criticism* (1957) Frye chooses to "not speak" of the collective unconscious as the source of archetypes. Instead, he emphasizes the literary tradition: "Poetry can only be made out of other poems; novels out of other novels" (97).[14] For him, an archetype is a "recurring image" or a "social fact" that "helps to unify and integrate our literary experience" (99).[15] In contrast, Hillman, who founded the school of archetypal psychology with the publication of *Re-Visioning Psychology* in 1975, brackets the collective unconscious by emphasizing the subject. For Hillman, an archetype—a term that he prefers to avoid—is not so much an archetype either because it emerges from the collective unconscious or because it is a "social fact" in the literary tradition; rather, Hillman argues that we experience the "archetypal"—his preferred term—because we view it archetypally ("Inquiry into Image").

Jung might say that Frye's approach is extraverted, and Hillman's is introverted. He might add that they both fail to explain the power of archetypes, which comes from a momentary unity of outer and inner, material reality and perception, culture and body, history and experience. As Erich Neumann says, archetypes are powerful because they represent a "unitary reality." The material world, culture, being, meaning all become "transparent" (174–75).

But perhaps we need not dance around the collective unconscious. What Jung actually wrote is not so problematic. He wrote that archetypes are ideas *in potential* that are fully realized only once they have emerged and taken on the content of a particular culture and historical epoch.[16] The influence of culture on archetypes, Jung says, is so great that the spirit archetype as it manifests itself in France cannot be substituted for the same archetype as it manifests itself in India. We cannot adopt the archetypes of another culture in the same way that we put on a new suit of clothes: "If we now try to cover our nakedness with the gorgeous trappings of the East, . . . we would be playing our own history false" (*CW* 9.1: 14). Archetypes develop historically and they can only be interpreted historically:

> The forms we use for assigning meaning are historical categories that reach back into the mists of time—a fact we do not take sufficiently into account. Interpretations make use of certain linguistic matrices that are themselves derived from primordial images. From whatever side we approach this question, everywhere we find ourselves confronted with the history of language, with images and motifs that lead straight back to the primitive wonder-world. (*CW* 9.1: 32–33)

Contrary to essentialist views of his theory, Jung argues that our knowledge of archetypes is anything but pure. Archetypes, which Jung says evolve over time, are constantly being transformed and reinterpreted by the individual's consciousness, and they are inseparable from language, history, and culture.

Rather than conceive of archetypes as fixed for millennia, it is perhaps much more appropriate to think that history is to archetypes as jazz is to melody. We might think that we know the melody to "Stormy Weather" or some other standard until a remarkable jazz artist transforms it. Indeed, one might even argue that what jazz has really taught us is that we can never know the melody; we can, however, be surprised. We can be repeatedly and endlessly surprised.

Certainly, it is female archetypes that are most in need of exploration. Jung himself encouraged Toni Wolff, Marie-Louise von Franz, and his wife in this task. More recently, in her study of mythic patterns

in novels authored by women, Pratt writes of the female imagination—
which is "not escapist but strategic"—as it rediscovers a means of transformation that patriarchy pushes into the unconscious:

> [F]or three centuries women novelists have been gathering around
> campfires where they have warned us with tales of patriarchal horror
> and encouraged us with stories of heroes undertaking quests that we
> may emulate. They have given us maps of the patriarchal battlefield
> and of the landscape of our ruined culture, and they have resurrected
> for our use codes and symbols of our potential power. . . . They have
> dug the goddess out of the ruins and cleansed the debris from her face,
> casting aside the gynophobic masks that have obscured her beauty, her
> power, and her benefice. (*Archetypal Patterns* 375)

Pratt and other scholars rightly demonstrate that archetypes are primordial and ever new (see also Elias-Button). Artists, often in consort
with scholars, rework archetypes of a previous age and discover archetypes that can only emerge in a new age (Neumann 90).

Unlike most theories of symbols or signs, however, Jung's theory
explains why archetypes carry such enduring power: although they are
a part of a cultural tradition, they are more than merely cultural creations. When archetypes function as cultural signs, they are meaningful because they connect with the archetype (as part of our heritage)
that remains within (Jung, *CW* 12: 11). This statement will not surprise those who have read Jung's essays—read *essays* in the sense of
"tries" or "attempts" here—to explain archetypes, but I would like to
suggest that everything we need to know about archetypes and the collective unconscious is in a simple poetic phrase, a style rare in Jung's
works: "Hunger makes food into gods" (8: 155). Let us unpack this
metaphor and see where it leads. For *hunger,* we could substitute the
body in the broadest possible sense, not as reduced to biology or
genetics.[17] For *food,* we can substitute the body's relation to its context. Any human who is denied food will experience hunger, which is
an emotion, what Jung calls a "feeling-toned" instinct. But would it be
accurate to say that we inherit hunger or that emotions are genetic?
Not entirely. These emerge as the body *lives* in its material context.[18]
However, once we do experience something like hunger, we make
some *food* into *gods* or archetypes, a transaction that occurs within a
historical and cultural context. As we follow this explanation of the
development of an archetype, we can see how it can be both universal
(emerging from hunger, the body) and variable (contingent on the
material, historical, and cultural context).[19] And, equally important,
we can understand why archetypes are so powerful. They do not sim-

ply come to us as socially constructed symbols from outside; they also connect with some emotionally charged aspect of our body. Indeed, when we experience the archetypal, there is no inner and outer or split between mind and history (Samuels, *Plural Psyche* 27). As Neumann writes, we experience "a unitary image" of the "unitary world" (173). Jungian criticism that ignores history is not very Jungian (for an example of the blending of archetypes and history, see Emma Jung and von Franz's *The Grail Legend*).

Jung's theory of archetypes, I have been arguing, needs to be viewed more fluidly, and Jung's emphasis on history, language, and culture needs to be acknowledged. We also need to recognize that Jung developed a model of the psyche that was dynamic and holistic, perhaps an unacknowledged debt to Hegel (see Kelley; Jensen, *Identities*). Jung wanted to embrace positions that, in current academic debates, are often considered irreconcilable: cognition and social construction, structure and history, mind and body, stability and fragmentation, idealism and materialism, form and culture. If we apply his theory of archetypes apart from the rest of his model, then we cannot appreciate its power. I will, in the remainder of this introduction, cover other aspects of Jung's work.

EGO

The ego, in most models of the psyche, is viewed as the core of the personality, the realm of consciousness and rationality, a "mechanism" for controlling instincts and bringing order to consciousness. In Jung's system, which is (as I have been arguing) closer to postmodern views of identity than is widely acknowledged, even the ego is fragmented. In *Mysterium Coniunctionis,* perhaps the most neglected of his works, Jung writes:

> The ego, ostensibly the thing we know the most about, is in fact a highly complex affair full of unfathomable obscurities. Indeed, one could even define it as a *relatively constant personification of the unconscious itself,* or as the Schopenhauerian mirror in which the unconscious becomes aware of its own face. (CW 14: 107; emphasis added)

Here, Jung hardly seems a structuralist. He does not seem to seek an orderly grammar beneath a random ego; rather, he looks to the ego, often considered the agent of order, and finds "unfathomable obscurities."

If we wish to consider Jung a phenomenologist, we could use this passage to discuss how he viewed the ego as the fragmented, disjointed perceptions of the thinking subject. If, however, we consider Jung a social constructionist, then we might find an ego that is created through language and signs:

> By ego I understood a complex of ideas which constitutes the centre of my field of consciousness and appears to possess a high degree of continuity and identity. Hence I also speak of an *ego-complex*. The ego-complex is as much a content as a condition of *consciousness,* for a psychic element is conscious to me only in so far as it is related to my ego-complex. (CW 6: 425; emphasis in original)

In this passage, Jung seems to be both a phenomenologist and a social constructionist. Jung writes of the ego as subject, the perceiving consciousness, which is highly fragmented, *and* the ego as object (a "complex of ideas which constitutes the centre of my field of consciousness"), the semiotic core of identity, the socially constructed "I" that brings, in moments of reflection, a bit of continuity to the chaos and multiplicity of the much broader concept, the self. Although the ego as object (one aspect of an individual's identity) is closely associated in healthy individuals with the persona (I am a banker, I play golf, I am a Buddhist, and so on) and is bolstered by a complex of signs (the clothes one wears, the way one decorates an office, the car one drives, and so on), its "content" may also be formed through negation, as a reaction to ideology. In more healthy individuals, the negations might result in an acceptance of the ways in which they do not fulfill some social expectations (e.g., gender roles, class status, and so on) or the formation of values that are at odds with the widely embraced ideologies (I do not hunt, I am a woman who likes football, I do not need a fancy car, and so on). For less healthy individuals, the negation may take the form of shame or guilt. The ego as object, the "complex of ideas" that we reflect upon, does provide some stability for the self in that it becomes a guide for action (it can be a foundation for resisting the push to conform to social norms even as it can be a foundation to which others appeal in their efforts to produce conformity), and it is this ego that dissolves and reforms during periods of developmental changes, such as midlife transition. In this sense, the ego—one might add, Jung's entire theory—is further relativized by the process of individuation, which Rowland calls "a deconstructive process, privileging the ungraspable unconscious over the limitations of the ego as it continually reshapes identity and perceptions of reality" (11).

Jung's ego, its fragmentation, indeterminancy, and instability, certainly sounds postmodern, that is, *if* postmodernists discussed anything like an ego. In the postmodern textual landscape, we tend to find personae that are not connected to authors and interpretations that are not connected to readers. Barthes says that intertextuality kills off authors, and Derrida says that the author is not a unified subject who can leave a "signature" on a text. Texts are disjointed webs of signifiers, which are tied to other texts but not so much to the material world. Postmodern critics demonstrate the fragmentation of texts, but they suggest—in an intriguing parallel to New Criticism—that their interpretations are in the text rather than emerging from the identity of readers. If Jung were responding to these developments in critical theory, he might say that the author can leave a recognizable "trace" in a text, which is not unified but nonetheless has a sense of shape, a dominant. The "trace" of the author in the text comes, in part, from the author's ego as subject, the author's perceptual tendencies, which might incompletely be described as the author's psychological type. As a reader encounters this "trace" in the text, he or she either identifies with it (saying, in short, "I am like this author") or fails to identify with it (saying, "I am not like this author"). The "I" of this transaction is the reader's ego as object, the socially constructed sense of self. This initial encounter with the text— an interpretation, actually an act of identification—can only be adequately explained if we employ a complex notion of the ego (Jensen, *Identities* 177–207).

The role of the ego in the interpretation of archetypes should also be acknowledged, for the ego can explain how archetypes change historically. Certainly, generations of artists rework archetypes, bring them into new historical eras, transforming them as culture shifts. Archetypes are even more protean once we look to the act of interpretation, for we even interpret archetypes through other archetypes. Here, we might draw from Peirce's theory of semiotics. Peirce believed, in short, that signs are related to other signs—and so have a social force of their own. Yet they are also interpreted and these interpretations become new signs, which are then also interpreted. Within a broader culture, interpretations continuously reshape signs. Similar to Peirce in his theory of semiotics, Jung emphasizes that archetypes have their own force, but they are also reinterpreted, a process that is both dialectical and dialogic (CW 9, 1: 40–41).

PERSONA

The persona, a concept Jung developed from his studies in anthropology, is a psychological mask, "the individual's system of adaptation to, or the manner he assumes in dealing with, the world" (CW 9.1: 122). It is in

his descriptions of the persona that Jung seems most clearly a social constructionist, for the persona is a social and historical role that is interpersonal and collective, not individualistic. Jung writes:

> The office I hold is certainly my special activity; but it is also a *collec-*
> *tive factor* that has come into existence *historically through the coop-*
> *eration of many people* and whose dignity rests solely on *collective*
> *approval.* When, therefore, I identity myself with my office or title, I
> behave as though I myself were the whole complex of social factors of
> which that office consists, or as though I were not only the bearer of
> the office, but also at the same time the approval of society. I have
> made an extraordinary *extension of myself and have usurped qualities*
> *which are not in me but outside me.* (CW 7: 143; emphasis added)

The persona's power comes from its ability to erase the shortcomings of
the self, at least temporarily, as the individual becomes absorbed into the
social role.[20] When acting out of the persona, we actually believe that we
are competent adults, far removed from the doubts that make us feel,
despite our age, yet little children. As Morse Peckham wrote in an essay
on Browning's use of dramatic personae in his dramatic monologues:
"Somehow, somewhere, Browning discovered that men wear masks not
merely to conceal their true characters from the world but for better reason, to conceal their true characters from themselves. . . . It is a platitude
that self-knowledge paralyzes; it should be a platitude that rationalization, only rationalization, enables us to act" (90–91).

Given the adaptive nature of the persona, it is not surprising that
we develop personae, many social roles that we fluidly move in and
out of during the course of a typical day. We are "the parent" one
moment, "the lawyer" the next, and "the religious pilgrim" still later.
Whenever we speak of persona, a singular mask, we are speaking only
of what occurs at a moment in time. We are many. At certain points of
our lives, one of these roles might be dominant, but psychologically
healthy individuals recognize both the multiplicity of their roles (as
well as the multiplicity of social demands on their inner lives) *and* the
difference between the self (the ego, as personal identity, and the
unconscious, as present but unrealized potentials) and their personae.
Healthy individuals realize that they are more than a single social role
even as they escape becoming lost in a mask (a way of being addressed
and addressing others, a stylistic register), play out a social ritual,
remove the mask, and then assume a different identity, or retreat and
reflect upon the ego, where they can recognize their limitations and
acknowledge their doubts about their ability to play those roles that
are larger than any individual.[21]

One of the most important aspects of the persona is that, as an adaption to the social, it is the portal through which ideology is introjected into the individual. Jung explains:

> No matter what obstacle we come up against—provided only it be a difficult one—the discord between our own purpose and the refractory object soon becomes a discord in ourselves. For, while I am striving to subordinate the object to my will, my whole being is gradually brought into relationship with it, following the strong libido investment which, as it were, draws a portion of my being across into the object. The result of this is a partial identification of certain portions of my personality with similar qualities in the object. As soon as this identification has taken place, the conflict is transferred into my own psyche. This "introjection" of the conflict with the object creates an inner discord, making me powerless against the object and also releasing affects, which are always symptomatic of inner disharmony. (CW 6: 89)

As we identify with social roles, we introject the conflict and ideology of our environment. Once the outer has been introjected, the entire psyche must adjust to it.

ANIMA AND ANIMUS

Feminist critics have been drawn to Jung's theory of the contrasexual Other within, the animus (the male Other within a female) and the anima (the female Other within a male) as frequently as they have been repulsed by his attempts to explain it. Even though Jung's theory provides terms for a cultural analysis of gender, his "characterizations" of the anima and animus seem essentialist. For example, consider the following description of the animus:

> In intellectual women the animus encourages disputatiousness and would-be highbrowism, which, however, consists essentially in harping on some irrelevant weak point and nonsensically making it the main one. Or a perfectly lucid discussion gets tangled up in the most maddening way through the introduction of a quite different and if possible perverse point of view. Without knowing it, such women are solely intent upon exasperating the man and are, in consequence, the more completely at the mercy of the animus. (CW 7: 208)

Such unflattering descriptions of the animus, more typical of Jung's middle career, certainly smack of patriarchy, and his descriptions of the anima are equally problematic. Jung variously describes the anima as an evil succubus, the male's beatific spiritual guide, or the idealized woman that heterosexual males project onto women they encounter.[22] The animus seems to devalue the feminine just as the anima seems to erase real women.

It could also be argued that, even during the middle years, when Jung was writing the descriptions of the anima and animus that seem so problematic, his theory is more historical than is widely acknowledged. He did explain, even during this period, that the individual forms a persona as an adaptation to the ideology of his or her culture, including, we could add, gender roles. The gender role that a female might embrace in her persona means that more masculine characteristics must be repressed, forming the animus. The animus and anima are formed, in part, as an unconscious compensation for gender roles. Thus, a cultural critique might focus on the material manifestation of gender roles, or it might consider gender roles *and* their relation to the anima and animus. Once we recognize that the anima and animus form as unconscious compensations for gender roles, we should not expect the anima in a warrior culture like the Norse to be the same as the anima in a culture with a professional military (see Jensen, *Identities* 97–127). We can, thus, use anima and animus to direct our attention toward the social.

Feminist critics have also acknowledged that Jung's theory contains the possibility of moving beyond gender limitations. Polly Young-Eisendrath writes that Jung's theory points to the importance of "the opposite sex as a projection-making factor." She explains:

> Jung's contrasexuality is a contribution to depth psychology that problematizes the "opposite sex," tracing the shadow of Otherness back to its owner. In contrast to Freud's narrowly focused theories of castration anxiety and penis envy (which centralize the penis, the phallus, and the power of the male), Jung's gender theory is fluid and expansive in its potential uses in a post-modern, decentered world. (224)

Jung's model of the psyche is ultimately about decentering the ego (which, in Jung's theory, is not all that centered), and his theory of human development, or individuation, is ultimately about learning to view the Other without projections. As females come to learn their animus and males their anima, typically during midlife, they no longer project an unconscious image onto the opposite gender. As they move beyond the limitations of cultural gender roles, women can come to know men and men can come to know women.

SHADOW

In "Psychology and Religion," Jung writes, "there can be no doubt that man is, on the whole, less good than he imagines himself" (*CW* 11: 76). We want to be good, or said another way, we need to be accepted. This might relate to the evolution of our species. The need to form groups and the behaviors that come with it—mutual protection, sharing food, and so on—certainly increased our chances of survival. To promote group cohesion, any aspect of our personality that does not relate to our cultural notion of "goodness" is generally negated or repressed. Through such negations, we begin to refine our conscious notion of who we are, how we should act, and what we are capable of doing, but we are, at the same time, relinquishing power over a complex within our broader self. Once repressed, this dark side or shadow "remains in the background, unsatisfied and resentful, only waiting for an opportunity to take its revenge in the most atrocious way" (*CW* 18: 587). Historically, the shadow probably formed as societies became more complex and needed ideology and a more stable social self to bring groups together. Personally, the shadow seems to form as we move toward adulthood, as we slowly construct a more durable sense of self that is defined, in part, by who we are not.

In "The Undiscovered Self," Jung describes the shadow as being the Other within. To explain, let us consider how the shadow has often functioned within the context of Western families in the aftermath of the industrial revolution. These families have experienced a progressive isolation (the nuclear family has come to be viewed as a unit apart from some broader community), an increased awareness of the class status of the family, and a progressive separation of the male and female spheres of influence. The typical middle-class father, if concerned about his responsibility as breadwinner outside of the family as well as his role in maintaining the image of an "ideal" family, may present his best persona when outside the home and frequently act out of his shadow when with his family. His children may, thus, perceive him as a threat; they will mesh their own "evil," which they wish to repress, with an image of the father. As they form their own identities, they will look to the father and say, "I will never be like him." Tragically, the shadow of the father may form the shadow of the children (as they struggle to be different than he), and so the shadow may be passed on from generation to generation, a common theme of Gothic literature.

As the personal shadow may develop through interaction with some specific person, so can a cultural shadow develop through a group interacting with a collective Other. As we become indoctrinated into the ideology of our culture, we repress the parts of our self that do not readily fit into our culture's views of the admirable, the sacred, and the acceptable. These repressed aspects of our selves mesh with the character of groups that our culture marginalizes. We then project the evil side of our culture onto these groups, seeing them as more different, more threatening, than they really are.

The cultural shadow, in this sense, is similar to what Lyotard calls "the jews," the Other within that represents what we have been culturally conditioned to despise. Lyotard refers to "the jews" in lower case and quotation marks to indicate that this is a symbolic Other, not the historical Jews, and he says

> "the jews" are within the "spirit" of the Occident that is preoccupied with foundational thinking, what resists this spirit; within its will, the will to want, what gets in the way of this will; within its accomplishments, projects, and progress, what never ceases to reopen the wound of the unaccomplished. . . . They are what cannot be domesticated in the obsession to dominate, in the compulsion to control domain, in the passion for empire, recurrent since Hellenistic Greece and Christian Rome. (22)

In other words, the identity of the Occident, even the project of modernism, is predicated on the repression of "the jews." One could add, following Homi K. Bhabha, that this fragile collective identity is also predicated on the repression of the colonial subject. "An important feature of colonial discourse," he writes, "is its dependence on the concept of 'fixity' in the ideological construction of otherness" (66). He says that "the image of post-Enlightenment man" is "tethered to, *not* confronted by, his dark reflection, the shadow of colonized man, that splits his presence, distorts his outline, breaches his boundaries" (44). To move past our colonial identities, we must "recognize ourselves doubly, as, at once, decentered in the solitary processes of the political group, and yet, ourself [sic] as a consciously committed, even individuated, agent [sic] of change—the bearer of belief." "We may," he continues, "have to force the limits of the social as we know it to rediscover a sense of political and personal agency through the unthought within the civic and the psychic realms" (65). Although neither Lyotard (a poststructuralist) or Bhabha (a postcolonial theorist) cite Jung as the source of their conception of cultural Otherness (and, I might add, they would probably dismiss Jung as a structuralist or a modernist), they find it necessary to reinvent (or unconsciously borrow) a Jungian concept. Their theories also point to the political importance of the shadow. The individual who has come to terms with his or her shadow, Jung believed, is less vulnerable to discourses that repress Others. They are more capable of discovering, in Bhabha's words, a "sense of political and personal agency."

PSYCHOLOGICAL TYPES

The most frequently cited concerns about Jung's theory of psychological types are that it is cognitive (focusing on the individual in isolation) and that it "boxes people in." Actually, as Jung wrote in *Memories, Dreams, Reflections,* his intent was to develop a theory of how the individual interacts with his or her context:

> The work sprang originally from my need to define the ways in which my outlook differed from Freud's and Adler's. In attempting to answer this question, I came across the problem of types, for it is one's psychological type which from the outset determines and limits a person's judgment. My book, therefore, was an effort to deal with the relationship of the individual to the world, to people and things. (207)

In *Psychological Types,* Jung explains how historical epochs have a certain "temperament," a psychological perspective that is similar to the psychological type of individuals. Thus type theory can explain why certain individuals—including writers—can emerge as emblems of their age and others are at odds with the norms of their culture. His theory directs our attention both to the power of social norms and trends (historical era, research methods, critical theories, ideologies, and so on) *and* to the differences within broad social movements (CW 6: 8–66). Among numerous applications, his typology can explain some of the differences that we find when we explore readers' reactions to texts. Psychological type can be viewed as one kind of "interpretant," to use Peirce's term, that influences the interpretation of signs.

If one understands type theory, then the claim that "it boxes individuals in" is equally fallacious. Jung's explanation of his typology begins with Extraversion and Introversion, which he calls attitudes. Extraverts are more outwardly directed, focusing their energy on the people or things of their environment. Introverts are more inwardly directed, spending more of their day reflecting, observing, or planning. An individual, Jung says, prefers one process over the other *only* in the sense that the preferred process is more automatic or habitual. All individuals move in and out of Extraversion and Introversion throughout the course of a day. The attitudes, thus, are actually moments in the flow of consciousness.

It is important to appreciate Jung's reason for emphasizing Extraversion and Introversion as he describes his typology. The fluidity of movement from Extraversion to Introversion within the flow of consciousness means that Jung's entire system is in constant flux, constantly undoing itself. Pure types, Jung says, do not exist, so to say "an individual is an Extravert" is simply a shorthand for saying that "the individual uses Extraversion habitually," even as the statement acknowledges that all individuals move in and out of Extraversion and Introversion from moment to moment, as a dialectic.

By the time that Jung wrote the preface to the Argentine edition of *Psychological Types*, five years after the book's publication, he offered the following caution:

> [E]ven in medical circles the opinion has got about that my method of treatment consists in fitting patients into this system and giving them corresponding "advice." This regrettable misunderstanding completely ignores the fact that this kind of classification is nothing but a childish parlour game. . . . My typology is far rather a critical apparatus serving to sort out and organize the welter of empirical material, but not in any sense to stick labels on people at first sight. (CW 6: xiv)

Jung's ultimate hope in developing his typology was that it could be used as a "critical apparatus" to move past egocentric world views. In *Methodological Approaches to Social Sciences*, Mitroff and Kilmann tie type theory to research methods, such as ethnography, empirical science, and case study; they, thus, make the claims of the superiority of one method over another highly suspect. In *Psychological Types*, Jung suggests that biographers might use his type theory; so, too, might the readers of biographies. Readers can conjecture about the psychological type of the subject of the biography *and* the type of the author of the biography. They can then read with more sophistication, as they analyze how author's type (say, an Extravert) interacted with the subject's type (an Introvert) and how the author's type might influence his interpretations (perhaps the author fails to understand Introverts and criticizes the subject for being withdrawn). Type theory is, thus, a "critical apparatus" for understanding interpersonal dynamics.

The rest of Jung's typology will, of necessity, be explained rather synoptically. Sensation and Intuition form a dialectic that relates to perception; individuals will exhibit a preference for one or the other. Sensation is "*sense perception*—perception mediated by the sense organs and 'body senses'"; it "conveys bodily changes to consciousness" (CW 6: 462). Sensation brings us in close contact with our immediate environment. Intuition is "a kind of instinctive apprehension," which "presents itself whole and complete, without our being able to explain or discover how this content came into existence" (*CW* 6: 453). It is the hunch about what might be that often takes us into the future. Jung calls Sensation and Intuition irrational functions to indicate that they are typically used automatically.

Thinking and Feeling form a dialectic that relates to making judgments. Here, also, individuals will exhibit a preference for one or the other, yet move in and out of both processes from moment to moment. Thinking "brings the contents of ideation into conceptual connection with one another" (*CW* 6: 481), that is, "it organizes the content of consciousness under concepts" (*CW* 6: 435). Feeling "is primarily a process that takes place between the ego and a given content, a process, moreover, that imparts to the content a definite value in the sense of acceptance or rejection ('like' or 'dislike')" (*CW* 6: 434). In other words, it arranges content according to some value. Jung calls Thinking and Feeling rational functions to indicate that they are typically used more actively as part of the process of making decisions.

The sophistication and fluidity of Jung's typology are certainly difficult to convey in limited space. Jung felt that type emerged historically, as did our manner of socially constructing the "individual." Each individual, furthermore, changes as he or she moves through the process of individuation. Throughout *Psychological Types*, Jung reminds us that he is explaining a model that should not be reified. For example, when describing the "rational types" (the Thinking and Feeling preferences), Jung wrote:

> I . . . base my judgment on what the individual feels to be his conscious psychology. But I am willing to grant that one could equally well conceive and present such a psychology from precisely the opposite angle. I am also convinced that, had I myself chanced to possess a different psychology, I would have described the rational types in the reverse way, from the standpoint of the unconscious—as irrational, therefore. This aggravates the difficulty of a lucid presentation of psychological matters and immeasurably increases the possibility of misunderstanding. (*CW* 6: 360)

If Jung's major contribution to depth psychology is building an interpersonal model of the psyche that decenters the ego, then his theory of psychological types could be considered the lynchpin of this model. One implication of type theory is that all thought is relative. Jung even acknowledges the relativity of descriptions of psychological type, including his own. "We naturally," he wrote, "tend to understand everything in terms of our own type" (*CW* 6: 3).

CONCLUSION

Anyone who has recently viewed Hitchcock's *Psycho,* or for that matter a videotape of Marie-Louise von Franz explaining Jung's theories, can appreciate how quickly psychological theories become dated. In some ways, Plato or Aristotle seem more our contemporaries than Freud or Jung. And so psychological theories need to be critiqued and reworked, explained in a new language, and dragged into a new age. Limitations of the theory, often a product of the culture in which the theory was constructed, need to be addressed. Latent potentials, maybe only marginally important to a previous age, need to be explored.

This volume will attempt to do, for Jung, what has already been done for Freud: Its contributors will read Jung with a hermeneutic of faith. Not blind faith, certainly, but faith nonetheless. As has been argued in this introduction, Jung's theory is as unavoidable as that of Darwin, Marx, or Freud. Even those who have never read Jung or those who claim to profess that they are not Jungians—even those who consciously attempt to excise his terms from their texts, not speak of persona, shadow, archetype, Extravert or Introvert, anima or animus—can hardly hope to avoid Jungian concepts.

As readers move through this volume, they will find that a more traditional approach to Jungian criticism, with some minor changes, is still viable. They will also discover authors who occasionally find Jungian thought essentialist but also surprisingly poststructuralist, authors who consider descriptions of anima and animus sexist yet the concept of a "transsexual Other within" transformative, and authors who feel that Jung's work embodies racism even while it can be used to resist racism. These authors have found new ways to read Jung.

These new ways of reading bring us to the "post-Jungian," a term that we borrowed from Andrew Samuels. His *Jung and the Post-Jungians* (1985) sought to make sense of the diverse, contrasting, even "chaotic" developments in analytical psychology since Jung's death in 1961. "I have used the term *post-Jungian,*" he writes, "in preference to *Jungian* to indicate both connectedness to Jung and distance from him" (19). Returning to this subject in a later essay (1997), "Jung and the post-Jungians," Samuels elaborates:

> I intended to indicate some connection to Jung and the traditions of thought and practice that had grown up around his name and also some distance or differentiation. In order to delineate post-Jungian analytical psychology, I adopt a pluralistic methodology in which *dispute* rather than consensus is permitted to define the field. The field is

defined by the debates and arguments that threaten to destroy it and not by the core of commonly agreed ideas. A post-Jungian is someone who can plug into, be interested in and energized by, and participate in post-Jungian debates whether on the basis of clinical interest, or intellectual exploration, or a combination of these. (7)

Earlier in this essay, Samuels sets out the broad basis of the post-Jungian "dispute":

> Jung's attitudes to women, blacks, so-called "primitive" cultures, and so forth are now outmoded and unacceptable. He converted prejudice into theory, and translated his perception of what was current into something supposed to be eternally valid. Here, too, it is the responsibility of the post-Jungians to discover these mistakes and contradictions and to correct Jung's faulty or amateur methods. When this is done, one can see that Jung had a remarkable capacity to intuit the themes and areas with which late twentieth-century psychology would be concerned: gender; race; nationalism; cultural analysis; the perseverance, reappearance and sociopolitical power of religious mentality in an apparently irreligious epoch; the unending search for meaning— all of these have turned out to be the problematics with which psychology has had to concern itself. Recognizing the soundness of Jung's intuitive vision facilitates a more interested but no less critical return to his texts. This is what is meant by "post-Jungian": correction of Jung's work and also critical distance from it. (2)

Revealing both their "connection" with and "critical distance" from traditional theory, the essays gathered together here seek to reinterpret, extend, and "correct," as well as "dispute" with, Jung in precisely those ways that Samuels terms post-Jungian. Specifically, our collection offers to carry the range and diversity of post-Jungian theory into the realm of literary and textual criticism.

Most closely "connected" to traditional theory are essays by Sophia Andres, Sally Porterfield, and J. R. Atfield, whose readings of archetypal images and characterizations—in Wilkie Collins, Anton Chekhov, and Seamus Heaney, respectively—nonetheless give careful attention to these authors' historical circumstances, thus demonstrating how archetypes assume the "cultural dress" of each age and culture. By exploring television programming and detective films set in the Orient, Keith Polette and Luke Hockley extend Jungian criticism to popular media (and to popular culture generally, an area left largely neglected by traditional archetypal criticism). Corrections of Jung's "attitudes to women, blacks, so-called 'primitive' cultures" are offered in several essays, including

Tita French Baumlin and James S. Baumlin's feminist revisioning of archetypes in *Jane Eyre*, Rebecca Meacham's postcolonialist reading of archetypes in LeRoi Jones/Imamu Amiri Baraka, and Andrew Elkins's reading of Jane Hirshfield's poetry as a Buddhist revision of Jung. James T. Jones brings post-Jungian and postmodernist themes together in a reading of the modern novelist Jack Kerouac. Standing at an even further "critical distance" from Jung are essays by Susan Rowland and Oliver Davis. Evincing the "textuality" of Jungian theory— that is, the interpretive problematic that Jung's own texts pose to readers—these and other authors in our collection offer critical rereadings that serve to "decenter" Jungian authority: no longer treated as a source of clear, univocal, authoritative pronouncement, Jung's writings become themselves the subject of deconstructive reading. Thus Rowland rereads the development of Jung's anima theory as a mode of storytelling (specifically, a "ghost story"), while Davis critiques recent attempts to reinterpret Jung as a "Lacanian" poststructuralist. Again, as Samuels writes, "a post-Jungian is someone who can plug into, be interested in and energized by, and participate in post-Jungian debates whether on the basis of clinical interest, or intellectual exploration, or a combination of these." Here, engaging in the "intellectual exploration" of literary-textual criticism, we are all clearly post-Jungian. To the essays we now turn.

Notes

1. A number of benchmark archetypal studies appeared during this period: Campbell's *The Hero with a Thousand Faces* (1949), Elizabeth Drew's *T. S. Eliot: The Design of His Poetry* (1949), Emma Jung and Marie-Louise von Franz's *The Grail Legend* (1960), and Frye's *Fearful Symmetry* (1969). I have, however, singled out Frye's *Anatomy of Criticism* because it was the most widely read.

2. As a general rule, scholars tend to read Freud or Jung, but not both. Certainly, the bifurcation of theorists into Freudians and Jungians is partially due to the difficulties of mastering more than one theorist, but it is also a continuation of the internecine battles that began when Jung split from Freud. See Phyllis Grosskurth's *The Secret Ring: Freud's Inner Circle and the Politics of Psychoanalysis*.

3. Jung's early experiments on memory are the most clearly cognitive of his works (see vol. 2 of *Collected Works*). In his mature work, Jung incorporated cognitive elements, but his attention to culture, archetypes, psychological type, family, and other themes set him apart from most cognitivists.

4. The *Standard Edition* of Freud's works is ordered chronologically. The *Collected Works* of Jung is not, which creates some difficulties in reading the development of Jung's thought. Homans writes:

> This breakdown of Jung's *Collected Works* and their correlation with major periods in his life, however valid it may be in a broad sense, is confusing at several important points. And titling each volume as if it were a self-contained—indeed, almost timeless—work, combined with Jung's penchant for revisions, has at points obscured the way the development of his work relates to his personal experience. (27)

5. For feminist appraisals of Jung's theory, see Lauter and Rupprecht's introduction to *Feminist Archetypal Theory* and Young-Eisendrath's "Gender and Contrasexuality." For a history and analysis of charges of anti-Semitism, see Andrew Samuels's *The Political Psyche* 287–339.

6. Similar to later proponents of philosophy without foundations, Jung argued that there exists no Archimedean point (*CW* 9.1: 69 n 27), but he did believe that, if a researcher were reflexive, he or she could approach validity through subjectivity rather than objectivity (*CW* 9.1: 182). Although this view applies to his entire system, it is particularly pertinent to his theory of type. Jung wrote:

> The recognition and taking to heart of the subjective determination of knowledge in general, and of psychological knowledge in particular, are basic conditions for the scientific and impartial evaluation of a psyche different from that of the observing subject. These conditions are fulfilled only when the observer is sufficiently informed about the nature and scope of his own personality. (*CW* 6: 10)

This view is similar to the epistemology of current anthropologists (see Sangren's "Rhetoric").

7. Jung often presented readers with instructions on how he wanted to be read and warnings that his ideas should not be reified. For example, in "On the Nature of the Psyche," he writes: "The moment one forms an idea of a thing and successfully catches one of its aspects, one invariably succumbs to the illusion of having caught the whole" (*CW* 8: 356). Among these instructions, the most frequently neglected relate to the importance of history and ideology, the difficulty of grasping the fluidity of reality, and the need to view reality as created interpersonally through interpretations.

8. For example, Jung would agree with social constructionists that "the individual" as we know it in our culture is a social and historical construction. In *Psychological Types*, he wrote:

> The further we go back into history, the more we see personality disappearing beneath the wrappings of collectivity. And if we go right back to primitive psychology, we find absolutely no trace of the concept of an individual. . . . What we understand by the concept of 'individual' is a relatively recent acquisition in the history of the human mind and human culture. (*CW* 6: 10)

9. While warning against the tendency of Jung to essentialize gender differences, Rowland writes: "Jung's insistence that the feminine has been disastrously suppressed in modern culture, religion and the psyches of the ruling gender, is a powerfully resonant theory for feminism" (16). See also Lauter and Rupprecht.

10. Pointing out that even a traditional reading of Jung suggests something of poststructuralism, Rowland writes: "Jung shares with Derrida a suspicion of metaphysical language when discussing psychological concepts" (19). Rowland continues that, once one begins to read Jung through Derrida, his work becomes even more poststructural: "Psychic images possess *différance* both in their difference and, importantly, in their infinite deferral of a full and sufficient signified to enforce closure. Jungian psychic imagery is 'writing' because it is a system of signs whose structure 'is determined by the trace or track of that other which is forever absent'" (21). She says: "Jungian theory is ripe for deconstruction and in some ways uncannily anticipates poststructuralist thought" (190). Of course, Jung's concept of enantiodramia ("the running away from opposites") might be viewed as a form of deconstruction, a working against the limitations of binary thought.

11. Jung tended to view the psyche as naturally disordered. Psychic order comes through hard work: at the social level, with rituals and ideology; at the personal level, with the individual's construction of an identity and the playing of social roles. Jung writes: "All man's strivings have . . . been directed toward consolidation of consciousness. This was the purpose of rite and dogma; they were dams and walls to keep back the dangers of the unconscious, the 'perils of the soul'" (9.1: 22). See also Andrew Samuels's *Jung and the Post-Jungians, The Plural Psyche,* and his introduction to Young-Eisendrath and Dawson's *The Cambridge Companion to Jung.*

12. For a discussion of Jung as postmodernist, see Griffin's introduction to *Archetypal Processes.* Jung might, however, be viewed as someone who has anticipated and moved past postmodernism in that he accounts for division and plurality while still maintaining some sense of order and structure. For example, in *Psychology and Alchemy,* Jung writes: "Not only is the self indefinite but— paradoxically enough—it also includes the quality of definiteness and even of uniqueness" (*CW* 12: 19; see also Jensen, *Identities* 1–22). The ability to conceive of unity and fluidity simultaneously is, perhaps, one of Jung's debts to Hegel. Both Maker's *Philosophy Without Foundations* and Rapp's *Fleeing the Universal* argue that Hegel anticipated and moved beyond the agenda of postmodernism.

13. In *The Black Atlantic,* Paul Gilroy argues that modernism's claim to rationality is challenged by "the way that slavery became internal to western civilisation and through the obvious complicity which both plantation slavery and colonial regimes revealed between rationality and the practice of racial terror" (39). In *The Location of Culture,* Homi K. Bhabha makes similar claims about critical theory and colonialism. Theories that assume a position or "loca-

tion" of power toward the colonial subject reproduce the history of colonialism by demanding that the colonial subject "be always the good object of knowledge, the docile body of difference" (31). In *Hitler's Willing Executioners,* Goldhagen writes of the long historical prelude of anti-Semitism that culminated in the Holocaust.

14. In *Anatomy of Criticism,* Frye wanted to create a systematic, even scientific, approach to criticism (7–8). He also opposed the Romantic notion of originality: "Originality returns to the origins of literature, as radicalism returns to its roots" (97–98). Jung's explanation of the collective unconscious struck him, no doubt, as too mysterious and too Romantic to be scientific.

15. Much of the appeal of Frye's work should be viewed within the context of the 1950s. Whereas New Critics tended to stay within the borders of single works, Frye's work was intertextual. He drew the idea of archetypes from Jung to catalog literature into a limited number of grand themes. Frye's work could also be viewed as an extension of formalism or structuralism, an attempt to articulate a grammar of literary themes in a way that was not so scientific (though he, at times, claims that criticism is a science) or reductive. Frye was not, however, a psychologist. He did not tie archetypes to the mind of the writer or reader. Similar to New Critics, formalists, and structuralists, Frye's approach to literature traverses a terrain that might include literary characters but is rather devoid of human beings.

16. Joseph Campbell has presented the most articulate defense of a traditional reading of Jung's theory of the collective unconscious and archetypes in "The Imprints of Experience," a chapter in *Primitive Mythology: The Masks of Gods* (50–131).

17. By using the term body rather than brain, mind, or biology, I hope to convey the sense of the collective aspects of humanity that account for the unity or permanence of our experience. I mean the "body" as Kenneth Burke uses the term in *Permanence and Change,* a book written when Burke was reading Jung. Burke writes:

> Insofar as the individual mind is a group product, we may look for the same patterns of relationship between the one and the many in any historical period. And however much we may question the terminology in which these patterns were expressed, the fact that man's neurological structure has remained pretty much of a constant through all the shifts of his environment would justify us in looking for permanencies beneath the differences, as the individual seeks by thought and act to confirm his solidarity with his group. (159)

Burke argues that it is the body that accounts for permanence and culture that brings about change.

18. While Jung did not believe that the mind is a tabula rasa at birth, he does not subscribe to the notion that we can ever speak of anything like genetically driven behavior. In *Psychological Types,* Jung stresses repeatedly that

modes of thought or patterns of behavior emerge historically. The Romantic movement, for example, developed a new world perspective and its own approach to understanding identity. Even though the Romantic movement is long past, some individuals, given their psychological type, might be still be prone to adopt Romantic views, but he hardly espouses anything close to a deterministic or purely genetic model.

19. One of the problems with a more traditional approach to archetypes is Jung's separation of "form" and "content." If we recognize that what Jung calls the "form" of an archetype might as easily be labeled as "emotions" or "affect," then the "form" and "content" of archetypes do not seem so separate. A complex of emotions comes together with a social scene, what Jung on a few occasions referred to as archetypal constellations, and distinctions between the "inner" and "outer" dissolve. The world, as Neumann describes it, becomes "transparent" (175).

20. A persona can be distinguished from a social role. The social role embodies the cultural norms and expectations that have developed historically; the persona is the individual's adaptation to that role.

21. One might argue that an important aspect of individuation is the development of multiple personae. Jensen suggests that basic writers tend to present a single persona in their works, a persona close to their psychological type (*Identities across Texts* 177–207). In Sudol's analysis of "Letter from a Birmingham Jail," he demonstrated how King moves through a series of personae. Certainly, much of the effectiveness of King's "Letter" is related to his ability to create a complex self that makes contact with a broad audience and is less likely to be stereotyped.

22. One could argue with some conviction that Jung was more aware of the historical and cultural construction of the anima and animus late in his career, in "Answer to Job," where he says that God is perfect but not complete because he has suppressed Sophia, or in *Mysterium Coniunctionis*, where he writes, "The alchemical texts were written exclusively by men, and their statements about the moon are therefore the products of masculine psychology" (*CW* 14: 178). Jung's awareness of the effects of patriarchy later in his career was, no doubt, a result of his work with a number of females, many of whom he encouraged to research feminine archetypes. The females include Esther Harding, Toni Wolff, Marie-Louise von Franz, and Emma Jung.

Works Cited

Baird, James. "'Preface' to *Ishmael*: Jungian Psychology in Criticism: Some Theoretical Problems." Sugg 38–53.

Basso, Ellen B. *In Favor of Deceit: A Study of the Trickster in an Amazonian Society.* Tucson: U of Arizona P, 1987.

Benjamin, Walter. *The Arcades Project.* 1972. Trans. Howard Eiland and Kevin McLaughlin. Ed. Rolf Tiedemann. Cambridge: Belknap, 1999.

Bhabha, Homi K. *The Location of Culture.* London: Routledge, 1994.

Burke, Kenneth. *Permanence and Change: An Anatomy of Purpose.* 1935. 3rd ed. Berkeley: U of California P, 1984.

Campbell, Joseph. *The Hero with a Thousand Faces.* Princeton: Princeton UP, 1949.

———. *Primitive Mythology: The Masks of Gods.* 1959. New York: Penguin, 1969.

Crews. Frederick. *The Memory Wars: Freud's Legacy in Dispute.* New York: New York Review of Books, 1995.

Dawson, Terence. "Jung, Literature, and Literary Criticism." Young-Eisendrath and Dawson 255–80.

Drew, Elizabeth. *T. S. Eliot: The Design of His Poetry.* New York: Scribner's, 1949.

Eliade, Mircea. *Images and Symbols: Studies in Religious Symbolism.* Trans. Philip Mairet. 1952. Princeton: Princeton UP, 1991.

Elias-Button, Karen. "Journey into an Archetype: The Dark Mother in Contemporary Women's Poetry." Sugg 355–66.

Freud, Sigmund. *The Standard Edition of the Complete Psychological Works of Sigmund Freud.* Trans. James Strachey. London: Hogarth, 1953–74.

Frye, Northrop. *Anatomy of Criticism: Four Essays.* Princeton: Princeton UP, 1957.

———. *Fearful Symmetry: A Study of William Blake.* Princeton: Princeton UP, 1969.

Gilroy, Paul. *The Black Atlantic: Modernity and Double Consciousness.* Cambridge: Harvard UP, 1993.

Goldhagen, Daniel Jonah. *Hitler's Willing Executioners: Ordinary Germans and the Holocaust.* New York: Knopf, 1996.

Griffin, David Ray. *Archetypal Processes: Self and Divine in Whitehead, Jung and Hillman.* Evanston, IL: Northwestern UP, 1989.

Grosskurth, Phyllis. *The Secret Ring: Freud's Inner Circle and the Politics of Psychoanalysis.* Reading, MA: Addison-Wesley, 1991.

Hillman, James. "An Inquiry into Image." *Spring* (1977): 62–88.

———. *Re-Visioning Psychology.* New York: Harper, 1975.

Homans, Peter. *Jung in Context: Modernity and the Making of Psychology.* Chicago: Chicago UP, 1979.

Horning, Alice S., and Ronald A. Sudol. *Understanding Literacy: Personality Preference in Rhetorical and Psycholinguistic Contexts.* Cresskill, NJ: Hampton P, 1997.

Jacoby, Mario. "The Analytical Psychology of C. G. Jung and the Problem of Literary Evaluation." Sugg 59–74.

Jensen, George H. *Identities across Texts.* Cresskill, NJ: Hampton P, 2001.

Jensen, George H., and John K. DiTiberio. *Personality and the Teaching of Composition.* Norwood, NJ: Ablex, 1989.

Jung, C. G. *The Collected Works of C.G. Jung.* Ed. Sir Herbert Read, Michael Fordham, and Gerhard Adler. Trans. R. F. C. Hull. 20 vols. Princeton: Princeton UP, 1953–91.

———. *Essays on Contemporary Events: The Psychology of Nazism.* 1947. Trans. R. F. C. Hull. Princeton: Princeton UP, 1989.

———. *Memories, Dreams, Reflections.* 1961. Ed. Aniela Jaffe. Trans. Richard Winston and Clara Winston. New York: Vintage, 1989.

Jung, Emma, and Marie-Louise von Franz. *The Grail Legend.* 1960. Trans. Andrea Dykes. 2nd ed. Princeton: Princeton UP, 1970.

Kelley, Sean. *Individuation and the Absolute: Hegel, Jung and the Path toward Wholeness.* New York: Paulist Press, 1993.

Lauter, Estella, and Carol Schreier Rupprecht, eds. *Feminist Archetypal Theory: Interdisciplinary Re-Visions of Jungian Thought.* Knoxville: U Tennessee P, 1985.

Lyotard, Jean-François. *Heidegger and "the Jews."* 1988. Trans. Andreas Michel and Mark Roberts. Minneapolis: Minneapolis UP, 1990.

MacCurdy, Marian M. "From Trauma to Writing: A Theoretical Model for Practical Use." *Writing and Healing: Toward an Informed Practice.* Ed. Charles M. Anderson and Marian M. MacCurdy. Urbana, IL: National Council of Teachers of English, 2000.

Mahony, Patrick J. *Cries of the Wolf Man.* New York: International UP, 1984.

Maker, William. *Philosophy without Foundations: Rethinking Hegel.* Albany: State U of New York P, 1994.

Marie-Louise von Franz: Remembering Jung. Dir. Suzanne Wagner. Videotape. Direct Cinema, 1991.

Masson, Jeffrey Moussaieff. *The Assault on Truth: Freud's Suppression of the Seduction Theory.* New York: HarperPerennial, 1992.

Mitroff, Ian, and Ralph Kilmann. *Methodological Approaches to Social Sciences.* San Francisco: Jossey-Bass, 1978.

Neumann, Erich. *Art and the Creative Unconscious: Four Essays.* Trans. Ralph Manheim. Princeton: Princeton UP, 1959.

Noll, Richard. *The Jung Cult: Origins of a Charismatic Movement.* Princeton: Princeton UP, 1994.

Peckham, Morse. "Personality and the Mask of Knowledge." *Victorian Revolutionaries.* New York: George Braziller, 1970. 84–129.

Peirce, Charles Sanders. *Writings of Charles S. Peirce: A Chronological Edition.* 5 vols. to date. Bloomington: Indiana UP, 1982– .

Pratt, Annis V. *Archetypal Patterns in Women's Fiction.* Bloomington: Indiana UP, 1981.

———. "Spinning among Fields: Jung, Frye, Lévi-Strauss and Feminist Archetypal Theory." Lauter and Ruprecht 93–136.

Provost, Judith A. and Scott Anchors. *Applications of the Myers-Briggs Type Indicator in Higher Education.* Palo Alto, CA: Consulting Psychologists P, 1987.

Psycho. Dir. Alfred Hitchcock. Universal Pictures, 1960.

Rapp, Carl. *Fleeing the Universal: The Critique of Post-Rational Criticism.* Albany: State U of New York P, 1998.

Rorty, Richard. *Essays on Heidegger and Others: Philosophical Papers.* 3 vols. Cambridge: Cambridge UP, 1991.

Rowland, Susan. *C. G. Jung and Literary Theory: The Challenge from Fiction.* New York: St. Martin's, 1999.

Samuels, Andrew. "Jung and the post-Jungians." *The Cambridge Companion to Jung.* Ed. Polly Young-Eisendrath and Terence Dawson. Cambridge: Cambridge UP, 1997. 1–13.

———. *The Plural Psyche: Personality, Morality, and the Father.* London: Routledge, 1989.

———. *The Political Psyche.* London: Routledge, 1993.

Samuels, Robert. *Between Philosophy and Psychoanalysis: Lacan's Reconstruction of Freud.* New York: Routledge, 1993.

Sangren, P. Steven. "Rhetoric and the Authority of Ethnography: 'Postmodernism' and the Social Reproduction of Texts." *Current Anthropology* 29 (1988): 405–37.

Sudol, Ronald A. "Self-Representation and Personality Type in 'Letter from Birmingham Jail.'" Horning and Sudol 37–54.

Sugg, Richard P. *Jungian Literary Criticism.* Evanston: Northwestern UP, 1992.

Thompson, Thomas C. *Most Excellent Differences: Essays on Using Type Theory in the Composition Classroom.* Gainesville, FL: Center for Applications of Psychological Type, 1996.

Volosinov, V. N. *Freudianism: A Critical Sketch.* Trans. I. R. Titunik. Ed. Neal H. Bruss. Bloomington: Bloomington UP, 1976.

von Franz, Marie-Louise, and James Hillman. *Lectures on Jung's Typology.* Dallas: Spring, 1971.

Wehr, Demaris S. *Jung and Feminism: Liberating Archetypes.* Boston: Beacon, 1987.

Young-Eisendrath, Polly. "Gender and Contrasexuality: Jung's Contribution and Beyond." Young-Eisendrath and Dawson 223–39.

Young-Eisendrath, Polly, and Terence Dawson, eds. *The Cambridge Companion to Jung.* Cambridge: Cambridge UP, 1997.

Jung's Ghost Stories

Jung for Literary Theory in Feminism, Poststructuralism, and Postmodernism

⤋

SUSAN ROWLAND

ANIMA

This is where Jung said "it all began":[1]

> I once asked myself, "What am I really doing? . . ." Whereupon a voice within me said, "It is art." I was astonished . . . I knew for a certainty that the voice had come from a woman. . . . Later I came to see that this inner feminine figure plays a typical, or archetypical, role in the unconscious of a man, and I called her the anima. . . . I was like a patient in analysis with a ghost and a woman! . . . The anima might then have easily seduced me into believing that I was a misunderstood artist. . . . If I had followed her voice, she would in all probability have said to me one day, "Do you imagine the nonsense you're engaged in is really art? Not a bit." (*Memories* 210–12)

A ghost and a woman. The story that Jung told late in life about the origin of his psychology places the feminine and the occult at the heart of his inner experience. Jung's ghostly inner feminine voice becomes the prototype for his concept of the anima as a male's archetypal unconscious femininity. His ghost reference is even more striking in the context of F. X. Charet's linking of Jung's description of the emergence of

31

his anima with one of his earliest published writings, his doctoral thesis. This intriguing work is based on the seances organized around a dramatic woman medium, who happened to be Jung's very young cousin, Hélène Preiswerk. Charet draws attention to Jung's use of mediumship practice to articulate the voice of the anima. Jung temporarily became the medium for her spirit-like utterance: "I reflected that the 'woman within me' did not have the speech centres I had. And so I suggested that she use mine" (*Memories* 210).

I have written elsewhere, in *C. G. Jung and Literary Theory*, about the gender politics at the crucial evolutionary moment for Jungian psychology described in the doctoral thesis. The wild, uncontrollable voice of the nineteenth-century female medium is domesticated by Jung within psychiatric literature as the unreliable anima. Jung seizes the medium position for male subjectivity and displaces the feminine into a form of representation dominated by the anima as "she" comes to contaminate the portrayal of women in Jungian writing. The qualities that Jung ascribes to his personal feminine, to *his* anima, too easily spill over in his work into a fatal stereotyping of women as possessing deficient intellectual powers.

The chief characteristics of the anima, both Jung's own and as a general concept, appear in the above quotations from *Memories, Dreams, Reflections*. "She" is marked as inferior in the face of masculine rationality. Yet one might turn this analysis the other way around and argue that what Jung reveals as crucial about the anima is a *resistance to theory*. In this section of the autobiography, the anima challenges conventional intellectual and disciplinary contexts, not allowing "science" or "nature" or "art" to be used to fix or define Jung's expedition into the unconscious (*Memories* 210–12).

Another aspect of this anima is the literariness of her representation. Jung says that it is essential to "personify" unconscious activities and refers to himself as "writing letters" to her (*Memories* 211). However much Jung rejects the perspective of art, the *writing* of the anima here bears an uncanny resemblance to the work of a novelist constructing literary characters. I do not mean simply to collapse Jung into a novelist: his medium-like, occult *and* literary attempt at self-analysis is not identical to the novelist's embrace of fiction. Even so, the casting of the anima in writing *resembles* a piece of not quite realist literature. There is something intrinsic within Jung's approach that is suggesting this sense of the literary. It proves to be his defining idea of the autonomy of the collective unconscious. In order to portray archetypal figures as spontaneous and independent of ego preoccupations, Jung has to draw upon literary techniques of personification in the course of his depiction.

The reader of *Memories, Dreams, Reflections* witnesses the building of the anima concept from a patchwork of psychic and intellectual sources: unconscious fantasy, Christian descriptions of the soul as feminine "anima," mediumship practice, and literary writing.

PERSONAL MYTH/GRAND THEORY

I would like to suggest that *Memories, Dreams, Reflections* constructs a narrative space in which stories from a life interact with something Jung called "personal myth." Jung then goes on to make tentative and ambiguous claims for the production of a wider theory of culture. Furthermore, I shall argue that away from the autobiography, Jung's writings are characterized by two distinct but interconnected ways of framing his psychology, which I call "personal myth" (his term) and "grand theory" (my term). *Memories, Dreams, Reflections* is where these two drives are most nakedly exposed in the portrayal of Jung's inner psychic being, but the feminine troubles both conceptual schemes and forms a ghostly gothic thread throughout the *Collected Works*.

In the autobiography, the ghostly anima voice is embedded among a number of visionary explorations of the unconscious. After Jung and his anima dismiss possible theoretical contexts of science and art, Jung supplies his own: these visitations from the unconscious form the crucial elements of his "personal myth" (*Memories* 195, 224). This phrase comes to stand for a complex weaving together of an individual's life story and the slow building of conceptual ideas into what is now known as Jungian psychology.

What is fascinating about the recorded construction of the personal myth is that unconscious fantasies are placed as *the* central ingredient of Jung's subjectivity and then become the "support" or "evidence" for his psychological beliefs. I am avoiding the term "Jungian theory" at this point because he insists that what is signified by "personal myth" is *personal* because it is true *to him* and is not a template for anybody else's subjectivity. He explicitly warns against "theoretical expressions" (*Memories* 153).

However, the word "myth" in *Memories, Dreams, Reflections* is not only a bridging term between "unconscious fantasy" and "ideas about that unconscious fantasy" in the "personal" sense. It also provides a transition between the Jung who promotes local truths in the personal myths of every individual and the Jung who makes large cultural claims for his ideas. Jung's work acts like a theory when it becomes a series of linked concepts that claim to explain both the subjectivities of human beings in general and large trends in history and culture. This occurs when "myth" from "personal myth" also stands for "mythology" and refers to existing religious narratives drawn from ancient and modern religions. I have already quoted one example in showing how Jung's personal feminine "ghost" becomes written up as the "anima" to be found in *every male* using a word drawn from Christian mythology. When Jung refers to a "personal myth," he limits the scope of his theoretical pretensions. What I want to call Jung's drive to "grand theory" expands them.

Jung tended to regard personal myth as the way forward for individual patients in analysis. He is most in the mode of grand theory when commenting upon the psychological deficiencies of Enlightenment rationality, or, as I will demonstrate later, in definitively ascribing ghosts to the projections of the unconscious. Unfortunately, he is also most likely to take on the mantle of grand theory in a reductive sense when commenting upon the social role and psychology of women. Jung's writing is haunted by these two drives that cannot be wholly separated: personal myth and grand theory. For both these aspects, the unconscious as autonomous and ultimately unknowable is fundamental and foundational. Where does this leave the anima?

On matters of gender, Jung fails to make sufficient distinction between bodily sex and the cultural shaping of masculine and feminine persons. Sex is regarded as connected to an innate gender. Consequently, gender is polarized oppositionally into masculine versus feminine. The anima appears to play a particular part in setting out this simple opposition. When Jung evokes "the astonishing assumptions and fantasies that women make about men" due to the function of their unconscious masculinity, their "illogical" animuses (*Aspects* 50), it becomes apparent that the irrationality of the anima deduced in the personal myth is being projected in terms of grand theory as a characteristic of *women*, not as the unconscious feminine of a man. The anima of *Memories, Dreams, Reflections* opposes Jung's attempt to be rational, conceptual, and, above all, theoretical about the unconscious. Such an opposition can be read in Enlightenment terms as the splitting off of irrationality in order to construct rationality: a binary creation habitually gendered, just as Jung does, as masculine reason opposing feminine unreason.

The irrational anima of personal myth is magnified in the formation of grand theory as the collapse of the feminine unconscious of males into generalized pronouncements about the psychology of women. Such a projection, rational/irrational opposition by means of gender, becomes the underlying rationale of a whole series of binaries that make up Jungian psychology when it is regarded as a coherent theory. In effect, gender opposition is the means by which grand theory can be structured. For example, virtually all the key concepts exist in gendered oppositional pairs, as masculine/Logos/consciousness opposes feminine/Eros/uncon-sciousness. In this sense, Jungian grand theory is essentialist on gender. An examination of personal myth reveals the fantasy lurking within the construction of this essentialism in the literary and occult apparition of the anima. I use the word "fantasy" here in two senses, what might be called the clinical and the skeptical. What seems to be happening in the writings about the anima is that a theoretical slippage, from personal myth (limiting conceptual ambition) to grand theory (claiming to account for large cultural phenomena) is also a cultural slippage on gender-irra-tional anima into irrational women. This is also arguable vice versa: the cultural slippage from anima to women may be the means of traversing the territory of personal myth into the epic landscape of grand theory.

A brief return to the anima as the resister of theory might be help-ful. As a signifier of the inappropriable unconscious, the anima has to resist "theory," since theory is the product of the supposedly rational ego. Once gender politics emerges *as an opposition,* the superior Jungian unconscious's challenge to ego pretensions becomes represented banally as an irrational woman nagging at the male theorist. Something pro-foundly challenging to the idea of theory as consistent and authoritative in a contemporary postmodern world is rendered abject through Jung's literary representation.

It is also important to notice that anima-inspired essentialism on gender is incoherent. Conscious gender in Jung's view (through individ-uation) relies upon interplay with a superior originating unconscious that is not always and not permanently reliant upon oppositions. Gen-der in the unconscious is fluid, just as the possibilities of the unconscious lie beyond ego comprehension and, therefore, social definition. Individ-uation means the polluting of the purity of gender opposition: the ego must take some of the otherness of its fantasy about the other gender into itself. Psychic health means ceasing to regard the other gender as distinctly separable from conscious identity. Jung's cultural and theoret-ical slippage into essentialism leads him to exactly the kind of dogmatic statements about the psychologies of men and women that elsewhere he repudiates in the face of the unknowable yet founding unconscious.

The role of Jung's ghost stories is pivotal in tracing the psychic pres-sures of gender politics embedded in personal myth and grand theory. His ghost stories are to be found in the medium writings of the early doctoral thesis, much later in a foreword to a book published in 1950 (to be examined below), and in the very late and mysterious *Memories, Dreams, Reflections.* They all trace a moment of crisis between the occult feminine as ghost or medium and Jung as masculine professional authority. Desire *for* the occult women, such as Hélène Preiswerk and her medium-like successors, in Jung's life (Sabina Spielrein, Toni Wolff) slides inexorably into the desire to *be* the medium. The medium position is concretized in the writing as that of the male subject facing his feminine anima. Jung's psychological theories are formed to meet the pressure to transform a feminine cultural position, characterized by the ghostly, to a masculine subject position structured by the displacement of the feminine into the overdetermined irrationality of the anima.

What I am suggesting can also be linked to Andrew Samuels's analysis in *The Plural Psyche* of the tension between gender certainty and gender ambivalence. Jung's ghost stories are locations at which he rehearses within himself shifting boundaries of gender between a feminized otherness and a masculinized desire to locate his identity within the comforting paradigms of grand theory. The slippage between personal myth and grand theory is one of gender uncertainty to gender certainty as Jung's ghostly anima becomes congealed into essentialist and dogmatic statements. These statements in turn produce a psychology stretched upon a framework of binary oppositions resting principally upon gender polarization or gender certainty. The tensions of a struggle to secure gender within and in the writing are inextricably bound up with the tensions of structuring the truth or "power" claims of Jung's ideas.

This excursion into gender interrupting theory demonstrates the need for a feminist criticism of Jung. In literary theory, feminism has developed several functions: it criticizes images of women in male-authored literature, in particular their claim to be unbiased and "natural" representations; it explores women's writing and, with poststructuralism and postmodernism, it investigates the troubled structuring of gender itself. Having taken the route of an "images of women" feminist literary analysis, the rest of this chapter will take a feminist poststructuralist approach to Jungian writing. Such a method of scrutinizing Jung's texts has hitherto been neglected by the literary establishment. One of my aims is to go beyond merely treating Jung as a textual body requiring literary criticism to be "done" to him. Could his writing also be a ghostly edifice in which valuable riches *for* feminist and literary argument lie concealed?

First of all, I will consider the existing tradition of Jungian literary criticism.

TRADITIONAL JUNGIAN LITERARY CRITICISM

What distinguishes many of the sophisticated works of what I am calling traditional Jungian literary criticism is that they take the grand theory approach to Jung and literature. This involves treating Jungian psychology as a theoretical frame sufficient to guarantee an authoritative reading of a literary text: in short, Jungian ideas are applied as a coherent theory to a literary work. Typically, traditional Jungian literary criticism seeks archetypal images in novels, plays, poems, and films. Such images may be deduced to relate psychologically to the author or to the characters. They are based on the model of individuation in the cause of an expanded and numinous subjectivity. "Anima," "animus," and "shadow" are terms frequently used to look at the psychological impact of romance, fantasy, and horror.

Such Jungian literary practice is often dismissed by non-Jungians, who claim to detect, amongst other cardinal errors, gender essentialism, the isolation of literature from history and culture, and the construction of Jungian ideas in the arts in ways designed to replicate a liberal humanist position. Yet those literary theorists who reject all traditional Jungian criticism because of its essentialism are both unfair and myopic. They are unfair to those "traditional" critics who nevertheless scrupulously explore the cultural dimension contained within Jung's depiction of archetypal images. Moreover, they miss altogether the function of Jung's unconscious as irreducible otherness even within grand theory. Jung may have written about archetypal images at times as if they consisted of unchanging (and so noncultural) content, but at other moments his argument is clear: archetypes as potential structures are inherited, contents are not. Archetypes are not inherited images.

Just as Jung is not always essentialist on gender, due to the unknowability of the unconscious, so traditional Jungian literary criticism need not be limited by Freud's lack of interest in the cultural and historical shaping of archetypal signifying. Such literary criticism looks at archetypes as a structuring of cultural forms within literary works and is careful to disavow Jung's personal limitations on gender and race. However, the practice of ignoring Jung's biased opinions for the purposes of a progressive literary criticism does raise another set of questions. Those opposed to the use of Jung at all in literary theory argue that it is not enough to strip away Jung's misogynistic and racist comments. One cannot take a body of work, cut out the untenable bits, and claim to retain an egalitarian core entirely purified of what has been cast out. Culturally oriented theories are far too alert to the lingering costs of removing or marginalizing the uncomfortable parts of texts to readily accept a neutered Jung.

It comes down to a question of authority, to a hierarchy among writings. To use Jungian concepts as a coherent literary theory, as a sufficient "explanation" for literary texts, is to use them as "grand theory"—and so claim authority for that theory. To remove parts of Jung's work, such as the insistence upon women's intellectual inferiority due to their Eros-dominated consciousnesses, is not to treat it as grand theory. It is to act more on the lines of "personal myth," in cutting out some personal lapse.

At this point, Jung's writings are no longer being treated as grand theory, so they cannot assert the same authority they once had over the literary text. A way out of this literary theoretical impasse would be to adopt poststructuralism's alternative approach to hierarchies of texts: instead, to read Jung's writing *alongside* a piece of literature in order to look for echoes, correspondences, gaps, and slippages in both. With such a practice, the Jungian text might well help to illuminate the literary one. The reverse is also permissible: that literary works cast light on the writing of Jung. With the dethroning of Jungian psychology as a grand theory of literature to become a writing of internal slippages and literary ghosts, Jung is reimagined *within* literature and within poststructuralism.

Jung in Poststructuralism, Deconstruction, and Feminism

The benefit gained by taking Jung and literature into poststructuralism is that the critic may address Jung's slippages head-on, in particular his cultural and gender bias. Instead of being something to ignore, the ambiguities of personal myth/grand theory within the writing are regarded as a pressure point where claims to "truth" and authority are constructed rather than revealed. Indeed, Jung's peculiar openness about the dimension of personal myth in his practice, in addition to the potency of his unconscious Other, may prove advantageous for feminist poststructuralist theory.

In considering Jung's slippages, poststructuralism critically examines strategies for "authorizing" grand theory as in the first two parts of this chapter. Such a dismantling of transcendent claims for truth also permits Jung's work to be read with other psychologies that have been taken into modern literary theory. For example, Jung can be read alongside the writing of Jacques Lacan and the succeeding so-called French feminism of Luce Irigaray, Julia Kristeva, and Hélène Cixous.

As well as drawing upon the general principles of poststructuralism, feminist theory has also adapted the specific work of Jacques Derrida, known as deconstruction. Combined with Freudian concepts of the unconscious, deconstruction has proved a powerful tool for the post-Lacanian French feminisms, which have come to dominate feminist literary theory. I aim to show in the remaining space that it is possible to read Jung in the light of these movements and to suggest that the resulting poststructuralist Jung might have something to offer a feminist postmodernism. As a first move, I will discuss Jung in deconstruction. Then, by means of Lacan and French feminism, I shall suggest that the writing of Jung's irrational anima betrays some, but not all, of the characteristics of Lacan's phallus.

Derridean deconstruction rests upon rejecting as metaphysical any beliefs about language as a stable system of meaning. Traditionally, philosophy has relied upon a binary opposition between speech and writing in which speech is regarded as superior because the presence of the speaker acts as a guarantor of "his" meaning. Writing, on the other hand, without the author present to back up his words, is all too often open to misinterpretation. Speech therefore takes precedence over writing. Such a binary opposition gives rise to "logocentrism," which is the idea that there can be a full and *present* meaning of the word. After all, in speech the originator of the word is present and must know/control his meaning. A word can unambiguously mean what it says and say what it means. Such logocentrism, argues Derrida, is *metaphysical* because it is an object of belief rather than a logical consequence. This is because, in fact, speech does *not* precede writing. The system of language enshrined in writing gives speech its capacity to "mean" anything in the first place. Logocentrism relies on an assumption of secure meaning that the slippery nature of the language system cannot supply. Hence logocentrism is metaphysical, something posited as outside the verifiable world.

Against metaphysical logocentrism, Derrida demonstrates slippage of meaning in the sliding of the signifiers over signifieds, of words over their meanings. Any cultural system that desires to maintain some semblance of unity between signifier and signified requires a powerful "god-term," a word of ultimate significance (like God, Truth, Man, Materialism) that purports to pin the rest of the system of meanings together. The god-term acts as a "transcendental signifier/signified," since it tries to "transcend" the inherent capacity of language to slip and spill out its cargo of meaning. Once the transcendental sign can be shown to be a myth (a form of metaphysical logocentrism), signs are revealed as operating upon principles of difference from each other (the structuralist position) and deferral (the poststructuralist addition). They will defer a fixed meaning infinitely in a continual sliding of signifier over signified. Instead of a "set" system of signifying relations— as if language were a crystalline, interconnected structure—language has the ever-moving quality of a liquid, spilling and disseminating meaning. This "liquid quality" of difference and deferral Derrida put together in his term *"différance."* It expresses his perception of a radical instability of language, and therefore of culture, knowledge, and human subjectivity.

The systems and underlying cultural codes that structuralists were proud of discovering are, in fact, very fragile fictions in their claims to organize truth and significance. Deconstruction does what the word indicates: it shows a text simultaneously constructing and destructing in its claim to offer knowledge and meaning. Derrida's deconstruction of the ways in which a text sets up a notion of "truth" shows that binary oppositions are not "natural" categories but fictions. Binary oppositions always require "supplement" or something from "outside" (and so something metaphysical) that then is offered as the originating principle. Yet this supplement, as metaphysical originary, is not a fixed point of authorization: deconstruction reveals that it is produced by the text itself. The so-called "origin" is, in actuality, a supplement generated by the text or cultural system in a vain attempt to stabilize its capacity for meaning. In deconstruction's view, all texts can do is to demonstrate their own metaphorical nature, never able to give a fixed, transparent version of "truth." Theories of all kinds become another variety of "literature" or "fiction." Read deconstructively, theories are criticisms of their own attempts to speak authoritatively.

At this point, feminism's interest in deconstruction becomes explicable. As a technique for dissolving the potential of powerful philosophies and literary works to rest upon binary oppositions that suppress the feminine, deconstruction is invaluable. It has become a literary critical tool, a sure-fire method that always serves to destabilize every textual meaning except its own. Against such assimilation, Derrida has stressed that such a characterizing of deconstruction as a mere critical tool to be applied indiscriminately everywhere has missed the full implications of his work:

> [D]econstruction is . . . not a method, nor is it a set of rules or tools; it cannot be separated from performatives. . . . On the one hand, there is no "applied deconstruction." But on the other hand, there is nothing else, since deconstruction doesn't consist in a set of theorems, axioms, tools, rules, techniques, and methods. If deconstruction, then, is nothing by itself, the only thing it can do is apply, to be applied, to something else. . . . There is no deconstruction, deconstruction has no specific object. . . . Deconstruction cannot be applied and cannot *not* be applied. (qtd. in Wolfreys 270)

In this understanding of deconstruction, it is not a technique but, as Julian Wolfreys puts it, an "event" within texts and structures (278). It is there whether we are aware of it or not, and deconstructive readings are the revelation of unrepeatable crises of meaning within/upon texts. In addition, Derrida stresses a limit to the "play" of deconstruction when he argues that metaphysical thinking is inescapable. There will always be, in every deconstructive reading, an irreducible metaphysical residue that is impermeable to deconstruction. If feminism has had a hand in domesticating Derrida's philosophy as a critical method whose radical nature can be restricted, then it is worth considering both deconstruction as a technique and as an "event" in relation to Jung.

JUNG, POSTSTRUCTURALISM, AND DECONSTRUCTION

Jung's writings, particularly in what I have called the "personal myth" mode, are both aware and not aware of their own deconstructive potential. This ambivalent state of awareness is part of Jung's unique properties for psychology and feminism, as it is fundamental to his conception of the psyche. Therefore, I am going to look at the possibilities for Jung to become a thinker in deconstruction (not a deconstructionist, per se), always in tension with his logocentric drive to be also a grand theorist.

When Jung writes authoritatively about the anima, animus, the female psyche attuned to Eros, and so forth, he is being logocentric in assuming that these names have a full, present, and stable meaning. He is being metaphysical in Derrida's sense, in mine, a grand theorist. Of course, as I have argued, grand theory has a "gap" in its logocentrism in the decentering role of the unconscious, compelling Jung to say: "The names I give do not imply a philosophy, although I cannot prevent people from barking at these terminological phantoms as if they were metaphysical" (CW 16: 320). On the other hand, the Jung of personal myth is not a simple deconstructionist. What I have called "personal myth" covers a number of nontotalizing attitudes. Frequently, writing in the style of personal myth, Jung is least poststructuralist in tone, more apt to claim "fixed" knowledge of his unconscious and anima. An essentialist attitude to gender, especially claiming the "knowledge" that "all women are like this," is, of course, crudely logocentric and metaphysical in deconstructionist terms.

When Jung described the beginning of his distinct theory in the discovery of the anima, the struggle for meaning took the form of a struggle with the feminine. In a move that is simultaneously both profoundly deconstructionist and essentializing-metaphysical, the anima is characterized as an unreliable woman, insisting on "art" when Jung wants to found/fund a "science." "She" is portrayed as the *origin* of

Jung's psychology, in the dual sense—as the inner source of his interior psyche and of his system of ideas.

The unconscious possesses an irreducible otherness to the definition and systematization of theory. This must be so because the whole idea of theory as a reassuring organizer of knowable facts is a creature of the ego. In founding his theory upon the unconscious other as feminine, Jung makes two contradictory moves. He allows the essentializing slippage in his writings between feminine other as *his* unconscious and female other as more "unconscious" than men, yet also situates feminine otherness as beyond the scope of his ego perceptions. The feminine is inside the theory as the anima (as his irrational inferiority) and outside as that which is unconscious in the theory: the unconsciousness of Jungian psychology as grand theory. The feminine other is Jung's supplement generated in his psyche that purports to originate both his psyche and his theory. The feminine does so because the anima stands for the unconscious as the *source* of the psyche, including the source of the ego.

In this sense, the feminine is the irreducible metaphysics that cannot be deconstructed out of Jung's psychology—his personal myth, his interior self, and his grand theory—because it is both the origin and the absolute other, the beyond of it. The irreducible femininity is the other everywhere deconstructing Jung's metaphysical concepts, or god-terms, in the form of unknowable "outside" or as nagging interior anima. This feminine deconstructs firstly because the unconscious cannot be wholly defined by the ego and will challenge the ego's attempt securely to map the psyche. Secondly, the feminine other challenges conceptual authority as the nagging "woman" within, through being congealed in Jung's thinking as the otherness-as-inferiority of the feminine as women.

Both the grand theory and personal myth aspects of Jung's writing generate this dichotomy between a radical femininity refusing definition and limitation for the ego (including that of gender) and sexist essentialism. Grand theory and personal myth, mutually implicated and intertwined, contain theory's internal deconstructive drive in the creative, irreducible otherness of the unconscious. Yet, in addition to deconstructive elements, grand theory produces metaphysical concepts in its urge to organize meanings of psyche and culture into a system that can then seek to become an authority.

A last word on the unconscious as the irreducible metaphysics of Jungian psychology may be useful. The concept of the unconscious remains metaphysical as it is the proposition that Jungian writings cannot escape. The unconscious is unknowable, ungraspable; therefore, it cannot be theorized or translated into ego (rational terms). Jung was explicit about this: "[T]he concept of the unconscious posits nothing; it designates only my unknowing" (*Letters* 411). Since its metaphysical irreducibility is "unknowableness," Jungian theory becomes deconstructive to the point of challenging deconstruction as a "method" and revealing it as an "event," always and everywhere within Jungian writings. For if the irreducible metaphysical of Jungian theory is the intrinsically deconstructive "feminine" unconscious, then that is like saying that deconstruction itself is metaphysical, which it is when it is a "method," a set of valued tools to be applied, rather than an "event." It reveals the metaphysical residue within deconstruction. To put it another way, Jung's founding presence (his metaphysical unconscious) is a founding absence. To the extent that this presence/absence is feminized, there may be possibilities for a postmodern feminine sublime, as I shall show later.

JUNGIAN DECONSTRUCTION AS AN EVENT

To Derrida, deconstruction cannot be applied and cannot not be applied. This notion of something only existing "in action" or in practice, and therefore not as a separate set of principles, reverberates strongly in Jung. Jungian psychic imagery and dreams do show correspondences with Derrida's thinking about language, its slippages and *différance*. Although the notion of archetypes and archetypal images is logocentric, Jung believed in keeping the images primary as the irreducible "language" of the unconscious. Psychic images thereby direct attention to the unknowable "deconstructive" aspects of the psyche. Archetypal images demonstrate *différance*, differing from each other and infinitely deferring a fixed meaning. In addition, Jung frequently reminds readers that archetypal imagery must be considered in the context, the personal circumstances, of the person generating it. Psychic imagery should not be ripped out of its place and used to demonstrate general principles, however much Jung, the grand theorist, was prepared to do precisely this.

Therefore, it would be possible to argue for this deconstructive echo: that Jungian psychology cannot be applied and cannot not be applied. The Jung who insists on context is thinking not just about an individual's cultural history but about the necessary, living rootedness of dreams and images to the radical unknowableness of the unconscious (of the analyst as well as the analysand). For this Jung, Jungian psychology does not exist except in application to a particular psychic text because of the deconstructive presence (and "presence" here shows the metaphysical residue) of the unconscious, the "other," within the theory.

Jungian practice, working with dreams, is deconstruction as an "event": "The picture is concrete . . . only when it is seen in its habitual context. . . . In order to understand its living function, we must let it remain an organic thing in all its complexity and not try to examine the anatomy of its corpse in the manner of a scientist" (CW 9.1: 182).

Jung in Literary Deconstruction and Feminism

Given Jung's permeability to deconstruction, both within his conceptual scheme and in his way of writing personal myth and grand theory, a totally different literary practice is possible from that of traditional Jungian criticism. The principle of treating psychic images as a primary form of signifying could similarly be applied to literary works. It would involve treating the actual words and literary images as so radically contextual as to forbear from lifting them out of the dream text/literary work or from transferring them to conventional schemes of meaning (logocentric "theory"), including even the conventional scheme of Jungian ideas. Thus the Jungian approach no longer provides the "theory" by which to "frame" literature. Rather, it is instead the means to dissolve institutionalized forms of meaning. Jungian literary deconstruction operates in the cause of seeking the radical otherness of the unconscious in the spillage of literary signification. Such poststructuralist Jungian literary practice can be oriented towards the text or towards the reader. Of course, it retains what it depends upon, the "metaphysical" absence-presence of the unconscious as unknowable, always in excess to the social symbolic.

Under the rubric of Jungian deconstruction as an event, there is a reader response theory that considers every specific reading of a literary text as a unique engagement between an individuating psyche suspended in its own evolving social history and a piece of literature. Every reading will be different, even those performed by the same critic, because the stream of images generated by reading will be entering a different moment of individuation. Such a nonliberal humanist and radical form of Jungian literary theory is merely one possible example of a deconstructive Jung for literature, or for feminism.

To summarize my arguments: firstly, Jung's writings are peculiarly receptive to deconstruction and feminist criticisms because his founding (metaphysical) belief in the autonomous unconscious radically reduces the possibility for any system of ideas, any theory so to speak, to claim comprehensiveness, comprehensibility, truth, and authority. Secondly, Jung's work feminizes the unconscious other in ways that are not helpful to women or feminists. In personal myth, the anima is a nagging, anti-intellectual, feminine interior. In grand theory, the slippage between anima as a male's femininity and actual women licenses a series of binary oppositions that has the dual effect of designating female intellect as inferior and continuing to feminize the position of the unconscious. A third position may have something to offer feminist theory. It is the interesting paradox that feminizing the *autonomous* unconscious suggests the possibility of the feminine as radically unknowable and generative, as sublime. At the same time, it is clear that the anima is the point in Jung's work where he most resists the efforts of the unconscious to undermine logocentric oppositions and where the grand theory hangs its pretensions to become an Enlightenment grand narrative, since characteristic of Enlightenment grand narratives is the gendered opposition between masculine reason and feminine irrationality.

JUNG IN THE CONTEXT OF POST-LACANIAN FEMINISM

Considerations of space preclude extensive consideration of Jung in relation to the work of Irigaray, Kristeva, and Cixous. Nevertheless, I want to suggest some future possibilities by drawing upon Irigaray's criticism of Lacan's concept of the phallus. In a famous statement, Irigaray contends that women do not exist in Lacanian psychoanalysis. The feminine sex is not "one" because feminine sexuality is multiple and diffuse. Furthermore, the feminine is "not one" because women are not representable in Lacan's symbolic under the regime of the binary-producing phallus. Without being construed as an essentialist body part, the phallus as a privileged signifier does effectively privilege masculinity in the symbolic by aligning it with the intelligible. Masculine subjects, ambiguously, are said to "have" the phallus, while feminine subjects must "be" the phallus for the masculine. Where is the symbolic feminine?

A regrettable answer to that question might be Jung's anima, unless its toxic properties can be neutralized by further scrutiny. Placing Lacan's concepts alongside Jung's, I would argue that the anima demonstrates phallic qualities. In order to align an unconscious archetype with a symbolic signifier, it is necessary to recall crucial differences between the unconscious of Freud-Lacan and that of Jung. Unlike the psychoanalytic unconscious, the Jungian unconscious is not simply repressed into subjectivity: it is also a creative and generative partner. As a chief signifier of the unconscious in males, the anima fulfills a similar function to Lacan's phallus in structuring sexual difference in the binary mode, beloved of both Lacan's and Jung's models of gender.

The anima is also phallic in that it is what males must "have" and females must "be," or rather must symbolize for males in relationships and in the wider society. It is the slippage between "anima" and "women" that causes the anima to proliferate as a privileged signifier of gender and subjectivity in Jung's texts. Crucially, the consequence, as Irigaray would put it, is that women do not exist in Jung's writing. The anima is a phallic signifier that works to repress the feminine as other and replace it with cultural stereotypes.

However, the anima as phallus is not a perfect analogy. Reading Jung with post-Freudian feminism allows not only a feminist criticism of Jung but also the situating of a productive Jungian difference for feminism. Given the poststructuralist aspects of Jung, however much the phallic anima contaminates notions of the feminine, the unknowable unconscious is continually going to challenge any pretension to secure signifying. Jung's desire to interpret that anima as "proof" of female inferiority may be tenacious, but just like any other essentialist belief, it falls before the metaphysical foundation of the unconscious. To say that woman does not exist in Jungian writing is not the same as saying that woman cannot exist.

The anima ceases to be totally phallic if we consider that the Jungian symbolic differs vitally from the Lacanian symbolic adopted by French feminism. An examination of Kristeva's opposition of the phallic symbolic with a maternal realm of unconscious semiotic reveals that Jung's symbolic is far more intimately involved with semiotic pulsations than what underpins post-Lacanian feminist theory. The Jungian symbolic cannot be structured wholly through repression because it is also formed and continually fed by the fluidly gendered archetypal unconscious. Androgynous archetypal energies are as easily realized in feminine images as masculine ones. A Jungian symbolic may have to contend with a society that privileges masculinity, of which the Jungian phallic anima is a symptom, yet it does not deny the possibility of feminine representation. Unlike the Lacanian phallus, the phallic anima is rampant in Jung's writing but is less indigenous to the ideas, since they are reliant upon the founding presence as absence. In effect, the anima is a phallus of Jungian textuality that simultaneously represses and reveals something quite "other" haunting *The Collected Works*.

JUNG IN POSTMODERNISM AND FEMINISM

Under the assumptions of the Englightenment, human beings are characterized by a stable, rational, conscious self; reason provides reliable foundations for knowledge and truth, and such truths are not subject to history, culture, or the body. Knowledge grounded in reason is said to be politically neutral. In turn, reason grounds science, so providing an objective, socially beneficial understanding of the world. To communicate the gifts of reason, human beings are provided with language that functions as a transparent medium for truth and representation. Postmodernism is a philosophical system and cultural condition that disputes such assumptions.

As Christopher Hauke has argued so convincingly, Jung's psychology is devoted to criticizing the limitations of Enlightenment rationality. Jung never ceases to lament the fatal consequences of relying wholly upon reason and to point to the resultant split of the psyche when the irrational is denied. Nevertheless, as my preceding analysis has shown, feminist-oriented literary criticism cannot simply regard Jung as a boon to postmodernism. Nor is postmodernism itself considered without skepticism by feminist thinkers. The key engines driving the postmodern condition have been postmodern philosophy, psychoanalysis, and feminism. Despite such heavyweight assaults upon the Enlightenment habit of gendering masculine reason against feminine irrationality, such binarism is still detectable in postmodernism, albeit with a reverse hierarchy: now the irrational, the sublime, the "veiled woman" is the truth sought for.

A ghostly outline of Jung is here visible. The tenacious (phallic) anima pulls Jung's writings back into the Enlightenment naturalization of reason as masculine. At the same time, Jung's radically unknowable feminine unconscious (destabilizing rationality) situates him in postmodernity. This is the Jung whose grand narrative contains its own deconstructive "core" in the potency of the unknowable unconscious: the metaphysical presence as absence. Feminist theory participates in postmodernism by revealing that grand narratives, supposedly based on reason as transcendent of history and culture, are actually dependent upon contingent historical contradictions. I have adopted this practice when suggesting that Jung's anima writing needs to be linked to the context of nineteenth-century female mediums as well as to his own erotic history. Jung's attempt to align rational theorizing against feminine "romances" in the doctoral thesis is replicated in the conception of the anima as an antitheoretical, feminine voice within. Jung becomes haunted by feminine ghosts speaking fictions to him. On the other hand, female fictions make some sort of reply to Jung, the author, in feminist novels. Recent works reveal the postmodern possibilities of taking Jungian psychology not as grand theory but as a historically contingent and antifoundational narrative. Margaret Atwood's *Alias Grace* (1996) is an example of a literary work that exposes through fiction the historical nature of the phallic anima, while it simultaneously draws upon the Jungian unconscious to represent gender as never completely certain, never completely knowable or finished.

GOTHIC JUNG AND GHOST STORY: JUNG FOR LITERATURE IN POSTSTRUCTURALISM, POSTMODERNISM, AND FEMINISM

This chapter has argued for the practice of feminist, poststructuralist, and postmodern literary analysis upon the body of Jung's writings. It has also sought to identify ways in which such an approach can construe Jung as a positive contributor to a pro-feminist, postmodern literary theory. Before ending with a discussion of Jung's least-studied ghost story, I will set out the possible gains to be achieved by reading Jung in these ways. Firstly, by looking at how gender contributes to the tensions between personal myth and grand theory, we may open up Jung's writings to a variety of contexts, including post-Freudian feminism and poststructuralist literary theory.

Secondly, the postmodern-friendly and deconstructive strands in Jung's work provide reasons for the psychic demand for "a theory" and also reasons for the simultaneous desirability to resist such total closure. For literary criticism, literature can be so positioned as something that speaks to and that exceeds the potential of psychological writing to contain it. This is equally true of the psychic interior of the reader of literature or of the subject in analysis. In this sense, Jung's writing offers a notion of the sublime as outside Jungian theory that is also a constituent inside as the Jungian subject remains in a continual dialogue with the unknowable. A Jungian sublime can be of use to feminism and the wider culture in its irreducible openness to otherness of all kinds. For literature, poststructuralist Jung can be part of a heterogeneous spectrum of modern literary theory.

The literariness in Jung (in his ghost stories for example) removes the possibility of rigid boundaries between psychology and literature. I am not suggesting that there are *no* boundaries, no "differences," but rather that the boundaries between these two disciplines are a negotiation between an internalized otherness drawn from each. Just as literature has an internal border region of psychology, so Jungian psychology has a literary region inside, as well as "outside"—and the struggle over the otherness of literature marks the contested and shifting nature of that boundary.

Given the above, my final contention is that when feminist literary readings of Jung structure the borderlands between Jung and literature, they do so in the realm of the literary Gothic far more than they do in "pure" postmodernism. For literary theory, Jung is a Gothic author among Gothic novelists. Gothic writers at the zenith of the Enlightenment struggled with the wild *otherness* of the feminine as they explored what had been suppressed or left out of rational accounts of modernity. Like the Gothic novelists, Jung appears to domesticate his feminine ghosts in his works in an attempt to recuperate binary paradigms. Also like the Gothic novelists, his feminine ghosts prove recurring and intractable. Below is a particular example.

JUNG'S GHOST STORY

In the course of writing a foreword to a book on the paranormal, Jung told his own ghost story, purporting to describe events that actually happened to him during a visit to England thirty years earlier (*Psychology* 143–52). At this period, Jung was staying in a rented country cottage with a male English colleague, Dr. X., and was attended by female servants. Jung was most disturbed to discover that he alone was assailed in bed at night by a terrible, unexplainable smell. After searching through his memory, Jung could only conclude that the smell resembled that of an open carcinoma of an elderly female patient of many years ago. After the sickly smell, Jung's sleep was next disrupted by the sound of a dripping tap. No such tap could be located. The following weekend, the smell and the tap were joined by a loud knocking and the impression of a dog rushing around the room. By this time Jung was feeling distinctly unwell, afflicted by what seemed to him to be an unnatural "torpor" (*Psychology* 148). He had noticed that the servants appeared afraid of the cottage; they confirmed his suspicions that it was known locally to be haunted. Noises and smells continued until the horrific climax: in bed Jung opened his eyes to discover that "There, beside me on the pillow, I saw the head of an old woman, and the right eye, wide open, glared at me. The left half of the face was missing below the eye" (*Psychology* 150). Jung "leapt out of bed with one bound" (*Psychology* 150). On succeeding nights he moved to another bedroom where he had no more trouble. Yet he does not end his tale until the skepticism of Dr X. is defeated. Challenged by Jung to spend a night in the cottage alone, Dr. X. is so perturbed by strange noises that he gives up the accommodation. Jung remarks: "It gave me considerable satisfaction after my colleague had laughed so loudly at my fear of ghosts" (*Psychology* 151). No buyer could be found for the cottage, and so eventually it had to be demolished.

What makes this small tale of great interest within Jung's works is that, like the doctoral seances and the account of the emergence of his anima, he attempts to absorb these occult manifestations within his theoretical concepts. What makes this text an example of Jung's Gothic is his difficulty in doing just that. This whole short text is prefaced by his commitment to challenging the limitations of Enlightenment reason: the more we exalt rationality, "the more alive becomes the spectral world of the unconscious" (*Psychology* 144). Yet the ability of Jung's own ideas to be a coherent container of otherness to rationality and science is itself obstinately troubled by the banal. Jung produces a "Jungian" explanation for all the phenomena *except* the dripping tap (*Psychology* 151)!

A look at his attempts to translate his ghostly experience into theorizing reveals a fascinating elaboration of Jung's notions of the function of the body within the psyche. Jung "explains" the smell, the knocking noises, and the dog as the unconscious psyche mapping the body onto the exterior surroundings. The hyper-aware unconscious, sensing that a sick person has been in the bedroom, manifests itself through a sick smell just as Jung's own lassitude is described as a bodily registering of fear. This fear does not become recognizable as an emotion until the ghostly vision erupts into the drowsing mind. The unconscious's corporeality also generates the "dog" as it "noses" out an illness (*Psychology* 151) and finally produces an optical hallucination based upon the incomplete memory of an actual cancer patient.

What is fascinating to the literary critic here is that the psyche is said to use the medium of a conventional ghost story in the haunted country house in order to map the body. In this text, it is impossible to locate a secure origin of the manifestations that would remove this tale from the literary Gothic. Does the body invoke or *cause* the psychic imagination by picking up a subliminal smell? Conversely, is the psyche reacting here to stress and unfamiliar surroundings and so activating bodily responses? Is the body or the psyche the origin of the assaults upon Jung's physical and mental health?

Also noticeable is the way that the abject feminine body is negotiated uncannily to constitute the masculine healthy body-mind continuum. Jung is afflicted in body because he cannot sleep and in mind because he cannot be sure of his sanity while unable to account for apparently exterior experiences that prove unique to him. Through the narrative of the ghost story, "sickness" becomes conflated with the occult as feminine in the final vision of the old woman. Jung breaks with his afflictions by leaping out of bed and away from proximity to the sick-feminine. He is not going to remain lying down in the manner of a patient, himself, with a sick female ghost on his pillow. His body refuses to stay close to a feminine force perceived as incomplete (a partial face), sick, and occult—an overdetermined gender other.

The leap is bodily, but it is also a mental and conceptual leap. After this active participation, Jung is able both to sleep and to put most of the ghost story into his own conceptual categories. The male theorist has been restored in the face of the abject feminine patient by his establishing a physical and mental distinction to the occult feminine realm. The ghost story serves as a deconstruction and a resituating of Jung as a "sane" male theorist confronting and structuring himself as distinct from a sick female. The move from a dangerous blurring of identity and gender boundaries is accomplished theoretically by shifting the occult feminine otherness to the feminine patient safely under the control of the masculine professional. Here, when Jung links the female ghost to his memory of his cancer patient, he is revisiting the strategy of his doctoral thesis. Hélène Preiswerk, the occult medium, is redefined as hysteria patient and eventually becomes the model for the unreliable anima.

There is a poignant quality to Jung's ghost story as it reveals both his persistent psychic involvement with the occult feminine and, in the partial face of the apparition, his inability to write of women as full subjects. The whole tale portrays Jung as suspended in a gender binary between female inferiority (in the patient, servants, and ghosts) and masculine scientific skepticism (in the scoffing Dr. X). Like Gothic ghost stories, this tale is built upon the erosion and recuperation of boundaries between natural and supernatural as well as between masculine and feminine. Jung's gender trouble lies in his need to mediate the otherness within his identity; an otherness that is coded in a gender binary that represses feminine otherness as inferior social status (the servants, the patient) and occult while it overidentifies the masculine subject position (Dr. X) with Enlightenment rationality.

It is crucial, I think, that Jung is here on foreign ground, both in terms of being in England, away from his native country, and being professionally engaged in speaking to the not yet, or not definitively, "converted" to his theories of psychology. Jung's identity can only be made secure if the ghost story can be absorbed into *his* conceptual ideas. It must become personal myth with the transitional possibilities of flowering into grand theory. The leap out of bed and into Jungian psychology restores, Gothically, masculinity and rational understanding as able to contain, to account for, otherness as feminine, abject, and supernatural.

Yet it is entirely consistent with the Gothic nature of Jung's writing that some excess to theorizing remains—in the dripping tap!—and that the ghost story reveals so nakedly the highly gendered efforts required to constitute grand theory out of personal myth: the need to structure masculine authority by casting out an abject, feminine body.

This is not to dismiss the feminist possibilities of this text, which go beyond the unraveling of its hyper-gendered strategies. What Jung's Gothic writing does here is to replace a theory of Enlightenment reason that dismisses all otherness from representative potential (the skepticism of Dr. X) with a theory constituted by feminine otherness within and without. The dripping tap is the most obvious loose thread in a text that celebrates the powers of the unconscious to disrupt ego-dominated, conceptual neatness. Although the feminine is finally abjected (if you read the text merely as one of Jung's perennial struggles with the feminine-occult), the fact that it is structured as a ghost story, as literary, and remains resistant to complete absorption in Jung's concepts is suggestive. Literature is not, of course, a feminine phenomenon to be set against masculine psychology. However, the gendering of psychology in Jung's ghost story bestows upon the Gothic literary excess a feminine position. In the hinterland between literature and psychology in this piece of writing, a feminine sublime is possible as feminine otherness evades complete imprisonment in masculine theory's abjection. The aesthetic takes the position of the feminine and refuses to submit to the philosophical-scientific.

By taking grand theory into the aesthetic, Gothic Jung opens up a discursive space for the feminine sublime. Unlike some arguments about the aesthetic nature of postmodernism as de-politicizing, Jung's Gothic feminine is an empowering of the Jungian symbolic in the direction of inexhaustible renegotiation of the meaning of the term "feminine." Put simply, Gothic Jung places the potential meanings of gender beyond the possibility of closure within existing and future social conventions. Jung's ghost stories reflect his struggles with theory and with gender as mutually entwined. In the literariness of the ghostly texts (that are not presented as conventional fiction) is staged what is at stake in both the writing of psychology and the psychology of writing.

NOTE

1. Jung writes, "it all began then" (*Memories* 210)—that is, his mythological and anima fantasies generated after his break with Freud.

WORKS CITED

Atwood, Margaret. *Alias Grace*. Great Britain: Bloomsbury, 1996.

Charet, F. X. *Spiritualism and the Foundations of C. G. Jung's Psychology*. New York: State U of New York P, 1993.

Derrida, Jacques. "As If I Were Dead: An Interview with Jacques Derrida." *Applying: To Derrida*. Ed. John Brannigan, Ruth Robbins, and Julian Wolfreys. London: Macmillan, 1996. 212–26.

Hauke, Christopher. *Jung and the Postmodern: The Interpretation of Realities*. London: Routledge, 2000.

Irigaray, Luce. *This Sex Which Is Not One*. Trans. Catherine Porter with Carolyn Burke. Ithaca, NY: Cornell UP, 1985.

Jung, C.G. *Aspects of the Feminine*. Trans. R. F. C. Hull. London: Ark, 1986.

———. *The Collected Works of C. G. Jung*. Ed. Sir Herbert Read, Michael Fordham, and Gerhard Adler. Trans. R. F. C. Hull. 20 vols. Princeton: Princeton UP, 1953–91.

———. *Letters: 1906–1961*. Ed. Gerhard Adler and Aniela Jaffe. Trans. R. F. C. Hull. 2 vols. Princeton: Princeton UP, 1973–75.

———. *Memories, Dreams, Reflections*. Ed. Aniela Jaffe. Trans. Richard Winston and Clara Winston. Great Britain: Routledge, 1963.

———. *Psychology and the Occult*. Trans. R. F. C. Hull. London: Ark, 1982.

Kristeva, Julia. *The Kristeva Reader*. Ed. Toril Moi. Oxford: Blackwell, 1986.

Lacan, Jacques. *Ecrits: A Selection*. Trans. Alan Sheridan. New York: Norton, 1977.

Rowland, Susan. *C. G. Jung and Literary Theory: The Challenge From Fiction*. New York: St Martin's, 1999.

Samuels, Andrew. *The Plural Psyche: Personality, Morality, and the Father*. London: Routledge, 1989.

Wolfreys, Julian, ed. *Literary Theories: A Reader and Guide*. Edinburgh: Edinburgh UP, 1999.

Theorizing Writerly Creativity

Jung with Lacan?

⌒⌒⌒

OLIVER DAVIS

This chapter compares the place of literature—the creative use of the written word—in Jungian and Lacanian theory. I shall analyze and argue against a tendency in recent Jungian scholarship to overemphasize the similarities between the two thinkers. Whereas Jung is primarily concerned, in the literary work as in the consulting room, with images—symbols and archetypes—the focus of Lacan's psychoanalytic interest is on language. I shall argue that this basic and familiar difference has far-reaching implications for the relevance of the two thinkers to the literary scholar, although my intention in what follows is primarily to offer a theoretical survey of the question, rather than a recipe for future work in the field.

A SHARED AMBIVALENCE

But perhaps the pairing of Jung with Lacan, even for the purposes of discussion, is merely arbitrary. In this section I shall endeavor to show that this is not the case by pointing to a shared ambivalence about the value and significance of the literary work. In his paper entitled "On the Relation of Analytical Psychology to Poetry," Jung takes a rather cautious view of the ground of this relation: "the practice of art is a psychological activity and, as such, can be approached from a psychological angle"

(*CW* 15: 65). Literature is a "psychological activity," but this does not distinguish it in principle from any other activity: on this rather conservative estimate, works of literature are no more or less interesting to the analytical psychologist than the products of any other field of human endeavor. Thus it would seem that art, literature included, has no special privileges for Jung the analytical psychologist: its value and interest are not intrinsically greater than those of any other human artifact or phenomenon. The analytical psychologist may very well place a work of literature and the rise of fascism on the same plane, viewing both as "compensatory" reactions to social imbalance. This is not, however, the end of the matter, for Jung also displays a very different writing persona: that of the cultural critic. In this mode, by contrast, he is keen to pay due deference to art; he recognizes and even inflates its prestige, railing against the alleged Freudian "reduction" of great art "to personal factors" (see "Psychology and Literature" and "On the Relation of Analytical Psychology to Poetry," *CW* 15) and waxing lyrical about the "golden gleam of artistic creation" (*CW* 15: 69). There is a tension, or split, between the extreme caution of the analytical psychologist and the sheer exuberance of the cultural critic: one never goes quite far enough while the other usually goes much too far. The former is radically indifferent to the claims of art to value, while the latter incessantly talks these up in a way that may seem both precious and dated to an unsympathetic reader.

Lacan's attitude to literature is similarly ambivalent. Lacan's own writing displays a concentration of wide-ranging allusions, demonstrating a mastery of both the elliptical and the utterly direct; in short, Lacan's writing evinces a concern for style and language that has prompted many to describe it as "literary" and recommend that it be treated accordingly.[1] Perhaps unsurprisingly, the most vocal advocates of a literary Lacan have tended to be those already engaged in the study of literature; practicing Lacanian analysts have quite rightly resisted the limitation of Lacan's clinical potential that such moves have often implied. Yet Lacan himself is perhaps to blame here: he seems at times to suggest provocatively that psychoanalysis has learned all it knows from literature. Thus he famously suggested that Freud's key notions from *The Interpretation of Dreams*—condensation and displacement—may be understood as metaphor and metonymy; he described the unconscious as "the censored chapter" (*Ecrits* 50), and in the "Seminar on the Purloined Letter," he seemed to suggest that Poe's story was an allegorical anticipation, or early formalization, of the psychoanalytic encounter. Yet closer attention to this latter paper suggests that many of those gestures of deference, both explicit and allusive, to the prescience and penetrative insights of literary works that crowd Lacan's pages, do in fact conceal a no less forceful reassertion of the ultimate primacy of psychoanalytic interpretation. As Malcolm Bowie has observed:

> The epistemic claims of imaginative literature are thus asserted, denied, forcibly re-asserted and equally forcibly re-denied as the paper proceeds. The psychoanalytic paradigm visible in the literary text must by definition be visible elsewhere too, and literature must be reminded it has no enduring prerogatives. (*Freud, Proust* 157)

The value of literature for the psychoanalyst consists, Lacan suggests, in its providing a vast compendium of variously combinable contents and in exemplifying those compositional, or rhetorical, modes of combination. Literary study, for Lacan's psychoanalyst, is ultimately neither more nor less than an object lesson in verbal/conceptual connection-building.

So Lacan and Jung are both highly ambivalent about the value and the claims of literature. Lacan seems at times to court the literary scholar, suggesting that his or her activity is almost psychoanalysis, and Jung, at times, is a passionate advocate of the princely immunity of the aesthetic object from reductive psychoanalytic explanation. Just as Poe's short story seems—miraculously—to have prefigured certain aspects of psychoanalytic experience, so works of what Jung terms "visionary" literature are held to offer a privileged glimpse of the collective unconscious at work. Yet for Lacan we find that, ultimately, it is less literature itself that is of interest and more the capacity for verbal/conceptual connectivity that it demonstrates so magisterially. For Jung in (over)cautiously scientific temper, literature is simply one field of human activity. It is in this mood that he can assert, in strictly psychological terms, that, "Between an artistic inspiration and an invasion there is absolutely no difference" ("Tavistock Lectures"; *CW* 18: 34). And "invasions," as Jung explains, are strong affects of unconscious origin, which "eclipse" consciousness (*CW* 18: 24, 32). Yet both Jung and Lacan also assume writing personae as cultural critics; both are, at times, drawn simply by the prestige of the literary, and to some extent both sponsor this misconception in their own work by accrediting certain works of literature with powers of insight so formidable as to rival only those of their own discipline.

This shared ambivalence as to the value of literature has, not surprisingly, had distorting effects on later literary criticism, Jungian and Lacanian alike. As was the case with early attempts at self-declaredly "Freudian" literary exegesis, it would not be unfair to say that both traditional "Jungian" interpretation (the industry that is archetype-extraction) and most avowedly "Lacanian" literary studies have reproduced and indeed accentuated some of the more regrettable aspects of their sponsoring analysts' respective approaches, even including their written styles. Thus, although it might be argued that Freud's work is largely free of the crudely automatic reduction-to-complex of which Jung so frequently accuses him, this is undeniably a feature of such early "Freudianism" as exemplified in (and widely disseminated by) Marie Bonaparte's prolonged 1927 literary-critical "application" of Freud's discoveries.[2] In the case of archetype-spotting Jungian interpretation, the tendency inherent in Jung's theorizing toward indifference to the sociopolitical situation of the subject is likewise much exaggerated, as Christine Gallant has rightly argued:

> The unspoken and unexamined assumptions of this criticism exclude any consideration of the marginalized experience. All—writer, reader, and critic—are assumed to share a process of individuation that is not scarred or deformed by a social evaluation of oneself as being innately inferior. Participation in the hegemony is taken for granted. (145)

I shall return to this and other accusations that have been leveled against "traditional" Jungian criticism. In the case of much "Lacanian" literary criticism, exegetes have usually striven both to emulate the master's written style and to achieve the highest possible concentration of abstruse "Lacanian" terminology, including those pseudo-mathematical formulae and schemata that already present a very considerable challenge to the interpreter in their original context.[3] It has not seemed to matter much that this is all profoundly anti-Lacanian: for Lacan, style and individuality are one and the same. Accordingly, he was quick to criticize those of his pupils whom he considered guilty of ostentatiously and unthinkingly parroting his terminology and theoretical models.[4] He devoted a great deal of attention to criticizing what he saw as the psychoanalytic establishment's thoughtless reliance on Freudian concepts in the routine of their daily work; one of the functions of his weekly seminar was to revisit and rethink many of these principles.[5]

So not only is an extreme ambivalence about the value of the literary work common to Jung and Lacan, but early attempts at literary criticism in the wake of both thinkers also tended to reproduce and accentuate some of the more regrettable tendencies in Jungian and Lacanian theoretical writing. Having established that there are indeed certain overall similarities between the place accorded to literature in the works of the two writers and the ways in which these works have in turn influenced literary critics, in the following section I shall discuss a selection of those comparisons between Jung and Lacan that have proliferated in recent Jungian scholarship.

THE APPROPRIATION OF LACAN:
A POST-JUNGIAN TEMPTATION

It is not insignificant that discussions of Jung in conjunction with Lacan have, to my knowledge, thus far been ventured exclusively by Jungian scholars—overwhelmingly literary or cultural theorists, workers in academic fields in which the prestige of Lacan is, for many reasons, considerably greater. By contrast, that I am aware, no Lacanian has yet felt it worth his or her while to investigate even Lacan's several *overt* references to Jung. There are, then, certain marginalizing institutional pressures operating against literary and other critics who describe their work as "Jungian," pressures that the insertion of the "post" into "post-Jungian" has in itself done little to relieve; non-Jungians, moreover, have been slow to recognize the importance of the post-Jungian project. Post-Jungian theory at its best has endeavored to open Jung's work to that of related thinkers, notably Lacan. The inventiveness and indeed the courage of pioneers in this field should not be underestimated. Yet it is important for the success of the post-Jungian project that claims made on behalf of Jung are not exaggerated at the expense of other thinkers: the risk inherent in overemphasizing similarities is one of appropriation. I aim in this section to substantiate these reservations with reference to the work of two of the most distinguished contributors to the post-Jungian project.

Andrew Samuels, writing in the *Cambridge Companion to Jung*, maintains:

> Lacan's decentering of the ego exposes as delusive the fantasy of mastery and unification of the personality. . . . The recognition that there are limits to the ego's consciousness, and that there are other kinds of consciousness, are anticipated by Jung's notion of the Self—the totality of psychic processes, somehow "bigger" than the ego and carrying humanity's apparatus of aspiration and imagination. (Introduction 5–6)

My question is simply: in what sense can Jung really be said to "anticipate" Lacan's position? The "decentering of the ego" can only be described as "Lacan's" in a kind of shorthand: this decentering of the ego that Lacan does indeed emphasize had already been posited by Freud. Bound up with Freud's discovery of the unconscious is the realization that the ego is no longer at the center, is no longer master in its house. Neither Jung nor Lacan was the first to suggest that "there are limits to the ego's consciousness." The credit for this fundamental insight must, I think, go to Freud. It should come as no surprise that there are certain fundamental similarities between thinkers who use (even if very differently) the concept of the unconscious as their foundation and these are properly to be explained, I would argue, by their shared *Freudian* inheritance. I would argue that the same can also be said for many of the other items in Samuels's list of Jung's intuitive "anticipations" of the work of later psychoanalytic theorists: a semblance of likeness is achieved either by withdrawing to a level of excessive generality or by isolating common features that ought in all honesty to be seen in the light of the common Freudian influence, however uncomfortable this recognition may be for a Jungian.

In his pioneering earlier work, *Jung and the Post-Jungians*, Samuels evokes in passing another point of convergence between Jung and Lacan: "Lacan's Symbolic and Imaginary orders may be aligned with Jung's archetypal theory (collective unconscious) and personal unconscious respectively. . . . Lacan's concept of the Real . . . approaches Jung's elaboration of the psychoid unconscious" (40–41). Such point-by-point terminological matching suggests that Lacan's theoretical language is far more static than is actually the case: it neglects the tantalizingly evanescent and mutually interconnected character of each order in the Symbolic-Imaginary-Real triad as it functions in the economy of Lacan's own work.[6] The assumption of fixity that such terminological matching presupposes runs counter, as I have already suggested, to the very sense of Lacan's persistently destabilizing, re-dynamizing, approach. Similarly, but perhaps less stridently, Jung often insists on the primarily heuristic character of his own theoretical formulations and is always alert to the risk that particular ways of describing and understanding psychic processes may unwittingly serve to reify and trivialize them.[7]

Susan Rowland, in her groundbreaking *C. G. Jung and Literary Theory*, undertakes a sustained and thought-provoking comparison between Jung and Lacan (among other prominent figures in contemporary literary theory). She is convinced that Jungian theory has a genuine contribution to make to current debates, though she is also committed to a "post-Jungian" revision of many of the more objectionable aspects of Jung's own writing: she wrestles in particular with his presentation of women, striving to salvage a Jungian discourse free from Jung's misogyny. My concern about Rowland's approach is whether the affinities that she claims to have identified between Jungian theory and Lacanian analysis are not in fact more produced by than represented in the language in which she chooses to rephrase key Jungian insights. In the following passage, for example, she casts individuation in that language of otherness so prevalent in contemporary poststructuralist discourse, Lacanian theory included:

What appears to be more promising in the concept of individuation is the privileging of Otherness in the construction of subjectivity. Since the Other within, the unconscious, can be constructed as the Other without, the Other gender or simply Other people, then Jungian theory could form a flexible ethical model that counteracts the model of ego psychology as heroism. (12)

Paradoxically, this redeployment on Jung's behalf of the language of alterity so very familiar from poststructuralism risks suppressing certain differences and resistances to such thinking that are characteristic of the Jungian perspective: one of the effects of this attempt to "rephrase" Jung in a language of otherness is, ironically, to limit the otherness and the difference of Jungian theory. Moreover, this deployment of a poststructuralist idiom of otherness does not in itself make it any clearer how the link from individuation to ethics is to be made in conceptual terms.[8]

The second phase of Rowland's engagement with Lacan is her argument for what she suggests is a Jungian feminist reading of Lacan:

If Lacan sees a female "lack" built into the system of gender formation, then Jungian theory could suggest that the cultural Symbolic is distorted by patriarchal discourses of which the phallus-as-signifier is a key ingredient. . . . This enables Lacan to be characterized as a product and producer of patriarchy. (32)

Yet the fact that this very charge had already been leveled against Lacan, incessantly—and indeed there is a sizeable body of feminist discussion of Lacan already in existence[9]—must surely raise questions about the status and value of this post-Jungian contribution to the debate, at least for non-Jungians: is it recognizably (post-)Jungian and does it add anything new to the existing discussion? And what about the other view of Lacan, which Juliet Mitchell and others have voiced, namely, that he is analyzing how patriarchy operates, which makes his work a useful propaedeutic to feminist projects for change?

Rowland's post-Jungian engagement with Lacan is, then, a bold attempt to map out theoretical interconnections. Yet both her and Samuels's work come dangerously close to appropriating Lacan on Jung's behalf, and, in an understandable desire to open Jungian theory to wider intellectual debates, they tend to ignore key points of real antagonism between the two thinkers. Having surveyed existing attempts to bring Jungian and Lacanian theory into productive dialogue, which have to varying degrees tended to elide or gloss over distinctive differences, I shall now return to my own examination of this relation-ship, in the specific domain of literary art, while striving to remain atten-tive to points of resistance and mismatch.

SELF-DIVESTITURE: THE COMMON GROUND

I shall contend that it is in Jung's view of the creative process that his work is most readily comparable with that of Lacan. Jung has a view of creativity that involves self-divestiture or self-dispossession. He describes how works of what he calls "visionary" art[10] are written:

> These works positively force themselves upon the author; his hand is seized, his pen writes things that his mind contemplates with amaze-ment. The work brings with it its own form . . . while his conscious mind stands amazed and empty before this phenomenon, he is over-whelmed by a flood of thoughts and images which he never intended to create and which his own will could never have brought into being. (*CW* 15: 73)

He characterizes the work of visionary art as follows: "One might almost describe it as a living being that uses man only as a nutrient medium, employing his capacities according to its own laws and shap-ing itself to the fulfilment of its own creative purpose (*CW* 15: 72). This view of the artist as mere vessel, the mere site at which archetypal pat-terns express themselves—which, in Jung's case, it has become custom-ary to tag and dismiss as Romantic—is in fact strikingly similar to Lacan's celebrated poststructuralist view of the human subject as mere plaything of linguistic forces: "Man speaks, then, but it is because the symbol has made him man" (*Ecrits* 65). The Lacanian subject is made, "spoken," by language—s/he is formed by words more than s/he forms them, even as s/he forms them—just as the Jungian artist is subjected to the particular essence of the work fashioned by the collective uncon-scious. The collective unconscious makes the work of art *with* the artist just as, in the following description, Lacan characterizes neurosis as a question that the unconscious asks *with* the subject:

> A question that being poses for the subject "from where it was before the subject came into the world" . . . it poses the question for the sub-ject. . . . It does not pose it *before* the subject, since the subject cannot come to the place where it is posed, but it poses it *in place* of the sub-ject, that is to say, in that place it poses the question *with* the subject, as one poses a problem *with* a pen. (*Ecrits* 168)

I cannot be concerned here with the plausibility of the Jungian account of the creative process any more than with that of this Lacanian characterization of neurosis or his view of the primacy of the symbolic. What is of interest to me here, rather, is this convergence of the two thinkers. I would suggest that Jung's account of a certain mode of writerly creativity corresponds to Lacan's general view of the way in which language determines the human subject. This correspondence is based upon the idea that subjectivity is conditioned by imposed structures that have preceded and will outlast it. Both Jung's visionary artist and Lacan's neurotic have an experience of being manipulated, *articulated*, by forces foreign to and greater than themselves.

Yet what, if any, are the broader implications of this convergence? Jung's visionary artist cannot be an inherently privileged individual—he is merely the vehicle for creative forces over which he exercises neither ownership nor influence. Indeed, in Jung's account, the very reason why the work of visionary art is held to be *great* art—the ground of its meaning and value—lies in the fact that it expresses aspects of those creative psychic forces that ultimately determine the subjective experience of all human beings but that, in their intimate workings, happen to be inaccessible to the vast majority. Thus, in Jung's account, the visionary artist simply experiences and (somehow) represents in symbolic form something that any human being could experience. The element of self-divesture in this artist's experience is not merely an incidental and dispensable feature of the Jungian account: Jung's very point is that the essence of human subjectivity is the self's being articulated by forces greater than it.[11] Art is "great" to the extent that it manifests this truth of subjectivity.

In Jung's account, then, the artist's experience of self-divesture must be conceived as an experience of how things really are for us all, as a universal truth about the human psyche. Similarly, in the Lacanian account of neurosis, the way in which the unconscious asks a question *with* the subject—articulates the subject—is (somehow) merely a more intense experience of what Lacan holds to be universally true of the role of language in the formation of subjectivity. So, this point of convergence between Jungian and Lacanian theory, which we isolated initially in the similarity between Jung's description of the visionary artist and Lacan's characterization of the neurotic, may indeed be extrapolated further on both sides. Indeed, there is a sense in which this extension is irresistible, for both thinkers have theoretical difficulties containing the extreme cases that are the visionary artist and the neurotic: neither can quite pinpoint the distinguishing difference between these cases and ordinary experience, the nature of which these extremes are held to illuminate all too brightly. Jung cannot ultimately distinguish between art and mental disturbance. He states, as I have already noted, in brute psychological terms, "Between an artistic inspiration and an invasion there is absolutely no difference" (CW 18: 34). And in the case of the patient who is judged to be mentally ill, Jacques-Alain Miller reports this question of Lacan's:

> "How do we not sense," Lacan asked, "that the words we depend upon are imposed on us, that speech is an overlay, a parasite, the form of cancer with which human beings are afflicted?" If we identify ourselves with the psychotic, it is insofar as he is, like ourselves, prey to language, or better, that this is what he teaches us. (49)

From this perspective, the difference between the patient and the analyst is not essential or ontic but is, rather, one of position or one of intensity of experience. As Miller glosses: the patient who "hears voices" is someone who encounters "the emergence of the discourse of the Other, but directly, without this soothing misapprehension of the reversal that makes us believe that we speak, when in fact we are spoken" (49). In psychoanalytic terms, the patient just experiences directly—*too* directly—something universally true about the dependence of human subjectivity upon language. For both Jung and Lacan, delicate and ultimately undecidable must be the boundary between intense, "extreme," experience—artistic or pathological—and the dulled, or "normal," experience that this is held to illuminate.

By focusing on Jung's view of writerly creativity, I have isolated a point of convergence between his and Lacan's theories. I have argued that this is more than a question of superficial similarity or a forced marriage of terminology and that this convergence has wider (indeed irresistible) ramifications in the theoretical work of both thinkers. Yet this is only one side of the story: I have now to address certain other aspects of Jung's view of literature that seem steadfastly hostile to a number of key Lacanian insights.

THE RESISTANCE OF JUNGIAN ANTI-TEXTUALISM

If some claim to have discovered in Jung's work all the hallmarks of a typically poststructuralist thematization of textuality, I can only suggest that this is because they set out to find it there. Jung's work in general, and most strikingly that concerned with literature, is remarkable precisely for what I would call its *anti*-textual bearing. In "Psychology and Literature," although the examples of visionary art that Jung cites happen to be literary works, what he says of them could equally well have been said of works in any other art form. Form is secondary: Jung claims in his review of "The Tale of the Otter" that this story "is only a literary form for a content that could have been expressed in quite other words and in quite another way" (*CW* 18: 762). Examples of the higher of Jung's two kinds of art, visionary art, when these are books, prove curiously independent of their very medium—the written word. Indeed, the more prominent the textuality—the language, style, narrative technique, or other formal features of the work—the more likely that we are dealing with a second-rate work, one of the "psychological" type. This anti-textual approach is clearly apparent later in the review already quoted:

> What the heart hears are the great, all-embracing things of life, the experiences which we do not arrange ourselves but which happen to us. All the pyrotechnics of reason and literary skill pale beside this and language returns to the naive and childlike. Simplicity of style is justified only by significance of content, and the content acquires its significance only from the revelation of experience. (*CW* 18: 763)

Thus for Jung, the experience is paramount and the form that "clothes" and communicates this to others chiefly concerns him when it threatens to distract attention from the experiential content with its vain (pyro)technicality. Form always risks betraying content and is envisaged as a necessary evil, at its least noxious when kept simple ("naive and childlike"); nowhere in Jung's writings on art is it suggested that form might fulfill a positive, potentially enhancing role.[12] As Elizabeth Wright has noted, "there is a disregard of the text's articulation of its verbal elements. Jungian literary criticism does not go by the letter" (68). Jung's anti-textual bias is not confined to his engagement with literature, though it is perhaps most striking there. To read his remarks about engaging with "history" and alchemy, it is as though texts had never been involved. Even in his extended analysis of Nietzsche's *Thus Spoke Zarathustra,* as in his *Answer to Job,* Jung has scarce little to say about the compelling extremes of form and language that are such striking features of the works in question. Terence Dawson has perceptively remarked that what I have called Jung's anti-textualism is "disappointing" in view of the fact that "many of his major ideas were derived from his interpretation of a remarkable range of *texts*" (255). Not that Jung's anti-textualism prevents him from using textual tropes, which may mislead:

> I handle the dream as if it were a text which I do not understand properly, say a Latin or a Greek or a Sanskrit text, where certain

words are unknown to me or the text is fragmentary, and I merely apply the ordinary method any philologist would apply in reading such a text. (*CW* 18: 83)

Yet, as Jung's many accounts of dream analysis clearly show, he approaches a dream less as a philologist trying to read a text and more as a curator of paintings attempting to identify and narrativize obscured images. In the context of our discussion of Jungian anti-textualism, Jung's own description of his procedure in terms of reading characters is potentially misleading, for he strictly sees dreams not as texts, as networks of written characters, but primarily as arrangements of visual images. As we shall now see, it is in Jung's overwhelmingly anti-textual approach, and in particular in his indifference to, or outright suspicion of, the very medium of the literary work—language—that he is most plainly at odds with Lacanian thinking.

In the early 1950s, in some of his most widely read work, Lacan continually emphasized the centrality of language to psychoanalysis. This foregrounding of language will probably be remembered as Lacan's most important, original, and enduring contribution to psychoanalysis. In addition to his celebrated principle, "the unconscious is structured like a language," he asserted that "psychoanalysis has only a single medium: the patient's speech" (*Ecrits* 40). Lacan was to insist in his theory and in his rhetoric, as "Anna O." had once remarked, that psychoanalysis was essentially the "talking cure." The thrust of his argument in this period was, in Elizabeth Grosz's words, "Psychoanalysis has no other aim, object, procedure, or techniques other than those given by language" (114). In its essence, psychoanalysis is about the relationship between the human being and language: "Freud's discovery was that of the field of the effects in the nature of man of his relations to the symbolic order" (Lacan, *Ecrits* 64). All this will be familiar to the reader who has even a passing acquaintance with Lacan. My concern here is not to rerun arguments that have been amply developed elsewhere but rather to ask: For literary study informed by Jungian theory, what are the implications of the fact that this theory, quite unlike Lacan's, is by turns indifferent and hostile to both language and form?

WORDS OR IMAGES?

Whereas the Lacanian unconscious is composed of potentially word-forming linguistic structures, the Jungian (collective) unconscious is made up of structures with a potential for image formation. According to Jung, it is the presence of images formed by these "archetypes" or "archetypal patterns" that characterizes the true work of art. Such "archetypal images" are expressed in "symbols." Jung characterizes symbols as preverbal: "attempts to express something for which no verbal concept yet exists" (*CW* 15: 70). Symbolic expression is top-heavy with meaning: "A term or image is symbolic when it means more than it denotes or expresses" (*CW* 18: 185). By contrast with the brutish straightforwardness of rational discourse, symbolism works on the oblique, by indirections: "One could say that this dream-image was symbolic, for it did not state the situation directly but in a roundabout way" (*CW* 18: 204). Each of these characterizations of the symbol is suggestive of a distinct interpretive route through Jung's *Collected Works*. There is, however, another feature of the Jungian archetypal image, or symbol, upon which Jung does not tend to dwell but which is crucial to this comparative analysis and which has far-reaching implications for the literary scholar. Images and symbols are, in themselves, single and *static;* by contrast, the narratives, myths, to which they are in some way connected are *extended* in time or text. Jung never actually makes clear how the static images are related to the extended narratives. Their connection is usually asserted in a frustratingly vague way, for example: "This symbol *brings up* the hero myth" (*CW* 18: 102; emphasis added). Moreover, it is not clear from Jung's many descriptions whether he thinks of these images or symbols as freeze-frames from the myth, which "bring up" or suggest the absent remainder by synecdoche, or whether they are thought of as somehow resuming the myth in its entirety. Either way, the archetypal images or symbols have ontic and epistemic priority over the myths that they suggest and constitute, for it is only by means of the archetypal images that myths are anchored in the collective unconscious and thereby acquire their significance. The static image is the basic unit of meaning.

All this poses a problem for the Jungian literary critic: being narrative, the global structure of works of literature resembles far more closely that of what Jung calls myth than it does that of the static archetypal image or the symbol. Yet the specific quality of myths, as opposed to images—the "narrative difference"—does not seem to have interested Jung. And indeed many of the excesses of "traditional" Jungian criticism can be traced back to Jung's own disregard for the structural and linguistic specificity of written texts. It is entirely wrong to assume that the mere act of identifying the figure of the Great Mother, for example, in a literary text is to have interpreted that text: locating the Great Mother is, if anything, preliminary to interpretation proper, which would go on to examine the way in which this figure is incorporated into and *rearticulated* by the kinds of language and narrative structure in combinations and inflections peculiar to the work in question. In particular, this interpretative work would have to determine—in a close look at form, language, and narrative structure—precisely which of the multifarious and opposing faces of the archetype were foregrounded in the text under examination.

Narrative appears to fare very much better in Lacan's work. Indeed, a certain Lacan (considerably in advance of Hillman's argument in *Healing Fiction*) is apt to characterize psychoanalysis itself in terms of story-telling: "It is certainly this assumption of his history by the subject, in so far as it is constituted by the speech addressed to the other, that constitutes the ground of the new method that Freud called psychoanalysis" (*Ecrits* 48). And anamnesis he characterizes as a fictive and future-orientated rewriting of the subject's past:

> I might as well be categorical: in psychoanalytic anamnesis, it is not a question of reality, but of truth, because the effect of full speech is to reorder past contingencies by conferring on them the sense of necessities to come, such as they are constituted by the little freedom through which the subject makes them present. (*Ecrits* 48)

Yet we are bound to wonder whether the overemphasis on similarity of material content that has afflicted Jungian criticism is perhaps mirrored—inverted and reflected—by the (over)privileging of form and narrative structure that we find in Lacan. Thus he writes that while the ancients sometimes saw in dreams the messages of the gods, "What interests us is the fabric in which these messages are incorporated, the web in which, sometimes, something is caught" (*Les Quatre Concepts* 45; my translation). It is mainly in this fabric—this surface texture, the mode and manner in which the dream (and by extension the literary text) operates—that its significance lies. The reader may suspect at this point that such a privileging of form at the expense of content is no more helpful to the literary critic than the Jungian preference for the opposing position.

But what precisely is Lacan's view of the status of the image content of dreams and of its role in their interpretation? He writes that dream images "are to be taken only for their value as signifiers, that is to say, in so far as they allow us to spell out the 'proverb' presented by the rebus of the dream" (*Ecrits* 159). The visual images of the dream in themselves are meaningless; they only acquire meaning, Lacan argues, when placed in the verbal context of the analysand's account of the dream and his or her associations with its particular parts. The dream is a rebus, or "proverb"—a network of images given in place of their linguistic meaning. Now it is well known that Jung advocated interpreting the dream "on its own terms"—with and through its own imagery—and it may appear as though Jung must be diametrically opposed to Lacan on this matter. Yet, although the divergence is wide in theoretical terms, it is not clear that the practical (clinical) difference is at all as great: after all, Jung and Lacan both agree that a dream in itself is a series of images, and Jung, no less than Lacan, offers an interpretation of the dream that is essentially verbal, an interpretation that narrativizes, establishing language-based connections, that supplies linguistic meaning where previously there had only been images. A more telling practical consequence of this theoretical divergence lies in the attitude toward the dream images *after* interpretation. In the Lacanian account, there is no further use for them once their linguistic meaning has been fully expressed: they may as well be discarded. From a Jungian perspective, by contrast, they remain intrinsically interesting, not only because the verbal interpretation must inevitably have failed to do them full justice, but also because they are to be prized as things of value, the treasured elaborations of a creative inner life, and not treated merely as disposable signifying matter.

(POST-)JUNG WITH LACAN?
IMPLICATIONS FOR THE STUDY OF LITERATURE

Even if Lacan may be thought to place too exclusive an emphasis on the connecting fabric of dreams and texts for the liking of the literary critic, his unswerving commitment to the power of language was always destined to endear him to anyone whose business is the study of texts, and all the more so in preference to a Jung whose anti-textualism is so prominently displayed. Yet to descend at this point into a merely competitive comparison, to abandon Jung for Lacan, would be unfortunate indeed. I want to ask instead what it is about Jung that attracts literary scholars in the first place, in spite of the anti-textualism of which they are surely well aware. Why have Jungian literary critics embraced Jung in spite of his pronounced anti-textualism? What is it about Jungian theory that has appealed to literary critics?

When addressing what might seem to be the paradoxical appeal of Jungian theory, I am reminded of this remark of Lacan's in another context: "the strength of the churches resides in the language they have been able to maintain" (*Ecrits* 72). Rather than poring over the techniques (or indeed the prejudices) that are to be found in Jung's work—in short, aspects of its content—it might be more productive to ask what sort of *language* the tradition, or "church," of Jungian and post-Jungian theory has fostered. A language of interiority, certainly, one in which inner experience is valued and real: this is the force of Jung's insistence on the reality of psychic phenomena. And the tradition has fostered an imaginative language circumscribing a universe of inexhaustible creative resourcefulness—even "mental illness," Jung remarked, is simply what "we" call the psyche's attempt at self-cure (*CW* 18: 169). Of course, it is important to recognize that there are areas in which this language is unsuitable (lest even the dictator be explained away as the attempt of the collective unconscious at compensatory correction). Yet there is no need to demand that any one kind of language either be valid in every domain or in none. And there are aspects of this language of interiority that are entirely appropriate to the literary encounter: reading is a solitary pursuit, even in company, and involves according reality and value to phenomena experienced in creative isolation. Reading involves an attentiveness to experience that is, in one respect, "inner." Reading is, indeed, more closely allied to the Jungian perspective's enduring care for the dream images than to the Lacanian assumption that they are redundant once "processed." The relevance of Jung to the study of literature lies less in his explicit theorizations of writerly creativity and more in the affinities of his language and approach with the reading encounter. Jung's work provides us, then, with an *analogy* of the reading encounter.

By way of conclusion, I should like to set out what I see as the relevance of my argument here to the post-Jungian enterprise. The preceding discussion is not intended to offer a complete blueprint for some future practical "application." Rather, it is informed by a Lacanian sense of the need to keep on theorizing, without the expectation of reward (which is not at all the same as believing that no reward will come). It is to be expected that such an approach will irritate those who remain committed to Jung's ostentatious impatience with "theorizing." Yet the *post*-Jungian project must involve an encounter with theory, even with theory for theory's sake, without the expectation of a practical payoff and without prior commitments as to the meaning and value of the "practical." My claim in this chapter that the notion of self-divestiture lies at the heart of both the Jungian view of artistic creativity and the Lacanian theory of the subject suggests at least that both stand together in their opposition to Ego Psychology's attempt to form the individual into a productive member of late-capitalist society. For both, pure theory should perhaps be seen as a means of resisting—creatively and meaningfully—the Ego Psychologist's insistence on productivity and, by extension, that of the society s/he aspires to represent.

Within the post-Jungian attempt to open Jung's work to the wider intellectual environment, the danger of reduction is great indeed. I have endeavored to demonstrate in this short study of self-divestiture that to bring Jung into meaningful exchange with another thinker requires, paradoxically, a large measure of self-restraint: the temptation is strong to overemphasize similarities in order to clinch a comparison. And it is stronger still when, for whatever reason, the academic prestige of the thinker in question is higher than that of Jung himself.

Jung with Lacan, yes—literary study needs both or neither—but tentatively.

NOTES

1. I cannot discuss here the array of different responses which this single recommendation has actually engendered. Suffice it to say that one uniting assumption has been that to view Lacan's work "as literature" implies not also viewing it as the outline of a coherent mode of clinical practice. Perhaps the most intelligent of these responses is that of Shoshana Felman, who argues for the importance of recognizing the "interimplication" of Lacanian psychoanalysis and literature, a mutually invigorating relationship which denies priority to either term.

2. The first English edition is John Rodker's translation in 1949 of Marie Bonaparte's *The Life and Works of Edgar Allan Poe, A Psycho-analytic Interpretation*.

3. This is not a challenge that can be met by taking them literally—that is, mathematically—which was plain to most readers of Lacan long before they encountered the patronizing pamphlet that is Sokal's *Intellectual Impostures*.

4. In his 1954–55 seminar, Lacan voiced his concern over the abuse of the mirror stage: "The mirror stage isn't a magic word. It's already a bit dated. . . . In order to make progress, one should know how to go back over things" (*Seminar* 102).

5. Lacan's self-appointed task was to reinvigorate psychoanalysis by discovering anew the incisive strangeness native to Freudian theory, much of the force of which he thought had been lost in years of unthinkingly orthodox "application" within the psychoanalytic establishment. He writes: "I consider it to be an urgent task to disengage from concepts that are being deadened by routine use the meaning they regain both from a re-examination of their history and from a reflexion on their subjective foundations" (*Ecrits* 33).

6. Malcolm Bowie argues that "Each of Lacan's orders is better thought of as a shifting gravitational centre for his arguments than as a stable concept" (*Freud, Proust and Lacan* 115). Even if this characterization somewhat overemphasizes the fluidity or instability of Lacan's theoretical formulations, this is surely the side on which readerly caution errs.

7. The reservations—from a Lacanian perspective—about some of Samuels's remarks that I have voiced here could also be raised in the case of Christopher Hauke's *Jung and the Postmodern*. For example, in a gesture to the mirror stage, Hauke claims that:

> The importance of Lacan's psychoanalytic view to the present argument is how it situates the formation of subjectivity in the *particular context of modernity:* as for Jung, <u>the modern ego or subject</u> suffers a partial and distorted experience of 'humanity'—an experience where much has been withdrawn, excluded or levelled out. (166; underlining added)

Yet the notion that the ego and the subject are identical, as Hauke dangerously implies in the passage underlined, is precisely what Lacan denies most vigorously of all in his paper on the mirror stage. Furthermore, it is entirely unclear why this theory of Lacan's should be thought particularly to explain, still less to be confined to, the formation of the *modern* subject. And as for the view that Jung and Lacan are similar in that both hold that the ego is only a small part of the picture, there is nothing here (as in the first of Samuels's formulations discussed above) that cannot be explained simply as an immediate consequence of Freud's discovery of the unconscious, a discovery to which both thinkers are evidently indebted. Hauke's comparison is flawed and frustrating.

    8. Rowland's description of the relationship between Jungian theory and deconstruction is similarly contestable. She writes that "what is productive for contemporary literary theory in Jungian writings is an awareness of an Otherness to theory embedded in textuality. Of course, it is Jung's affinities, not identity with, deconstruction which bring the discourse into a relationship with contemporary literary theory" (24). However, not only do these alleged "affinities" owe much (again) to the shared Freudian inheritance—Derrida acknowledged Freud's formative influence on deconstruction, along with Nietzsche and Heidegger (in *Writing and Difference,* Ch. 10)—but Rowland seems to suggest that the mere fact that the Jungian text can be subjected to a deconstructive reading implies that it has affinities with deconstruction; but *any* text can be deconstructed. She writes that, "Feminist deconstruction of Jungian texts is facilitated by the affinities of Jungian discourse with deconstruction" (36). Yet even if Jung's work did have meaningful affinities with deconstruction, there is every reason to suspect that these relationships would *complicate* rather than facilitate the business of a deconstructive reading; it would be rather like treating an analysand who had read a great deal of psychoanalytic theory—by no means impossible but perhaps rather more difficult.

    9. See chapter 6 of Elizabeth Grosz's excellent *Lacan: A Feminist Introduction* for an intelligent overview of the debate.

    10. In "Psychology and Literature" and "On the Relation of Analytical Psychology to Poetry" (both in *CW,* vol. 15), Jung's principal theoretical writings on literature, he divides works of literary art into two categories: (i) "psychological," or works that straightforwardly "spring wholly from the author's intention to produce a particular result" (72), and (ii) "visionary" works, which are described above. Jung has comparatively little to say about the former category in either essay and it seems clear to me that this is because, in his understanding, "visionary" art is the superior, the true and essential, form of art. From

the way in which Jung briefly describes the prominence of planning and technique in works of the "psychological" type, we can infer that he views these to be grossly inferior: overstylized and drily deliberate exercises in verbal virtuosity. We shall be concentrating here on what Jung has to say about "visionary" works.

11. Thus any attempt to tone down Jung's account of artistic creativity by removing the element of radical self-divestiture is to be rejected. Henderson, for example, thinks that the Jungian artist can be turned into a placidly industrious craftsman:

> We are more likely to find today that a true artist, far from seeking self-divestiture, discovers his identity, that which makes him most real to himself and to others, by means of an aesthetic attitude which has all the continuity and consistency of a conscious vocational commitment. From this point of view, the artist is not merely a mouthpiece for the unconscious; he functions as a craftsman or artificer whose actual technique is just as important to his work as its content. (57)

12. There is, however, an isolated reference to formal accomplishment in Jung's preface to *Ulysses*, albeit a rather disapproving one: "Joyce's inexpressibly rich and myriad-faceted language unfolds itself in passages that creep along in tapeworm fashion" (*CW* 15: 128).

WORKS CITED

Bonaparte, Marie. *The Life and Works of Edgar Allan Poe, A Psycho-Analytical Interpretation*. Trans. John Rodker. London: Imago, 1949.

Bowie, Malcolm. *Freud, Proust and Lacan: Theory as Fiction*. Cambridge: Cambridge UP, 1987.

———. *Lacan*. London: Fontana, 1991.

Dawson, Terence. "Jung, Literature, and Literary Criticism." Young-Eisendrath and Dawson 255–80.

Derrida, Jacques. *Writing and Difference*. Trans. Alan Bass. Chicago: U of Chicago P, 1978.

Felman, Shoshana. *Jacques Lacan and the Adventure of Insight*. Cambridge, MA: Harvard UP, 1987.

Gallant, Christine. *Tabooed Jung: Marginality as Power*. Basingstoke: Macmillan, 1996.

Grosz, Elizabeth. *Lacan: A Feminist Introduction*. London: Routledge, 1990.

Hauke, Christopher. *Jung and the Postmodern: The Interpretation of Realities*. London: Routledge, 2000.

Henderson, Joseph L. "The Artist's Relation to the Unconscious." Sugg 54–58.

Hillman, James. *Healing Fiction*. Woodstock, CT: Spring, 1983.

Jung, C. G. *The Collected Works of C. G. Jung*. Ed. Sir Herbert Read, Michael Fordham, and Gerhard Adler. Trans. R. F. C. Hull. 20 vols. Princeton: Princeton UP, 1953–91.

Lacan, Jacques. *Ecrits: A Selection*. Trans. Alan Sheridan. London: Tavistock, 1977.

———. *Les Quatre Concepts fondamentaux de la psychanalyse*. Paris: Seuil, 1973.

———. *The Seminar of Jacques Lacan*. Trans. Sylvana Tomaselli. Cambridge: Cambridge UP, 1988.

Miller, Jacques-Alain. "Teachings of the Case Presentation." Schneiderman 42–52.

Mitchell, Juliet, and Jacqueline Rose. *Feminine Sexuality: Jacques Lacan and the école freudienne*. London: Macmillan, 1982.

Rowland, Susan. *C. G. Jung and Literary Theory: The Challenge from Fiction*. Basingstoke: Macmillan, 1992.

Samuels, Andrew. Introduction. Young-Eisendrath and Dawson 1–13.

———. *Jung and the Post-Jungians*. London: Routledge, 1985.

Schneiderman, Stuart, ed. and trans. *Returning to Freud. Clinical Psychoanalysis in the School of Lacan*. New Haven: Yale UP, 1980.

Sokal, Alan D. *Intellectual Impostures. Postmodern Philosophers' Abuse of Science*. London: Profile, 1998.

Sugg, Richard P., ed. *Jungian Literary Criticism*. Evanston: Northwestern UP, 1992.

Wright, Elizabeth. *Psychoanalytic Criticism: A Reappraisal*. Cambridge: Polity, 1998.

Young-Eisendrath, Polly, and Terence Dawson, eds. *The Cambridge Companion to Jung*. Cambridge: Cambridge UP, 1997.

Detective Films and Images of the Orient

A Post-Jungian Reflection

∽∾∽

LUKE HOCKLEY

Walsh (Joe Mantell) to J. J. Gittes (Jack Nicholson):
Forget it, Jake. It's Chinatown.
—*Chinatown*

INTRODUCTION

The purpose of this chapter is to examine detective films from the perspective that is offered by analytical psychology. It will focus on the centrality of the act of detection, as both a narrative and psychological
activity, and will examine the relationship of the detective to the Orient.
More specifically, it will explore the way that images of Oriental cultures
and Chinatown permeate detective films. Moving among questions of
race, post-Jungian critiques of Jung's analytical psychology, and detective films, the chapter will reposition the work of detection away from
the legal realm of law and order and closer to the psychological world
of self-investigation and individuation. At the same time, it will suggest
that the work of psychological development, which Jung called the individuation process, lies at the heart of analytical psychology and involves
the acceptance of both personal and collective responsibilities.

DETECTION: THE POLITICAL AND SELF-UNDERSTANDING

Whether it is a film or a book, a newspaper article or a television program, the activities of reading and viewing are similar, insomuch as both
involve the activity of detection. For the detective, following clues to
eliminate the impossible and then, no matter how improbable, using the
evidence at hand to reveal "who done it," is all part of a day's work.
This is work that brings the detective into contact with the quasi-mytho-
logical underworld of crime and murder and with the imagery of the
unconscious. Jung was alert to the idea that "detection" can be an archetypal activity, and he also understood that one of the ways in which we
make sense of our lives is through images. Jung encouraged his patients
to paint, sculpt, and build; he wanted them to be creative and to put
their images to good therapeutic use. Like detectives, analysands worked
at understanding what their images might mean, what these clues might
say about their psyche and about their relationships with others. In
devising the process of "active imagination" (in which analysand and
analyst enter into the images of the analysand's fantasy world, and, in so
doing, come to a better understanding of real world problems) Jung was
breaking new ground. In establishing the bond between analyst and analyzed in the therapeutic relationship, Jung suggested that meanings were
not arbitrary but rather the result of a negotiation between analyst and
client. In short, if Jungian psychology is anything, it is a psychology of
images. As Jung put it in 1934, "The symbolic process is an experience
in images and of images" (CW 9.1: 82; emphasis in original). Images
have the potential to challenge our self-perceptions and help us to
understand the various elements of our social identity, race, gender,
class, age, family relations, and sexual orientation—all of which affect
our sense of who we are and how we relate. Understanding these is integral to the work of individuation.

   Yet Jungian psychology has come in for its fair share of attacks: the
terms "mystical" and "otherworldly" have been applied, and not without some justification. Among other commentators, Ellwood has noted
the lack of attention that analytical psychology has paid to politics and
its significance in shaping human existence and experience:

> From the Jungian perspective, real life is not, on the profoundest level,
> one's worldly life of homes, marriages, or jobs, but is the flow of a
> mighty underground river to which life's surface phenomena are but
> reflections or diversions. Politics as such are the least of concerns to the
> god of this river, yet the river is the ultimate source of all that happens
> in politics, as in everything else. (37)

Some post-Jungian theorists, notably Andrew Samuels, have openly sought to redress this imbalance, and with some success. In fact, while many Jungians might not want to acknowledge this, there lies at the heart of analytical psychology an intrinsically political project. In his writing about individuation, Jung was constantly at pains to stress that individuation is about gathering the world to oneself; it is about *not* shutting it out. The individual exists in relationship to history and culture, and individuation involves accepting our collective responsibilities and ties.

That Jung was not aware, we might say conscious, of the political importance of his psychological observations suggests that something was afoot in his own unconscious; that he vigorously denied that political symbols and ideologies could be powerful and play a role in a healthy psychological life smacks of repression. Take, for example, the following statement from a 1921 article on the psychology of types: "The great events of world history are, at bottom, profoundly unimportant. In the last analysis, the essential thing is the life of the individual. This alone makes history, here alone do the great transformations take place" (*CW* 6: 119). By 1935, in the article "Archetypes of the Collective Unconscious," Jung was writing:

> Anyone who has lost the historical symbols and cannot be satisfied with substitutes is certainly in a very difficult position today: before him yawns the void, and he turns away from it in horror. What is worse, the vacuum gets filled with absurd political and social ideas, which one and all are distinguished by their spiritual bleakness. (*CW* 9.1: 28)

Never one to play down a point, Jung even more dramatically wrote in an article from 1939, "Our blight is ideologies—they are the long-expected Antichrist!" (*CW* 11: 778). Of course, it is important to locate this remark historically in the context of the developments in Germany. But Jung's blind spot, when it came to recognizing the potential of his analytical psychology to embrace and critique political events and relationships, should not deter us from exploring the interrelationships that exist between unconscious forces and the realities of human existence. These realities are embedded in social and economic relations but can also be viewed from a psychological perspective. They are also, in part, played out on the cinema screen. Thus the two views—that life is built on unconscious dynamics, and that experience is the result of power relationships—are equally important.

The detective, as we are familiar with him, might initially seem to operate in a world that is outside politics. But in fact he is intimately embroiled with power and definitions of normality. In narrative terms, he acts as an agent of law and order who, with the solution to a crime, seemingly restores the textual world to a state of balance and harmony. But the situation is not so straightforward. The detective does not operate in a vacuum, and his world is one in which murders are commonplace. And at the heart of his experience is Chinatown. Images of the Orient permeate detective films, and in their evocation of the Other they are less representational than they are mythic in their quality. As symbols, they stand for something other than themselves. To borrow a couple of terms from linguistic theory, they are more connotative than denotative.

DETECTIVE FILMS AND INDIVIDUATION

While remaining alert to the dangers of overstating the case, it may be that films give a symbolic expression to elements of the psyche that have been repressed. Unwittingly, we recognize on the screen images of our unconscious. The literal form of projection in the cinema turns out to mirror the process of psychological projection. Jung remarks that "projections change the world into the replica of one's own unknown face" (*CW* 9.2: 17). So, too, we can recognize elements of unconscious lives, emotional, political, social, and so forth, on the silver screen. This may partly explain why figures such as the detective and the femme fatale, with their setting in the underworld of crime, murder, and corruption, have proved enduring. Their appeal lies not just in their role as narrative agents but also in their psychological qualities.

A traditional way to interpret the topography of detective stories is to reconstruct their narrative elements in psychoanalytic terms. The article "Detective Stories and the Primal Scene," by Geraldine Pederson-Krag, does precisely that. The crime the detective seeks to solve is embodied in the primal scene and develops into the impossibility of the Oedipal situation. The act of detection carried out by the child involves piecing together from matters overheard, glimpsed, and imagined, what the parents are up to. However, the perspective of analytical psychology offers an alternative view. Here, the detective is on a more personal search: the elements of the story operate as symbols and represent the quest for self-awareness. Hauke draws attention to the importance of Jung's idea of individuation, which is

> probably one of the most central defining concepts of Jung's psychology and one that distinguishes his perspective from those of the other depth psychologies. . . . Individuation is about the dual struggle of the

subject with, on the one hand, the "inner world" of the unconscious in its infantile, personal and collective aspects, and, on the other hand, the struggle with the "outer world" of collective society. (169)

However, from a post-Jungian perspective we might also think of individuation itself as a fantasy or illusion. Individuation is not a literal process; instead, it can better be thought of as metaphor. To borrow a term from James Hillman, but to use it slightly differently, what individuation offers is an "ideational perspective" (116–31). When we use the language of individuation, archetype, symbol, myth, consciousness, and so forth, we are using a metaphorical terminology. Yet there is a clear tendency within Jungian thought to treat these elements as though they were literally true, whereas actually they offer a way of describing and understanding experience. This is important, because I want to argue that this view of the world is of help in understanding that cinema films are inherently psychological. My intention is to shift the debate about cinematic representation away from a literal, almost documentary view of cinema towards a more metaphorical position. In a curious way, this is also an appropriately political project, because it aims to make us aware of how the process of psychological projection can shape and determine our views of the world. Indeed, in the end it may be more revealing not to engage in what amounts to a fantasy of opposites and instead to see inner and outer worlds as inextricably linked. Dissolving the projections and becoming aware of how our unconscious selves exert an influence will help us to engage with society in a more meaningful manner or, to put it psychologically, will serve to make us more conscious.

Seen like this, the city in detective films stands as a potent image of individuation. Echoing this, the Jungian analyst Carotenuto has drawn attention to the relationship between the city or town and the labyrinth:

> The structure of the little town, with all those intersecting streets, calls to mind the archetypal image of the labyrinth, which fundamentally expresses the path of life. Indeed, our existence, if it is to proceed individually and responsibly, cannot be linear as is commonly believed; a life lived in an authentically human way requires continual choices among various directions and different possibilities. (48)

If the city is an image of individuation, then the characters that people its streets take on something of an archetypal character. The criminal becomes a personification of the shadow of the detective. This archetype stands for the underdeveloped and weaker side of our psyche and also embodies those elements of our psyche that we would rather repress; it

acts out the potentially destructive and chthonic aspect of human existence. It is important to remind ourselves that here we are reflecting not
on real crime in the "outer world" (although our perception of such
events is influenced by psychological material) but rather on the inner,
symbolic world of the objective psyche, of the unconscious.

CHINATOWN: THE ORIENT IN DETECTIVE FILMS

The quest for truth draws the detective inexorably towards the Orient. Frequently, what the detective finds at the heart of the cinematic city is Chinatown, almost a city within a city. The Chinatowns encountered in detective films are strong communities. There is little sense in which these
societies represent a repressed, downtrodden minority; in fact, if anything,
they are strong, secretive communities. What they are is different, they are
"other," and they mark everyone who enters them as different. In some
ways, Orson Welles's *The Lady from Shanghai* (1948) is not a typical
detective film, although it shares many of the characteristics of that genre.
Michael O'Hara (Orson Welles) is the character that has to make sense of
what is happening, as well as the person that the other characters in the
film believe to be the most malleable and open to manipulation. The character of Elsa Bannister (Rita Hayworth) is the femme fatale and also the
"lady from Shanghai" of the film's title. Most of the characters in the film
are shot in shadow, suggesting the dark, largely unknowable side to the
psyche. By contrast, Elsa Bannister is given the full-Hollywood, diffused,
backlit, key-and-fill treatment—she appears to be the innocent abroad, her
white dresses seeming to reinforce her purity. Indeed, that Hayworth had
her hair cut short and dyed blonde caused something of a stir at the time.
    The realization that Elsa is not what she seems comes close to the
end of the film and, significantly, takes place during a brief scene set in
San Francisco's Chinatown. By this point, O'Hara has discovered that
he has been set up as a murderer by Arthur Bannister (Everett Sloane),
a top-class lawyer and husband of Elsa. After taking a drug overdose,
O'Hara flees the courtroom and takes refuge in a Chinese theater. The
audience consists mainly of old Chinese men, and O'Hara looks completely out of place, but he evidently feels safe. Elsa tracks him down to
the theater and, speaking fluent Chinese, finds her way inside. We realize that she has more control of her life than we had been led to believe.
Curiously, as Elsa and O'Hara talk with each other, nobody in the audience seems much bothered; indeed, the audience remains equally impas-
sive when the police storm the theater. In her biography of Welles, Barbara Leaming interprets this as a deliberately Brechtian statement:

> Gravely disappointed at not having been able to work with Brecht,
> Orson had, by way of compensation, made a film that very subtly
> embodied key principles of Brechtian theatrical theory: most notably
> the actor's distance from his role, which also prohibits the spectator's
> identification with the action. (336)

This is a useful insight and in a curious way supports the interpretation of the scene as being in some way different from the rest of the film—even though Leaming does go on to suggest that all the performances in the film are subtly alienating. The symbolic quality of the scene prepares for O'Hara's discovery, in Elsa's handbag, of the gun that killed Grisby, Elsa's husband's business partner. These elements make us reinterpret our view of Elsa: the lighting, which appeared to symbolize purity, now takes on an ironic quality, as we realize that Welles was showing us that she was, after all, too good to be true; it seems that purity, if it exists at all, is defined in relationship to corruption—something of a consistent theme in detective films. From the psychological perspective, this acts as a metaphor for the dialogue between consciousness and the unconscious. The film is perhaps best known for its ending, which is set in a house of mirrors. Having passed out in the Chinese theater, O'Hara wakes up commenting, "I came to in the crazy house and for a while there I thought it was me that was crazy." The mirrors distort and fragment, causing multiple images of Elsa to fill the screen. While this is alienating for the viewer, it also symbolizes that O'Hara's view of Elsa had been based on illusions.

Frequently, Chinatown provides a source of inspiration for the detective and is a fruitful hunting ground for case-breaking clues. For example, soon after the start of Howard Hawks's 1946 film, *The Big Sleep,* comes an important sequence: Philip Marlow (Humphrey Bogart) arrives at the house of Geiger; after a couple of shots are fired, he rushes in to find Carmen Sternwood (Martha Vickers) with Geiger, dead on the floor. Carmen (described as "high as a kite" by Marlow) is dressed in clothing with Oriental motifs and is sitting on an Oriental-looking chair; a camera concealed inside a Balinese-style head has photographed her. The sequence introduces the pornography subplot, and the house itself becomes an important location in the film, providing the final location in which Marlow shoots the Oriental head. Even the less successful remake (*The Big Sleep,* directed by Michael Winner, 1978), which transposed the location to London, preserves the Oriental decor in Geiger's home. Other characters in Hawks's film are tinged with the Orient, as well, for example, Agnes Lowzier (Sonia Darrin), who works in the undercover pornographic bookshop. As Branson notes: "Agnes is briefly juxtaposed with an Oriental-like statue. She also wears a small Oriental deity there, on her blouse, and at a later point, Marlow describes her (in his policeman-like way) as 'brunette; green eyes—rather slanted'" (163). This type of Oriental *mise en scène* can also be seen in *Farewell My Lovely,* directed by Dick Richards in 1975, in which part of the plot revolves around the theft of a valuable jade necklace. In searching for it, Philip Marlow (Robert Mitchum) is sent to Chinatown. References to the Orient pervade the film: Marlow describes Helen Grayle (Charlotte Rampling) as "dragon-lady," and the brothel in which the drugged Marlow wakes up is called the White Orchid Club. In a similar vein, it is San Francisco's Chinatown that provides the setting for the end of Roman Polanski's *Chinatown* (1974). The audience has already discovered the dreadful truth that the daughter of Evelyn Cross Mulwray (Faye Dunaway) is also her sister, Katherine (Belinda Palmer). The final sequence in which Evelyn is shot and killed as she attempts to drive out of Chinatown with Katherine represents the punishment for the crime of incest.

JUNG AND THE ORIENT

The association of the Orient with the detective inevitably makes us wonder why this has come about and what its possible significance might be. Can a Jungian view of race and cultural identity be useful to us? This is a sensitive topic, not least because Jung was not always sensitive in the way that he dealt with racial matters. Indeed, if we approach his writing on this subject from a fundamentalist perspective, then it becomes largely unusable. But there is another approach, which is to identify what is useful in analytical psychology as the basis upon which to reflect on how a post-Jungian view of cultural identity can be developed. Adams points out:

> [I]t seems to me that Jungians are under no duress to accept uncritically everything that Jung may have said on the topic of "race." They *are* under a scientific and ethical obligation to scrutinize and revise Jungian theory and practice when experience and evidence contradict it. To be a "Jungian" does not mean to be "Jung" any more than to be a "Freudian" means to be "Freud." (131; emphasis in original)

There is little question that Jung was interested in the East, in Oriental religious teaching and in the more esoteric aspects of ancient Oriental spiritual practices. He had a particular interest in the *I Ching*, a Chinese system for divination, and he wrote the foreword to Richard Wilhelm's translation. Wilhelm also translated and wrote an explanation of *The Secret of the Golden Flower: A Chinese Book of Life,* which is concerned with Chinese yoga. It is also an alchemical treatise that contains details of mystical practices and, according to Jung, insights into the human psyche. Jung provided the psychological commentary (CW 13: 1–84) and, indicating the friendship between the two men, gave the principal address at Wilhelm's funeral on 1 March 1930. Jung had received the book in 1928, and it proved influential in shaping his thinking on the nature of the objective psyche; in his 1929 commentary, Jung is at pains to stress the value that he attributes to Oriental life in providing a counterbalance to the extraverted rationalism of the West:

> The East teaches us another, broader, more profound, and higher understanding—understanding through life. We know this only by hearsay, as a shadowy sentiment expressing a vague religiosity, and we are fond of putting "Oriental wisdom" in quotation marks and banishing it to the dim region of faith and superstition. But that is wholly to misunderstand the realism of the East. Texts of this kind . . . are based on the practical insights of highly evolved Chinese minds, which we have not the slightest justification for undervaluing. (*CW* 13: 2)

Because he was writing in the 1920s, the way in which Jung adopts a non-Eurocentric approach and was prepared to learn from other cultures marked an informed and enlightened attitude. However, there is a problem. When Jung writes about societies he tends to generalize and use the term "character." In so doing, he blurs the distinction between the individual and the collective and conflates the notions of race and nation. Samuels comments on this problem, and, while he refers specifically to Jung's writing on "African character," the general point holds: "But when Jung generalizes about African *character,* and does so from a solely psychological point of view, ignoring economic, social, political and historical factors, then he spoils his own work, inviting the severe criticism he has received" (*Political Psyche* 310). This actually marks a fairly constant pattern in Jung's writing, where he focuses on the mythological and spiritual dimensions of a society, while at the same time assiduously ignoring the social and political. There is a lack of focus on history and culture as contributing factors in human development. As Adams puts it, "[h]istorically, Jungian analysis has tended to regard the typical components of the psyche as strictly archetypal, not stereotypical. That is, it has tended to reduce the stereotypical to the archetypal, the cultural to the natural" (39–40).

To be fair, Jung explains differences in culture by references sometimes to race, sometimes to history, sometimes to culture, and at other times by reference to evolution. This is typical of Jung: that he was breaking new ground is reflected in the considerable fluidity of his writing. Unsurprisingly, as his thinking developed, he quite naturally refined what the terminology of analytical psychology meant. For example, Jung uses the terms image, symbol, and archetype in different ways at different times. We also see the same idea expressed in different ways, and even a core concept such as the objective psyche is referred to variously as "the collective unconscious" and "the psychic organ." This leaves us with the challenge of identifying where the strength of his argument lies. One of the key points that I want to identify is Jung's insistence in 1929 that the archetype is a psychosomatic concept, that body and psyche cannot be considered independently of each other: "it must be pointed out that just as the human body shows a common anatomy over and above all racial differences, so, too, the human psyche possesses a common substratum transcending all differences in culture and consciousness" (*CW* 13: 11). This clearly positions the concept of the objective psyche as a human, not racial, theory of the unconscious. As Adams observes, "[l]ike Lévi-Strauss, Jung argues that if skin color matters at all, it matters not as natural or 'racial' phenomenon but as a strictly cultural or historical phenomenon. Ultimately, it is history, not 'race' or skin color, that matters. If there is 'psychological' stratification, it is not 'racial' but historical" (119).

The historical influences can be seen in the interaction between archetypal material and personal experience. While the archetypal patterns may remain outside time and history, the images that these patterns assume are affected by our upbringing, by societal and cultural experiences, by class, race, family, sexual orientation, and so forth. Jung not only realized this but also actually suggested that it was important for the analysand to accept personal factors and recognize the role that the seemingly impersonal elements of culture at large play in shaping our psychological relationship to the world. As Jung notes,

> [F]or it often happens that, when a problem which is at the bottom personal, and therefore apparently subjective, coincides with external events that contain the same psychological elements as the personal conflict, it is suddenly transformed into a general question embracing the whole of society. . . . [I]f the connection between the personal problem and the larger contemporary events is discerned and understood, it brings a release from the loneliness of the purely personal, and the subjective problem is magnified into a general question of our society. (*CW* 6: 119)

This provides us with a clue on how to interpret Jung's writing on the Orient. Instead of seeing his view of the East in documentary terms, we need to reposition it as an archetypal fantasy, and, as we shall see, this fantasy—not something that is pathological, but a necessary part of psychological apperception—is alive and well in contemporary detective films. If we take Jung at face value, then the observations of critics such as Ellwood, who level the charge of "Orientalism" at Jung, are not unreasonable. He notes: "One product of the European mentality was what has more recently been called colonialist if not imperialist scholarship, or 'Orientalism,' readings of non-European peoples in terms that justified the political and spiritual hegemony of the imperial powers" (49). As Ellwood goes on to make clear, his claim can easily be justified. But another way of thinking about Jung's remarks is to reframe them as a psychological projection. What happens in this projection is that there is a failure to recognize how the extraverted rationalism of Western thought masks the intuitive and spiritual dimension of the psyche, which is consequently projected onto the Orient. Jung hints at this: "Because the European does not know his own unconscious, he does not understand the East and projects into it everything he fears and despises in himself" (*CW* 18: 8). The result is a projection that has two faces, both of which become thrown onto the world: one is fear and the other is a deep attraction. This goes some way to explaining why Jung wrote as though the entire Orient was made up of individuated, spiritual individuals. It also provides an insight into the reason Jung was adamant that Oriental spiritual practices were useless for Westerners:

> There could be no greater mistake than for a Westerner to take up the direct practice of Chinese yoga, for that would merely strengthen his will and consciousness against the unconscious and bring about the very effect to be avoided. The neurosis would then simply be intensified. It cannot be emphasized enough that we are not Orientals, and that we have an entirely different point of departure in these matters. (*CW* 13: 16)

RISING SUN: DETECTING THE ORIENT

Rising Sun is an adaptation of a Michael Crichton novel of the same name. The film follows the plot of the book fairly closely, but significantly it introduces and develops one theme in particular, namely racism. The film revolves around the murder of a young white woman in the Los Angeles office of the high-tech company Nakamoto. The murder takes place during a lavish reception that is being held by the Japanese corporation to mark the opening of their new tower. The building is equipped with state of the art surveillance technology that captures the murder on digital videodisk, but subsequently the images on the disks are doctored to incriminate Eddie Sakamura (Cary-Hiroyuki Tagawa). It is the task of John Conner (Sean Connery) and Web Smith (Wesley Snipes) to uncover the truth. Interwoven with this story is another that deals with the business relationships among Nakamoto, MicroCon (an American high-tech company involved in defense), and a U.S. senator, who turns out to be implicated in the murder. In true Hollywood style, corruption and deception abound and Conner and Smith expose this as they solve the case.

The solution of the crime is largely due to the efforts of John Conner. He is the only Westerner in the film who understands Japanese culture. He lived in Japan, can speak fluent Japanese, and understands the cultural nuances of how business there is carried out. Other cops do not like him because he solves cases "Japanese style." Like most detectives in films, Conner is an outsider. Played by Sean Connery, he is a Scot, and as such he is part of neither the Japanese nor the American cultures. The location of his apartment, near San Francisco's Chinatown, suggests this ambiguity, as do his personal relationships. His partner is a beautiful dual-race woman, Jingo Asakuma (Tia Carrere). While she has a deformed hand, her real "deformity" is her parentage—a Negro father and a Japanese mother. The film comes dangerously close to promoting racism towards Japanese people by noting how unwelcome this made her in Japan. She comments, "I was deformed. I fell in love with a Caucasian who was living there." Further reinforcing how out of touch with the "real world" Conner is, he is the only person to argue that "their way is better"—a comment that is somehow neutralized by his sense of not belonging. As an archetypal figure, he embodies many of the qualities of the trickster and wise person. He uses his *chokkan* (intuition) to understand what is going on, and his dialogue emphasizes this as it is peppered with phrases such as, "If you sit by the river long enough, you will see the body of your enemy floating by." And, "When something looks too good to be true, it is untrue." Yet these comments are tinged with a knowing irony; this type of wisdom is indeed too simple, too easy, and too good to be true.

His character provides a counterbalance to Tom Graham (Harvey Keitel), a racist, corrupt cop with no interest or understanding of Japanese culture. His racism towards the Japanese is couched in both economic and cultural terms. He notes of the Nakamoto Tower, "They built this building in six months, not one American worker." The inference is clear, as it is in his comment that the murderer left Cheryl Lynn (Totjana Patitz) "lying dead on the boardroom table, like a piece of sushi." The film stereotypes Japanese culture as high-tech, other, mysterious, powerful, dangerous, cold, and callous. Somehow this notion of good other (Conner) and bad other (Japan) suggests the potential of the psyche for health and creativity; at the same time it encompasses the capacity of the psyche for fear, xenophobia, and greed. The film takes murder, the traditional business of the detective, and relocates it to a contemporary business setting. This re-mythologizing suggests something potent about the myth of detection, something that has a psychological relevance for our current cultural condition.

Different again is the partnership between Web Smith and John Conner. This is presented in terms of a *kohai* (young man)/*sempai* (older and more senior man) relationship. When Conner tells Smith that he is going to be his *sempai,* Smith is quick to observe caustically, "That wouldn't be anything like Masa, now would it?" Later, when someone mistakes him for a parking valet, he rightly puts him firmly in his place: "No. You get the senator's car. Wrong guy, wrong fucking century." The message is clear: racism toward African Americans will not be tolerated. Racism towards the Japanese is, of course, an altogether different matter. As the truth begins to emerge, the narrative suggests that the Nakamoto corporation is quite comfortable engaging in dirty tricks. As Eddie Sakamura remarks, "Business is war. I know you understand." Showing that indeed he does understand, later in the film Conner remarks, "The war is never over . . . we're in the war zone." It therefore comes as little surprise when Nakamoto uses its political connections to bring pressure to bear on the investigation. What is surprising is that it takes the form of racist accusations:

> Web Smith: Japan bashing. What will they think of next?
> John Conner: Next. Next they'll call you a racist.

I am suggesting that played out in the film is both an actual real-world fear, which is expressed in terms of the economic power of Japanese corporations, and a psychological fear of a different culture. At the same time, this is an inner-world psychological fear of the unconscious, and of course the two become mixed up. This type of projection is commonplace: we choose to make our psychological projections onto receptive material. Here we have to be careful; we must be alert to the difference between inner- and outer-world fears. We must distinguish between the archetypal fantasy of the Orient, expressed in the film using the mythology of capitalist business and the sense of a real-world Japan, and the proper condemnation of anything racist:

> When considering national psychologies, we need to remember that these do not need to be taken absolutely literally. When one talks in general terms of the national psychology of Britain or Japan, one is engaging in a kind of fantasizing process: Britons are reserved, ironic, emotionally repressed, and possessed of "grace under pressure"; Japanese people are disciplined, obedient, courteous, and unimaginative. Such fantasy needs to be valued as psychically real, even if arguable from a factual point of view. (Samuels, *Politics* 190)

Coupled with this is a sense in the film in which capitalism has let us down: it has not bought the prosperity, the contentment, or equality it promised. The poorest group in *Rising Sun* are some young African American men; their power, such as it is, manifests itself as destructive aggression. The film offers little by way of alternatives. However, it does suggest the need for different economic relationships that enable tolerance and inclusivity, which again implies that there is a relationship between the political and the psychological (see Samuels). In the film, no one can be trusted. *Rising Sun* expresses disillusionment with the police, big business, the senate, and interpersonal relationships. Everything seems dysfunctional.

CONCLUSION

At the heart of this chapter has been the attempt to see the detective as a potent psychological figure, as much concerned with the inner work of individuation as he or she is with the outer world of work and detection. The mythological world of the detective is changing; it is now less involved with a murky underworld and more focused on the failure of capitalist business. But underneath this change remains a connection to an archetypal fantasy about the Orient. Understood from a post-Jungian perspective, this can be interpreted as a rejoinder to pay attention to the potentially change-making, psychological dimension of human life:

> We must couple a less simplistic methodology and a more sensitive set of political values to Jung's intuitions about the centrality of a psychology of cultural difference. If we do so, then analytical psychology has something to offer depth psychology that is concerned with processes of political and cultural transformation. (Samuels, *Political* 336)

In this chapter I have tried to heed this advice and to blur the distinction between inner and outer worlds: to see that films can refer to our everyday, lived reality and can also maintain the capacity to be metaphorical—sometimes at the same time. If analytical psychology has something to offer film analysis, then it lies in the area of understanding that images belong to both the conscious *and* the unconscious. From a psychological perspective, this may seem like a rather obvious claim, but much film theory finds its roots in an approach to cinema that is overtly materialistic. Even psychoanalytic cinema theory has been heavily influenced by a Marxist approach to structural linguistics. Indeed, when film theorists have paid any attention to analytical psychology, one of their criticisms is that Jungian thought is otherworldly and insufficiently rooted in the political realities of contemporary society. For example, Miller suggests in his overview of critical approaches to Hitchcock's *Psycho* that this perspective lacks the capacity for a political engagement with society: "Lastly, I turn to myth criticism, derived from the legacy of Carl Jung, which adopts a semi-spiritual stance on the text. Such an approach cannot understand feminist concerns" (331). Admittedly, in context he is making a specific point, but this example serves to illustrate that there are two arguments that still need to be won. First, a post-Jungian approach to film studies has the capacity to make a significant contribution to film theory. Second, analytical psychology is not a mystical, self-indulgent approach to life. Rather, it offers a valuable perspective through which to engage with actual events and issues in contemporary society. The hope is that by reflecting on films in this way we can come to a fuller understanding of our relationship with the "real world."

WORKS CITED

Adams, Michael Vannoy. *The Multicultural Imagination: "Race," Color and the Unconscious.* London: Routledge, 1996.

Barthes, Roland. *The Pleasure of the Text.* Trans. Richard Miller. New York: Hill and Wang, 1975.

Baudrillard, Jean. *Simulacra and Simulation.* Trans. Sheila Faria Glazer. Ann Arbor: U of Michigan P, 1994.

The Big Sleep. Dir. Howard Hawks. Warner Bros., 1946.

The Big Sleep. Dir. Michael Winner. United Artists, 1978.

Branson, Howard. *Howard Hawks: A Jungian Study.* Santa Barbara: Capra, 1987.

Camus, Albert. *The Outsider.* Trans. Joseph Loredo. Harmondsworth: Penguin, 1981.

Carotenuto, Aldo. *The Vertical Labyrinth: Individuation in Jungian Psychology.* Toronto: Inner City, 1981.

Chinatown. Dir. Roman Polanski. Paramount Pictures, 1974.

Dalal, Farhad. "Jung, a Racist." *Journal of Psychotherapy* 4. 3 (1988): 263–79.

Deconstructing Harry. Dir. Woody Allen. Jean Doumanian Productions/Sweetland Films, 1997.

Ellwood, Robert S. *The Politics of Myth: A Study of C. G. Jung, Mircea Eliade and Joseph Campbell.* New York: State U of New York P, 1999.

Farewell, My Lovely. Dir. Dick Richards. AVCO Embassy Pictures, 1975.

Hauke, Christopher. *Jung and the Postmodern: The Interpretation of Realities.* London: Routledge, 2000.

Hillman, James. *Re-Visioning Psychology.* New York: Harper, 1975.

Hockley, Luke. *Cinematic Projections: The Analytical Psychology of C. G. Jung and Film Theory.* Luton: Uof Luton P, 2001.

Jung, C. G. *The Collected Works of C. G. Jung.* Ed. Sir Herbert Read, Michael Fordham, and Gerhard Adler. Trans. R. F. C. Hull. 20 vols. Princeton: Princeton UP, 1953–91.

———. Foreword. *The I Ching or Book of Changes.* Trans. Richard Wilhelm and Cary F. Baynes. 3rd ed. Bollingen Series 9. Princeton: Princeton UP, 1950. xxi–xxxix.

The Lady from Shanghai. Dir. Orson Welles. Columbia Pictures, 1948.

Leaming, Barbara. *Orson Welles: A Biography.* Harmondsworth: Penguin, 1985.

Miller, Toby. "*Psycho*'s Bad Timing: The Sensual Obsessions of Film Theory." *Companion to Film Theory.* Ed. Toby Miller and Robert Stam. Oxford: Blackwell, 1999. 323–32.

Papadopoulos, Renos. "Jung and the Concept of the Other." *Jung in Modern Perspective.* Ed. Renos Papadopoulos and Graham Saayman. Hounslow: Wildwood, 1984. 54–88.

Pederson-Krag, Geraldine. "Detective Stories and the Primal Scene." *The Poetics of Murder: Detective Fiction and Literary Theory.* Ed. Glen Most and William Stowe. New York: Harcourt, 1983. 13–20.

Rising Sun. Dir. Philip Kaufman. Twentieth Century Fox, 1993.

Sammon, Paul, M. *Future Noir: The Making of Blade Runner.* London: Orion, 1996.

Samuels, Andrew. *The Political Psyche.* London: Routledge, 1993.

————. *Politics on the Couch: Citizenship and the Internal Life*. London: Profile, 2001.

Wilhelm, Richard, and Carl G. Jung. *The Secret of the Golden Flower: A Chinese Book of Life*. Trans. Richard Wilhelm and Cary F. Baynes. London: Kegan, Paul, 1931.

The Woman in the Window. Dir. Fritz Lang. RKO Radio Pictures, 1944.

Airing (Erring) the Soul

An Archetypal View of Television

❦

KEITH POLETTE

Taste is the only morality. . . . Tell me what you like, and I'll
tell you what you are.
> —John Ruskin, *The Crown of Wild Olive*

We identify so much with the fleeting consciousness of the
present that we forget the "timelessness" of our psychic
foundations.
> —C. G. Jung, "Flying Saucers"

The cult of TV is not due to a natural human need; man is not
naturally oriented toward entertainment.
> —Roberts Avens, "Reflections on Wolfgang Giegerich's
> 'The Burial of the Soul in Technological Civilization'"

Every night millions of Americans are abducted by an alien presence.
These abductions, however, are not the stuff of tabloid journalism. We
will not see a host of UFOs hovering in skies over suburbia and secretly
spiriting Americans into their disc-shaped bellies for the purposes of
enigmatic experimentation. No, what abducts myriad Americans nightly
is something we have eagerly invited into our homes: it is that luminous
presence called TV.

Even though most of us have, at some point, been abducted by TV, do we really know what this abducting presence is and why so many of us long for abduction so often? To attempt to answer these questions, we will employ Jung's archetypal approach. At first glance, this may seem an odd choice, as Jung did not write about TV but about the archetypal intricacies of the enigmatic, image-based psyche. But he does offer us a method to follow, one that is fecund with imaginal possibilities because it is grounded in the notion of subversion, that is, in the conscious move to disrupt, disturb, undermine, and see through our accepted notions of "what is" in order to discover the archetypal dynamics informing the underlying structures of appearances. And because TV is so many things to so many people, we need to approach it with a flexible and multilayered method that is equal to the task of discerning what lies beneath its disparate faces, multiple channels, and numerous fantasies.[1]

Our first turn at understanding the archetypal dynamics of TV will take the form of a question: which mythical figures stand behind TV? The question centers us in Jungian thinking and assumes that if we know who or what informs the structure and function of TV, we will then better understand what TV means—and thus we will understand how to renegotiate our relationship with it. This approach will place us in the world of myth and mythical thinking, a world and mode of thought that Jung discovered, both personally and professionally, as foundational to all psychic processes and all aspects of knowledge. He writes that "the psyche creates reality every day" (*CW* 6: 52) and that "archetypal explanatory principles . . . are the sine qua non of the cognitive process" (*CW* 12: 288–89). He adds that "all mythical figures correspond to inner psychic experiences and originally sprang from them" (*CW* 9.1: 154). Hence, to catch sight of, and relate to, the "archetypal principles" underlying TV, we must look to the mythic figures—"the psychic experiences"—that stand behind it. To think mythically, then, is to discover that behind everything we think, do, and say is an imaginal figure, an archetypal entity—in a word, a god. James Hillman writes, "There is no place without Gods and no activity that does not enact them. Every fantasy, every experience has its archetypal reason. There is nothing that does not belong to one God or another" (*Re-Visioning* 168–69). To find the gods of TV, then, we will use the mythic method of discovery; for if we do not identify the mythic figures—the gods—who drive TV and our need to watch it, we will never penetrate to the core archetypal patterns that give rise to our ideas, actions, and fixations about what TV is and how we relate to it. As such, we must move backwards and downwards, away from a strict adherence to logos and towards an appreciative employment of mythos.

TV: BACKED BY AN OMNIPRESENT, OMNIPOTENT DEITY

Following Jung's dictum to "stick with the image," we will examine TV initially by seeing where it is and what it does. In other words, we will not look initially at TV's programs but at TV's position and energetics; and in so doing we will bring into relief one of its archetypal dimensions, that is, a god who stands behind it.

By reconnoitering ninety-two million American households—which equals ninety-eight percent of the population (Allen, "More Talk" 1)—we will spot at least one television set, usually in a position that commands the focal attention of each living or family room. We will also notice that, more often than not, the furniture in those rooms is arranged to afford the best view of TV rather than to accommodate social integration or to facilitate easy conversation. Other sets in over seventy percent of American households will be found in bedrooms, kitchens, bathrooms, basements, and attics—as well as in vans and SUVs. Because we have surrounded ourselves with TVs, we want one always to be instantly near-to-hand—and near-to-eye. Sandy Flitterman-Lewis writes, "The television set occupies a space that is nearby—just across the room, at the end of the bed, in the palm of our hand, or elsewhere. The television screen thus takes up a much-reduced, and more intimate, part of the spectator's visual field and seems available at a moment's notice" (218). Not only has TV secured a strong position in our homes, but it has broken out of the house and invaded restaurants, taverns, airports, bus stations, stores, hair salons, and service stations, to name just a few. TV in America is nearly everywhere. It has become our near-constant companion and our unconscious master; it occupies prominent places in our lives, and it demands that we look long and longingly at it.

TV is nearly everywhere in America, but why? Most of our discussions about TV focus on human actions as the manifestations of social or cultural influences that can be deduced and articulated. And while such an approach has merit, it misses the deeper point. It fails to see the god that puts itself eternally in the sightlines of our eyes. Hillman writes that "the main image of God in our culture [is] omniscient, omnipotent, eternal, seated. . . . The high god of our culture is a senex god" (*Blue Fire* 208). TV is reproduced endlessly in shapes that range from palm-size to giant-size; it is everywhere. As such, TV fulfills the fantasy of omnipresence, an all-pervasive position that was once reserved for the "senex god of our culture."

Not only do we see TV as omnipresent, but we regard it as omnipotent, as well. It overpowers the eyes and paralyzes the movement of the imagination. Consider: as soon as a person enters a room lit by TV, his or her eyes, like moths to a porch light, are drawn to its flickering, flat face. With bright, ever-changing spectacles of light and color, TV lures us to look. Jane Healy tells us that TV uses such "salient features" as "bright colors, quick movements, or sudden noises [to] get attention fast, since brains are programmed to be extremely sensitive to such changes that might signal danger" (200). And Neil Postman writes that "the average length of a shot on a network television program is somewhere between three and four seconds" (78). A flashy, quick-cut artist, TV entices us to watch, lest we miss something bright, fast, colorful— or dangerous.

TV's colorful quick-cuts certainly conflate the differences between signals of danger and signals of pleasure. But TV also cuts the image of the senex god, as well as all other interior archetypal figures, literally out of sight by using the techniques of flash and color to dominate the eyes and keep them locked on the set. TV keeps our eyes tracked and paralyzed along a flat, horizontal line. Jung writes that in the world of mythology, the eyes are often associated with the "motif of polyophthalmia," and they "point to the peculiar nature of the unconscious, which can be regarded as a 'multiple consciousness'" (CW 9.1: 346). TV-entranced eyes, however, do not look up or down, do not extend themselves to search out what is above, below, or to the side. In short, TV eyes are blinded to multiple points of view that exist outside of the rectangular frame of reference. When eyes adopt the TV outlook, they confine themselves to a linear and limited view and necessarily ignore the possibilities of investigating and employing the "multiple consciousness" that, metaphorically, results from multiple movements of the eyes. And, when the eyes are focused on TV and held within its frame, mono-consciousness is the only mode experienced. Vertical dimensions are closed; images of the mythic figures who soar through the imaginal sky of the mind or dwell deeply in the chthonic underground of the psyche are shunned. Hillman writes:

> If our society suffers from failures of imagination, of leadership, of far-sighted perspectives, then we must attend to the places and moments where these interior faculties of the human mind begin. Remember the psalm: "I shall lift up mine eyes—from whence cometh my help." That primordial gesture toward the upper dimension, that glance above ourselves, yet not lofty, spacey, and dizzy, may be where the first bits of interior change take place. (*Blue Fire* 111)

So long as TV restricts the movement and the awareness of the eyes, up or down, it assumes an omnipotent position that successfully shuts down access to the imagination. When the eyes are overpowered by TV's flat-line trajectory, the "I" is similarly flattened and reduced. Subjectivity shrinks, restricting the ability of the "I" to venture into deep imaginative places in order to initiate important "interior changes."

TV's dominance extends to the ears, as well. Like the senex of old, TV is jealous of any voice that is not sanctioned as its own. David Marc writes: "By manufacturing norms and by announcing the parameters of acceptable manners, styles, and language usage, [television] stimulates and constricts behavior, setting contexts and expectations for future events" (49). And Mimi White writes that "television can be seen as working to contain minority positions or deviations from the mainstream" (185), because "the range of ideological positions to be found on television is ultimately limited to sets of cultural and social beliefs that are not extreme" (190–91). By harnessing any voice that would declaim an extreme position—especially a position that works against simplistic ideas or capitalist notions—TV-as-senex tells its viewers only what's best for them to hear. And TV, being owned and operated by the moneyed few, doesn't allow viewers to hear voices that do not happily converge with conservative capitalist or religious thought. On TV one will not find, for instance, commercially supported airings of radical Marxist, anarchist, existential, feminist, or minority thought. In this way, TV marginalizes any group whose ideological perspective does not match its own. Moreover, TV actively works against, for instance, Jung's notion that for consciousness to evolve, it must come into contact with, and learn to relate to, disparate, divergent, and disregarded voices from within and without. In Jung's view, when one encounters such voices, especially those from the interior, one will find that they frequently reveal positions that are disturbingly antithetical to ego-bound, collective thought.[2] Jung writes: "The Other may be just as one-sided in one way as the ego is in another. And yet the conflict between them may give rise to truth and meaning—but only if ego is willing to grant the other its rightful personality" (*CW* 9.1: 132). By banning extreme voices, TV silences all Others who, one-sided or not, would act as counterbalancing, meaningful forces. The senex in TV will admit no voices that do not harmonize with its dominant, one-sided voice: the voice that is simple, spare, specific, dramatic, feeling-oriented, sensational, nonreflective, bipolar, judgmental, conservative, and capitalistic. Jung writes, "Ultimate truth, if there be such a thing, demands the concert of many voices" (Foreword to *Origins* xiv): when one monolithic voice reigns, the concert of truth perishes. As such, TV never speaks the truth, which is necessarily polysemous.

The postmodern equivalent of the premodern household altar, TV-as-senex is the site where the eyes and ears give their time and attention in regular, unconscious ceremonies of worship. TV's omnipotence does not stop with the domination and redirection of the eyes and ears; it also colonizes our notions of, and participation in, time. Measured by the amount of time it commands (second only to the amount of time people spend sleeping), TV has become the recipient of widespread "eye-dolatry." Mihaly Csikszentmihalyi argues that "the most ubiquitous medium for the exchange of information is television. It is the one that takes up the most of our psychic energy. . . . [I]n every culture where TV is accessible, people watch it more than they pursue any other activity in their free time" (135–36). And Robert Allen substantiates the argument: "Today, around the world, 3.5 billion hours will be devoted to watching television" ("More Talk" 1). One thing that distinguishes us as human beings, as opposed to animals, is our awareness of time. Animals, as far as we know, display no metacognitive sense of past, present, or future—or of the highly relative, interwoven status of each within each. Humans, however, are keenly aware of time's trinity of faces. Moreover, if we hold with Heidegger and allow the notion of time being in us, rather than our being in time, we see that our tripartite sense of time—the not-yet, the no-longer, and the here-and-now—is not so much an attempt to create fixed positions within time (and by extension, within ourselves) as it is an effort to hollow out imaginative places and spaces in our experience of time (and in our experiences of ourselves as both changing and nonchanging). We need to be able to step out of ourselves-as-time, paradoxically, to step more deeply into ourselves in a kind of time not predicated on the ticking of the clock: Jung's synchronicity, for instance, and the non–clock-driven experiences of musing, dreaming, or interacting with figures in the archetypal imagination.

TV, always "on the clock," blunts our awareness of anything other than its presentation of time. First, TV appears to have placed itself beyond time: unlike the 1950s when TV was young and the handful of broadcast stations actually went off the air at night, TV today does not rest, does not sleep; instead, today "most television stations broadcast around the clock or nearly so" (Kozloff 90). We view TV as a heroic, hypermanical insomniac that wants us to believe it has overcome time and obliterated all dead air space: "Surely television's unfailing effort to appear as if trying to tell all and show all, no matter that it fails, suggests that television not only wants to be on everywhere, but also wants to be on all the time" (Clough 70). A continually active presence, TV, in a muscular display of electronic omnipotence, sends the message that it has replaced finitude with infinitude and has collapsed past and future into an eternally transmittable present.

Furthermore, by keeping us viewing, TV colonizes our time, too. On average, Americans watch TV for seven hours per day (Allen, "More Talk" 1), and by the time an American child has reached the age of five, he or she has spent, on average, over six thousand hours watching TV (Sanders 39). All told, Americans, on average, spend seven years of their lives watching TV (Allen, "More Talk" 1). If we are watching TV one-fourth of each day, we are not, for instance, thinking, musing, creating, or interacting with real or imagined others:

> television has made us so thoroughly interested in drama, current events, spectator sports, illustrated music, monology, travelogues, the weather, old movies, new movies, gastronomy, animated cartoons, shopping, politically didactic religious sermons, sexual voyeurism, gossip, home improvement techniques, and Jeopardy that we are too busy for almost anything else, such as, say reading. (Marc 22)

More importantly, however, when we watch TV, we are unaware of the varieties of time itself, regressing to a state of mind that is little more than animalistic.

That TV induces a kind of animalistic lethargy is clear enough. Viewers of television display a variety of receding postures: some slouch in an overstuffed easy chair, others lounge on the sofa, and still others sprawl on the floor with a bag of chips within easy reach. Eyes glaze and breathing shallows as the sensibilities are numbed by a flood of predictable sights, sounds, and structures. Conversation is sporadic; words between viewers, usually uttered at commercial breaks, glance from person to person like rocks skipping across still pools. Through the unconscious unity of lethargy and the camaraderie induced by a TV-delivered, consciousness-stunting coma, viewers allow themselves to be lulled into the lotus-land of tele-vision—or what we might more appropriately call "the land of the long-distance look":

> Television the world over seems to have the following effects on viewers: It makes them feel very relaxed, but also significantly less active, alert, mentally focused, satisfied, or creative. . . . Like drugs, watching TV initially produces a positive experience. But after the viewer is hooked, the medium uses consciousness without providing further benefits. . . . [T]he more one watches TV in one sitting the worse one's moods progressively get. (Csikszentmihalyi 136)

Jane Healy, who has done extensive research in the relationship between brain development and the emergence of cognitive skills, tells us that TV promotes a "zombie-like affect" of "intentional inertia" among viewers—and especially among children (204). Marian Diamond and Janet Hopson note that "television's most pernicious quality is the tendency for even its best shows to encourage mental passivity—to dull the imagination and stifle active thought" (219). Similarly, Barry Sanders argues that TV is structured to promote "viewer passivity" (228).

Jung writes that "overvaluation of the object is one of the things most liable to prejudice the development of the subject. . . . [I]ndividual differentiation cannot possibly be maintained if external factors 'magically' interfere with the psychic mechanism" (*CW* 9.1: 275). By giving TV so much of our time, we overvalue it. What follows is a loss of subjectivity as we allow ourselves to become animal-eyed, zombie-gazers of reductive images that we did not create, and that we do not react or relate to, but that we have beckoned into our houses nonetheless:

> by organizing the "free time" of persons into end-to-end interchangeable units, broadcasting extends, and harmonizes with, the industrialization of time. . . . Leisure is industrialized, duration is homogenized, even excitement is routinized, and the standard repeated TV format is an important component in the process. . . . Time and attention are not one's own; the established powers have the capacity to colonize consciousness and unconsciousness. (Gitlin, "Prime Time" 578–79)

Entranced by TV's cool, glimmering eye, we place our imaginative responses in the freezer sections of our minds as we hold an iced Pepsi or Budweiser in one hand and the remote control in the other. We might wonder, though, why so many of us yearn for the numbing that TV regularly visits upon us.

TV'S GROUND OF HALF-FORGETFULNESS

A clue about the archetypal dynamics inherent in our desire to "TV" ourselves into animalistic and colonized numbness lies in the actionless action of TV viewing. When we switch on the TV and plop down in front of it to let its light flicker us into a simplified state, we are unconsciously attempting to move towards an archetypal reality, one wherein we hope to slip into deep, imaginative forgetfulness by sliding into what the Greeks mythologically referred to as the underworld waters of "Lethe." This is where Shakespeare's Richard II yearned to find the deep rinse of forgetfulness: "[O] that I could forget what I have been, / Or not remember what I must be now" (III, iii, 138–39). Under Lethe's influence, we relax our grip on the daylight world of troubles, particularities, and necessities; we loosen our hold on objects and intentions; we free ourselves from our paralyzed positions. When we drop into Lethe's wet regions, into the moist forgetfulness of archetypal territories, we thus make room for what James Hillman calls "the inflow of another sort of remembrance" (*Dream* 155).

This "remembrance" is the archetypal kind that Mnemosyne offers: a reminiscence of the often-ignored images of the deep self unencumbered by references to daily events; a memory unwilling to serve conscious designs or fit into the day world's schemata of necessities; a recollection that rises from a source beyond conscious construction. When we enter into watery concert with Lethe and Mnemosyne, we place ourselves in a position to re-member the movements of archetypal life-giving waters surging our way.

While TV viewing may seem to induce us towards Lethe's regions, it almost never takes us into the kind of archetypal forgetfulness for which we are unconsciously longing, for it is only, as Jeffrey Scheuer writes, "a phosphorescent rabbit hole for escaping reality" whose "very physical presence is an invitation to something nonpresent" (100). Although we may hope to "escape" our conscious selves by diving towards Lethe's depths—or by jumping into "the phosphorescent rabbit hole"—by watching TV, such dives are often less like plunges into unlit realms and more like belly flops into puddles lit by flashlights. Scheuer adds: "TV promotes narcissism and regression in the viewer: mental states that are inimical to complex, critical, and other-directed modes of thought. . . . Television literally diminishes the world for us" (35). And while we may enjoy a degree of forgetting via TV—that is, we may temporarily turn away the demands of our jobs, our concerns with our relationships, our fears for our futures—we have simply shifted from one horizontal plane to another, for television "is not Plato's cave . . . but a privitized electronic grotto, a miniature sound and light show to distract our attention from the pressure without or within" (Stam 27). However, by seeking distraction we may be finding too much of it: Jung argues that "The strains and stresses of twentieth-century living have so affected the modern mind that in many countries children are no longer able to concentrate. . . . The same distractions affect adults as well. . . . Worst of all is television" (*C. G. Jung Speaking* 248–49). Caught in a viewing experience that promotes distraction and regressive narcissism, viewers veer away from the archetypal imagination and the sites of awareness that would lead to a more fecund recognition of those aspects of the self that are often unseen.

Jung writes that "The psyche consists essentially of images. It is a series of images in the truest sense, not an accidental juxtaposition or sequence, but a structure that is throughout full of meaning and purpose;

it is a 'picturing' of vital activities" (*CW* 8: 325). There is within us a demand for active recognition of, and imaginative relationship with, those vigorous "psychic images" that reveal and express who we are. If we do recognize and relate to them, these images offer us the prospect of becoming via increased self-knowledge, as Jung reminds us, the persons that "nature intended us to be": "The process of coming to terms with the Other in us is well worth while, because in this way we get to know aspects of our nature which we would not allow anybody else to show us and which we ourselves would never have admitted" (*CW* 14: 496). However, when viewers wade into TV's Lethe-like—and Lethe-lite—half-world, they do not place themselves in a position to "recall" the images of those archetypal selves who inhabit and constitute their dynamic, unconscious psyches. By substituting Lethe's purge of memory for TV's hypnotic effect, viewers also trade the mysterious faces of Mnemosyne—the psyche's inborn images—for a night's worth of non-numinous images. Barry Sanders writes, "Watching TV . . . makes a person more suscepti-ble to manufactured images by diminishing that person's ability to gen-erate his [or her] own, a condition akin to the suppression of the immune system" (42).

Under the influence of the TV's slim semblance of Lethe, we are greeted with de-ranged images that are little more than cheap, cardboard cutouts of Mnemosyne's children. As David Marc laments of the effect of TV: "Oh, Mnemosyne, why have you deserted me?" (136). Starving orphans, hastily fabricated, these images are lost and homeless things. Indeed, it is one of TV's chief projects to elide the fact that nearly all of its images are necessarily one-sided—what Jung called "neurotic"—because they dwell in a consciously constructed universe, not an arche-typally depicted one. Patricia Clough describes TV's agenda this way:

> [A]ny reality [TV] enframes, and therefore brings forth, is readily dis-placed by another framing. The cycle of revealing and concealing, of placing and displacing every enframement of the real, is repeated with such rapidity that what is real seems to be nothing but framing. There is nothing left but frames and frames of nothing—nothing but the reproductive technology of framing. (88)

As such, TV-as-event ruptures the possibility of developing an authentic sense of subjectivity grounded in the archetypal imagination. Rather, TV viewing works to keep us framed within the larger realm of collective subjectivity, one wherein we are all equally interchangeable because we are constructed and reproduced as consumers of framed images—not imaginers of archetypal ones.

In fact, TV, as it now exists, is not designed to take viewers into the places where the internal Others dwell because those trips are necessarily individual—or individuated—ones. (Besides, such trips usually do not photograph well.) Moreover, because the vast majority of American TV programming is fabricated to appeal to the widest demographic possible, the electronically constructed replacements of Mnemosyne must be so generic and so stereotypical that they will be palatable to millions of viewers. As Pierre Bourdieu puts it, "The televised event is a commercial, marketable product that must be designed to reach the largest audience and hold on to it the longest" (79). Consequently, TV most often enforces a monocular perspective that does not admit numinous images, complex ideas, or indeterminate meanings: "for all its technological and social complexity, television's main systematic effect on human thinking is that of simplification" (Scheuer 62). Were TV to offer multiple, archetypal perspectives, it would force viewers to grapple with startling, polyvalent images, but such images cannot be stuffed into sitcoms and such multifaceted ideas cannot be squeezed into sound bites.

The archetypal Menelaus grappled an answer from the shape-shifting Proteus, but TV's current programming is designed to keep viewers from grappling with any of its simulated, protean images. Neil Postman writes, "[W]atching television requires instantaneous pattern-recognition, not delayed analytic decoding. It requires perception, not conception. . . . [It] not only requires no skills but develops no skills" (78–79). Similarly, Jeffrey Scheuer argues:

> Television . . . simplifies the world by systematically filtering out complex modes and dimensions of understanding. . . . Television . . . thrives on action, immediacy, specificity, and certainty. It filters out 1) more abstract and conceptual structures or relationships, including systems . . . ; 2) causality, particularly remote causal histories and destinies, evolutionary change, and uncertain or incomplete processes of change; 3) context, which is likewise relational and causative; and 4) ambiguity, i.e., uncertainty of meaning, and ambivalence, or uncertainty of value. (121–22)

TV makes viewing mindlessly easy by presenting a kaleidoscope of images that are risk-free: in a word, TV never places viewers in a position to make them feel stupid. Rather than ask viewers to wrestle with the slippery images of a dangerous, water-soaked deity, TV presents an eyeful of shape-shifting images that are thin, but safe, illusions of dangerous deities.

THE NEWS FAULT

Newscasts are little more than emotionless catalogues of disconnected, image-laden mini-stories. Hence TV news is "a litany of events with no beginning and no real end, thrown together only because they occurred at the same time. So an earthquake in Turkey turns up next to proposed budget cuts, and a championship sports team is featured alongside a big murder trial" (Bourdieu 6). Further, "violence and moral degeneracy . . . are the staples of TV news shows" (Postman and Powers 149). TV news allows its hunger for stories to override the necessity to create narrative order or to reveal complex associations. And so, when a nightly news-cast cuts from an image of burnt bodies in a worn-torn country to a commercial of char-broiled burgers, it instantly equates tragedies with trivialities and the horrific and the familiar, similar to Jung's account of schizophrenia, a condition whose "dissociated products" are "fragments with vestiges of meaning" because they are the result of psychic "disin-tegration" (*CW* 8: 122). News stories, in their flashy, dramatic disunion, are little more than "fragments" of larger stories that have only "ves-tiges of meaning" because they are not complete and because they do not cohere. The nightly newscast might more appropriately be thought of as a network-sanctioned psychic rupture on display.[3]

Additionally, James Hillman argues that "The manner in which we tell ourselves about what is going on is the genre through which events become experiences" (*Healing Fiction* 23). And since "a very high pro-portion of the population . . . is dependent on television as the sole source of news" (Bourdieu 18), we should not be surprised to find that "people who are heavy television viewers, including viewers of television news shows, believe their communities are much more dangerous than do light television viewers" (Postman and Powers 23). By obliterating important categorical distinctions among stories, by presenting a world where chaos reigns, and by reducing complicated events to their simplest and most salacious possible presentations, TV news feeds viewers a skewed version of the world and how to comprehend it.

Neil Postman writes that TV news reveals the idea "that there are no important differences between one day and another, that the same emotions that were called for yesterday are called for today, and that in any case, the events of the day are meaningless" (103). Newscasters thus enter into an unconscious participation mystique with the archetype of Saturn, a temperament that is "cold. . . . It is outside of things. . . . Cold-ness is also cold reality, things just as they are, dry data, unchangeable cold hard facts. And coldness is cruel, without the warmth of the heart" (Hillman, "On Senex Consciousness" 20). Like Saturn, newscasters sit "outside of things," removed—both physically and emotionally—from the fragmented events they are articulating, displaying all the hallmarks of an inferior feeling type function, which, according to Jung, manifests itself as a "highly impersonal" attitude that devalues people and things (*Psychological Types* 350).

LIVING IN TELEVISED ILLUSIONS

Daniel Boorstin writes, "We are the first people in history to make their illusions so vivid, so persuasive, so 'realistic' that we can live in them" (240). When viewers are enticed to "live in" TV's illusions, they do little more than emulate simulations. By emulating the self-referential images of TV's illusions, viewers slide into a narcissistic world of self-reflexive appearances where images are stuck in their reflections. Unable or unwilling to detach themselves from a preponderance of images that have no imaginal essence because they are little more than simulacra (images that mark the absence of a true signified), viewers become psychologically indistinguishable from the images they are aping. Jung describes the dire consequences of imitation:

> we see everyday how people use, or rather abuse, the mechanism of imitation: . . . they are content to ape some eminent personality, some striking characteristic or mode of behavior. . . . We could almost say that as a punishment for this the uniformity of their minds . . . is intensified into an unconscious, compulsive bondage to the environment. As a rule these specious attempts at individual differentiation stiffen into a pose, and the imitator remains at the same level as he always was, only several degrees more sterile than before. (*CW* 7: 155)

Viewers thus introject TV's sterile images and use them as psychic compasses to negotiate their way through a self-reflexive world of likenesses. Jung writes: "Identity does not make consciousness possible; it is only separation, detachment, and agonizing confrontation through opposition that produce consciousness and insight" (*CW* 9.1: 171). Through the mechanism of imitation, viewers refuse the call to consciousness via "confrontation through opposition" and instead fuse themselves to interchangeable images and lose touch with the only thing that might beckon them back to the psychic underworld of their souls: the invisible, insistent, and often oppositional voices of the archetypal imagination.

Furthermore, as viewers come to identify with simulated images, they do not notice that their visual attention is being held by images:

all pictures make us look. They seduce us into looking. The gaze stimulates the other senses and arouses. Arousal fetishizes the object. We are fixed by it, to it. What holds the gaze is this demonic power in the image. . . . Images draw us into participation with them. (Hillman, "Pink Madness" 51)

Much of TV's force rests in the "demonic power" of its images to capture its viewers' eyes and imaginations, a power that generally quashes a conscious relationship with images and inserts in its place an unconscious, fetish-fueled participation with them. When viewers are sucked into a participation mystique with TV's pictures, they are not animated by—or anima-mated to—them. Rather, they are seduced and reduced into craving only the surface of what they see. Sandy Flitterman-Lewis writes, "In TV, it is the viewer who does the absorbing, taking in programs like a sponge. . . . An explosion of stimulation replaces directed fascination" (218). Viewers find themselves caught in an endless loop of wanting to view and viewing to want—and never getting enough of either.

As TV's programs (most of which are commercially driven) hook viewers with a hunger for images, it also lures them into "amputating"[4] access to their archetypal imaginations. As viewers hack off the routes to the image-producing psyche, TV then offers itself as a technological replacement to masses of imaginative amputees and promises to provide endless hours of trouble-free imaging. Tom Englehardt writes that TV programs'

lack of inspiration, their authorless, randomly repetitive, interchangeable quality give them a strange sort of fascination. Just as the industry as been deregulated economically, so in some sense what appears on the screen has been deregulated emotionally to produce a sort of crude twilight zone of present-day American consciousness. (86)

Thus TV functions as the imaginative prosthetic of the mass-psyche: it gives the metaphoric no room to move, no time to air. Archibald MacLeash offers a poignant description of what happens when images are severed from their metaphorical roots: "A world ends when its metaphor has died. / It perishes when those images, though seen, / No longer mean" (173–74).

When Jung wrote that "the gods have become diseases" (*CW* 13: 37), he was suggesting, among other things, that archetypal images turn into pathological symptoms when they are downgraded into literalisms. In our time the gods have been projected into TV and have been flattened into pixelated patterns. Television-as-prosthesis thus replaces the metaphoric with the literal and sells viewers the notion that the gods have been tamed and now serve them—that viewers can control the gods by merely pressing the button on the remote control. In this way, viewers create the constant replacement of archetype with stereotype. Thus, for example, the meaningfully directed actions of Ares become images of people brutalizing one another; Athena's well-wrought plans and superb speech become acts of mindless vengeance and vitriolic blatherings; the deep attractions and soulful connections of Eros become simulations of sex; Aphrodite's essential beauty becomes a parade of Ken and Barbie doll bodies sculpted by plastic surgeons; Hermes's divine tricks become laugh-track-punctuated sitcoms; and the dark domain of Hades becomes pictures of people killing people.

THE GREAT AND TERRIBLE MOTHER

TV also attempts to assume the role of what Jung referred to as "the Great Mother." Jung writes:

> The qualities associated with [the mother archetype] are maternal solicitude and sympathy; . . . any helpful instinct or impulse; all that is benign, all that cherishes and sustains, that fosters growth and fertility. . . . On the negative side the mother archetype may connote anything secret, hidden, dark, the abyss, the world of the dead, anything that devours, seduces, and poisons. (*CW* 9.1: 82)

By presenting itself as a "helpful" entity, one that "sustains" and "fosters" the desires of its viewers with endless images of things desirable, TV usurps the archetypal mother by supplying viewers imaginatively with everything that they will ever want or need. Patricia Clough writes: "Television offers itself as the machine metaphor for representing the structuration of capitalism in its effects; it also is the machine that produces the effects—that is, value" (97). Entranced by the "machine metaphor" of TV-as-mother, viewers become sucked into a wish-fulfillment fantasy of endless proportions. In this fantasy, viewers attend to a TV-mother who tells them that everything she displays on her cold, pulsing face is literally desirable and obtainable. Moreover, TV offers "a coherent story concerning how to live in the world. It provides . . . a steady stream of allegories, suggestions, and didactic pep talks on the subject of success and how to achieve it under a set of rules" (Marc 146). TV-as-mother structures the desires of, and "produce effects" in, her viewers—if, that is, they follow the set rules. TV implies, moreover, that if "she" cannot display a thing, then the thing either does not exist or else it is not worthy of desire. Inveigled by TV's literalisms, however, viewers are taught not to kill the literal by nourishing themselves with the archetypal underworld's metaphorical stuff. Rather, they are told to stuff themselves with upper-world images: luxury SUVs instead of Pegasus-drawn chariots, fast food instead of ambrosia, a talk show's gossip instead of Teiresias's oracles, MTV's assorted howls instead of Orpheus's splendid songs, a comfortable Carnival cruise instead of an Odyssean harrowing voyage, and the caustic remarks of talk show guests instead of the daemonic speech of Hecate. By compacting metaphoric images into stylized, literal ones, TV, as the Big Mom, displays and helps maintain the narrow limits of collective consciousness. Todd Gitlin argues that TV in general, and commercials in particular, have gotten viewers "accustomed to thinking of [them]selves and behaving as a market rather than a public, as consumers rather than citizens" ("Prime Time" 579).[5] Viewers are thus led away from the realization that they are (conscious) citizens and into a situation where they are (unconscious) consumers.

Moreover, as a stand-in for the Great Mother, TV reduces her viewers to children. Gitlin describes the bulk of TV's images this way: "Surface is all; what you see is what you get. [TV's] images are proud of their standing as images. They suggest that the highest destiny of our time is to become cleansed of depth and specificity altogether" (139). TV's images of "what you see is what you get" transform viewers into children by appealing to that aspect of psyche that wants everything rendered in simple terms, that is constantly craving something, and that responds to images with condensed, explicit, and highly polarized emotions.

In Jungian terms, TV's surface-only images evoke that childish side of the psyche—one side of the puer/puella archetype—that "feels" but fails to differentiate the subtleties and perplexities of feeling. In describing the dynamics of this archetype, Jung writes that it reflects in us "something that is always becoming, is never completed, and calls for unceasing care, attention, and education" (*CW* 17: 170). One of the dominant aspects of the puer archetype is a focus on immediacy, that is, on achieving immediate gratification of his or her needs. And because a person under the influence of this archetype craves "maternal solicitude and sympathy," he or she will most often display impatience, diminished thinking, and overblown emotions—especially when such "solicitude and sympathy" are not forthcoming. When constellated, moreover, this childish side of the psyche "that is always becoming, is never completed, and [that] calls for unceasing care [and] attention" impatiently resolves complex issues by collapsing the distinctions between the literal and the metaphoric, between the stereotypical and the archetypal. Jung writes that when the psyche is dominated by the child archetype it has formed an "identification with the mother," which then leads "to paralysis" (*CW* 9.1: 29). Such a paralysis manifests itself in the inability to differentiate one thing from another, or in this case, one TV image from another. Additionally, Jung writes that "consciousness can only exist through continual recognition of the unconscious" (*CW* 9.1: 96). By abdicating clear-sighted "recognition of the unconscious"—its moods, movements, and images—in favor of feeling-induced identification with TV-as-mother, the child-dominated psyche defines reality as an either/or proposition, one that is either desirable or repulsive, and says, "I like the appearance of this and I don't like the appearance of that."

Furthermore, TV also keeps its viewers in a childish state by spewing out an avalanche of images at breakneck speed. As it does, it reinforces a childish perspective in its viewers by overwhelming them on two fronts: first, because the vast majority of its images are designed to arouse basic instincts and nondifferentiated feelings, TV keeps the psyche mired in an animalistic, mass-minded configuration; and second, by continually jumping from image to image, from cut to cut, and from shot to shot, TV disrupts the natural slowness the psyche needs to reflect upon new images and new information. Jung writes that "environmental influences place all sorts of unsuperable obstacles in the way of individuation" (*CW* 9.1: 166). And since "on TV, something happens all the time" (Sanders 43), the psyche is unable either to discriminate one environmental influence from another or to see their structural dynamics. As a result, in the face of TV's "unsuperable obstacles" and its whirling images, the psyche most often finds itself like Vasalisa in the house of Baba Yaga, as he said to her, "Take this sack of millet and pick it over seed by seed. And mind that you take out all the black bits, for if you don't, I shall eat you up" (Moss 76). In the house of the TV-witch-mother (the antithesis of the Great Mother), the child-psyche is ordered to pick through whirling images and separate them into clearly differentiated psychic piles. Such a task, however, is nearly impossible for two reasons: first, most TV images occur too rapidly for the mind to recall and differentiate; second, because the images usually appeal to the instincts, the psyche will most likely be unable to find the mother-given "doll" (as did Vasalisa) of intuition to help it distinguish one image from another.

Another way that TV's mother-myth locks her viewers into a childish condition is by placing most of its images, events, and stories inside simplistic aesthetic frames. Howard Gardner argues: "Although the artistic productions of young children are often notable for their imagination and subtlety, children's tastes tend to the most elemental works.

Popular taste and mass culture *build directly upon these early predilections*" (111; emphasis added). By building directly upon childish tastes that "tend to the most elemental works," the bulk of TV's stories and images do not foster an archetypally individuated psyche but instead reinforce the undifferentiated, childish mind of popular culture. Most of TV's programs and images are underdeveloped and infantile because they present emotionally "immediate," simple narratives and eschew intellectually discordant and complex ones:

> TV is essentially narrative and episodic rather than thematic or analytical in character. It can show and tell, but is best at showing; unlike the written word, it cannot readily escape its own immediacy in the here-and-now to examine, define, deconstruct, infer, deduce, analyze, hypothesize, suggest relations among ostensibly remote entities, or glide across different levels of abstraction. (Scheuer 71–72)

Because they must fit within strict time frames that are neatly structured for commercial breaks, TV's shows do not have the unrestricted freedom to range into unstructured time. Thus the mind that produces the script for any TV show is already hampered because it must keep the action within preestablished parameters.

The reductiveness in segments of time also forces a reductiveness in genres. Jim Collins, however, argues that TV is, in fact, a fecund post-modern device, one that offers a wealth of program variety:

> the eclecticism of television textuality operates on a technological/institutional level . . . because it has been institutionalized by cable television and the VCR, which together produce infinite programing variations. . . . Television, like the postmodern subject, must be conceived as a site—an intersection of multiple, conflicting cultural messages. (338)

From a Jungian perspective, we can see that Collins is arguing that the god behind TV is Hermes: the god who is notable for his change-abilities, his polysemy, his delight in multiple messages from multiple realms, and his skill in transgressing boundaries. (Interestingly, Hermes is the only god who is able to travel into the realms of the other gods.) However, it may be countered that American TV is more premodern than postmodern because it is influenced more by the archetypal mother's reductiveness (bringing things down to their material appearances, to mater) than by Hermes's disruptiveness. Being a device that works to insure "normalcy" (Caldwell 664), TV precludes Hermes's unpredictablity and insubstantiality. And the move towards normalcy is most clearly evident in the way that TV's programs stay tightly within the straitjackets of their respective genres.

Were they driven by Hermes, programs on TV would disrupt themselves, would startle us with something new and unexpected each week. But they do not. Indeed, if there's one word that can be applied to TV's programming it is "predictable": viewers "bring to TV a set of more or less precise expectations, which are rarely upset. . . . TV hardly ever surprises us" (Scheuer 73). TV's programs, unlike most postmodern cultural artifacts, stay within rigid, easily identifiable, and genre-specific parameters. According to Sarah Kozloff, "most television shows . . . are narrative texts. . . . [N]arratives are not only the dominant type of text on television, but narrative structure is, to a large extent, the portal or grid through which even nonnarrative television must pass" (68–69). One result of narrative dominance on TV is the shaping of expectation and desire. If viewers see mostly narratives on TV, then they will expect to see narratives and little else. Indeed, a medium where narrative predominates is not a postmodern medium because it follows the archetypal mother's dictum that predictable connections (either positive or negative) must be made and maintained. For such a medium as TV to be postmodern, to spring from the domain of Hermes, it would necessarily have to entertain multiple nonnarrative formats, most of which would call into question the very nature and purpose of narration as the legitimate, dominant media form. Failing that, however, the narrative hegemony of TV continues to shape the viewing consciousness, leading necessarily to a habituated consciousness, and, as Jung writes, "Nothing is more deleterious than a routine understanding of everything" (CW 16: 87).

The central dictum for nearly all TV shows is that all problems—no matter how small or large—must display the conflict of easily identifiable opposites and must be clearly resolved within the space of (usually) a half hour to two hours. Importantly, nearly all problems on TV are solved not with imaginative synthesis or poetic graciousness but with an overwhelming application of violence, sentimentality, or technical wizardry (the deus ex machina is alive and well and airing regularly on TV). The result of such a simplistic and unimaginative approach to problem solving is an assurance that mediocrity will prevail, that TV will not rise above its own "elemental" level, and that individuals who cannot free themselves from viewing will not shut off the TV in order to exercise the individuating imagination. Jung writes:

> Society, by automatically stressing all the collective qualities in its individual representatives, puts a premium on mediocrity, on everything

that settles down to vegetate in an easy, irresponsible way. . . . The man of today, who resembles more or less the collective ideal, has made his heart into a den of murderers. (*CW* 7: 153–54)

Jung fittingly describes the dynamic between TV and those viewers who represent "the collective ideal." When they allow TV to frame their thoughts and supply them with images to emulate, viewers then buy into a herd-bound, commodified version of reality. And while their TV-shaped personalities may appear to be the "ideals" of popular culture, their individual souls, which have come to resemble a stockpile of shadows churning in a dark place, will find ways to break through the surface of mass-mindedness with symptoms that demand attention. Such symptoms can be seen circulating in the TV-shaped, collective psyche as the fear of any underworld image that cannot be easily imitated, dominated, or explained away; the inability to see the literal self as a variety of metaphoric selves; the general suspicion of all that is strange or unusual; the pervasive discomfort with anything grotesque; the endless search for numinosity in external objects; the growing ignorance of complexity; and the childish desire to reduce everything to simple, seeable, binary opposites.

Perhaps TV could be a medium where Lethe and Mnemosyne could safely find a home and where the world soul, the Anima Mundi, not the simulated glitz of popular culture, could aesthetically reveal herself in fullness and plenitude. By blunting access to images and messages that are spontaneous, irrational, ambiguous, indeterminate, marginal, complex, and archetypal, however, television has trapped itself in a self-structured battle between the Apollonian drive towards light and order and the Dionysian drive towards reverie and chaos. In this battle of opposites, virtual order nearly always overcomes simulated chaos and enshrines the literal-minded mass-psyche on the altar of popular culture, beneath which seethes a polymorphous world of shape-shifting shadows. As long as TV keeps sending out one-sided images of itself, it will air only gaunt glitter in place of soul—and in the airing, err.

NOTES

1. The reader will notice the interplay of two rhetorical styles in this chapter: the serious (academic) and the playful (poetic). The yoking of these styles is a deliberate choice, which reflects Jung's notion that the psyche must be approached from more than one perspective and written about in more than one rhetorical style. Jung writes that "the psyche remains completely refractory to all methods that approach it from a single exclusive standpoint" (*CW* 8: 260). And

James Hillman adds: "Jung varies. . . . Jung's style is precisely the one required for soul-making. Its variety reflects the need to have different styles for different archetypal constellations" (*Re-Visioning* 215–16).

2. Todd Gitlin describes the standardization in scope and format of most TV programs:

[T]he standard curve of narrative action—stock characters encounter new version of stock situation; the plot thickens, allowing stock characters to show their standard stuff; the plot resolves—over twenty-two or fifty minutes is itself a source of rigidity and forced regularity. . . . [U]sual programs are performances that rehearse social fixity: they express and cement the obduracy of a social world impervious to substantial change. ("Prime Time" 578)

3. Howard Nemerov offers an apt description of TV's reality-reducing nature:

> The straying lens across the battlefield,
> The cameraman's quivering hand considering death,
> The instant replay—all of them shopworn,
> All soiled and secondhand goods of this world
> Shaken in God's wavering attention just
> An instant before we see it as out there. (502)

4. TV's replacement of the imaginal is what Robert Sardello calls "the auto-amputation of thinking" where "information . . . comes to imitate thought." He adds: "Along with the imitation, or double of thought, comes the hope that this dummy thought will produce complete satisfaction" (103).

5. Robert Allen writes:

It is not coincidental that commercial television has developed a sophisticated rhetorical mode of viewer engagement within which much energy is expended to give the viewer at home an image of himself or herself on screen and to make sure the viewer knows that he or she is the person to whom the show (and its accompanying commercials) is offered. By conflating addresser and addressee under the regime of the fictive We, commercial television softens the bluntness of its rhetorical thrust. ("Audience-Oriented" 125)

Works Cited

Allen, Robert C. "Audience-Oriented Criticism and Television." Allen, *Channels of Discourse, Reassembled* 101–37.

———, ed. *Channels of Discourse, Reassembled: Television and Contemporary Criticism.* Ed. Robert C. Allen. Chapel Hill: U of North Carolina P, 1992.

———. "More Talk About TV." *Channels of Discourse, Reassembled* 1–30.

Avens, Roberts. "Reflections on Wolfgang Giegerich's 'The Burial of the Soul in Technological Civilization.'" *Sulfur: A Literary Quarterly of the Whole Art* 20 (1987): 34–54.

Boorstin, Daniel. *The Image; or, What Happened to the American Dream.* New York: Antheneum, 1962.

Bourdieu, Pierre. *On Television.* Trans. Priscilla Parkhurst Ferguson. New York: New P, 1996.

Caldwell, John Thornton. "Excessive Style: The Crisis of Network Television." *Television: The Critical View.* Ed. Horace Newcomb. New York: Oxford UP, 2000.

Clough, Patricia. *Auto Affection: Unconscious Thought in the Age of Teletechnology.* Minneapolis: U of Minnesota P, 2000.

Collins, Jim. "Postmodernism and Television." Allen, *Channels of Discourse, Reassembled* 327–53.

Csikszentmihalyi, Mihaly. *The Evolving Self.* New York: HarperPerennial, 1993.

Diamond, Marian, and Janet Hopson. *Magic Trees of the Mind.* New York: Dutton, 1998.

Englehardt, Tom. "The Shortcake Strategy." Gitlin, *Watching Television* 68–110.

Flitterman-Lewis, Sandy. "Psychoanalysis, Film, and Television." Allen, *Channels of Discourse, Reassembled* 203–46.

Gardner, Howard. *The Unschooled Mind.* New York: HarperCollins, 1991.

Gitlin, Todd. "Prime Time Ideology: The Hegemonic Process in Television Entertainment." *Television: The Critical View.* Ed. Horace Newcomb. New York: Oxford UP, 2000. 574–94.

———, ed. *Watching Television.* New York: Pantheon Books, 1986.

———. "We Build Excitement." Gitlin, *Watching Television* 136–61.

Healy, Jane. *Endangered Minds.* New York: Simon, 1990.

Hillman, James. *Blue Fire: Selected Writings.* New York: Harper, 1989.

———. *The Dream and the Underworld.* New York: Harper, 1979.

———. *Healing Fiction.* Woodstock, CT: Spring, 1983.

———. "Pink Madness." *Spring* 57 (1995): 39–72.

———. *Re-Visioning Psychology.* New York: Harper, 1975.

———. "On Senex Consciousness." *Mothers and Fathers.* Ed. Patricia Berry. Dallas: Spring, 1991.

Jung, C. G. *Alchemical Studies.* Trans. R. F. C. Hull. Princeton: Princeton UP, 1967.

———. *Analytical Psychology: Its Theory and Practice.* New York: Random, 1970.

———. *The Archetypes and the Collective Unconscious.* Trans. R. F. C. Hull. Princeton: Princeton UP, 1969.

———. *C. G. Jung Speaking.* Ed. William McGuire and R. F. C. Hull. Princeton: Princeton UP, 1977.

———. *The Development of Personality.* Trans. R. F. C. Hull. Princeton: Princeton UP, 1969.

———. *Four Archetypes.* Trans. R. F. C. Hull. Princeton: Princeton UP, 1959.

———. *Flying Saucers: A Modern Myth of Things Seen in the Skies.* Trans. R. F. C. Hull. Princeton: Princeton UP, 1978.

———. *Mysterium Coniunctionis.* Trans. R. F. C. Hull. Princeton: Princeton UP, 1963.

———. Foreword. *The Origins and History of Consciousness.* Eric Neumann. Trans. R. F. C. Hull. Princeton: Princeton UP, 1970. xiii–xiv.

———. *The Practice of Psychotherapy.* Trans. R. F. C. Hull. Princeton: Princeton UP, 1966.

———. *Psychological Types.* Trans. R. F. C. Hull. Princeton: Princeton UP, 1971.

———. *Psychology and Alchemy.* Trans. R. F. C. Hull. Princeton: Princeton UP, 1968.

———. *Psychology and Western Religion.* Trans. R. F. C. Hull. Princeton: Princeton UP, 1984.

———. *The Structure and Dynamics of the Psyche.* Trans. R. F. C. Hull. Princeton: Princeton UP, 1969.

———. *Two Essays on Analytical Psychology.* Trans. R. F. C. Hull. Princeton: Princeton UP, 1953.

Kozloff, Sarah. "Narrative Theory and Television." Allen, *Channels of Discourse, Reassembled* 67–100.

Lynch, William. *Christ and Apollo.* New York: Mentor, 1966.

Marc, David. *Bonfire of the Humanities: Television, Subliteracy, and Long-Term Memory Loss.* Syracuse: Syracuse UP, 1995.

MacLeash, Archibald. *Collected Poems 1917–1952.* Boston: Houghton, 1952.

Moss, Anita, and Jon C. Stott, eds. *The Family of Stories.* New York: Holt, 1986.

Nemerov, Howard. *The Collected Poems of Howard Nemerov.* Chicago: U of Chicago P, 1977.

Neumann, Erich. *The Origins and History of Consciousness.* Trans. R. F. C. Hull. Princeton: Princeton UP, 1970.

Postman, Neil. *The Disappearance of Childhood*. New York: Vintage, 1994.

Postman, Neil, and Steve Powers. *How to Watch TV News*. New York: Penguin, 1992.

Ruskin, John. *The Crown of Wild Olive*. New York: J. M. Dent, 1908.

Sanders, Barry. *A Is for Ox: The Collapse of Literacy and the Rise of Violence in an Electronic Age*. New York: Vintage, 1995.

Sardello, Robert. *Facing the World with Soul: The Reimagination of Modern Life*. New York: HarperPerennial, 1994.

Scheuer, Jeffrey. *The Soundbite Society: Television and the American Mind*. New York: Four Walls Eight Windows, 1999.

Shakespeare, William. *The Complete Works of William Shakespeare*. Ed. Hardin Craig and David Bevington. Glenview, IL: Scott Foresman, 1973.

Sorkin, Michael. "Faking It." Gitlin, *Watching Television* 162–82.

Stam, Robert. "Television News and Its Spectator." *Regarding Television—Critical Approaches: An Anthology*. Ed. E. Ann Kaplan. American Film Institute Monograph Series, vol. 2. Frederick, MD: American Film Institute, 1983.

White, Mimi. "Ideological Analysis and Television." *Channels of Discourse, Reassembled* 161–202.

Jane Iterare

Jane Eyre *as a Feminist Revision*
of the Hero's Journey

❦

TITA FRENCH BAUMLIN
AND
JAMES S. BAUMLIN

Learning to cherish and emphasize feminine values is the primary condition of our holding our own against the masculine
principle which is mighty in a double sense—both within the
psyche and without. . . . But when women succeed in maintaining themselves against the animus, instead of allowing
themselves to be devoured by it, then it ceases to be only a
danger and becomes a creative power.
    —Emma Jung, *Animus and Anima*

Women heroes are seldom able to assimilate these animus-
shadow constellations which embody proscriptions against
women's maturation. The green world lover, who embodies
a powerful and amarital feminine eroticism, and the anima,
often represented in the strong mother or goddess archetype, remain inaccessible. Thus novels in which women go
mad or die at the hands of "perfectly nice" husbands out-
number by far novels in which women achieve rebirth and
transformation.
    —Annis V. Pratt, "Spinning among Fields"

> To return now to my opening questions: what fantasy struc-
> tures do girls take away from reading *Jane Eyre?* [A]nd what
> accounts for readers' passionate attachment to the novel?
> One cannot ignore the testimony of readers like Rich and
> Lazarre, who say that *Jane Eyre* gave them alternative ideals
> of female autonomy and female solidarity. Jane's refusals to
> be contained within gender categories, in the face of countless
> pressures and temptations to accept a subordinate role, can
> inspire her reader with a determination to make the fantasy
> of defiant autonomy her own.
>
> —Jean Wyatt, *Reconstructing Desire*

Since its 1847 publication, *Jane Eyre* has remained among the most popular novels in English, influencing generations of appreciative readers.
Why so? What accounts for its fascination for, and hold upon, readers,
women especially? Part of its appeal, surely, lies in its deep exploration
of female psychology, its charting (through various archetypal figures
and symbols) of a heroine's complex psychological development.
Whereas her sister Emily's *Wuthering Heights* is "multipersonal"
(Williams 63) in narrative structure, Charlotte Brontë's novel is first person "in a radical way," as Raymond Williams notes: reflecting aspects
of her life (Scargill; Langbridge; Moglen), *Jane Eyre* is a novel of personal experience and "private confidence," in effect a "mode of confes-
sion" (Williams 63) in which Jane "is the whole of the novel in which
she appears" (Craik 107). Over the whole, indeed, reigns the personality of its autobiographical narrator. Not surprisingly, then, *Jane Eyre* has
been the subject of numerous psychoanalytic studies (Burkhart; Chase;
Dooley; Langbridge; Lodge; Maynard; Schreiber; Wyatt); in contrast,
the novel's archetypal dimensions remain relatively uncharted. And
whereas Harold Bloom asserts that "Rochester has enough of the daemonic to call into question any feminist reading of *Jane Eyre*" (5), we
believe that post-Jungian archetypal theory can make contributions
toward an original and distinctively feminist analysis.[1]

Though we stay largely within the traditional Jungian vocabulary,
our chapter seeks a post-Jungian revaluation of the varied roles the animus plays in women's psychological development. Also, we take it as a
given that a literary text's archetypal images are shaped by history and
culture and, thus, that Jane's personal psychology (particularly the projected images of her animus and shadow) incorporates the ideologies of
Victorian patriarchy. "Throughout the patriarchal period," as Edward
C. Whitmont writes, the ego "was conditioned by the collective super-
ego and persona of that time":

Our identity, our personal choices, decisions, and value judgments, are determined—certainly initially and, to a large extent, throughout our lives—by the ways we endeavor to be seen. We express the ideals of our family group and cultural environment, even when we hate or rebel against them or consciously disregard them. Genuinely individual values are more often than not carried by the shadow. (337)

Whitmont's observations certainly hold true for Brontë's narrator, whose "plain Jane" persona reflects Victorian injunctions against female vanity, sexual appetite, and power. To discover our heroine's "genuinely individual values," we must look elsewhere: perhaps surprisingly, to Jane's shadow-image, the "madwoman" Bertha.

As Annis V. Pratt observes, "Jung's male shadow, or antiself, is antisocial, for man's dark impulses spring from rebellion against cultural norms and mores," whereas women's shadows tend to be "socially conformist, incorporating women's self-loathing for their deviations from social norms, specifically the norms of femininity" (103). Though true for most Victorian literary protagonists, Pratt's description only partially pertains to Brontë's heroine. Bertha does symbolize Jane's "self-loathing" and "deviations from social norms" regarding her self-appearance and sexuality; nonetheless, Jane's persona is "socially conformist," though her shadow's beauty and sensuality—qualities rejected by Jane's ego-consciousness—belong to the "green world" of female physical "nature." But this should not surprise, given that dream-representations of one's shadow and greater Self are often blurred together. As M.-L. von Franz notes, "sometimes the shadow is powerful because the urge of the Self is pointing in the same direction, and so one does not know whether it is the Self or the shadow that is behind the inner pressure" (173). Von Franz continues:

If the shadow figure contains valuable, vital forces, they ought to be assimilated into actual experience and not repressed. It is up to the ego to give up its pride and priggishness and to live out something that seems to be dark, but actually may not be. This can require a sacrifice just as heroic as the conquest of passion, but in an opposite sense. . . .

When dark figures turn up in our dreams and seem to want something, we cannot be sure whether they personify merely a shadowy part of ourselves, or the self, or both at the same time. Divining in advance whether our dark partner symbolizes a shortcoming that we should overcome or a meaningful bit of life that we should accept—this is one of the most difficult problems that we encounter on the way to individuation. (175)

One of our aims, thus, is to reinterpret and revalue Bertha as a projection of Jane's shadow: from an archetypal perspective, Bertha's violent "madness" symbolizes her distance from the heroine's ego-identification with her humble, sexless, "plain Jane" persona. Of course, Rochester mediates in Jane's discovery and assimilation of her repressed sexuality. Our further aim is to explore the various transformations that Jane's animus-image undergoes, from patriarchal tyrant to "demon lover" to domestic helpmate. Though some have read the novel's ending as naive, mere wish fulfillment, and even "delusional" in its projection of a perfect, happy ending (Tromly; Wyatt), nonetheless *Jane Eyre* triumphs over Victorian patriarchy by envisioning an absolute equality in marriage. Unlike Emily Brontë's Catherine, who is driven by her "demon lover," Heathcliff, "to a socially correct marriage and later to her death" (Pratt 102), Jane *does not* suffer or die in marriage, nor does her sexual awakening lead to social isolation or madness. In these respects, Charlotte Brontë's novel is exceptional, even revolutionary for its age. Annis V. Pratt describes the more common results of such "dangerous" animus encounters:

> Whenever women encounter erotic, godlike figures in literature, the encounters are often natural, antisocial, and above all antimarital; the women end up mad, dead, or socially outcast. An integrated feminine self, particularly when it includes full-fledged Eros, is frightening to society. Thus women's rebirth literature casts its heroes *out of* the social community rather than, as in men's rebirth literature, elevating them to the status of hero. (102–03)

In contrast with other Victorian women's novels, *Jane Eyre* displays, if not a fully "integrated feminine self," then a youthful heroine well on the journey toward individuation. The novel depicts a woman's overcoming of the "natural, antisocial, and above all antimarital" aspects of her animus "lover" by assimilating her own sexuality or "full-fledged Eros" while remaining, at the same time, within "the social community" represented by marriage. In short, we read *Jane Eyre* as a positive instance of women's "rebirth literature," in which the protagonist is indeed elevated to the status of "hero." In its "birth of Venus" mythology, *Jane Eyre* offers a compensatory myth to the desexualized "angel in the house" dominant throughout English Victorian culture. For "'I am not an angel,'" Jane tells Rochester time and again throughout: "'I will be myself'" (Brontë 228).

That Jane narrates an allegorical journey of "Everywoman" (Gilbert and Gubar 339) every bit as psychologically compelling as the male Odyssean journey-myth is suggested even in the symbolism of her name. Deriving from the Latin *iterare*, "to journey," the word *eyre* was used through the nineteenth century to denote "circuit" or "itinerant" (as in the "eyre of justices"); further, *eyre* was a spelling variant of *aerie* which, in the language of falconry, meant "to breed" or "nest." Archetypally, then, Jane narrates the *eyre*, or journey, of the female ego toward its nest of Self—as Ulanov describes it, toward a "spiritual transformation" marked by "a searching out and accepting of the manifestations of the spirit that have taken refuge in the despised and rejected parts of one's psyche" (*Feminine* 182). Indeed, each woman is challenged to achieve an active, conscious relationship with the "feminine principle," a relationship necessarily marked by ambivalence since the principle itself embraces several dualities: for example, the paradigm of the "mother" earth is both the fertile field, where all life is born and nurtured, and the dark, devouring pit of the grave. And though masculine in its representations, the animus serves primarily to awaken the female ego to the fullness of the feminine principle and its positive transformations. "To be a whole person," Ulanov writes,

> we must come to terms with our own physical, sexual identity and with all those psychic factors which are represented to us by means of the symbolism of the masculine-feminine polarity. Without wrestling with this task of differentiation, we fall into formlessness and a cheap imitation of current persona roles. We miss our chance to become unique persons. Furthermore, we miss the spiritual significance of physical sexuality. (*Feminine* 147)

The "persona roles" that Ulanov warns against derive from the "mask" that an individual wears in social life, the persona ensuring that one's appearance and behaviors conform to the expectations of society and one's conscious self-image.[2] But just as the persona performs the necessary (and oftentimes positive) role of mediating between one's ego and the outer world, so the ego requires a mediator in its negotiations with the inner world or unconscious. For a woman, the archetype guiding one on this journey—a journey toward individuation, toward establishing a conscious ego-Self relation—is the animus, the masculine "Other" within.

Just as women mature physically, cognitively, and emotionally through distinctive developmental stages, so they experience stages of animus development. In the first stage (Ulanov, *Feminine* 242–46), a young girl experiences self-discovery, initially through *identification* with the unconscious "maternal feminine" and then through *differentiation*, the latter marking a frail ego's "self-conservation" against the potentially devouring powers of the so-called "matriarchal unity" (consisting of material from the collective unconscious as well as from the girl's personal unconscious, with its introjected mother-image). For Jane, the devouring "matriarchal unity" is represented by the Reed family relations of her dead mother—who, while they supposedly feed and nurture the young girl in accordance with her Uncle Reed's dying request, threaten to rob Jane of any developing sense of a unique, valued self. To her foster family, Jane's every act of self-preservation against matriarchal power becomes an act of rebellion and willful pride.

Jane's early years are thus marked by ambivalence, by a series of oscillating negative and positive images of the masculine Other within. As she says of her nemesis, the young John Reed, "I really saw in him a tyrant: a murderer" (Brontë 9): this conflict with the animus (and thus with the deeper feminine) culminates in the red-room scene, in which Mrs. Reed locks the terrified Jane in "the dark and haunted chamber" (62) where the child loses consciousness, believing she sees the ghost of her deceased uncle, Mr. Reed—significantly, Jane's mother's brother. In the red room, Jane is briefly overwhelmed by the contents of the feminine unconscious, symbolized by the remnants of her mother's family; yet the scene suggests, at the same time, a powerful opening of contact with her animus. Critics have argued over the scene's sexual imagery. The phallic proportions of the "tabernacle" of the bed, with its "massive pillars of mahogany," and Mr. Reed's throne-like chair (10–11) seem to assert a masculine force (Maynard 101–02); at the same time, the room's womblike color and appearance evoke feminist symbolisms of sexuality and woman's "inner space" (Showalter 113–16). Clearly, too, the scene expresses Jane's terrified fascination with her own divided self-image: staring "involuntarily" into a mirror, she encounters "the strange little figure there gazing at me, with . . . glittering eyes of fear moving where all else was still, . . . like one of the tiny phantoms, half fairy, half imp" (Brontë 11).

Here, in this early fantasy-projection of her animus, the young Jane experiences much the same ambivalence that Rochester later will evoke in her. As she imagines him, Mr. Reed appears alternately as a potential protector and as a sexually oppressive and suffocating presence. The child has "never doubted" that "if Mr. Reed had been alive he would have treated me kindly," and she fantasizes that his spirit, "harassed by the wrongs of his sister's child," might "rise before me in this chamber" to "comfort me"—a thought that, though "consolatory in theory," would be "terrible if realised" (Brontë 13). At the same time, she wishes that his spirit would revisit "the earth to punish the perjured and avenge the oppressed" (13). Still, when she envisions the ghost "penetrating" (14) the room, she responds physically, with "all the signs of a kind of sexual overload," as John Maynard (102–03) interprets it: "My heart beat thick, my head grew hot; . . . I was oppressed, suffocated:

endurance broke down" (Brontë 14). The fact that her uncle represents both a sexually charged Other and an avenging hero surely suggests an animus-projection. And it is a masculine force—the ghost of a mother's brother in a room that itself has a "masculine majesty" (Maynard 102)—that liberates her from the "matriarchal unity" (Ulanov, *Feminine* 242) of Gateshead Hall. Here, we also note the symbolism of liminality or rite of passage, Gateshead being a "gate" or threshold through which Everywoman must pass on her journey toward adulthood. Soon after the red-room scene, she is sent to the Lowood school, upon the concerned advice of Mr. Lloyd, another masculine intercessor with Mrs. Reed.

There, continuing to differentiate herself from early matriarchal dominance, the child Jane begins to identify with her persona—the "mask" society expects her to assume, though stifling to her greater Self. Yet she continues to encounter the deeper, oppositional principles of femininity and masculinity within her, as the very name "Lowood" implies a descent into the dark "wood" or *materia* of the unconscious. Accordingly, this section of the novel is dominated by a constellation of archetypes that Jane now encounters in her psychic growth: the nurturing mother figure, Miss Temple, the tyrannical "step-father," Mr. Brocklehurst (who, representative of "paternal Logos," also serves as a projection of Jane's still-undeveloped animus), and Helen Burns, Jane's older, wiser, "heroic" alter ego and a projection of the narrator's unconscious (yet emerging) Self.[3]

In contrast to earlier images of devouring matriarchy, Miss Temple represents another aspect of the feminine principle: the warm, enfolding mother who offers to care for Jane's insecure ego, teaching her to nurture her greater Self and, later, her own children. Indeed, Miss Temple's name suggests the sanctity of Jane's total personality, the Self being a "temple" of divine nurturing. Not surprisingly, Jane carries to church a prayer book in which Miss Temple's name is inscribed (Brontë 41). And, as befits her goddess mother, Miss Temple's "larger-than-life" appearance inspires always "a controlling sense of awe" (63), for Miss Temple is "stately" (41), "tall, fair, and shapely" with a large, white face and a "benignant light" radiating from her eyes (40). As the adult narrator tells us, the child Jane notices that "a gold watch (watches were not so common then as now) shone at her girdle" (41): indeed, Miss Temple's connection with the gold watch and with the passage of time is an appropriate symbol, since Jane's own individuation can progress only with slow and careful attention to the steps of her journey. It seems appropriate, also, that in Jane's memory such attention to time was "not so common" as the "now" of her narrative, when she has reached a higher level of maturity and when her own "gold watch-chain" has become the "glittering ornament" (397) symbolizing her adulthood. At Lowood, Miss Temple is the mother-image, the Demeter figure who calls Jane and Helen "'my children'" (64), feeding them the "seed-cake" she has hidden in a locked drawer (63). "We feasted that evening as on nectar and ambrosia" (63), Jane recollects; such "seeds" of the divine, nurturing feminine will take root within Jane's psyche and help her produce, albeit slowly, the self-nourishment needed in her further journey toward individuation. Significantly, it is under Miss Temple's tutelage that Jane completes her first accomplishments at Lowood, where "I learned the first two tenses of the verb *Etre,* and sketched my first cottage" (65). Clearly, learning "to be" involves learning what "is" and what "was," both necessary steps toward building the "cottage" or nest of the Self. And yet Jane's connection with the feminine principle remains immature. As she admits, "I derived a child's pleasure from the contemplation of [Miss Temple's] face, her . . . white forehead . . . and beaming dark eyes" (62).

Yet, pitted against the maternal nurturing of Miss Temple is Mr. Brocklehurst, the owner of Lowood and an early, undeveloped projection of Jane's animus. Jane's description of his first appearance emphasizes Brocklehurst's stiff, alien masculinity:

> A long stride measured the schoolroom, and presently beside Miss Temple . . . stood the same black column which had frowned on me so ominously from the hearth-rug of Gateshead. . . . [I]t was Mr. Brocklehurst, buttoned up in a surtout, and looking longer, narrower, and more rigid than ever. (Brontë 53)

Representing her animus at an immature, even negative stage, he is no more than an "apparition" (53)—another ghost, like her mother's brother. Indeed, as Ulanov might suggest, Jane's later description of Brocklehurst's speech characterizes him as a "tyrannizing animus," a figure serving to "stifle initiative and . . . create a growing sense of inferiority" (*Feminine* 263) in women. As Emma Jung explains the dynamics of animus-possession,

> If the possibility of spiritual functioning is not taken up by the conscious mind, the psychic energy intended for it falls into the unconscious, and there activates the archetype of the animus. Possessed of the energy that has flowed back into the unconscious, the animus figure becomes autonomous, so powerful, indeed, that it can overwhelm the conscious ego, and thus finally dominate the whole personality. (6)

In such manner, Brocklehurst threatens to dominate Jane's still frail personality. As Ulanov suggests, such an animus tends to "echo the traditional patriarchal ideal that women ought only to be wives and mothers, haranguing a woman at every moment" (*Feminine* 263), bombarding the ego with platitudes, banalities, and dogmatic, rigid judgments, all parading as one's own firmly held "beliefs." Clearly, Brocklehurst symbolizes such a figure, berating the young girls with platitudes about Christian martyrdom and a woman's duty to learn self-denial, conforming "'not . . . to nature'" (Brontë 55) but to society's demands. His "'plan in bringing up these girls,'" he announces to Miss Temple, is "'not to accustom them to habits of luxury and indulgence, but to render them hardy, patient, self-denying'" (54).

At such a stage in her development, a young woman may perceive the animus as a personal destroyer; this is especially the case here, since bringing up the dark contents of the unconscious threatens to inundate Jane's childish ego with material as yet unassimilable. Thus Jane says of Mr. Brocklehurst that she must look out "daily for the 'Coming Man,' whose information respecting my past life and conversation was to brand me as a bad child for ever" (Brontë 53). Yet his first appearance suggests the mediating role—albeit here undeveloped and negative—that the animus assumes in relation to the feminine unconscious: "He stood at Miss Temple's side; he was speaking low in her ear: I did not doubt he was making disclosures of my villainy; and I watched her eye with painful anxiety, expecting every moment to see its dark orb turn on me a glance of repugnance and contempt" (53). Miss Temple intervenes to protect Jane and the other girls from this animus-tyrant's overbearing rigidity; still, she cannot prevent their self-effacement when he orders that their "naturally" curly hair be cut to conform to the "modesty" of his "charitable establishment" (55). "These words fell like the knell of doom—'All those top-knots must be cut off'" (56), Jane recalls. The "knell of doom" extends well beyond this moment of mutilation, for Brocklehurst's demand that the girls' hair "'be arranged closely, modestly, plainly'" (55) echoes throughout Jane's adolescence and early adulthood, Jane believing herself plain in spite of protests to the contrary.

At Lowood, nonetheless, Jane has the good fortune to encounter a projected aspect of her "hero" (Brontë 58) or greater Self. Helen Burns is older than Jane and taller—symbolic of the total personality's strength and power, which the ego has yet to realize consciously. Jane's early description of Helen shows the older girl standing on a stool before the class, bearing with equanimity a punishment "in a high degree ignominious, especially for so great a girl":

> I expected she would show signs of great distress and shame, but to my surprise she neither wept nor blushed: composed, though grave, she

stood, the central mark of all eyes. "How can she bear it so quietly—
so firmly?" I asked of myself. "Were I in her place, it seems to me I
should wish the earth to open and swallow me up. She looks as if she
were thinking of something beyond her punishment—beyond her situation: of something not round her nor before her. . . . [H]er sight seems
turned in, gone down into her heart: she is looking at what she can
remember, I believe; not at what is really present." (44–45)

An image of Jane's later maturity, Helen admits her faults and accepts
their consequences with stoicism and a transcendent splendor. When she
speaks, Helen acquires "a beauty more singular than that of Miss Temple's—a beauty . . . of meaning, of movement, of radiance. Then her soul
sat on her lips, and language flowed, from what source I cannot tell"
(63). The language flowing from Helen bespeaks the psychic terrain of
both the personal and the collective unconscious, a realm more expan-
sive, resourceful, and creative than the conscious child can envision.
"'Hush,' Helen admonishes Jane, 'you think too much of the love of
human beings.'"

> You are too impulsive, too vehement: the sovereign hand that created
> your frame, and put life into it, has provided you with other resources
> than your feeble self. . . . Besides this earth, and besides the race of
> men, there is an invisible world and a kingdom of spirits: that world is
> round us, for it is everywhere; and those spirits watch us, for they are
> commissioned to guard us. (60)

Helen's projection of Jane's greater Self—not to mention her connection with the deepest wellspring of human soul-consciousness—is symbolized by a tendency that Helen deems, paradoxically, her own great
flaw: Often, she says, she falls into a trance-like daydream of a place near
her home, a place in nature called (suggestively) Deepden (Brontë 49),
where a bubbling little "visionary brook" obscures the sound of her teachers' voices in the classroom. Revealing the regenerating depth of this Deepden reverie, Helen teaches Jane of a wisdom far deeper than the vengeful,
bitter, immature credo Jane has followed thus far. "I must dislike those
who, whatever I do to please them, persist in disliking me," Jane says, suggesting her own inability to confront and assimilate the shadow within her
own psyche: "I must resist those who punish me unjustly" (50). Helen's
wise reply suggests the self-forgiveness necessary for the ego to encounter
and, ultimately, to assimilate her own inner "enemies." "It is not violence
that best overcomes hate," Helen observes: "Life appears to me to be too
short to be spent in nursing animosity. . . . [I]njustice never crushes me too
low: I live in calm, looking to the end" (50–51).

Though Jane admits, "I was no Helen Burns" (Brontë 57), still Helen's calm influence—her "looking to the end," which is the essence of the psychic journey—has its effect. With Helen's assistance, Jane is able to endure her greatest fear, public punishment, with equanimity:

> There was I, then, mounted aloft: I, who had said I could not bear the shame of standing on my natural feet in the middle of the room, was now exposed to general view on a pedestal of infamy. What my sensations were, no language can describe: but just as they all rose, stifling my breath and constricting my throat, [Helen] came up and passed me: in passing, she lifted her eyes. What a strange light inspired them! What an extraordinary sensation that ray sent through me! How the new feeling bore me up! It was as if a martyr, a hero, had passed a slave or victim, and imparted strength in the transit. I mastered the rising hysteria, lifted up my head, and took a firm stand on the stool. (58)

And later, with "far less of gall and wormwood than ordinary" (62), Jane is able to defend herself against Mr. Brocklehurst's destructive charges. These victories usher in springtime, when her injuries begin "to heal and subside under the gentler breathings of April," and she is more consciously autonomous, able to "set to work afresh, resolved to pioneer my way through every difficulty" (65).

A youthful projection of the deeper Self, Helen is not destined to live, for the ego-consciousness must wrestle with other forces of the psyche in order to establish a fuller, richer contact with the Self in maturity. "Disease" having become "an inhabitant of Lowood" (Brontë 67), the feminine principle must now direct its strength and nurturance to ensure the psyche's further growth. "Miss Temple's whole attention was absorbed by the patients," Jane tells us: "[S]he lived in the sick-room, never quitting it" (66–67). The consumptive Helen is "removed from my sight," Jane says, to "I knew not what room upstairs" (68), an upper room of the psyche that, appropriately, turns out to be Miss Temple's own (69)—symbolically, the home of our heroine's unconscious. And Jane is not allowed to speak with Helen, except to say goodbye at her death. That this repository of strength and faith does not live to merge into Jane's conscious ego proves significant, since it is precisely from the "upper room" of the unconscious that repressed aspects of the Self will later re-emerge, symbolized by Bertha Mason. Soon, Miss Temple marries and even she leaves Jane, who reports that "gone" was "every settled feeling, every association that had made Lowood in some degree a home to me" (73). Though Jane writes in sorrow, her loss of Lowood is in fact her gain, for, having first identified with the maternal principle and then differentiated herself from it, Jane's youthful ego is now ready for the second stage of animus development. In this stage, a woman confronts the animus as a "transpersonal ravishing penetrator," as Ulanov describes it: such an animus figure "breaks into her consciousness, overpowers her, transports her outside herself, connects her to her own instinctual nature, and fundamentally changes her personality" (*Feminine* 247). Throughout most of the remaining novel, Jane works through this second stage.

After the loss of Miss Temple and Lowood, Jane finds employment at Thornfield, whose very name symbolizes her struggle with the animus's masculine force: the phallic thorn will pierce her "field" of self-absorption, the thorn symbolizing a conjunction of "thesis and antithesis, . . . existence and non-existence, ecstasy and anguish, pleasure and pain" (Cirlot 322–23). A "thorn *field*" offers a further conjunction of opposites, particularly of masculine and feminine symbols. During her early days at Thornfield, Jane knows only Adele, an immature young female who, Jane says, is "a dependent like myself" (Brontë 88) and neither wholly good nor bad; and the elderly Mrs. Fairfax, the "beau ideal of domestic comfort" (83). Jane's conscious world thus embraces only the quiet, safe, and comfortable cultural stereotypes of the early Victorian feminine persona. Yet Jane remains strangely restless, drawn to explore the house's third floor: there, from the attic—"black as a vault"—emanates a "mirthless" (93) and "preternatural" (94) laugh, soon revealed to belong to "that living enigma, that mystery of mysteries" (178), Bertha Mason. Jane at first believes the laugh belongs to Grace Poole, whose name, as we have come to expect, suggests her symbolic influence on Jane's ego: a power of grace bringing the ego to encounter the as-yet hidden depths—the unrippled pool—of her unconscious. Before meeting Rochester, Jane's "sole relief' when feeling restless and lonely is to go to the third floor corridor, where she turns her "inward ear to a tale . . . [full of] incident, life, fire, feeling, that I desired and had not in my actual existence" (95–96). Unconsciously, Jane yearns to experience her shadow-Self, with its dangerously alluring murmurings of "incident, life, fire, feeling." Such an introduction follows upon her fateful confrontation with Rochester.

In Rochester, Jane confronts a maturer animus figure, though (as Ulanov leads us to anticipate) he first appears as an interloper, a stranger on the road, approaching with "rude noise" and accompanied by his dog, a curious "lion-like creature" with "strange pretercanine eyes" (Brontë 98), all symbolic of the conjunctive force that Rochester becomes in her development. And though Rochester appears threatening, Jane feels "set . . . at ease" by his "frown, the roughness of the traveller" (100), his face being "dissimilar" to all the other pictures in her "gallery of memory . . . firstly, because it was masculine; and, secondly, because it was dark, strong, and stern" (101). However unconscious her longing may be, Jane apparently longs for the partnership of her own masculine force, that alien Other she has thus far fearfully renounced. But the encounter on the road soon ends. Assuming that she leaves this "traveller" behind, Jane returns to Thornfield, where "to cross the silent hall, to ascend the darksome staircase, to seek my own lonely little room, and then to meet tranquil Mrs. Fairfax and spend the long winter evening with her, and her only," is to "return to stagnation" (102).

Yet Rochester again invades Jane's world with a Dionysian force, his rough power matched only by his strange moodiness. And Jane reacts to him with a mixture of fascination and fear. He is "dread, but adored" (Brontë 252), as she describes him after agreeing to marry: "if I loved him less I should have thought his accent and look of exultation savage" (224). Jane struggles against Rochester's invasion "like a wild, frantic bird that is rending its own plumage in its desperation" (223). Yet Rochester fulfills his archetypal role as mediator and guide, calling her "my equal . . . my likeness" (223) and advising her, in his disguise (female, appropriately) as a gypsy fortuneteller, of the sources of her feelings of incompleteness: "You are cold, because you are alone: no contact strikes the fire from you that is in you. You are sick: because the best of feelings . . . keeps far away from you. You are silly, because, suffer as you may, you will not beckon it to approach; nor will you stir one step to meet it where it waits you" (173). Cold, sick, silly, suffering: thus the animus views the one-sided ego, imperiled through its own self-imposed isolation. Appropriately, Jane describes her slowly dawning discovery (that the gypsy is Rochester in disguise) as a mirror gaze or self-recognition: "her gesture, and all were familiar to me as my own face in a glass—as the speech of my own tongue" (177).

Jane's animus relationship remains fraught with conflict, with compelling urges and fears, with "annoyance and degradation" (Brontë 236) and discord; for the closer she comes to embracing her masculine Other, the more pressing becomes her need to accept the repressed shadow aspects of herself, particularly regarding sexuality. Throughout her adolescence, Jane has identified with her persona as fashioned at Lowood: the prim, proper image of a dutiful Victorian working-class female. Accordingly, Jane holds austere and self-effacing opinions about her appearance, continually telling us that she is physically plain—for all practical purposes, quite ugly—though Rochester tells her she is "'truly pretty'" (226). In keeping with her negative (yet socially sanctioned) self-image, Jane can only answer, "Don't address me as if I were a beauty; I am your plain, Quakerish governess" (227). As long as she remains bound to her persona—symbolized in part by her plain clothing—Jane cannot change to fit her new status as Rochester's prospective wife; indeed, she rejects all jewelry and a beautiful wedding veil, saying to Rochester, "I thought how I would carry down to you the square of unembroidered blond I had myself prepared as a covering for my low-born head" (247).

Significantly, the jewelry that Jane refuses belonged (by a "previous marriage") to her shadow-image, Bertha Mason. The notorious Victorian "madwoman in the attic," Bertha has occasionally been treated as a projection of Rochester's unconscious (Kinkead-Weakes; Scargill), while feminist critics have seen her as symbolic both of Jane's repressed anger against Rochester and of Brontë's anger against patriarchy (Gilbert and Gubar; Rigney; Wyatt). There is, indeed, a poignant cultural symbolism in her attic imprisonment: given Victorian sexual strictures, Bertha expressed an independent, uncontrolled and, hence, "dangerous" sexual appetite that English patriarchal culture sought by all means to repress. It is no wonder that Bertha Mason was deemed a beautiful woman, "the boast of Spanish Town for her beauty[,] . . . tall, dark, and majestic" (Brontë 268). A native of the West Indies (and, thus, Jane's cultural Other), Bertha embodied, before the onset of madness, those aspects of the total personality that Jane's prim Victorian persona most fears and rejects: sensuality, vanity, and violent temper (268–69), as well as physical beauty, social grace, and charm. As Jane's shadow-projection, Bertha's insanity represents no less than the narrator's own fear over the loss of ego control, madness symbolizing a submersion (and disabling) of the ego within the greater Self. In short, Bertha's sexuality, untamed beauty, and guiltless sensuality pose too great a threat to the sanitized cultural stereotype of the Victorian woman.

Jane's physical confrontation with Bertha follows two dreams of frightening intensity in which, separated from Rochester, she is heavily burdened with a child "'too young and feeble to walk'" and who "'wailed piteously in my ear'" (Brontë 247). In the first dream, she is fettered and cannot run after Rochester; in the second, both she and the child fall into the crumbling ruins of Thornfield. Symbolically, both dreams warn Jane that separation from her animus, at this point, could mean regression and a crumbling of her personality. Upon waking, she sees Bertha looming over her, an image "fearful and ghastly" (249) and reminiscent of a "Vampyre" (250), though wearing Jane's wedding veil. Here, again, the ego's fear of the unconscious is a fear of symbolic death, of losing itself in the engulfing wave of all that is repressed and instinctual; thus, when Bertha tears the wedding veil, she offers a compelling image of all that Jane fears in her own repressed sexuality, the veil being the "hymeneal symbol of the bride's giving herself to the groom, who lifts it in the ceremony to kiss her" (Maynard 108). Suddenly confronting the prospects of living with Rochester and Bertha together (that is, in conscious relation with her shadow-animus constellation), Jane becomes increasingly agitated, even appalled by a man who "seemed to devour me with his flaming glance: physically, I felt, at the moment, powerless as stubble exposed to the draught and glow of a furnace" (279).

Ignoring her warning dreams, Jane fears and resists submission to the transformative "fire" that Rochester represents—a fire symbolizing both her own repressed sexuality and the gradually emerging aspects of her unconscious feminine principle.[4] Thus she flees Thornfield: "Up the blood rushed to his face; forth flashed the fire from his eyes; erect he sprang; he held his arms out; but I evaded the embrace, and at once quitted the room. 'Farewell!' was the cry of my heart as I left him" (Brontë 281). During the ensuing night, Jane says, "I dreamt I lay in the red room at Gateshead," where a curious "white human form . . . spoke to my spirit: . . . 'My daughter, flee temptation!' 'Mother, I will!'" (281). Coming in reaction to her newly discovered sexuality—part of the unconscious feminine principle that Jane must consciously assimilate—such a dream reveals Jane's perilous wish to return to the "matriarchal unity" of her childhood, as well as a regression back to the animus-tyranny of her earlier years.

The effect of this animus-tyranny may be traced through her "speeches" while starving on the heath, all pseudo-rational, platitudinous mouthings of Christian dogma (Brontë 285). "In a state of identification with the animus," writes Emma Jung, "we think, say, or do something in the full conviction that it is we who are doing it, while in reality, without our having been aware of it, the animus has been speaking through us" (14). Such seems the case here with Jane, and it is only a small step from such platitudes to St. John at Moor House, who represents her return to the animus-tyranny earlier epitomized in Mr. Brocklehurst. Though the two men differ in appearance, their rhetoric—platitudes, dogma, rigidity—and repressive patriarchal attitudes are all too similar. Moor House, then, represents Jane's regression to Lowood, but during a more perilous stage of development, when the young woman is challenged to explore and assimilate her sexuality. Studying books among other young women, Jane finds herself passionless and desexualized, ruled over by yet another austere Brocklehurst.[5] Proposing a marriage based not on romantic love and sexual pleasure but on "service," "assistance," and "labour" (354–55), St. John responds to Jane's warning that he seek a wife "elsewhere than in me" (357): "Again I tell you it is not the insignificant private individual—the mere man, with the man's selfish senses—I wish to mate: it is the missionary. . . . It is the cause of God I advocate . . . I cannot accept on His behalf a divided allegiance: it must be entire" (357). As she reports, Jane feels "his influence in my marrow—his hold on my limbs" (357): "I felt veneration for St. John—veneration so strong that its impetus thrust me at once to the point I had so long shunned. I was tempted to cease struggling with him—to rush down the torrent of his will into the gulf of his existence, and there lose my own" (368). Yet Jane comes to realize that union with St. John would be "almost equivalent to committing suicide" (364).

Immediately after rejecting St. John, Jane hears Rochester calling "wildly, eerily, urgently" (Brontë 369); as if awakened from a "torpor," she responds, "I am coming! Wait for me! Oh, I will come!" (369). On the road back to Thornfield, she recognizes the rightness of her choice, feeling "like the messenger-pigeon flying home" (372). Yet Jane returns to a world transformed, Thornfield having burned to the ground at "harvest time" (375). Indeed, the incident symbolizes a fruitful "harvest" in many aspects, suggesting the alchemical medium of transformation—the Heraclitean fire being agent not simply of destruction but also of regeneration (Cirlot 100–01). Set by Bertha, the fire becomes, symbolically, a Self-willed transformation arising from the depths of Jane's own unconscious. The symbolic connection between Bertha's action and that earlier representation of Jane's Self, Helen *Burns,* should also be noted, for it is fire that unites shadow and Self, driving Bertha out of the dark attic of the unconscious and down to the brighter pavement of ego-consciousness. The fire changes Rochester, too, transforming him from a driven, Dionysian figure into the calmed, though blind and lame, partner Jane can now embrace without threat or fear: "Delightful consciousness!" Jane writes: "It brought to life and light my whole nature: in his presence I thoroughly lived; and he lived in mine. Blind as he was, smiles played over his face, joy dawned on his forehead; his lineaments softened and warmed" (384).

Though (from a Freudian perspective) critics have interpreted Rochester's blinding as a symbolic castration,[6] we choose to interpret the fire's archetypal symbolism more positively, for it has transformed the unstable animus figure earlier described as "'stand[ing] on a crater-crust which may crack and spue fire any day'" (190). Contrasted with the coldly intellectual St. John, the "Apollo" (389) of her recollections, Rochester has become Jane's "Vulcan" (389), mythic husband to Venus. As the god of fire and forge, of artistic creativity and domestic labor, Rochester's Vulcan-transformation suggests a further maturing of Jane's animus-image and, thus, of her own developing ego-Self relation. Having married her Vulcan, Jane can enjoy, guiltfree, her newly discovered identification as goddess of sexual pleasure and procreation.

"Conclusion," writes Jane: "Reader, I married him" (Brontë 395). From a Jungian perspective, such a terse, memorable summation of Jane's story expresses a supreme psychic achievement, for the fruitful union or "marriage" of ego-consciousness with archetypes of the unconscious has opened new paths toward individuation. Significantly, too, we are told that *she* married *him:* given her bold use of "active voice," one can no longer detect any sense of fear, sacrifice, compromise, or passivity on her part. Jane's later description of their marriage relationship is similarly without struggle, fear, or conflict:

> I have now been married ten years. . . . No woman was ever nearer to her mate than I am; ever more absolutely bone of his bone and flesh of his flesh. . . . We talk, I believe, all day long: to talk to each other is but a more animated and an audible thinking. All my confidence is bestowed on him, all his confidence is devoted to me. . . . (396–97)

The imagery of wholeness, of effortless and unimpeded communication, underscores the implicit achievement of what Ulanov calls the third stage of development: a conscious partnership with the animus (*Feminine* 255) that leads, ultimately, to the self-discovery and self-giving of individuation, Ulanov's fourth and final stage (*Feminine* 268).[7] Yet it is here, in the "perfect concord" (397) of their marriage, that Jane leaves off her personal narrative. Brontë's story of the "eyre" or allegorical journey of Everywoman remains unfinished: individuation has yet to be fully achieved. Jane has reached, nonetheless, a moment of rest and refreshment on a plateau of vision and clarity, having assimilated her once-repressed sexuality and entered into an active, conscious relationship with her masculine Other, one now capable of assisting her on the difficult, though fruitful and generative, path toward wholeness.

"There is, in the naive resolution of *Jane Eyre,* an idealization of Jane and Rochester's life together which is part of the logic of the psychosexual romance" (Moglen 144). Though somewhat disparaging, Helene Moglen's Freudian reading acknowledges the revolutionary, "visionary" nature of Brontë's feminist mythology:

> The last chapter begins with an extraordinary statement that places Jane at the center of the relationship. "Reader, I married him," she says. . . . But the truth of this relation is an interior truth, as remote from social reality as are Gateshead, Lowood, Thornfield, Marsh End, and Ferndean—themselves all landscapes of psychological development. It is the truth of Charlotte Brontë's dream that we have here: the

truth of her fantasy. To the extent that it dramatizes the conflict of
larger social and psychological forces, it offers also the larger truth of
myth. But what is extraordinary is that this novel, born of repression
and frustration, of limited experience and less hope, should have
offered an insight into psychosexual relations that was visionary in its
own time and remains active in ours. (144–45)

Hardly naive, the "truth" of Jane's "myth" lies not in Brontë's own wish
fulfillment fantasy but in the depth of its exploration of the archetypal
dimensions of the heroine's personal and cultural experience. As a distinctively Victorian "rebirth myth," *Jane Eyre* directly challenges the
gender ideologies of nineteenth-century English patriarchal culture. And
"therein lies the social significance of art," as Jung suggests: "it is constantly at work educating the spirit of the age, conjuring up the forms in
which the age is most lacking. The unsatisfied yearning of the artist
reaches back to the primordial image in the unconscious which is best
fitted to compensate the inadequacy and one-sidedness of the present"
("Relation of Analytical Psychology to Poetry," *CW* 15 par. 130). Its
nineteenth-century trappings notwithstanding, *Jane Eyre* remains a most
potent, generative, and regenerative myth for any century in its depiction of woman as hero, travailing the journey from immature ineffectu-
ality to confident possession of true power: the "plain Jane" who is able
to regenerate herself into no less than Venus, the generative goddess.

NOTES

1. Quotations from *Jane Eyre* are taken from the Norton Critical Edition,
edited by Richard J. Dunn. For feminist readings of *Jane Eyre,* see Gilbert and
Gubar; Moglen; Nestor; Rigney; and Tromly. Our analysis follows Ann Belford
Ulanov's "Stages of Animus Development" (241–85), a chapter from her seminal work, *The Feminine* (1971); to a lesser extent, we make use of her later work
with Barry Ulanov, *Transforming Sexuality* (1994). A further influence is Annis
V. Pratt's "Spinning among Fields," a post-Jungian exploration of the conflict-
ing patriarchal and pre-patriarchal (or proto-feminist) mythologies operant
within Victorian women's novels.

2. It is for this reason that "the realization of the shadow is inhibited by the
persona," as Sharp notes: "To the degree that we identify with a bright persona,
the shadow is correspondingly dark Thus shadow and persona stand in a compensatory relationship, and the conflict between them is invariably present in an
outbreak of neurosis" (124). This is certainly the case with Jane Eyre, whose idealized and, thereby, one-sided self-image affirms Victorian sexual mores and
strictures against female behavior. And yet the shadow "does not consist only of
morally reprehensible tendencies," Jung tells us, "but also displays a number of

good qualities, such as normal instincts, appropriate reactions, realistic insights, creative impulses" (Conclusion, *CW* 9.2 par. 423). Much of the shadow's "darkness," then, reflects the extent to which its qualities are undervalued, feared, or socially condemned. As part of the task of individuation, the ego must confront, acknowledge, and enter into conscious relationship with all such aspects of the total personality. Through Rochester's mediation, Jane must meet Bertha.

3. Here, then, in a constellation of the archetypal family, Jane will find herself playing "bad" (that is, abused) "child" to Miss Temple's forgiving mother and Mr Brocklehurst's tyrannizing father, a constellation that will become further complicated by Jane's fantasy-projection of a rival, "ghostly" father, the deceased Mr. Reed. A further constellation (that of sibling witness, long-suffering martyr, and parental persecutor) arises when Jane "bears witness" to Helen's classroom punishment. Donald F. Sandner and John Beebe describe the causes and effects of such archetypal constellations:

> An archetype provides the implicit structure for an image, an affect, and a pattern of behavior. When these appear, an archetype is said to be constellated, and typical preoccupations, feelings, and situations tend to recur. . . . [A]rchetypes "come up" when they are needed, and they are needed when an adaptation demand cannot be met by an individual's ego. For example, archetypal behavior must emerge in adolescence because the ego that has been shaped by childhood experience simply is not adequate to meet the demands placed upon it when social and biological adulthood approach. The first steps in the adult direction are then, necessarily, structured by archetypes. (318)

Jane Eyre's narrative, we believe, confirms the "necessarily" archetypal structure of adolescent experience. Of course, Jane's task is to grow beyond such unconscious roles and identifications. Such growth in ego-consciousness will prove particularly crucial during a later constellation when Jane, still largely identified with her adolescent persona, confronts her animus-image in Rochester and shadow-Self in Bertha.

4. As Barbara Hill Rigney writes, "what Brontë fears for Jane is that marriage with Rochester will not be a union of equals, but rather a loss of self, an engulfment in the identity of another" (20) This, indeed, represents Jane's conscious fears, though her motives for fleeing Thornfield are somewhat more complex. As Ulanov and Ulanov write,

> A woman may really fear the tremendous force of her own sexual arousal. Its power may make her tremble. She may repress this instinctive response, which will only force it underground and may occasion a destructive frigidity in her. Her unclaimed fear may act itself out by estranging her from any response as just too risky. Or she may try to control her instinctive fear by developing relation only to the logos end of the masculine archetype—all word, transcendence, and order—to avoid the eros end of active poking, pushing, arousing, opening, penetrating. (112)

5. As Emma Jung writes of such regressive behavior: "the animus is expert at sketching in and making plausible a picture that represents us as we would like to be seen, for example, as the 'ideal lover,' the 'appealing, helpless child,' the 'selfless handmaiden,'" This activity, she adds, "naturally lends the animus power over us until we voluntarily, or perforce, make up our minds to sacrifice the highly colored picture and see ourselves as we really are" (18)

6. Dooley was first to interpret Rochester's blinding as symbolic castration (268), though Chase popularized (indeed, sensationalized) this Freudian perspective Schreiber, in contrast, reads Rochester's lameness as symbolic of the author's own frigidity. Moglen offers a suggestive alternative: "Rochester's mutilation is, in terms of this nascent feminist myth, the necessary counterpart of Jane's independence: the terrible condition of a relationship of inequality" (142). Given the obvious fruitfulness of their marriage, Rochester's sacrifice is of male aggressivity, and not sexual potency. See Maynard (138–44 and 249–50) for further discussion of the castration myth and, conversely, of sexual growth and fulfillment in the novel's ending.

7. A further transformation occurs two years later, when Rochester, seeing Jane's "gold watch-chain" (Brontë 397)—reminiscent of the watch Miss Temple wore during her first meeting with Jane (41)—recovers sight in one eye And Jane's physical union with Rochester is fruitful, producing offspring—a visionary boy-child whose eyes are as "large and brilliant" as Rochester's own (397).

WORKS CITED

Bloom, Harold, ed. *The Brontës: Modern Critical Views.* New York: Chelsea, 1987.

Burkhart, Charles. *Charlotte Brontë: A Psychosexual Study of Her Novels.* London: Gollancz, 1973.

Calder, Jenni. *Women and Marriage in Victorian Fiction.* London: Thames and Hudson, 1976.

Chase, Richard. "The Brontës, or Myth Domesticated." Dunn 462–71.

Cirlot, J. E. *A Dictionary of Symbols.* Trans. Jack Sage. New York: Philosophical Library, 1962.

Craik, W. A. *The Brontë Novels.* London: Methuen, 1968.

Dooley, Lucile. "Psychoanalysis of Charlotte Brontë, as a Type of the Woman of Genius." *American Journal of Psychology* 31 (1920): 221–72.

Dunn, Richard J., ed. *Jane Eyre: An Authoritative Text, Backgrounds, Criticism.* New York: Norton, 1971.

Gilbert, Sandra M., and Susan Gubar. *The Madwoman in the Attic: The Woman Writer and the Nineteenth-Century Literary Imagination.* New Haven: Yale UP, 1979.

Gliserman, Martin J. *Psychoanalysis, Language, and the Body of the Text.* Gainesville: UP of Florida, 1996.

Gregor, Ian, ed. *The Brontës: A Collection of Critical Essays.* Englewood Cliffs: Prentice, 1970.

Hughes, R. E. "Jane Eyre: The Unbaptized Dionysos." *Nineteenth-Century Fiction* 18 (1964): 347–64.

Jung, Carl G. *The Collected Works of C. G. Jung.* Ed. Sir Herbert Read, Michael Fordham, and Gerhard Adler. Trans. R. F. C. Hull. 20 vols. Princeton: Princeton UP, 1953–77.

Jung, Emma. *Animus and Anima.* Trans. Cary F. Baynes and Hildegard Nagel. Zurich: Spring, 1974.

Kinkead-Weakes, Mark. "The Place of Love in *Jane Eyre* and *Wuthering Heights.*" Gregor 76–95.

Langbridge, Rosamond. *Charlotte Brontë: A Psychological Study.* London: Heinemann, 1929.

Lodge, David. "Fire and Eyre: Charlotte Brontë's War of Earthly Elements." Gregory 110–36.

Maynard, John. *Charlotte Brontë and Sexuality.* Cambridge: Cambridge UP, 1984.

Moglen, Helene. *Charlotte Brontë: The Self Conceived.* New York: Norton, 1976.

Nestor, Pauline. *Charlotte Brontë.* Totowa, NJ: Barnes and Noble, 1987.

Pratt, Annis V. "Spinning among Fields: Jung, Frye, Lévi-Strauss and Feminist Archetypal Theory." Lauter and Rupprecht 93–136.

Rigney, Barbara Hill. *Madness and Sexual Politics in the Feminist Novel: Studies in Brontë, Woolf, Lessing, and Atwood.* Madison: U of Wisconsin P, 1978.

Sandner, Donald F., and John Beebe. "Psychopathology and Analysis." Stein 294–334.

Scargill, M. H. "All Passion Spent: A Revaluation of *Jane Eyre.*" *University of Toronto Quarterly* 19 (1949): 120–25.

Schreiber, Annette. "The Myth in Charlotte Brontë." *Literature and Psychology* 18 (1968): 48–67.

Sharp, Daryl. *Jung Lexicon: A Primer of Terms and Concepts.* Toronto: Inner City, 1991.

Showalter, Elaine. *A Literature of Their Own: British Women Novelists from Brontë to Lessing.* Princeton: Princeton UP, 1977.

Stein, Murray, ed. *Jungian Analysis.* Boston: Shambhala, 1985.

Tromly, Annette. *The Cover of the Mask: The Autobiographers in Charlotte Brontë's Fiction.* Victoria, BC: U of Victoria P, 1982.

Ulanov, Ann Belford. *The Feminine in Jungian Psychology and in Christian Theology.* Evanston: Northwestern UP, 1971.

Ulanov, Ann Belford, and Barry Ulanov. *Transforming Sexuality: The Archetypal World of Anima and Animus.* Boston: Shambala, 1994.

von Franz, Marie-Louise. "The Process of Individuation." *Man and His Symbols.* Ed. Carl G. Jung. Garden City, NY: Doubleday, 1964. 158–229.

Whitmont, Edward C. "Recent Influences on Jungian Analysis." Stein 335–66.

Williams, Raymond. "Charlotte and Emily Brontë." Bloom 57–68.

Wyatt, Jean. *Reconstructing Desire: The Role of the Unconscious in Women's Reading and Writing.* Chapel Hill: U of North Carolina P, 1990.

Jungian Insights into Victorian Cultural Ambiguities

Wilkie Collins's The Woman in White

⌒⌒⌒

SOPHIA ANDRES

Following trends in postmodern thought, Jungian literary criticism has given increasing attention to the convergence between the psychological and the cultural. Applying Jung's concepts of individuation, anima, animus, and shadow, I wish to explore such a convergence in one of the most popular novels of Victorian England, Wilkie Collins's *The Woman in White* (published in four editions within the first month of its publication).[1] Recently, critics have focused on Collins's subversion of Victorian stereotypes (Balee, Bernstein, Elam, Langbauer, Williams) but have overlooked the Pre-Raphaelites' influence on Collins's challenges to gender constructs. Beginning with some Pre-Raphaelite paintings that served as possible inspirations, I would like first to explore the affinities that Pre-Raphaelite paintings and Collins's narrative images share and then to demonstrate how Collins's Pre-Raphaelite concern with the rendering of light and shadow leads him to explore the workings of the unconscious.

Even before the appearance of the woman in white at the outset of the novel, while Walter Hartright is walking in a moonlit landscape, Collins masterfully interweaves the real and the imaginative in Pre-Raphaelite interplays of light with shadow. Collins captures the fluidity of the liberating space between waking and dreaming. In this eerie and mysterious setting, the sudden appearance of the woman in white, an "extraordinary apparition" (Collins, *Woman in White* 47)—a shadow—partakes of the substantial and the ethereal, the real and the possible, the conscious and the unconscious. Thus Collins's choice of the moonlit landscape seems extremely appropriate, especially when considered in light of M.-L. von Franz's description of the unconscious as a "moonlit landscape," in which "all the contents are blurred and merge into one another, and one never knows exactly what or where anything is" (173). Although Hartright does not explicitly refer to Anne Catherick as a shadow when he first meets her, he describes her as such at the end of the novel, when he hears about her death: "So the ghostly figure which has haunted these pages, as it haunted my life, goes down into impenetrable gloom. Like a shadow she first came to me in the loneliness of the night. Like a shadow she passes away in the loneliness of the dead" (Collins, *Woman in White* 576).

Thus Collins, in an attempt to draw his narrative in Pre-Raphaelite interplays of light with shadow, transforms the social imaginary, the fear of the Other—the outcast, the displaced—into an essential phase in the protagonist's (the typical Victorian's) psyche. Eventually, the shadowy figure becomes an integral part of Hartright's quest for psychic integration. In the process Collins illustrates that psychic integration is not possible without an active interaction of the masculine with the feminine, of the self with the Other, of the personal with the cultural. Thus in Collins's renowned novel we may discern the same Jungian structures operative across artistic forms. In this case literature and art combined might have enabled Victorians, and may enable postmodern readers, vicariously to explore their own shadows.

Cultural Relevance and Transcendence: Jung's Cross-Gendered Shadow

Unlike most literary critics who develop their theories within the boundaries of cultural specificity or textual relevance, Jung's perspective on literature often transcends yet does not entirely disregard cultural boundaries. Indeed the literary manifestation of his psychology becomes most intriguing and fascinating in the convergence of psychological consequence with cultural relevance. Throughout his works, his definitions of key terms are not static, limited within the psychological, the universal, or the cultural arenas; rather, they fluctuate among these spheres and partake of qualities of all three. His definition of the unconscious, for instance, distinguishes between the personal and the collective unconscious, designating the contents of the former as having been "acquired during the individual's lifetime"—thus allowing for its cultural uniqueness—and of the latter as "archetypes that were present from the beginning" (*CW* 9.2: 8).

Similarly, Jung's definition of the shadow relies on the convergence of the psychological with the cultural and the universal. Thus he defines the shadow as a "moral problem that challenges the whole ego-personality, for no one can become conscious of the shadow without considerable moral effort" (*CW* 9.2: 8). In this respect, the shadow is of individual consequence and involves "a recognition of the dark aspects of personality as present and real" (*CW* 9.2: 8). But this personal relevance is quickly broadened as Jung relates the shadow to projections that are bound up with resistances but are not recognized as such, and "their recognition is a moral achievement, beyond the ordinary" (*CW* 9.2: 8). Whereas one may recognize some aspects of the shadow as one's own negative qualities, such recognition becomes almost impossible when "the cause of the emotion appears to lie, beyond all possibility of doubt, in the *other person*" (emphasis in original; *CW* 9.2: 9). In this respect, the shadow partakes qualities of the cultural context, since the personal is shaped and modified by ideology. Once again, though, Jung locates the shadow in the convergence of the psychological with the cultural and the universal: "with a little self-criticism one can see through the shadow—so far as its nature is personal. But when it appears as an archetype, one encounters the same difficulties as with the anima and animus" (*CW* 9.2: 10).

Although he seems to limit the shadow within gender boundaries by designating it as "the same sex as the subject" (*CW* 9.2: 10), Jung elides gender distinctions when he relates the shadow to projections: "One might assume that projections like these, which are so very difficult if not impossible to dissolve, would belong to the realm of the shadow. . . . This assumption becomes untenable after a certain point, because the symbols that then appear no longer refer to the same but to the opposite sex, in a man's case to a woman and vice versa" (*CW* 9. 2: 10). As the concept of the shadow becomes interwoven with projections and these projections acquire contrasexual qualities, the concept of the shadow may also display a contrasexual quality. In broadening the meaning of the shadow and thus moving beyond gender boundaries, Jung seems to anticipate postmodern theorists who deal with the complexity of our projections on the Other. Terry Eagleton, for instance, discusses the man-woman antithesis in terms of the Other, what Jung would regard as the contrasexual aspects of the shadow:

Woman is the opposite, the "other" of man: she is non-man, defective
man, assigned a chiefly negative value in relation to the male first principle. But equally man is what he is only by virtue of ceaselessly shutting this other or opposite, defining himself in antithesis to it, and his
whole identity is therefore caught up and put at risk in the very gesture
by which he seeks to assert his unique, autonomous existence. Woman
is not just an other in the sense of something beyond his ken, but an
other intimately related to him as the image of what he is not, and
therefore as an essential reminder of what he is. Man therefore needs
this other as he spurns it. . . . Not only is his own being parasitically
dependent upon the woman, and upon the act of excluding and subor-
dinating her, but one reason why such exclusion is necessary is because
she may not be quite so other after all. Perhaps what is outside is also
somehow inside. (132–33)

Thus Eagleton transgresses the gender boundaries Jung ascribes to the
shadow but at the same time, like Jung, perceives the Other as a projection that, in pointing outward, originates within.

THE PRE-RAPHAELITE SHADOW IN THE WOMAN IN WHITE

Through his brother, Charley Collins, himself a Pre-Raphaelite, Wilkie
Collins came to know Dante Gabriel Rossetti and became intimate
friends with John Everett Millais and William Holman Hunt. His close
friendship with these three founders of the Pre-Raphaelite Brotherhood
is evident in his correspondence with them (Baker and Clarke). In his
Pre-Raphaelitism and Pre-Raphaelite Brotherhood, William Holman
Hunt mentions Wilkie Collins's intention to write an article about the
Pre-Raphaelite principles (1: 304). Besides, in a long review of the 1851
Royal Academy Summer Exhibition, Collins claimed that he admired
the Pre-Raphaelites' "earnestness of purpose, their originality of
thought, their close and reverent study of nature" (624–25). Indeed
Collins's interest in the Pre-Raphaelites' "strict adherence to the truth as
it is in Nature," as Patricia Frick has demonstrated, "provided Collins
with a sense of landscape, which enabled him, in his later writings, to
establish his scenes with vivid effect" (12–13).

In addition to vivid, detailed landscapes, women in white abound
in Pre-Raphaelite paintings. These women in white often represent
archetypal images which simultaneously depict Victorian binary oppositions: the virgin and the fallen woman. Charley Collins's *Convent
Thoughts* (1852), for instance, which Ruskin described as "Mr. Collins'
lady in white" (12: 320–21), and the vulnerable divine figure in Ros-

setti's *Ecce Ancilla Domini* (1850) represent idealist conceptions of the Victorian woman as a virginal, pure, inaccessible figure. Yet the women in white in such paintings as Ford Madox Brown's *Take Your Son, Sir* (1856–57) or William Holman Hunt's *The Awakening Conscience* (1853–54) disclose cultural anxieties about the Other, in this case the fallen woman, the outcast—a collective shadow. Besides these figures, even a cursory look at Rossetti's "haunting and somewhat bizarre drawing" *How They Met Themselves* (1850–60), which depicts a couple in medieval costume meeting their doubles in a dark wood (Faxon 140–41), seems but an illustration of Collins's rendering of the Doppelgänger theme in *The Woman in White*. By transposing the illegitimate Anne Catherick with her respectable half-sister Laura Fairlie-Glyde—the outcast with the privileged—Collins seems to undermine contemporary gender ideology, demonstrating that women, as long as they are kept uninformed, run the same risks whether they be outcasts or honored members of the upper classes.

On the other hand, an illustration of the ironic reversals in *The Woman in White* can also be seen in John Everett Millais's drawing *Retribution* (1854), which, as Susan Casteras points out, depicts an ironic reversal of roles: the fallen woman is portrayed as a regal figure and the respectable wife as a pitiful suppliant in a society ruled by sexual double standards (30–31). Certainly the central situation in the novel seems to duplicate this tableau. Whereas Laura Fairlie, the upper middle-class woman, is imprisoned in her own house by her husband, Sir Percival Glyde (who later commits her to an asylum where she is deprived of her own identity and property), Mrs. Catherick, the fallen woman and the mother of Laura's half-sister Anne, enjoys respectability. And because of Mr. Fairlie's hidden infidelity, Anne Catherick and Laura Fairlie never know that they are sisters. Hartright's passionate commitment to "unknown Retribution" (Collins, *Woman in White* 296)—his pursuit of Sir Percival, which his love for Laura engenders—is a theme that unifies the various seemingly disparate narratives of the novel.

In addition to themes for the novel, I believe that Pre-Raphaelite paintings also provided Collins with ideas for his primary narrative technique, namely his treatment of light and shadow. Early reviews of Pre-Raphaelite exhibitions note the Pre-Raphaelites' departure from traditional modes of perspective and treatments of light and shadow. In 1849, for instance, a reviewer for *Athenaeum,* responding to John Everett Millais's *Isabella* (1849) and William Holman Hunt's *Rienzi* (1849), complains that "the faults of the two pictures under consideration are the results of the partial views which have led their authors to the practice of a time when knowledge of light and shade and of the means of imparting due relief by the systematic conduct of aerial per-spective had not been obtained," and concludes that "the hard monot-ony of contour in Isabella is due to the absence of shadow" (Hunt 1: 178–79). Two years later, in *Times* of 7 May 1851, an outraged reviewer responded to an exhibition of Millais's *Mariana,* Collins's *Convent Thoughts,* and William Holman Hunt's *Valentine Rescuing Sylvia from Proteus,* by censuring the painters' eccentric techniques: "Their faith seems to consist in an absolute contempt for perspective and the known laws of light and shade" (Hunt 1: 249). On 29 April 1854, a reviewer of Hunt's *The Awakening Conscience* also focused on the shadow in the background, a relatively minor detail in such a heav-ily cluttered painting: "The complicated compound shadow in the mir-ror is also a mere piece of intricacy without any good or valuable effort" (Hunt 1: 404–06).

Brushstrokes of light and shadow indeed sharpen the visual effect of key events in *The Woman in White,* accentuating their impact. But besides enhancing the sensational quality of the novel, these Pre-Raphaelite touches of light and shadow reveal Collins's concern with human psychology, in particular his perspicacious understanding of the mysterious workings of the unconscious. Such an understanding is inter-woven with his subtle and astute subversion of Victorian bourgeois men-tality and Victorian gender constructs. By placing Anne Catherick, the illegitimate daughter of a fallen woman, in the novel's center, Collins, like his Pre-Raphaelite friends, aroused and allayed the fear of the Other. Initially presenting the illegitimate figure of Anne Catherick as the threat of the Other to Hartright, Collins eventually transforms her into his personal shadow. It is curious that in a novel supposedly about a woman, the "effective protagonist" (Dawson 257) is a man whose quest for psychic integration becomes possible through his encounters with women. Thus Collins anticipates postmodern theorists in demon-strating that masculinity "does not exist in isolation from femininity—it will always be an expression of the current images that men have of themselves in relation to women. And these images are often contradic-tory and ambivalent (Brittan 2–3).

INDIVIDUATION: THE INDIVIDUAL IN
DIALOGUE WITH THE COLLECTIVE

Even before the woman in white appears to Hartright at the opening of the novel, we are aware of a landscape suffused with light and shade. As a teacher of drawing, Walter is naturally sensitive and receptive to his surroundings, describing them in Pre-Raphaelite–like details: "the long hot summer was drawing to a close; and we, the weary pilgrims of the London pavement, were beginning to think of the cloud-shadows on the corn-fields, and the autumn breezes on the sea-shore" (Collins, *Woman in White* 34). Soon after this scene, Walter appears against a Pre-Raphaelite background of light and shadow. Oppressed by the humidity, he decides to "stroll home in the purer air . . . to follow the white winding paths across the lonely heath" in the "mysterious light" of the moon; and as he enjoys "the divine stillness of the scene," admiring "the soft alternations of light and shade . . . over the broken ground," he is startled by the sudden appearance of the solitary figure of Anne Catherick, the woman in white: "there, as if it had that moment sprung out of the earth or dropped from the heaven—stood the figure of a solitary Woman, dressed from head to foot in white garments, her face bent in grave inquiry on mine, her hand pointing to the dark cloud over London, as I faced her" (46–47).

Anyone familiar with William Holman Hunt's popular painting, *The Light of the World* (fig. 1), would have no difficulty seeing that Collins's woman in white, silhouetted in the moonlight, her hand raised, pointing toward London, evokes this painting, "the most famous of all Victorian religious images" (Wood 43). In this painting Christ, his hand raised, knocking on the sinner's door, is captured in the moonlight, with the moon in the background serving as his halo. It is entirely possible that Wilkie Collins had this painting in mind when he drew its literary transformation in *The Woman in White*. After all, he had observed Hunt working on this painting when he spent time with his brother Charley, John Everett Millais, and William Holman Hunt at Rectory Farm in Ewell in 1851 (Hunt 1: 304). Collins must have also known that "the character of the head was a composite taken from several male sitters . . . while Lizzie Siddal and Christina Rossetti sat for its colouring" (Parris 119). In the hands of a Pre-Raphaelite artist the creation of the image of the ultimate patriarchal figure became possible through the fusion of opposite genders. It is not surprising, then, that Collins would transform this representation of Christ into the image of a destitute woman—the Other.

Simultaneously, Collins's readers, who saw his woman in white as the narrative redrawing of *The Light of the World*, would have also been aware of Collins's allusion to *The Awakening Conscience* (fig. 2). This painting was conceived as the "material counterpart [to *The Light of the World*] . . . to show how the still small voice speaks to a human soul in the turmoil of life" (Hunt 1: 347). Like *The Light of the World*, *The Awakening Conscience* presents a figure in white fraught with cultural

As he that taketh away a garment in cold weather,
so is he that singeth songs to an heavy heart.

FIGURE 1. William Holman Hunt, *The Awakening Conscience* (1853–54), oil on canvas, 30 x 23 1/2 in. Tate Gallery, London.

FIGURE 2. William Holman Hunt, *The Light of the World*
(1851–53), oil on canvas, 49 2/8 x 23 1/2 in. Warden and
Fellows of Keble College, Oxford.

contradictions and ambivalent messages. Although a fallen woman, the figure is represented in childlike innocence as she reaches a revelation through the childhood memories evoked by the sound of the song her lover plays on the piano. Thus Collins, like his Pre-Raphaelite friends, further complicates the concept of the shadow by interweaving it with projections of cultural anxieties and contradictions.

The shock Hartright experiences during this extraordinary meeting is characteristic of the first phase in the process of individuation, a phase that involves the establishment of one's uniqueness beyond social or cultural constructs. According to Jung, individuation means "becoming an 'in-dividual,' and in so far as 'individuality' embraces our innermost, last, and incomparable uniqueness, it also implies becoming one's own self. We could therefore translate individuation as 'coming to selfhood' or self-realization" (*CW* 7: 173). Yet the establishment of one's uniqueness does not occur in isolation from a social context. Rather, as with the quest of the hero, the process of individuation begins with a call that draws an individual into the social sphere. In an attempt to master his bewilderment, Hartright responds to the call by resorting to Victorian standards of respectability and conventional gender constructs: "There was nothing wild, nothing immodest in her manner: it was quiet and self-controlled . . . not exactly the manner of a lady, and, at the same time, not the manner of a woman in the humblest rank of life" (Collins, *Woman in White* 48). Since the mysterious figure eludes conventional standards, Hartright, in his response to her, has to rely on his own unconscious rather than on established social or cultural values.

Simultaneously, though, he feels compelled to justify his rash impulse to help her in terms of conventional gender constructs: "the loneliness and helplessness of the woman touched me. The natural impulse to assist her and to spare her got the better of the judgement, the caution, . . . which an older, wiser, and colder man might have summoned to help him in this strange emergency" (Collins, *Woman in White* 49). In his spontaneous decision to help Anne, Hartright exhibits his individualism, his uniqueness as a human being, which also is requisite to individuation. In his distinction of individualism from individuation, Jung also relates their integration:

> Individualism means deliberately stressing and giving prominence to some supposed peculiarity rather than to collective considerations and obligations. But individuation means precisely the better and more complete fulfillment of the collective qualities of the human being, since adequate consideration of the peculiarity of the individual is more conducive to a better social performance than when the peculiarity is neglected or suppressed. (*CW* 7: 173–74)

According to Jung, then, a social system that cultivates the uniqueness of its individual members will ultimately flourish. As Christopher Hauke points out, "the denial or suppression of individual characteristics is not only limiting and distorting of individuals . . . but it also impoverishes the social collective of accessing the full range of human possibilities" (170).

The shock of Hartright's intriguing encounter initiates an identity crisis. "Was I Walter Hartright?" he asks himself; "had I really left, little more than an hour since, the quiet, decent, conventionally domestic atmosphere of my mother's cottage?" (Collins, *Woman in White* 50). His bewilderment may be partly explained by Anne Catherick's transgression of conventional gender and class boundaries. Whereas the meeting creates a conventional situation—a woman in distress and a man coming to her rescue—Collins, like his Pre-Raphaelite friends, opts for the unconventional, depriving Hartright the opportunity to act out the traditional role of rescuer and affirm his masculinity. Thus Collins intimates that Hartright's identity crisis is bound to this suspension of gender constructs during Hartright's extraordinary meeting with the woman in white. Simultaneously, this bewildering experience prefigures Walter's confrontation with his unconscious. The dreamlike qualities of the woman, this "extraordinary apparition" (47) that was "like a dream" (50), are important, for "through dreams," M.-L. von Franz explains, "one becomes acquainted with aspects of one's own personality that for various reasons one has preferred not to look at too closely. That is what Jung called 'the realization of the shadow'" (168).

After Walter assists the woman in white to find a cab and get away, he is uneasy about his decision and confesses that he "was perplexed and distressed by an uneasy sense of having done wrong, which yet left me confusedly ignorant of how I could have done right" (54). Hartright's perplexity and bewilderment also characterize the encounter with the unconscious, since, as von Franz points out in her discussion of the shadow, "divining [sic] in advance whether our dark partner symbolizes a shortcoming that we should overcome or a meaningful bit of life that we should accept—this is one of the most difficult problems that we encounter on the way to individuation" (175–76). His doubts become torments when he realizes, after he sees her pursuers, that she has escaped from an asylum: "What had I done? Assisted the victim of the most horrible of all false imprisonments to escape; or cast loose on the wide world of London an unfortunate creature, whose actions it was my duty, and every man's duty to control?" (Collins, *Woman in White* 55).

In the beginning of his journey towards psychic integration, Walter is unable to bring the process of individuation into reality, for the extraordinary encounter with the Other cannot be explained in terms of conventional morality within traditional class or gender boundaries. According to Jung, an individual must be willing to "surrender consciously to the power of the unconscious, instead of thinking in terms of what one should do, or of what is generally thought right. . . . One must simply listen, in order to learn what the inner totality—the Self—wants one to do here and now" (von Franz 164). At this point Walter lacks, in psychoanalytic terms, the courage "to take the unconscious seriously and to tackle the problems it raises" (von Franz 176). As Susan Rowland explains, individuation involves the constant reshaping of identity; in a way, individuation can be conceived as "a deconstructive process, privileging the ungraspable unconscious over the limitations of the ego as it continually reshapes identity and perceptions of reality" (11). But at this point, Walter disregards his unconscious as he attempts to repress the memory of the encounter and hopes to start a new life at Limmeridge, teaching Laura Fairlie and her half-sister, Marian Halcombe, drawing and painting.

Yet the image of the woman in white becomes imperceptibly fused with Laura's when Walter first meets Laura in the summerhouse at Limmeridge. With a Pre-Raphaelite sensitivity to light and shadow, Walter draws attention to the shadows in Laura's portrait: "a little straw hat . . . covers her head, and throws its soft pearly shadow over the upper part of her face. Her hair is of so faint and pale a brown . . . that it nearly melts here and there into the shadow of the hat" (Collins, *Woman in White* 74–75). Even before Walter is aware of the resemblance of Laura to Anne, the narrator subtly merges the two figures. In the process, Collins fuses the social with the private. In this scene, Laura's function as Walter's anima is revealed in his frustrated attempt to account for his irrational attraction. Drawn in brushstrokes of light and shadow, Laura becomes for Walter an archetype and the ideal Victorian angel, "the woman who first gives life, light, and form to our shadowy conceptions of beauty, fills a void in our spiritual nature that has remained unknown to us till she appeared" (75–76). Collins's insight into human psychology is even more striking when Walter describes the fatality of his attraction in terms of the siren archetype: "Lulled by the Syren-song that my own heart sung to me, with eyes shut to all sight, and ears closed to all sound of danger, I drifted nearer and nearer to the fatal rocks" (90). In Jungian terms, "it is the presence of the anima that causes a man to fall suddenly in love when he sees a woman for the first time and knows at once that this is 'she.' . . . The

Greek Sirens . . . personify this dangerous aspect of the anima, which in this form symbolizes destructive illusion" (von Franz 180, 178).

On the evening of the same day, a few hours after his first meeting with Laura, Walter and Marian try to fathom the mystery of the connection of the woman in white to Laura's mother. Walter is stunned to see Laura dressed in white, walking on the terrace, bathed in moonlight—a Pre-Raphaelite figure enveloped in light and shadow:

> A thrill of the same feeling which ran through me when the touch was laid upon my shoulder on the lonely high-road chilled me again. There stood Miss Fairlie, a white figure, alone in the moonlight; in her attitude, in the turn of her head, in her complexion, in the shape of her face, the living image . . . of the woman in white! The doubt which had troubled my mind for hours and hours past flashed into conviction in an instant. That "something wanting" was my own recognition of the ominous likeness between the fugitive from the asylum and my pupil at Limmeridge House. (Collins, *Woman in White* 86)

Immediately he regrets his recognition of a resemblance between Anne and Laura, for, he thinks, "to associate that forlorn, friendless lost woman, even by accidental likeness only, with Miss Fairlie, seems like casting a shadow on the future of the bright creature" (86). His detachment from Anne and identification with Laura could be seen as "the mystique of projective identification," as Polly Young-Eisendrath terms it, marked by "its uncanny capacity to evoke in another . . . the most dreaded or idealized aspect of the self" (227). Thus Walter's endeavor to extricate himself from the social responsibility to the "forlorn figure" is futile the moment Laura's and Anne's images are interchanged. His condition here represents yet another important phase in his journey to psychic integration; indeed, the Jungian analysis of this phase seems to correspond to Walter's predicament: "if the shadow figure contains valuable, vital forces, they ought to be assimilated. . . . It is up to the ego to give up its pride and priggishness and to live out something that seems to be dark, but actually may not be. This can require a sacrifice just as heroic as the conquest of passion, but in an opposite sense" (von Franz 175).

In Jung's view, then, when traditional values do not apply to unique cases, the individual must resort to his/her own unconscious for guidance. Walter exhibits such a reliance on his unconscious later in the novel when he becomes suspicious of Sir Percival (after reading Anne Catherick's letter to Laura, in which she accuses Percival of imprisoning her in an asylum lest she reveal his secret of illegitimacy), and though unable to find incriminating evidence, he nevertheless believes in Anne's innocence. As Michael Adams observes, "the unconscious redresses what the conscious either excludes or omits from consideration" (107). Even Anne herself perceives the change in Walter when she meets him at the cemetery later. Instead of experiencing fear, as she did during her first encounter with him, Anne looks at Walter "eagerly, without a shadow of [the] . . . former distrust left in her expression" (Collins, *Woman in White* 120).

Undermining ideology, Collins seems to enjoy playing with contrasts and ironic situations, thus destabilizing traditional class and gender constructs. A destitute, vulnerable, seemingly outcast figure, Anne Catherick could be easily perceived as the guilty party. Wealthy, respectable, "a really irresistible man—courteous, considerate, delightfully free from pride—a gentleman, every inch of him" (Collins, *Woman in White* 169), Sir Percival Glyde, on the other hand, is beyond suspicion. Contrasted with Walter's response is Mr. Gilmore's conventional reaction, representative of the suppression of individualism to the social collective. Justifying his conduct as "practical" by juxtaposing it with Walter's "romantic" view, Mr. Gilmore—Laura's lawyer—resists any doubts he himself experiences about Sir Percival's defense against Catherick. When made uneasy by Marian's suspicions, Mr. Gilmore muses complacently, "in my youth, I should have chafed and fretted under the irritation of my own unreasonable state of mind. In my age, I knew better, and went out philosophically to walk it off" (159). Like Laura's uncle, who refuses to participate in drawing up a marriage settlement that would protect Laura from Sir Percival's abuse and who later on prefers her dead lest a legal action to establish her identity would disturb his "fragile nerves," Mr. Gilmore prefers peace of mind to the pursuit of justice, the solipsist cocoon of individual complacency to social responsibility. In this respect he prefigures his successor, Mr. Kyle, who, though believing that Laura has been the victim of a gross deception—imprisoned in an asylum as Anne Catherick and, after Catherick's death, declared dead and deprived of all her legal rights—tells Walter that he does not have "the shadow of a case" (462).

Collins, then, seems to expose the average human mind that shrinks from contact with the unconscious, because the "recognition of its unconscious reality involves honest self-examination and reorganization of one's life," a formidable task that people would rather avoid, continuing "to behave as if nothing at all has happened" (von Franz 176). Even Walter is tempted to disengage himself from Catherick's cumbersome problem, and the second time he meets her at the cemetery he hopes, as on the first occasion, to never see her again (Collins, *Woman in White* 130). Yet her mystery haunts him during his adventure in Central America, where he believed the distance and time would efface his shadow and the physical journey might obviate the anxiety of his psychic journey. During that time, Marian's prophetic dream depicts Walter's struggle, prefiguring his eventual rebirth; simultaneously, the dream conveys a fusion of the real and the imaginative or possible. In this exotic dream, Walter appears in a landscape drawn in Pre-Raphaelite touches of light and shadows cast by immense tropical trees that "shut out the sky, and threw a *dismal shadow* over the forlorn band of men on the steps. *White exhalations* twisted and curled up stealthily from the ground" (295). Later in the same dream, Walter appears "kneeling by a tomb of *white* marble, and the *shadow* of a veiled woman rose out of the grave beneath and waited by his side" (296; emphasis added). Again, the Pre-Raphaelite "soft alternations of light and shade," against which Walter's meeting of the woman in white first occurred, highlight this important episode that prefigures Sir Percival's deception, the burial of Anne Catherick as Lady Glyde.

When Walter resumes the narrative, after his return from Central America, he seems to celebrate his higher state of consciousness, which was signaled by his symbolic death in Marian's dream. Indeed, the acceptance of his unconscious initiates his social involvement, his determination to vindicate Laura and thus become fully involved in exposing the deplorable inefficiency of the legal system. After this Walter emerges as a reborn figure, a self-reliant, self-assured individual, who believes that "in the stern school of extremity and danger my will had learnt to be strong, my heart resolute, my mind to rely on itself" (Collins, *Woman in White* 427). After this recognition, the following scene in the cemetery, where he believes Laura is buried, is yet another transformation of his encounter with the woman in white; in fact, his reaction to Laura's touch is almost identical to his reaction to the touch by the mysterious shadow: "the springs of my life fell low, and the shuddering of an unutterable dread crept over me from head to foot" (431). In this case, however, Walter does not resist the call, does not attempt to extricate himself from social responsibility, but undertakes the seemingly impossible task of vindicating Laura "through all risks and all sacrifices—through the hopeless struggle against Rank and Power, . . . through the waste of my reputation, through the loss of any friends, through the hazard of my life" (435).

His journey toward psychic integration concludes with the most important event in Hartright's struggle for Laura's vindication, an event that coincides with a crucial phase in his process of individuation. In the nightmarish scene of the fire at the church vestry, where Sir Percival (the secret of his illegitimacy having been discovered) tries surreptitiously to

add the names of his parents to the church marriage register but acci-
dentally starts a fire with his lantern, Hartright responds to his unconscious by renouncing his passionate commitment to retribution. Like the
sudden appearance of the woman in white, the sudden fire represents
another call, another temptation to gratify the ego by letting Sir Percival
burn to death. But unlike during the first occasion, when Walter's ego
takes over and seeks to ascertain Anne Catherick's respectability before
he offers help, this time Walter immediately responds to his unconscious
and tries to rescue Sir Percival:

> I rushed to the door. The one absorbing purpose that had filled all my
> thoughts, that had controlled all my actions, for weeks and weeks past,
> vanished in an instant from my mind. All remembrance of the heartless
> injury the man's crimes had inflicted—of the love, the innocence, the
> happiness he had pitilessly laid waste—of the oath I had sworn in my
> own heart to summon him to the terrible reckoning that he deserved—
> passed from my memory like a dream. I remembered nothing but the
> horror of his situation. (Collins, *Woman in White* 535)

Thus Collins, like Jung, demonstrates the convergence of the psychological with the social sphere at the end of the novel. "As the individual is
not just a single, separate being," Jung asserts, "but by his very existence
presupposes a collective relationship, it follows that the process of individuation must lead to more intense and broader collective relationships
and not to isolation" (*CW* 6: 448).

In Jung's view, the development of personality is an ongoing process,
and a new or higher level of consciousness is at times initiated by symbolic death or rebirth (von Franz 222). Indeed, rebirth follows death as
the novel closes in the springtime, and Walter traces the full circle of his
journey: "From the long slumber, on her side and on mine, those imper-
ishable memories of our past life in Cumberland now awoke, which
were one and all alike, the memories of our love" (Collins, *Woman in
White* 577). Ironically, Walter chooses Laura, the woman who has
undergone no mental or psychological growth, the figure Nina Auerbach appropriately calls "the nebulous, incompetent heroine" (135).
Carl Jung's explanation of a man's love choice could help us understand
Hartright's marriage to Laura: "man, in his love-choice, is strongly
tempted to win the woman who best corresponds to his own unconscious femininity—a woman, in short, who can unhesitatingly receive
the projection of his soul. Although such a choice is often regarded and
felt as altogether ideal, it may turn out that the man has manifestly married his own worst weakness" (*Aspects* 78). No reader would dispute
that Laura represents Hartright's worst weakness—lack of individual-

ism. Perhaps for this reason the strong-minded and independent Marian, Laura's half-sister and protector, becomes the focal point of the closing scene of the novel as she holds Laura's and Hartright's child: "So she spoke. In writing those last words, I have written all. The pen falters in my hand. The long, happy labour of many months is over. Marian was the good angel of our lives—let Marian end our Story" (Collins, *Woman in White* 646). Yet the traditional Victorian closure of the novel, the marriage of Hartright to Laura, discloses Collins's keen sensitivity to the forces of the marketplace, revealing his exquisite ability to gratify his middle-class readers while simultaneously criticizing them.

Wilkie Collins often attempted to gain recognition as a literary artist, the founder of the sensation novel that moved beyond the limits of the realistic without violating realism. As Jenny Bourne Taylor states, Collins has been recognized as a novelist who "breaks down stable boundaries between wildness and domesticity, self and other, masculinity and femininity, 'black' and 'white.' Moreover, his stories involve not only complex explorations of forms of perception, of consciousness and cognition, but also of the shaping of social identity" (1). In the liberating dream space of the sensation novel, Collins successfully undermines contemporary ideology that displaces women by either apotheosizing them as angels or condemning them as outcasts. Through his emphasis on Walter's mysterious entanglement in someone else's fate—an outcast, the illegitimate daughter of a fallen woman—Collins, like his Pre-Raphaelite friends, fuses the shadow of the Other with the self, exploring psychological anxieties generated by cultural incongruities. Collins's understanding of Hartright's individualism and individuation anticipates Jung's conviction that "if a single individual devotes himself to individuation, he frequently has a positive contagious effect on the people around him. It is as if a spark leaps from one to another" (von Franz 224). In his attempt to draw, like his Pre-Raphaelite friends, landscapes and portraits in alternations of light and shade, Collins discovers the shadow of the unconscious. And through the struggle of the ego with the unconscious towards psychic growth and integration, individualism and individuation, he expresses his faith in the role of individuals, rather than legislative measures, in effecting social reforms.

By relating shadow images to artistic, literary, psychological, and cultural phenomena, Collins engages not only Victorians who need to come to terms with their own shadows, but postmodern readers as well. Thus the novel involves cultural specificity and transcendence. As Jung maintains, the literary artist "lifts the idea he is seeking to express out of the occasional and the transitory into the realm of the ever-enduring. He transmutes our personal destiny into the destiny of mankind" (*CW* 15: 82).

NOTE

1. Collins is considered the founder of the sensation and detective novel. Like his other popular novels, *The Woman in White* is constructed with an intricate plot, a mystery which is not solved till the end. Walter Hartright, a drawing master, meets Anne Catherick on his way to the Fairlie home where he is to teach Laura Fairlie and her half-sister, Marian Halcombe. To his surprise, Laura strikingly resembles Anne, who, we discover later on, is her illegitimate sister. Hartright falls in love with Laura, who reciprocates his feelings but is engaged to and marries Sir Percival Glyde. Marian later discovers that Sir Percival has married Laura for her wealth and is responsible for confining Anne Catherick in an asylum, lest she disclose a dreadful secret about him. When Laura refuses to sign a document that would entitle him to her wealth, Sir Percival and his friend, Count Fosco, confine Laura in an asylum. When Catherick dies, they bury her as Laura Fairlie. With Marian's help, Hartright discovers Sir Percival's crime and forces Fosco to a testimony that restores Laura's identity. Sir Percival, whose secret is his illegitimacy, is burnt to death while tampering with a parish register in an attempt to rescue his title.

WORKS CITED

Adams, Michael Vannoy. "The Archetypal School." Young-Eisendrath and Dawson 101–18.

Auerbach, Nina. *Woman and the Demon: The Life of a Victorian Myth.* Cambridge: Harvard UP, 1982.

Baker, William, and William M. Clarke. *The Letters of Wilkie Collins, 1838–1889.* 2 vols. New York: St. Martin's, 1999.

Balee, Susan. "Wilkie Collins and Surplus Women: The Case of Marian Halcombe." *Victorian Literature and Culture* 20 (1992): 197–215.

Bernstein, Stephen. "Reading in Blackwater Park: Gothicism, Narrative and Ideology in *The Woman in White.*" *Studies in the Novel* 25 (1993): 291–305.

Brittan, Arthur. *Masculinity and Power.* Oxford, England: Blackwell, 1989.

Casteras, Susan. *Images of Victorian Womanhood in English Art.* London: Associated UPs, 1987.

Clarke, William. *The Secret Life of Wilkie Collins.* Chicago: Ivan Reo. 1991.

Collins, Wilkie. "The Exhibition of the Royal Academy." *Bentley's Miscellany* 29 (1851): 617–27.

———. *The Woman in White.* Ed. Julian Symons. Harmondsworth: Penguin, 1985.

Dawson, Terence. "Jung, Literature, and Literary Criticism." Young-Eisendrath and Dawson 255–80.

Eagleton, Terry. *Literary Theory.* Minneapolis: U of Minnesota P, 1983.

Elam, Diane. "White Narratology: Gender and Reference in Wilkie Collins's *The Woman in White.*" *Virginal Sexuality and Textuality in Victorian Literature.* Ed. Diane Elam. Albany: State U of New York P, 1993. 49–63.

Faxon, Alicia Craig. *Dante Gabriel Rossetti.* New York: Abbeville P, 1989.

Frick, Patricia. "Wilkie Collins and John Ruskin." *Victorians Institute Journal* 13 (1985): 11–22.

Hauke, Christopher. *Jung and the Postmodern: The Interpretation of Realities.* London: Routledge, 2000.

Hunt, William Holman. *The Awakening Conscience.* Tate Gallery, London. 1853–54. Tate Home Page. <http://www.tate.org.uk/servlet/Awork?id=6996>.

———. *The Light of the World.* Keble College, Oxford. 1851–53. William Hunt Home Page. <http://www.williamhunt.com/explorer/wsk.htm>.

———. *Pre-Raphaelitism and the Pre-Raphaelite Brotherhood.* 2 vols. London: Macmillan, 1905.

Jung, Carl G. *Aspects of the Feminine.* Trans. R. F. C. Hull. Princeton: Princeton UP, 1982.

———. *Collected Works of C. G. Jung.* Ed. Sir Herbert Read, Michael Fordham, and Gerhard Adler. Trans. R. F. C. Hull. 20 vols. Princeton: Princeton UP, 1953–91.

Langbauer, Laurie. "Women in White, Men in Feminism." *The Yale Journal in Criticism* 2 (1989): 219–43.

Parris, Leslie. Ed. *The Pre-Raphaelites.* New York: Crescent Books, 1981.

Rowland, Susan. *C. G. Jung and Literary Theory: The Challenge from Fiction.* New York: St. Martin's, 1999.

Ruskin, John. *The Works of John Ruskin.* Ed. E. T. Cook and Alexander Wedderburn. 39 vols. London: George Allen, 1903–12.

Taylor, Jenny Bourne. *In the Secret Theatre of Home: Wilkie Collins, Sensation Narrative, and Nineteenth-Century Psychology.* New York: Routledge: 1988.

von Franz, Marie-Louise. "The Process of Individuation." *Man and His Symbols.* Ed. Carl Jung. Garden City, NY: Doubleday, 1964. 158–229.

Williams, M. Kellen. "'Traced and Captured by the Men in the Chaise': Pursuing Sexual Difference in Wilkie Collins's *The Woman in White.*" *The Journal of Narrative Technique* 28 (1998): 91–110.

Wood, Christopher. *The Pre-Raphaelites*. New York: Crescent Books, 1981.

Young-Eisendrath, Polly. "Gender and Contrasexuality: Jung's Contribution and Beyond." Young-Eisendrath and Dawson 223–39.

Young-Eisendrath, Polly, and Terence Dawson, eds. *The Cambridge Companion to Jung*. Cambridge: Cambridge UP, 1997.

Drs. Jung and Chekhov

Physicians of the Soul

∽∾∽

SALLY PORTERFIELD

A funny thing has happened. Anton Chekhov, who was
judged in his own time to be a playwright narrowly culture-
bound, over-refined and obscure, whose drama was persistently characterized at home and abroad as "depressing" and
"pessimistic," has become second only to Shakespeare in
reputation and in frequency of production. Andrzej Wajda's
remark—"Theatre in our European tradition derives from
the word, from literature, the Greeks, Shakespeare,
Chekhov"—is typical of the regard in which Chekhov is
held. He is a synecdoche for all modern drama, indeed, in
Wajda's debatable overview, for all drama from the Eliza-
bethans to ourselves.

—Senelick, *The Chekhov Theatre*

What then, is responsible for this "funny happening"? Why does
Chekhov's relatively small, seemingly parochial body of work take its
place in the mythic cosmos of the Greeks and Shakespeare? What can
Jung tell us about the work of this man whose life and his own show
some interesting commonalities? To begin, in a collection that deals
largely with the written word, it is vital to record that the leap from
page to stage is never a solitary venture. The audience member sees only
the end result of the collaborative work that brings a piece of dramatic

literature to life on stage, while the solitary reader creates his own world from the text, his imagination, and his own experience. The two encounters might be likened to that of the contemplative in his cell and the public worshiper in church or temple.

ARCHETYPE AND CULTURE

The process of production begins in the individual conscious and unconscious workings of the director, the actors, and the designers. Those widely diverse sensibilities work together to create a synthesis that begins with the text and becomes something unique, not only in each production but in each performance, each moment of its life. Thus the ephemeral nature of the performing arts generates something as elusive as the unconscious itself and often as numinous, like the shimmer of currents beneath a moving stream, hints of truth in a language that can be grasped only by the unconscious mind. Jung's description of this process reframes Keats's notion of "negative capability" as he asserts that "The essence of a work of art is not to be found in the personal idiosyncrasies that creep into it—indeed, the more there are of them, the less it is a work of art—but in its rising above the personal and speaking from the mind and heart of the artist to the mind and heart of mankind" (*Spirit* 19). He continues later in the same essay: "Art is a kind of innate drive that seizes a human being and makes him its instrument. The artist is not a person endowed with free will who seeks his own ends, but one who allows art to realize its purposes through him" (101).

Since art emanates from the unconscious, very often the artist has no conscious awareness of the process that produces it. Great dramatic characters have the ability to come to life only through actors who allow themselves to be vessels for that incarnation. There is no Hamlet, no Oedipus, no Uncle Vanya, just as there is no sounding glory in a Beethoven manuscript. Hamlet, Oedipus, and Vanya come alive only in the merger of character and actor that is the transcendent function of great theater. This incarnation becomes an experience of enormous power, for both actor and audience, a sort of group descent into the collective unconscious.

We are discussing here, then, not only the private versus the public but the unmediated versus the mediated transaction between the work of art and the individual. How much influence do time, place, and culture wield over the strength of archetypal patterns? We can agree that specifics alter with these variables, as Jung himself asserts with uncharacteristic consistency. A casual perusal of photographs and drawings from various productions of Shakespeare or the Greeks shows an enormous difference in aesthetic values, from set and costumes to body language and attitude, even among those that are performed in a generally "traditional" style, according to the popular notions of what that tradition is. Acting styles themselves change so quickly that a film or television program of ten or fifteen years ago often seems already dated. Often, attempts to "update" classics merely serve to strip them of their grandeur, and the attempt to cut archetypal themes into bite-sized pieces becomes a way of courting the conscious mind at the expense of the unconscious, thereby losing the very mystery that confers their power.

With those elements in mind, let us now turn to Chekhov, whose archetypal characters come, decked not in the grandeur of Greek tragedy, nor in the majesty of Shakespeare's poetry, but as ordinary turn-of-the-century Russians. Chekhov prefigures Arthur Miller's manifesto "Tragedy and the Common Man," as he, along with Ibsen and Strindberg, lays the foundation for the twentieth century's plunge into realism as its dominant theatrical mode, particularly in the United States. Do Chekhov's realism, his poetic selection, and his impressionistic approach to the human condition make his work less relevant or lasting from an archetypal viewpoint? Clearly, his characters still have enormous impact on actors, directors, and audiences, an impact that cannot be attributed to some sort of antique or ethnic appeal any more than can the appeal of the Greeks or of Shakespeare.

Sisyphus, the Neglected Archetype

Chekhov provides an experience that, while culturally framed, deals with the existential pain inflicted by the stasis that grips us when fate blocks our path and forces us to look inside for answers. Is it possible that we are neglecting the archetype that most closely embodies our own times? The alienation and existential angst that provide the climate of this postmodern world clearly evoke the archetypal existential hero, Sisyphus. In his essay on the myth of Sisyphus, Camus tells us we must think of Sisyphus as happy. Sisyphus, for Camus, is the absurd man: the man who has found freedom within the boundaries of a life that is perceived as futile only if we expect some exterior force to provide meaning. He gives shape to his fate and is defined by his work to the same extent that *he* defines *it*. This absurd man, having come to terms with his own fate, has developed a mind that "Frolics—in myths, to be sure, but myths with no other depth than that of human suffering and, like it, inexhaustible. Not the divine fable that amuses and blinds, but the terrestrial farce, gesture, and drama in which are summed up a difficult wisdom and an ephemeral passion" (Camus 87). This "difficult wisdom" and "ephemeral passion" might exemplify the "heroic pessimism" (Vandenbroucke 87) that seems to be central not only to many of Chekhov's characters but to his own gentle irony, given his constant battle with the tuberculosis that killed him at age forty-four, after twenty-odd years of struggle. Chekhov's cultural background—the social and political unrest that foreshadowed the cataclysmic changes to come in the fall of Czarist Russia—created the perfect climate for the constellation of this archetype, the existential hero who endures all in order to survive the unimaginable.

Nevertheless, the strength of Chekhov's women fuels much of the character development in his works. His men, often weak and dispirited, mirror the flaws of a failing patriarchy. In despair, unable to shoulder the burdens consigned to them as men, they become paralyzed by depression. Frequently, the women's pragmatic courage enables them to go on, pushing their rocks up the hill day after day. Emasculated by their society, they learn the patience that has historically been woman's only refuge. Just as Camus imagines Sisyphus happy, Chekhov allows us to imagine that the inner journey may become a reality for these souls stalled on the road toward fulfillment. Indeed, Chekhov leaps over the bounds of gender roles that imprisoned Jung's thinking in a nineteenth-century European trap. Even as the Germanic tradition of the "fatherland" stood in clear opposition to "Mother Russia," so does Chekhov's attitude about women differ from Jung's. Chekhov's attitude seems to be singularly unbiased toward either sex. Indeed, much of his appeal resides in that egalitarian posture.

Moreover, Chekhov's characters, so complex and quixotic, exemplify humanity in its unconscious state. Like Tantalus, they strain for that which is forever out of reach. Like Odysseus, they long for Ithaca, as a place which will fill the gnawing hunger of an existential void. Each day becomes a Sisyphean struggle for validity through work. The very life force of sexual desire sickens, like Phaedra's in her doomed love for Hippolytus. The unconsciousness of Chekhov's characters is one of their most seductive traits for both actor and director. Certainly no playwright has better captured the bewilderment and alienation of the twentieth-century's existential bog. Coupled with the unconsciousness of these characters, and possibly even more compelling, is their precarious liminality. So many of them spend their lives attempting to elude their obvious archetypal patterns, creating a sense of disorder and imbalance heightened by the constant motion of coming and going that is so much a part of Chekhov's universe.

THREE SISTERS: ELEUSIS REVISITED

The four most frequently performed works by Chekhov are familiar to most, at least in name: *Three Sisters, Uncle Vanya, The Cherry Orchard,* and *The Seagull.* Of these, the first is arguably the best known for a number of obvious reasons, including the sexual tension and drama created by the proximity of dashing army officers to three young, orphaned sisters in a dull, provincial town. Add an adulterous affair, a sociopathic suitor, a catastrophic fire, and a fatal duel, and you have enough material for any Greek or Shakespearian tragedy. Nonetheless, as any student of Chekhov knows, his plots are merely props upon which to display the vagaries of human behavior. In direct contrast to the day's dominant forms of drama, the heroic and the melodramatic, Chekhov attempted to craft a new form. This new form is outwardly built around the normal events of each day but deals essentially with the inner life and the ways in which we manage to go through the motions of everyday life, while inwardly traveling an entirely separate emotional and psychological landscape.

Thus the plot of *Three Sisters* is relatively simple in structure. Olga and Irina, oldest and youngest sisters, live in the family home with brother Andre. Andre is the family's white hope: he is expected to find a brilliant position as a university professor in Moscow, where they will all then move to a new and brighter life. Masha, the middle sister, is in a disastrously bad marriage with Kulygin, a village schoolmaster; she spends much of her time at home lamenting her self-imposed fate. Because of established custom, a group of bored army officers makes the Prozorov home their social headquarters while they are stationed nearby. Prozorov senior, dead a year at the play's point of attack, was father of the three girls and Andre. As senior officer in the area, Prozorov had always provided hospitality to his junior officers. When Andre marries Natasha, a vulgar village schemer, she takes over the house and ultimately destroys both Andre's ambition and the family. Olga's sad maidenhood, Masha's doomed affair with the glamorous, married Vershinin, Irina's gradual loss of innocence, and the eventual departure of the battalion trace the plot's essential outline but give no hint of the play's extraordinary power, which is, of course, where Jung comes in.

The crux of this piece seems to be located in the three women themselves, three being the traditional feminine number of myth. Variations on this triad feature the traditional stages of women—maiden/mother/crone—but also include three maidens (such as the Graces or the Muses) sometimes transformed from three crones, as in the Furies of *The*

Oresteia. Macbeth's three witches also tap into this mythic strain. But how do we classify Olga, Masha, and Irina? Irina clearly incarnates the maiden, young and idealistic. Masha, as the matron, should be the mother, but therein lies the first problem. Olga, still a maiden, seems to carry the burdens of both mother and crone in her behavior and her attitudes, while Masha defies convention in her affair with Vershinin, reforming the trio into two unequal parts: the virgin/whore dichotomy. Now that we have two virgins and one whore, the problem of archetypal balance emerges. Despite Olga's best attempts, she cannot fill the critical role of the missing mother.

With Andre's marriage to Natasha comes the possibility of a mother. This becomes physical reality in Natasha's rapid production of offspring. But, alas, it soon becomes obvious that here is not the good parent the unconscious seeks but the dreaded devouring mother, who quickly dominates and cuckolds the weak Andre while laying waste the formerly affectionate household. In Natasha, we have a spectacularly bad mother, a monster who succeeds in devouring all about her to satisfy her own unhealthy appetites. Not only does she spoil her children and abuse Andre, but she bullies the sisters and forces out of the family home Olga and the faithful old nursemaid, Anfisa, who has acted as surrogate for the Prozorovs' dead mother. Thus all remnants of the good mother are finally absent entirely. The epitome of female evil, Natasha incorporates all the qualities of the wicked stepmother, that stock figure of folklore and legend who represents the archetypal good mother's darkest shadow. Yet Natasha is merely a vulgar, selfish, banal woman, too stupid to comprehend the extent of the damage she causes, too insensitive to care. Her final appearance in the play shows her dreamily planning her garden while she bullies Irina ("Sweetie, that belt doesn't do a thing for you") and abuses the housemaid: "Who left this fork out here! *(Goes into the house, calling to the maid)* I want to know who left this fork out here! Do you hear me? Shut up when I'm talking to you!" (Chekhov, *Three Sisters* 317). In characters like Natasha, the banality of evil is fully manifested. The unconscious, Jung tells us, experiences these events as archetypal tragedies, despite the fact that they are not caused by dark, malignant forces.

Let us now look for the father in this world which is, like Hamlet's, distinctly out of joint. He is surely not to be found in the avuncular bachelor Dr. Chebutykin, who fails to fulfill his possibility as wise old man. Foolish and vain, he combines puer and senex through a cynical loss of faith in both himself and the world, claiming the benefits of family affection without paying the price of family responsibility. Andre is the son whose task is to take over the place of the father. A reticent and

unremarkable young man, he has been forced into an impossible position by his doting sisters. In the first act, we see him brought out to
demonstrate his imagined talents to the dashing Vershinin, who has
called to pay his respects to the household upon his first arrival in town.
Chekhov shows that poor Andre has no chance of fulfilling the impossible expectations of his family: "Andre's our intellectual," Olga tells
Vershinin, "and he plays the violin and he can carve almost anything in
wood. He's our genius" (Chekhov, *Three Sisters* 268). Trotted out like
some clever child to perform, he is on the other hand expected to act as
family protector and guardian, their ticket to Moscow and life. He himself, however, admits that "My father, God rest him, educated us with a
vengeance" (269) but succeeded in merely teaching them three foreign
languages which, as Masha says, "in a town like this" is "a useless luxury . . . an unnecessary appendage, like a sixth finger" (269). Andre is
the embodiment of every young man who is called upon to fill the
impossibly big shoes of a successful father who, in death, becomes even
larger than he was in life.

Frustrated by the impossible demands on him, Andre falls prey to
Natasha's wiles and proposes to her, seeing in her a simple, adoring village girl who will love him because of his superior social station. He
pays the price for his blindness a hundredfold when he becomes a weak,
emasculated victim of the woman he thought might be his rescuer. As
Natasha becomes the shadow of the mother, Andre becomes his own
shadow, embodying exactly those qualities that he most despises among
the townspeople. One of the most poignant images in all of Chekhov's
work is Andre, in the fourth act, as he paces to and fro with the peram-
bulator, a man unsexed, castrated by life, attempting to perform a
father's duties with no hope of enjoying a father's rewards:

> Oh, whatever happened to the past, when I was young and happy and
> intelligent. . . . We barely begin to live, and all of a sudden we're old
> and boring and lazy and useless and unhappy. This town has a hundred
> thousand people in it, and not one of them has ever amounted to a
> thing. Each one is just like all the others: they eat, drink, sleep, and
> then they die . . . and the children end up just as aimless and dead as
> their parents. (Chekhov, *Three Sisters* 313)

Here is Sisyphus revealed, without the hard-won wisdom that makes
such a life bearable. We can only hope that Andre, like the archetype,
can find meaning within what appears to be a meaningless existence.

As for Olga and Irina, they doggedly attempt to fulfill their duties.
Work as salvation, as raison d'être, forms a leitmotif in much of
Chekhov's drama, once more reminding us of the existential myth. Olga,

who has been promoted to school principal, finds the work even more grueling and less fulfilling than teaching. Clearly, she longs for a family and children of her own; she presents the melancholy spectacle of a woman who might indeed fill the role of mother but instead stands outside that archetype. She is the unwilling virgin caring for the offspring of others, never to be blessed with her own home. Irina, whose young idealism illuminates the first act ("Man must work, work in the sweat of his brow," she says. "No matter who he is, that's the whole point of his life. And all his happiness. How wonderful it must be to get up at dawn and pave streets, or be a shepard, or a schoolteacher" [Chekhov, *Three Sisters* 261]), also slips into disillusion as she learns the truth about daily work at the post office that, predictably to everyone but her, proves stifling rather than ennobling. Her romantic notions are dashed, as well, when the most serious suitor she attracts turns out to be only Baron Tuzenbach. An idealist and a decent man, he nonetheless fails to arouse her passion. She faces the prospect either of a dull marriage, like Masha, or of spinsterhood, like Olga. Her life is also complicated by the obsessive attentions of Solyony, a sociopathic officer who attempts to force himself on her. When Irina finally agrees to marry Tuzenbach, Solyony kills him in a duel, ending any immediate hope of escape for Irina. The male villain of this piece, Solyony presents interesting archetypal material. Like the Greeks in *Troilus and Cressida* (Porterfield 35), and like all armies forced to sit and wait, he is caught in a sort of stasis that fixes him in the archetype of the warrior, generally regarded as a stage in the hero's journey that is symbolic of Jung's individuation process. Solyony, then, might be read as a shadow of the hero—vicious, narcissistic, and nihilistic.

Masha, whose romance with Vershinin creates the play's emotional center, manages to find some stolen happiness in their illicit affair. But when he leaves with the battalion at play's end, her hopes, like those of her sisters', are dead. Vershinin is the classic dramatic type of the *miles gloriosus:* handsome, dashing, romantic, and dangerous. He and Masha create an irresistible archetypal combination of anima/animus attraction. She is a beautiful, sensuous woman in the prison of marriage to a dull pedant. She projects on him the epitome of the animus hero, arriving to free her from that prison. Unfortunately, the wrong archetypal formation asserts itself. The hero has children and a wife; the wife is prone to suicide attempts, occasioned by what we are led to believe are his habitual extramarital entanglements. Masha's captor is neither a dragon nor a bluebeard but a sadly foolish nonentity; his clownish efforts at affability make us blush as we recognize the work of the trickster in all of us, making us into sad parodies of that which we want to be.

For most of us, this trickster possession is an occasional affliction; for Masha's husband, Kulygin, however, it is a way of life. He is a man who hobbles and hops through life with his foot lodged firmly in his mouth. Kulygin, like Andre, knows he has been unmanned and betrayed, and, like Andre, he attempts to carry on in a pathetically inauthentic life, simply because no other way occurs to him. "You're my wife," he tells Masha after the affair has ended, "and I'm happy, no matter what happened. . . . I'll never say a single word about this, never" (Chekhov, *Three Sisters* 316). Thus he evolves, finally, through that magical trickster capacity for shape shifting, into a sort of holy fool, possibly even a savior figure, through his demonstration of compassion and understanding that had lain completely hidden under the fool's motley.

Stasis and its companion, a sense of frustrated movement, pervade Chekhov's drama. Perhaps Chekhov's illness was a factor in the constant coming and going of his characters, a restlessness that is part of the febrile condition that often accompanies tuberculosis. Chekhov himself demonstrated this tendency toward restlessness and frequent travel, particularly as he grew older and the illness became more severe. Thus the sisters' constant mantra of Moscow as the Mecca or Ithaca of their desires displays a universal drive for the place that will finally fulfill our longings. The investment of these physical places with mystical significance might translate quite logically into the Jungian search for self, that inner space where finally we come upon what has eluded us in the outer world.

At the play's end, the three sisters stand together, attempting to find some sort of solace in an absurd world. They are clearly existential heroes who manage to salvage a sense of purpose in the midst of chaos. In this they are much like their Greek counterparts, who did not avoid catastrophe but attempted to respond with whatever measure of dignity was left to them. As Camus describes it, "At the very conclusion of the absurd reasoning, in one of the attitudes dictated by its logic, it is not a matter of indifference to find hope coming back in under one of its most touching guises" (84). Chekhovian actor Austin Pendleton talks about Chekhov's knack for turning great pain into joy when he says, "*Three Sisters,* probably more than any play I know, is about the simple heroism of getting through the day. Not plodding through the day, but really, *really* getting through the day" (qtd. in Hackett 10). When Olga says, "The music sounds so happy, so positive, it makes you want to live. Oh, dear God. . . . My dears, my dear sisters, life isn't over yet. We'll go on living" (Chekhov, *Three Sisters* 318–19), Chekhov gives us hope about these women who persevere and attempt to find some measure of peace in their lives. The urge to live, to transcend despair, hints of a deeper purpose, one that does not depend on exterior events. Here we might perhaps return once more to the mystical ideal of three women, going beyond the maiden, mother, crone to the virgin goddesses like Athena and Artemis. Some versions of the Demeter myth equate Persephone with Artemis. Is there an alternative archetype here that we are missing, one that Jung never explored but that seems clearly present in myth and religion? Somewhere, hidden in the notion of the mother goddess, virgin/mother, solitary priestess, celibate nun, perhaps we have another version of what woman might be, an archetype of wholeness that depends on the fusion of opposites only as they exist within the individual. Perhaps it is Sophia we are seeking, the wisdom that can only come with resignation and the unaccountable happiness that Camus identifies as the product of absurd reasoning. Just as Camus argues that Sisyphus is happy, we would like to imagine that Olga, Masha, and Irina might be embarking on that inner voyage of discovery that goes beyond happiness to the beginnings of wisdom.

In *Three Sisters* we thus find archetypal patterns and themes that are unrelated to any specific time or place. Any one of these characters would be equally authentic in countless settings—the mother, the father, the anima and animus, the divided women's roles, the warrior without a war, the existential hero, Sisyphus, and, finally, Sophia, who rescues us from the patriarchal chains of Athena, the daughter who sprang from Zeus's forehead and supports the masculine world of war and strategy. Sophia not only reclaims the feminine principle but, like Sisyphus, transcends gender even as Chekhov's works do.

Uncle Vanya: Tyranny of the Persona

Closest to *Three Sisters* in mood, *Uncle Vanya,* on the other hand, has inspired several more contemporary adaptations,[1] partially because Uncle Vanya and his niece Sonia speak for everyone who has ever felt used and abused. The simple plot outline deals with the arrival of a retired professor, Serebriakov, and his beautiful twenty-seven-year-old wife, Yelena, to the estate that he inherited from his first wife. Vanya, brother of the dead wife, and her grown daughter, Sonia, run the farm and care for Voinitskaia, the aged grandmother. Frequent visitor and friend to Vanya is Dr. Astrov, the most memorable of all Chekhov's surrogates to be found in his work. Astrov, a visionary, acts as a voice for the playwright in articulating many of Chekhov's progressive views on land use and conservation. (In fact, the play's original title was *The Wood Demon*.) Astrov's views of himself and his world, expressed with great irony, also appear to echo those of his creator:

> Well, all right, you say, that's progress. Right; I agree; I could under-stand if in place of the trees we destroyed we had *something*. If there were communities, jobs, schools, then people might be better off, right, but none of that happened! We still have the same swamps, the same mosquitoes, the same poverty, the same diseases. . . . *(Suddenly cool.)* But none of this interests you, does it? I can tell. (Chekhov, *Uncle Vanya* 236)

Yelena and Serebriakov, like the army officers in *Three Sisters*, create the familiar friction that alters the flow of normal events. Both Vanya and Astrov predictably fall in love with Yelena, while being provoked by the incessant demands of the professor. Serebriakov is a chronic invalid and insufferable egotist who creates upheaval by his constant demands. The entire household falls into disarray and into a condition of stasis because of the presence of these disturbing visitors. What is happening here in the Jungian sense? Let us look at the dramatis personae in their archetypal identities. Yelena is the anima, in her most seductive, mysterious guise. Beautiful, languid, and unavailable, she becomes the princess in her tower, sadly captive to the aging king, a man old enough to be her father. We have the classic comedic scenario, celebrated in the commedia dell'arte and all its descendants: the old man and his young wife, who is waiting to be rescued by the young hero. Here, however, we have no young hero but instead two middle-aged bachelors, long entrenched in their habits, suddenly awakened to a suppressed sexuality and a suspicion that time has passed by and left them behind.

Add to this Sonia's doomed love for Astrov and you have a typical Chekhovian world: A loves B, B loves C, C loves D, and D either loves A or cares for no one at all. Chekhov refuses to give us happy families, which Tolstoi tells us are all alike anyway and therefore are not good subjects for drama. Astrov is the perfect target for Sonia's animus projection—wise, handsome, kind, and amusing—but with the dangerously attractive quality of decadence in his increasing inclination to substitute vodka for reflection. What more seductive animus can an inexperienced young girl seek? Like Heathcliff and Rochester, Astrov has that edge of danger that brings with it the irresistible possibility of salvation through the love of a good woman. Astrov is attracted to that same danger in the bewitching Yelena, rather than being attracted to the admirable but drab and predictable Sonia. Interestingly, *Uncle*

Vanya also contains the constellation of three women: Sonia, the maiden; Yelena, like Masha, neither mother nor virgin; and Voinit-skaia, the failed mother and foolish crone. In both plays, an old nurse shoulders the responsibilities of the absent mother physically, and in some measure psychologically, but it does not suffice. The evidence is clear, here and in other literature, of the void caused by the absence of parental archetypes, whether that absence be physical or psychological. In the remaining two plays to be examined here, the same void stands central to the situation, creating psychological orphans who show difficulty in integrating their own archetypes.

We look in vain for the mother and the father in this puzzle; those archetypes are sadly missing in the characters who should be representing them. Voinitskaia, mother and grandmother to Vanya and Sonia, seems indifferent to her own blood while lavishing sycophantic attentions, based on some imagined scholarly fame, on the odious professor Serebriakov: as Vanya laments, "His mother-in-law, my [own] mother, worships the ground he walks on; to this day she treats him like the second coming" (Chekhov, *Uncle Vanya* 212). We seem to be once more in the presence of misplaced archetypes in this crone, who not only seems to have neglected her mother's role but demonstrates an almost girlish infatuation with her son-in-law. And Serebriakov shows no more indication of fatherly affection toward Sonia than does her grandmother. Totally self-absorbed, he glories in the role of aged hero, oblivious to his daughter, his brother-in-law, and his wife, except for their use as servants to him. He has relinquished the role of the father and now masquerades as a sort of conquering hero cum wise old man, vying with the grandmother for the ultimate state of unconsciousness: "I'm repulsive, I'm an egotist, I'm a tyrant, but don't I have the right to a little ego in my old age?" (220). There is nothing, Chekhov shows us, so frustrating as the old, foolish, and powerful.

The heart of *Uncle Vanya* is the two men, Vanya and Astrov. In these two we find a sympathy and complexity not present in Chekhov's other male characters. How do we classify the two old friends whose obvious sensitivity and intelligence far surpass that of most of those around them? Certainly, Astrov functions as an animus for both Sonia and Yelena. Vanya fills the father role for Sonia and a sort of trickster-clown role for Yelena, so that in some slight respect Sonia and Yelena act as shadows for each other. But what seems most evident here is that the ego is badly detoured by life into a takeover by the persona. Vanya and Astrov's work has so engulfed them over the years that they speak constantly of having become nothing but that work. Astrov is on call for every medical problem in the district, which leaves him little or no time for the pursuit of his own life: "I'm on my feet from morning to night, I never get any rest, I go to bed at night and I can't sleep: I just lie there waiting for an emergency call" (Chekhov, *Uncle Vanya* 209). He discards the notion of marrying Sonia for lack of time. Vanya, on the other hand, has devoted his life to supporting Serebriakov. The whole family has idolized this man until his retirement, when it becomes clear that he was never the eminent scholar he claimed to be. Vanya's bitterness results from realizing that he has devoted his life and his passion to a selfish "complete fraud," who has never appreciated anyone's efforts on his behalf but who "walks around like he'd just stepped off Mount Olympus" (212).

The men are imprisoned in their personas of doctor and estate manager, chained by their own inability to break out and begin the process of individuation. Vanya cries impotently, "All I want is a new life. Tell me how to find one . . . where should I look?" to which Astrov snaps, "Will you listen to yourself? There is no new life! None for you, none for me. It's hopeless. . . . The only thing we have to look forward to is a little peace and quiet when we're finally in our graves" (Chekhov, *Uncle Vanya* 247). Vanya's ill-fated attempt to seek his anima in Yelena serves only to reinforce his sense of futility, while the shadow qualities called forth by his rage at Serebriakov only become ridiculous in their extremity. After Vanya's aborted and pathetic attempt to shoot the professor, Astrov wryly points out, "You're not crazy, you're just the comic relief around here. You're a freak, you know that? I used to think freaks were sick, but I've changed my mind. Now I think being a freak is the normal human condition. I think you're completely normal" (246–47). Perhaps this persona possession furnishes the key to much of our contemporary fascination with *Uncle Vanya*. The electronic jungle that we inhabit carries the perpetual threat of making us fall behind, should we stop for an instant to reflect on its significance. Here, perhaps, we can glimpse the trickster again, staring boldly out at us—this time from the mirror—declaring, " I am what I do." It also seems reasonable to speculate that Astrov and Vanya might represent to some extent two aspects of Chekhov's own personality. He was a hardworking physician who, unlike Astrov, nonetheless made time for all his other passions, from conservation to writing. Like Vanya, he was also the sole supporter of a large and frequently disappointing family. Perhaps he allowed his shadow to live in his art, in order to keep it from overtaking him in life.

Vanya's conclusion leaves us with a much bleaker prospect than *Three Sisters*. In this absurd world, Vanya is driven to distraction by Serebriakov's decision that the estate should be sold in order to provide him with every comfort, and he attempts to shoot the old man in a comic variation on Tuzenbach's tragic murder. Vanya misses several times, creating a ridiculous spectacle, then retires with dark threats about doing away with himself. The incident precipitates Serebriakov's departure, which signals the play's end. After all the guests have left the family alone, Sonia speaks these heartbreaking words of consolation to her uncle, but perhaps even more to herself:

> We have to go on living. You and I, Uncle Vanya, we have to go on living. The days will be slow, and the nights will be long, but we'll take whatever fate sends us. We'll spend most of our lives doing other people's work for them, we won't know a minute's rest, and then, when our time comes, we'll die. And when we're dead, we'll say that our lives were full of pain, that we wept and suffered, and God will have pity on us, and then, Uncle, dear Uncle Vanya, . . . then we'll rest. (Chekhov, *Uncle Vanya* 253)

She continues on, attempting to create a sense of purpose in heavenly reward, having been unable to rationalize the life she now leads. Very different from Olga's jubilant, "We'll go on living" (Chekhov, *Three Sisters* 319), Sonia's martyrdom only fills us with sadness for the wasted lives of these good people. Perhaps this is Chekhov's elegy for those who live such lives. Or perhaps once more we are left to hope that the Sisyphus archetype will be invoked, allowing these good people to find that strange joy that Camus describes, the contentment of those who find meaning through taking up their own existential challenges. At least Sonia gives us more hope than her uncle does, for, Sophia once again, she confers the wisdom, the gnosis that makes such heroism possible. We can hope that Yelena, too, through stoical adherence to her marriage, might eventually find that hard-won wisdom that seems to descend like divine grace but carries the familiar feel of that which we have always known and have only just released from its prison in the unconscious.

The Cherry Orchard: Send in the Clowns

We turn now to the most comedic and in some ways the most problematic of Chekhov's "big four." *The Cherry Orchard* provides us with characters who give the most exuberant display of unconsciousness since King Lear's opening speech. Briefly, the story line deals with the impending sale of a local landmark, the fabled cherry orchard belonging to Lyuba Andryeevna Ranevskaya, an absentee landowner. The property, which was the childhood home of Lyuba and her brother, Gaev, is a legacy from Lyuba's late husband, who bought it from their father. The play's point of attack occurs when Lyuba returns, brought home from a long sojourn in Paris by her seventeen-year-old daughter Anya. They are accompanied by Carlotta Ivanovna, an eccentric German governess, and Yasha, a brash, young, male servant. At home to greet them are Gaev, various neighbors and friends, and Varya, Lyuba's adopted daughter who acts as housekeeper. After much discussion and little comprehension, the cherry orchard is finally sold to Lopakhin, a local peasant-entrepreneur who destroys their fairy tale world of self-delusion.

Once more the archetypal structure is centered on the void where parental authority should exist. Ranevskaya is Chekhov's most captivating puella aeterna. Her personality is a blend of calculating self-serving charm and rueful self-awareness; it brings everyone under her spell. Although her self-indulgence and inappropriate largesse have been instrumental in bankrupting the estate, she manages to ignore those issues while beguiling everyone in the process. When told of the family's desperate financial situation, Ranevskaya remains in complete denial: "Cut down the cherry orchard? My dear man, you don't understand! Our cherry orchard is a landmark! It's famous for miles around" (Chekhov, *Cherry Orchard* 341). The mother's stubborn refusal to grow up forces both of her daughters, young Anya and long-suffering Varya, to assume the parental role. The position of the archetypes is thus reversed. Meanwhile, Anya's naive idealism attracts her to Trefimov, a perpetual student whose speeches on social activism are a substitute for action. In all Chekhov's work we find a variation of this character who prophesies a future that is finer and more beautiful than the present. Vershinin, Tuzenbach, and Astrov all assume that role at different times—but they are also men who act in other endeavors. Trefimov is the hero sans action, a man seemingly mired in his own mind. He is as delusional as Lyuba in his way, complaining ironically about the intellectuals at his university. They "take themselves so seriously," he says; "they're full of theories and ideas" but "certainly don't *do* much" (355).

Gaev is one of Chekhov's most bizarre creations. A man who makes speeches to furniture and people alike, Gaev is a perfect parody of the wise old man. He, like his sister, has lived a life of privilege, untroubled by practical considerations. Far from being a patriarchal figure in the household, he is an unwitting jester, a victim of trickster possession who has no idea of his own eccentricity. Another puer/senex, he bumbles through life, muttering about billiard shots—apparently the only subject on which he has any real knowledge—and admitting happily that "I've eaten up my entire inheritance in candy" (354).

Even the minor characters in this farce indulge in foolishness. Yasha, the footman who has acquired airs in Paris, seduces Dunyasha, the impressionable housemaid, who then rejects her bumptious suitor, Epihodov, the estate clerk. It has been often observed that much of Chekhov is about longing for that which is never within our reach. Perhaps that is what makes him the most human of playwrights, this acknowledgment of our universal search, which for Jung was a search for the self. In *The Cherry Orchard* that yearning becomes a burlesque, in that nearly all of these people are over-reachers. They inhabit a fantasy landscape in which there is no model of rational behavior. Only Firs, the ancient butler, seems satisfied with his lot in life, like the elderly nurses in *Three Sisters* and *Uncle Vanya*. Firs finds in his loyalty to his master "all the freedom I needed" (Chekhov, *Cherry Orchard* 355). For Chekhov, simple people who expect little from life seem to be happier than those with great ambition. Yet at the final curtain Firs, alone on stage, dimly comprehends the waste of his own life in service to people who have never really appreciated his efforts nor seen him as fully human: "Well, it's all over now," he mumbles, "and I never even had a life to live" (385). That, in itself, becomes a rent in the fabric of an unexamined life, and we see a vision of an unconscious Sisyphus comprehending too late that the rock has rolled down and crushed him.

Carlotta Ivanovna—the mysterious governess who was once a circus performer—is possibly the most enigmatic character in all Chekhov's work. Who is Carlotta Ivanovna? Even she doesn't know:

> I don't know how old I really am. I just think of myself as young. When I was a little girl, Mama and my father used to travel around to fairs and put on shows, good ones. I did back flips, things like that. . . . Where I'm from . . . who I am . . . no idea. Who my parents were— maybe they weren't even married—no idea. *(Takes a large cucumber pickle out of her pocket and takes a bite.)* No idea at all. And I feel like talking all the time, but there's no one to talk to. No one. (Chekhov, *Cherry Orchard* 349–50)

Carlotta performs parlor tricks, cares for her dog, and gives us no further indication about her function in the play. Can it be that Chekhov has posed through her a question to the audience about the nature of reality in our lives? She is clearly a trickster figure. The incarnation of illusion itself, she reminds us of the liminal quality of the lives around her and of our own, as well. The self-deception of these characters is nearly universal; amid them, we find the trickster unmasked, challenging our own honesty.

Finally, we come to Lopakhin, who, along with Ranevskaya, commands the play's center. A parvenu, Lopakhin attempts to explain to the foolish siblings their perilous financial situation. He offers to develop the land for them, in order to save it from auction, but both Ranevskaya and Gaev ignore any attempt to bring them to consciousness, financially or otherwise. When the property ultimately does reach the auction block, Lopakhin himself buys it. After a brief period of melodramatic protest, everyone adjusts to the new situation and goes off to a new life: Ranevskaya back to Paris, Gaev to a banking job, and the rest to their various destinations. Lopakhin stands astride this fading, feudal world as hero, conqueror, and king. But the trickster has once again unbalanced the scales. The dragon Lopakhin has slain is simply a ghost of his own wretched childhood:

> Ninety thousand plus the balance on the mortgage. And now the cherry orchard is mine! . . . My God, if my father and my grandfather could be here now and see this, see *me*, their Yermolai, the boy they beat, who went barefoot in winter and never went to school, see how that poor boy just bought the most beautiful estate in the whole world! I bought the estate where my father and my grandfather slaved away their lives, where they wouldn't even let them in the kitchen! (Chekhov, *Cherry Orchard* 373)

The people whose good opinion he craves despise him for his success, and he has rejected the love of Varya, the poor stepsister who never becomes Cinderella. Sisyphus and Sophia seem far removed from these people, all of them victims of their own delusional thinking. And yet, even here, Sophia's transcendent wisdom might lie ahead for young Anya. Like Irina and Sonia, she possesses the compassionate idealism that often signals the beginnings of understanding:

> Mama dear, I love you, I'll take care of you. The cherry orchard is sold, it's gone now, that's the truth, Mama, that's the truth, but don't cry. You still have your life to lead. . . . Come with me, Mama, we'll go away, someplace far away from here. We'll plant a new orchard, even better than this one, you'll see, Mama, you'll understand, and you'll feel a new kind of joy, like a light in your soul. . . . Let's go, Mama. Let's go! (374)

As a final ironic twist to the plot, Pischik, the bumbling neighborhood freeloader, comes into an inheritance and pays off all his debts. The trickster simply will not stay idle in this play. How then, does this conglomeration of clowns and mountebanks manage to touch us so deeply? Perhaps it is because we see our own world more clearly in this fun-house mirror, which, with its distortions, shows truth more clearly than literal reality.

THE SEAGULL: KILLING THE SHADOW

As the first of Chekhov's works to be produced by Stanislavski and the Moscow Art Theater, *The Seagull* holds a special place in the canon. It was a great success, and the fledgling theater company adopted the seagull as its symbol. This stands as a permanent homage to the collaboration between the playwright and the director who shaped so much of our approach to theater in succeeding years. Like *Uncle Vanya, The Seagull* has a small cast and a more tightly focused plot than *Three Sisters* or *The Cherry Orchard*. Arkadina, a famous actress, is visiting the estate of her brother Sorin; she is accompanied by her much younger lover, Trigorin, a writer. Trepliev, her son, has written a play that is about to be performed on a makeshift outdoor stage. Trepliev is in love with his leading lady, Nina, a young neighbor; he becomes distraught when she abandons him to pursue a romance with the glamorous Trigorin. The doctor in this play is called Dorn; he is involved in a long-standing affair with Polena, who is the wife of Shamrayev, Sorin's ill-tempered bailiff. Shamrayev's daughter, Masha, in despair over her unrequited love for Trepliev, marries Mediedenko, the local schoolmaster, in a situation very closely resembling that of Masha and Kulygin in *Three Sisters*.

In Arkadina, we find another version of Ranevskaya, the mother who refuses to accept her archetypal role and instead clings to her status as a young, desirable woman. She is annoyed by the presence of an adult child who, her son says is "a constant reminder she's not so young any more. . . . When I'm not around, she's only thirty-two" (Chekhov, *Seagull* 114). Consequently, she takes every opportunity to diminish and insult Trepliev, calling him an "amateur" writer and a "nobody" (141). Because of her taunts, he halts the performance of his play and stalks away in hurt and anger. She pretends innocence and accuses him of oversensitivity, clearly indifferent to his feelings or his desires. Her vanity is overweening, and she takes every opportunity to reassure herself by using others as foils. When she asks Dr. Dorn who looks the younger—she or the unhappy Masha—he responds as expected, supplying her with the flattery she craves. Like the wicked queen in Snow White, Narcissus incarnate, she uses the world as her mirror. "You're supposed to talk about *her*," Trepliev laments, "write about *her,* applaud *her,* tell *her* she was divine in *Camille,* or in a piece of trash like *The Fumes of Life.* And here she is in the country, where nobody knows who she is, so she's bored and then she gets mean, and of course it's all our fault" (113). Arkadina is a monster, another devouring mother who would happily eat her young in order to secure her own happiness. She does show signs of affection for Trepliev upon occasion, but she bristles when challenged in any of her opinions and seems to want his affection only as she wants the admiration of everyone else. Trepliev clearly suffers from her indifference and quite naturally longs for his mother's love, as he confides to both his uncle and the doctor.

Nina, of course, is the anima here, young, innocent and ripe for picking by the charming but irresponsible Trigorin. Trigorin becomes infatuated with Nina's youth, and longs for a virginal love in order to escape from the stale routine of his liaison with the middle-aged Arkadina. Sardonic Masha, chronically lovesick for Trepliev, invariably wears black because she claims to be "in mourning for my life" (Chekhov, *Seagull* 111). Her self-destructive behavior, such as drinking and taking snuff, makes her a precise shadow figure for Nina, the archetypal virgin-anima. Nina is appropriately dressed in white at play's beginning, and her innocence, joy, and optimism contrast with Masha's dark moods and somber clothing. Masha also serves as a double for her mother, whose longstanding affair with Dr. Dorn is an escape from her unhappy marriage to Masha's father.

By the same token, Trigorin serves as a shadow for Trepliev. This creates an unsavory sense of Oedipal confusion, when, as Arkadina's lover, Trigorin displaces the son in her affections, thus taking the place of the dead father and the son, as well. When he possesses Nina, too, it is the last straw. He has robbed Trepliev of all anima connection. Trepliev challenges him to a duel, which he refuses, and Trepliev succeeds only in wounding himself in a botched suicide attempt: psychologically, he attempts to kill his shadow, and when that fails, he attempts to kill himself. One of the play's most poignant moments occurs when Trepliev begs his mother to bandage his wounded forehead because she has "magic hands" (Chekhov, *Seagull* 140). He attempts to recall their earlier days when she was close to him, but they only argue about Trigorin once again.

When at play's end Nina returns after a two-year absence, she is a changed woman. Trigorin has grown tired of her; the child she bore him has died, and she has failed as an actress. Trepliev has become a successful writer who continues to love her as obsessively as ever, for, as he puts it, "I realized every minute [during her absence] that my soul was tied to you forever. I can't *not* love you, Nina. I can't. . . . Everywhere I turn, I see your face" (158). She, however, is still in love with Trigorin, who has gone back to Arkadina, and, when she hears this, she rushes out of the house, telling Trepliev, "I love him. I love him even more than before" (159).

Trepliev's suicide, which shocks audiences by its unexpectedness, is the result of a psychological deathblow. Before she exits, Nina tells him, "You have to keep on believing. I believe, and it helps. And now when I think about my vocation, I'm not afraid of life" (Chekhov, *Seagull* 159). But his shadow, Trigorin, has bested him in every respect, depriving him of both mother and lover, cutting him off from his anima and consequently from love and himself. Just before Trepliev destroys his manuscripts and leaves the stage to shoot himself, he says to Nina: "I *don't* believe, and I don't know what my vocation is. You've found your way in life, you know where you're heading, but I just go on drifting through a chaos of images and dreams, I don't know what my work is good for, or who needs it" (159). Although the play's title refers to Nina, as a result of her identification with a bird that Trepliev shoots early in the action, it is in fact Trepliev's tragedy that lies at the center of this tale. As Nina returns to the theater to continue her work as an artist, she seems to have begun her journey toward the self; she demonstrates the resilience of Chekhov's women and once more evokes the spirit of Sophia's wisdom. But Trepliev, completely stymied by his shadow, is the seagull destroyed by a hunter "because he has nothing better to do" (159).

ACTOR/AUDIENCE/ARTIST

Is an audience aware of the archetypal hold that these plays exert on it? Certainly, in most cases, those watching the play are not aware, and indeed many people find Chekhov dull, because the inner life of the drama is buried under a ponderous style and slow tempo. This is the eternal obstacle between artist and audience in the ephemeral arts such as theater, dance, and music. Sometimes the performance bears little relationship to the intent of the creator. But that is, conversely, what keeps the performing arts alive and well. Stanislavski's dictum to the actor to play the scene as if it were first time every time applies to all the lively arts. In each performance, the work is born again, like Dionysus in the archetype of rebirth that is so apt for theater, of whom he is the god. No bad performance can kill a good play, because it will rise again and speak its truth to different eras.

Countless acting teachers will affirm that the universality and time-lessness of Chekhov's themes become apparent every time a group of young actors approaches his plays. Abruptly, the mask of contemporary skepticism and wariness falls away. The mannered readings affected from film and television disappear to make room for honest human emotion, which then blasts its way through the cultural conventions and gives birth to human truth. This sometimes shocks the actors into tears of sudden recognition of themes that could just as easily have come from the Greeks or from Shakespeare.

How can Jung's work help the actor and the director? Both actors and directors need multiple approaches in their search for truth in the work. Jung can help this process through teaching us to work with per-sonality type, instead of against it. Strong thinking types need to under-stand the character intellectually first, while the opposite is true for strong feeling types, whose hearts understand the emotional truth first and work from there. Regardless of one's method of access, though, both functions have to come together in order to create the whole char-acter. Clearly, the unconscious is working in the intuitive actor, translat-ing the archetypal material into emotional understanding without con-scious thinking. An understanding of the deep layer of archetypal-mythic patterns can stimulate the process of emotional com-prehension for a thinking type, while it can aid the intellectual mastery necessary to complete the procedure for the primarily feeling type. For example, an actor may explore the despair of Trepliev by understanding the archetypal resonances of being cut off by the same person who rep-resents both the mother archetype (life) and the anima (soul). Trigorin takes on the aspect of an all-powerful destroyer who has stolen both life and soul. Trepliev's physical death is simply an inevitable coda to the psychic death that has already taken place. To be sure, not every actor will find this method helpful or will be open to the study of archetypal theory. Even so, for the director it will almost certainly prove a useful tool, since the director must seek to understand the play on every level available to him or her.

The deep structural analysis available to us through Jung's theories offers an incomparable insight into the reasons great literature remains great over the years. And so each generation of theatrical artists will thank Drs. Jung and Chekhov for adding greatly to our understanding of this human condition and for reminding us of our place within the *animus mundi,* the world soul of which Chekhov speaks wistfully through his surrogate, Dr. Dorn: "Evenings, when you left your hotel, the entire street was full of people. You drift along with the crowd, no destination in mind, just back and forth; it becomes a living thing, and you become part of it, spiritually as well as physically; you begin to believe that a universal world soul is possible" (Chekhov, *Seagull* 150).

NOTE

1. Professor Donald Eisen of the University of Pennsylvania furnished the following information through his Chekhov Web site, an invaluable resource:

The [version] with Sam Neill and Greta Scacchi is named 'Country Life.' Then there is a production of 'Uncle Vanya' with David Warner and Mary Elizabeth Mastroantonio which was a PBS Great Performances production. And most recently there was the film with Anthony Hopkins adapted from *Uncle Vanya* and titled 'August.' There is a film of an earlier production, called 'Uncle Vanya,' directed by Laurence Olivier in which he also stars. I loved 'Vanya on 42nd Street,' and I saw it in New York in its original production. It too, is available on videotape.

Vanya on 42nd Street is a film of the Andre Gregory play, starring Wallace Shawn in the title role. It is a wonderfully metatheatrical treatment of Chekhov that clearly shows his timelessness.

WORKS CITED

Camus, Albert. *The Myth of Sisyphus and Other Essays*. New York: Random, 1955.

Chekhov, Anton. *The Cherry Orchard*. Schmidt 331–87.

———. *The Seagull*. Schmidt 109–64.

———. *Three Sisters*. Schmidt 257–322.

———. *Uncle Vanya*. Schmidt 207–55.

Eisen, Donald. *Eisen's Web*. 3 March 2000. <http://home.adelphia.net/~dgeisen>.

Hackett, Jean. *The Actor's Chekhov*. Newbury, VT: Smith and Kraus, 1993.

Jung, C. G. *Memories, Dreams, Reflections*. Ed. Aniela Jaffé. Trans. Richard Winston and Clara Winston. New York: Vintage, 1969.

———. *The Spirit in Man, Art, and Literature*. Ed. Sir Herbert Read. Trans. R. F. C. Hull. Princeton: Bollingen, 1966.

Porterfield, Sally. *Jung's Advice to the Players: A Jungian Reading of Shakespeare's Problem Plays*. Westport: Greenwood, 1994.

Schmidt, Paul, trans. and ed. *The Plays of Anton Chekhov*. By Anton Chekhov. New York: HarperCollins, 1997.

Senelick, Laurence. *The Chekhov Theatre: A Century of Plays in Performance.* Cambridge: Cambridge UP, 1997.

Stanislavski, Constantin. Introduction. *Anton Chekhov: Plays.* Ed. and trans. Elisaveta Fen. London: Penguin, 1954.

Vandenbroucke, Russell. *Truths the Hand Can Touch: The Theatre of Athol Fugard.* New York: Theatre Communications Group, 1985.

Vanya on 42nd Street. Dir. Louis Malle. Play by Andre Gregory. Sony Pictures, 1994.

Opened Ground from a Jungian Perspective

The Father Archetype in the
Poetry of Seamus Heaney

ᐸᔱᐳ

J. R. ATFIELD

A self-declared "Jungian in religion" ("Artists" 409), Seamus Heaney has sought to re-establish in modern society something of the ancient religious quality of myth, the healing element of ritualistic connections with ancient powers. As Suzanne Langer has commented, "The ultimate end of myth is not wishful distortion of the world, but serious envisagement of its fundamental truths" (176); it is a "moral orientation, not escape" (176). Offering a means to explore self and society, myth becomes a potent reality in his poems, for "poetry," Heaney has claimed, and "the imaginative arts in general . . . strike and stake out the ore of the self which lies at the base of every individuated life" (*Government* 107). By mythologizing his father, Heaney's examination of self is powerfully extended through the father archetype and through what Jung has called (when considering the relation of analytical psychology to poetry) "the participation mystique of primitive man with the soil on which he dwells, and which contains the spirits of his ancestors" (*CW* 15: 82). By the fluent movement and articulacy of sound, Heaney connects with the "poet's music, derived not from the literate parts of his mind but from its illiterate parts" and reflecting "unconscious activity,

at the pre-verbal level" (Heaney, *Preoccupations* 62)—qualities more in
tune with his father's "earthy" taciturnity than with his own refined
skills of literacy.[1] In an interview in 1991, when asked about his relationship with his father, Heaney responded directly in Jungian terms, by
saying that Patrick Heaney "seemed more of an archetype" than an
actual person *(South Bank Show)!*

Though this volume enphasizes post-Jungian theory, the following
paragraphs offer to reassert the continuing relevance and vitality of "traditional" Jungian analysis.[2] Heaney's conscious espousal of a "Jungian
religion" warrants such a reading, since his use of archetypal symbolism
is deliberate and his own understanding of Jung entirely "traditional."
Without such a reading, the understanding and appreciation (not to
mention individual, psychological engagements with Heaney's work)
remain incomplete. Such a reading is not antithetical to a consideration
of Heaney's formal artistry and musicality, though "traditional" archetypal analyses have often been faulted, either for ignoring a poem's aesthetic qualities or for ignoring its historical/cultural contexts. Because
Heaney works deliberately with archetypal materials, these become part
of the formal artistry of his poetry, as well as a commentary upon his life
and times.

Heaney writes in the manner that he admired in Robert Lowell, who
"was and will remain a pattern for poets in this amphibiousness, this
ability to plunge into the downward reptilian welter of the individual
self and yet raise himself with whatever knowledge he gained there out
on to the hard ledges of the historical present, which he then appre-
hended with refreshed insight and intensity" ("Robert Lowell" 26).
Heaney, too, proves able to apprehend his own and Ireland's "historical
present" with the "refreshed insight and intensity" of a poet writing
from an archetypal, Jungian perspective; he uses archetypes not to
escape from Ireland's historical present but, rather, to enhance the life-
meaning of the individual poet and of the Irish as a people, a life-mean-
ing that grows collectively through generations.[3] As Terence Dawson has
emphasized, "A Jungian reading of a work of literature is one that,
whilst rooted in the exploration of ordinary human dilemmas, *also*
engages with social, political, national and cultural realities" (275).
Heaney reads Lowell in this manner and thus invites a similar reading of
his own work.

Heaney's own identification with the Father through his father (and
through his father before him, and his father before him) cannot be
experienced or understood in any way but archetypally. In a sense, Irish
identity is constituted by its living myths, which its poets have deliberately embraced, championed, and furthered by their writing. Referring

to his own generation of writers, Heaney suggests that "we all experienced a need to get certain unique and almost subcultural realities of
Ulster life into words. . . . [T]he writers could not altogether escape the
myth of their own importance in an ongoing work of definition and
transformation" (*Redress* 193).

Outlining "Jung's five stages in the withdrawal of projections,"
Dawson describes a stage of individuation "predominantly concerned
with . . . identity in relation to an 'other'/'others' . . . [and a later stage
concerned with] social reality/individual consciousness" (274). He also
emphasizes that these stages are "not intended to be seen as a fixed scale
of exclusive distinctions" (267). Dawson shows how, through these
"stages" suggested by Jung, self-identity grows in the movement
between identification with and separation from the "other," which can
be related to Heaney's employment and adaptation of the Father archetype, in which he explores the dialectical relations between "social reality" and "individual consciousness." The following analysis of Heaney's
poetry also acknowledges a distinction advocated by Dawson, which
Heaney implicitly employs, between *collective* and *personal* archetypes;
in this chapter, the Father archetype denoted with a capital letter refers
to the *collective* concept.

In particular, Heaney dramatizes the distance—created partly
through the advantages of education—between father and son, inartic-
ulateness and articulacy. By doing so, he points to the emergence of the
Ulster Catholic "voice" that parallels his own individuation, recalling
that "not just the household but the culture of rural Ulster, indeed
Ulster generally—were suspicious of speech" (Wilmer 78). In an interview he describes how, through poetry, he had "loosened the voice of
the self over the years" (Wilmer 82), at the same time describing "the
violence for people from Ulster [as] a manifestation of something that
was always latent and potential. . . . [M]y own generation of Catholics
perceived just that very emergence of themselves, as a generation into
the vocal world of the academy and the world of politics, as an aspect
of change itself" (Wilmer 80). Thus Heaney's work can be seen to have
as its underlying premise the "defining characteristics of modern literature," described by Dawson as "simultaneous engagement with personal *and* social issues" (256).

Feder has suggested that "A study of myth in the poetry of the generation following Lowell's would reveal some remarkable adaptations of
traditional mythical narratives and figures to accommodate the responses
of new poets to the disorder and brutality that have increased in immea-
surable proportions . . . and have deeply affected the poet's concept of his
art" (410). An admirer and elegist of Lowell, Heaney confirms this view.

His reaction to the disordered brutality of Northern Ireland during his generation has certainly led Heaney to take stock of his concept of his art and to employ myth as a means of articulating the tensions of the modern-day world. Jung himself provided the poet with the terms for this analogy: as Heaney states, "By the 1960s, in Jung's scenario, 'a higher consciousness' was manifesting itself in the form of poetry itself, an ideal towards which the poets turned in order to survive the stunting conditions" (*Government* xviii).

"Digging"—which Heaney has referred to (in a somewhat dismissive tone) as a "coarse-grained navvy of a poem" *(English File)*—has nonetheless always been featured as the opening poem in anthologies of his works, including his latest, *Opened Ground* (1998). In this admiring poetic celebration, the colloquial diction conveys the typical ambiguity of Heaney's relationship with his father, reflecting the casual, with the tender reference to "old man," as well as the more respectful acknowledgment of the "wise old man" as it manifests in the Father archetype and recurs with each generation. A skillful change of perspective from close-up to long shot, from present to past, dramatizes the poet's glance "down" to the flowerbeds at "my father, digging," who then "comes up twenty years away." The poetic enjambment, setting up the continuous movement of the poem, reflects the continuity of family tradition that Heaney was to break: "the old man could handle a spade. / Just like his old man." The father and grandfather embody attributes of the Father archetype: power, strength, and order. Working "in rhythm . . . firmly . . . neatly," they are described with the clarity and precision of active verbs, in both past ("levered," "rooted," "buried," "cut," "fell to") and continuous present tenses ("nicking," "slicing," "heaving"), implying further continuity. The contrast with the poet's observatory, "sedentary trade" is finally extended through the transmuted "pen" in the now famous, decisive declaration of the last line, "I'll dig with it."

As Jung has explained in *The Archetypes and the Collective Unconscious,* "The wise old man appears in dreams in the guise of a magician, doctor, priest, teacher, professor, grandfather, or any other person possessing authority" (*CW* 9.1: 216). The respect for this authority and the pride of the son in his elders is recaptured in childlike aggrandizement: "My grandfather cut more turf in a day / Than any other man on Toner's bog" ("Digging," *Opened Ground* 3 lines 17–18). This is evident also in "Follower" (*Opened Ground* 3), which expresses similar awe of the father as "an expert." Heaney emphasizes this phrase by setting it apart, yet still confining it within the strict limits of the half-rhyme and regular tetrameter rhythm used throughout most of the poem.[4] The form reflects the regularity and precision of the father's task, in the poet's re-creation of the order imposed on the "polished sod" and the team of horses. The enjambment of "a single pluck / Of reins" further recaptures both the revered mastery of the father and the unconscious resentment of the child, whose own "small imperfect limits would keep breaking" ("Poem," *Opened Ground* 14). Such an image confirms Maud Bodkin's suggestion that "The figures of both father and king tend to retain, within those deeper levels of the mind to which poetry may penetrate, something of the manna that invested the first representative of a power akin to, but vastly beyond, that of the individual emerging into self-consciousness" (17).

Heaney's father set limits and kept within them, providing an example that his son, as a child emulated, but failed to achieve. As an adult, however, Heaney redefines his own limits. Poetry needs to "go beyond conventional bounds" (*Redress* 192) in order to provide the hope of any kind of answer to social and political unrest. These views of the father presented in the early poems confirm the nurturing and yet ultimately restricting aspects of the archetypal Father, who conveys the moral boundaries and expectations of the society into which the child will integrate and enables the development of the adult's confidence in adapting these to his own self-image and relationships with others. Again Dawson's interpretation of Jungian theory of withdrawal of projections is relevant here, in particular the "fourth stage [which] begins with the realisation that the aura and authority with which one has invested all the collective norms and expectations within which one lives are of one's own making. The 'projection' is already broken . . . freeing the person to become the specific human being that he or she is" (267).

In his third volume, *Wintering Out* (1980), Heaney wrote some of the first poems connected with bogland and P. V. Glob's Scandinavian archaeological discoveries, both of which provided him with "symbols adequate to our predicament" (*Preoccupations* 56). In "Nerthus" (*Opened Ground* 66), the poet makes his first implicit reference to the ash plant as a symbol of his father's archetypal qualities and the idea of his being wedded to his land. The simplicity and conciseness of the poem conversely reflect the wealth of resonance that the symbol has for Heaney, not at all easily defined but related to the sense of rootedness that he feels his father possesses and that he can never attain; it is related also to the image of the goddess Nerthus (pictured in Glob's book, *The Bog People*, which so fascinated Heaney) as a long, thick, split stick. Relating this inspiration for his "individual self" to the "befitting emblems of adversity" in the "historical present," Heaney remarked thus of the rituals associated with the goddess: "Taken in relation to the tradition of Irish political martyrdom for that cause whose icon is Kathleen

Ni Houlihan, this . . . is an archetypal pattern" (*Preoccupations* 57). The reference to an *ash*-fork, however, is Heaney's interpolation; Glob refers merely to the "branch" representing the goddess.[5]

Clearly, for Heaney, this represents a kind of "beauty," a numinous quality attached to the practical, sturdy walking stick his father always carried. He re-creates a religious symbol through this reference in dialect to the "kesh" and "loaning"—the raised footway and space between untilled fields—in which the ash-fork is "staked" ("Nerthus," *Opened Ground* 66). Heaney thus invokes, through local and collo-quial rather than academic language, the "protean mythologem and the shimmering symbol" that, as Jung emphasized, "express the processes of the psyche far more trenchantly and, in the end, far more clearly than the clearest concept" (*CW* 13: 166). The tension between the father's pragmatism and the son's imaginative resonance results in a precise description with very imprecise associations, again supported by Jung's remarks that "in psychic matters we are dealing with processes of experience, that is, with transformations which should never be given hard and fast names if their living movement is not to petrify into something static" (*CW* 13: 66).

The poem can be read as a direct example of Jung's point: through the symbol of the ash-fork, Heaney's experiences of awe and reverence for the land and for the practical abilities of his father (as represented by his stick) are transformed into the living movement of the "grains gath-ering," deliberately described in the continuous present participle. Although the stick is fixed permanently in the earth, its symbolic reso-nance is anything but static. It is positioned "where kesh and loaning finger out to heather"; it reaches out to the wider stretches of land, as the symbol reaches out to a linguistic expression of the imaginative asso-ciations that Heaney brings to it. This occurs, significantly, through the suggestion, "*say* an ash-fork . . . ," emphasizing the verbal and written form in which the poet's reverence for the land is represented, rather than the father's nonverbal, active possession of the land as a farmer and cattle dealer.

In "The Harvest Bow" (*Opened Ground* 183), Heaney's father becomes a representative figure for all those whose lives are tied to the land and to physical labor, in contrast to the world of literary scholar-ship that the son has entered. As Anthony Stevens has remarked, with reference to the Jungian perspective, "the Father is concerned with events occurring in the tangible world in the context of space and time—events that are approached, controlled and modified through conscious-ness and the use of will" (107). The poet, who digs with his pen rather than with spade or plough, ventures beyond the limits of consciousness.

As Heaney suggests in *The Government of the Tongue,* "poetry, having to do with feelings and emotions, must not submit to the intellect's eagerness to foreclose. . . . [A]rt does not trace the given map of a better reality but improvises an inspired sketch of it" (9). In "The Harvest Bow," Heaney dramatizes this contrast: the opening poetic expression is of his father's practical artistic gift, the plaiting of wheat straw figures, a symbol of control of the material; the final image is of the escape of the "spirit of the corn" which will not be tied down.

"The Harvest Bow" (*Opened Ground* 183) also dramatizes one of Jung's descriptions of the creative process, which, "so far as we are able to follow it at all, consists of the unconscious activation of an archetypal image and in elaborating and shaping this image into the finished work" (*CW* 15: 110). The Father archetype is activated in Heaney's childhood walks with his own father along the riverbank; his shaping and reworking of the image results in the poem, which is itself left open-ended, suggesting the indefinable quality of creative power. An intricate twist of wheat straw, the harvest bow seems to symbolize the skill of the laborer's hands "that aged round ashplants and cane sticks." Heaney achieves a skillful balance between the material and the spiritual in these reminiscences, establishing his father more explicitly in terms of the motif of the ashplant. The "love-knot of straw" that he fashions seems to contain in its open pattern the silent presence of the inarticulate:

> As you plaited the harvest bow
> You implicated the mellowed silence in you
> In wheat that does not rust.

The "mellowed silence" emphasizes the difference between the reticence of the farmer father and the poet son whose life is words; the contrast between the two is fused in the intense image of the harvest bow, which becomes the medium in which their two worlds meet, as son interprets in word what the father had fashioned in deed: "I tell and finger it like braille, / Gleaning the unsaid off the palpable."

The bow embodies all that Heaney has left behind but which is still so much part of him, the tiny hamlet in which Mossbawn farm was situated, "that original townland / Still tongue-tied in the straw tied by your hand." Jung's comment on the creative process of the artist in relation to the archetype is relevant here: "By giving it shape, the artist translates it into the language of the present and so makes it possible for us to make our way back to the deepest springs of life" (*CW* 15: 10). If Heaney releases the tongue, however, the implication is that the reality of the place may escape him when he tries to capture it in words and pin it down, just as the spirit of the corn escapes when plucked, twisted, and put up artificially as an ornament. At this point, father and son meet both in endeavor and in failure: this spirit is other, separate, and not to be caught by either; it slips the "snare."

The reticence of Heaney's father, captured in a number of poems, links him to the archetypal Father, from whom any pronouncement will necessarily be significant; when he does speak, it is with the voice of authority, representative of collective wisdom. The touching tone of the sonnet "Clearances VII" (*Opened Ground* 313), in which the deathbed moments of Kathleen Heaney are affectionately recalled, emphasizes the silent years of sturdy love: "he said more to her /Almost than in all their life together." The slightly clumsy syntax used to create a half-rhyme recreates the awkwardness of endearments on the tongue of an outwardly gruff, taciturn man. The fluency of the following lines, in which the father recalls his courting, is contrasted with the stark bluntness of the actual moment of death, the caesura breaking the rhythm as the last breath breaks from the body: "He called her good and girl. Then she was dead." In describing the relief of the gathered family—"we were overjoyed"—Heaney ironically indicates that the words of the father are more significant to those remaining than to the loved one addressed, who "could not hear."

In "The Stone Verdict" (*Opened Ground* 304), the stone "cairn" built up around the exonerated Hermes is appropriately substituted with "a gate pillar / Or a tumbled wallstead" for Patrick Heaney, implying the moral rectitude of the archetypal Father. By projecting his father into surroundings more appropriate to his earthly role and by following Kavanagh (one of Heaney's models from an earlier generation of Irish poets) in creating "local heroes," Heaney achieves the "best application of Jung's archetypal theory," according to Russo—avoiding "reductionism": Heaney's archetypal imagery provides readers with a "mold flexible enough to permit context and local culture to refract the original image into its specific and distinctive variants" (Russo 244). Like the stones, the poet's words are piled up in the second stanza, with no end-stopped lines. They effectively create an ironic counterpart to the silence built up around the departed figure—an extraneous expression which Heaney self-reflectively acknowledges as "too much" comment on his father's death.

Heaney's work would seem to endorse Jung's comment that "it is not that 'God' is a myth, but that myth is the revelation of a divine life in man" (*Memories* 319). Heaney's own comment on the volume *Seeing Things* emphasizes his own personal development throughout the writing of this collection, composed after the death of his father: "I found myself using words like 'spirit' and 'soul,' words which I had disallowed myself for a long time, because there was so much prejudice against them in my literary education. Then you realise that's attenuating, and that there is a space that's covered by them" (Morrison 91). At this stage in his poetic career, Heaney finds the confidence to move beyond reductive elements of his education.

In "Man and Boy" (*Opened Ground* 337–38), Heaney conveys this numinous, spiritual quality: the experience of his father's death recalls that of his grandfather, emphasizing the archetypal quality of the inevitable death of former generations and the recurring need for descendants' adjustment and assimilation of their absence. A complex of déjà vu and prefiguration in the time continuum is both physically and spiritually re-created by the skillful use of enjambment to suggest time and space, distanced yet conflated:

> My father is a barefoot boy with news,
> Running at eye-level with weeds and stooks
> On the afternoon of his own father's death.
>
> . . . I feel his legs and quick heels far away
>
> And strange as my own.

These examples further confirm Jung's relevance to a reading of Heaney's work, especially when considered in relation to Jung's remarks that "the personal father inevitably embodies the archetype, which is what endows this figure with its fascinating power. The archetype acts as an amplifier, enhancing beyond measure the effects that proceed from the father, so far as these conform to the inherited pattern" (*CW* 4: 744).

Another repeated image in the poetry is of the father as protector and savior; this, too, is seen re-enacted through generations, in a reciprocated dramatization of the mythical visit to the world of the dead. Heaney-Aeneas pleads with the sibyl for "one face-to-face meeting with my / Dear father" (*Opened Ground* 333), recalling, with exactly the same phrase, the childhood experience when "I saw him face to face, he came to me / With his damp footprints out of the river" (*Opened Ground* 341):

> I pray for one look . . .
> Teach me the way and open the holy doors wide.
> I carried him on these shoulders and through flames
> And thousands of enemy spears.
>
> ("The Golden Bough," *Seeing Things* 1)

Aeneas is the archetype of filial piety and duty to the patria or fatherland. Heaney's reiteration of the Aeneas/Anchises relationship is an act
of filial heroism, as well as an admission of ultimate sorrow and sacrifice: the father he saves must die, and Aeneas must seek him in the
underworld himself—which is his own final destiny. The time shift effect
is extended again as Heaney suggests that his filial responsibility was
prepared for in his father's care of him, itself prefigured at the time of
Heaney's grandfather's death,

> . . . when he will piggyback me
> At a great height, light-headed and thin-boned,
> Like a witless elder rescued from the fire.
>
> (*Opened Ground* 338)

In an interview, Heaney explained his motivation for writing these
poems: "No, I haven't seen any ghosts. But at this stage of life you're
more surrounded by death than ever before, and you do have to people
the space, you do have to make up the meanings" (Morrison 26). The
experience of death activates the archetypes and releases Heaney to a
fuller acknowledgment of sprituality. Jung commented that archetypes
"only acquire solidity, influence, and eventual consciousness in the
empirical facts, which touch the unconscious aptitude and quicken it to
life" (*CW* 7: 204).

Heaney's progress in self-development and self-realization following his father's death is a release celebrated in many moments throughout the "Squarings" (*Opened Ground* 367) sequence, particularly in
relation to the creative energy of the poet's gift. In a review, B. Morrison observes that "death is presented less as a losing of life than as a
setting free of it" (Morrison 26). The father's spirit is set free, but
equally significantly the son's individuality and personal direction is
more fully untrammelled. Several poems emphasize the father's concern
for order and limit; others emphasize the poet's desire to transcend the
limits imposed. In "Markings" (*Opened Ground* 335), the alliteration
of "loved lines," the half-rhyme of "garden . . . open," and the repetition of "rod stuck" create a sense of regularity, within which the potential for expansion (in the enjambments of "open / From" and "rod /
Stuck") is contained:

> You also loved lines pegged out in the garden . . .
>
> A field of grazing, to be ploughed open
> From the rod stuck in one headrig to the rod
> Stuck in the other.

Through recognition of the archetypal significance of the superficially mundane, individuals gain a sense of value beyond the immediate, "in time that was extra, unforseen and free." Through dreams and imagination, individual lives are experienced as existing beyond time and history. As Jung observes,

> Ultimately, every individual life is at the same time the eternal life of the species. The individual is continuously "historical" because strictly time-bound; the relation of the type to time, on the other hand, is irrelevant. . . . [S]ince the archetype is the unconscious precondition of every human life, its life, when revealed, also reveals the hidden, unconscious ground-life of every individual. (*CW* 11: 89)

In *Seeing Things*, Heaney's memories of his father enable him to confront the archetypal experience of death. Jung's researches revealed that "it not infrequently happens that the archetype appears in the form of a spirit in dreams or fantasy-products, or even comports itself like a ghost. . . . [I]t mobilizes philosophical and religious convictions" (*CW* 8: 205). His memory having become a ghostly presence, Heaney's father remains embodied in the landscape he dominated. As an adult, the son finds that he "cannot mention keshes or the ford / Without my father's shade appearing to me / On a path towards sunset" (*Opened Ground* 377); in "Seeing Things," the young child

> . . . was inside the house
> And saw him out the window, scatter-eyed
> And daunted, strange without his hat,
> His step unguided, his ghosthood immanent.
>
> (*Opened Ground* 340)

Heaney's recollection of this incident reflects Jungian content: "I must have been three or four. I wasn't there, but it was as if I saw it all, him falling off, the cart going into the river. I remember him coming back and walking towards me in a dream, and the strangest thing was seeing him without his hat" (Morrison 26).

The frequently repeated motif of the ashplant becomes the father's badge of authority, creating a microcosm of the responsibility and respect accorded the cattle dealer:

> "Look for a man with an ashplant on the boat"
> My father told his sister setting out
> For London, "and stay near him all night
>
> And you'll be safe."
>
> (*Seeing Things* 85)

In a poem actually titled "The Ash Plant " (*Seeing Things* 19), Heaney movingly describes his father's urgent clinging to this symbol of authority while on his deathbed. The pitiful image of the once strong hand now "wasting" as it "Gropes desperately" reflects the son's equally desperate wish for the father's restoration. The "third leg," which for so long provided balance and sturdiness—literally and metaphorically—in the father's and son's life, is now a "phantom limb," insubstantial and intangible, as the father loses consciousness, "his head go[ing] light with light." The steady monosyllables of the next line suggest a regaining of conscious control, as if once he has it "in his grasp" he is himself again, his powers restored through contact with reality, re-established through "touch" and the rigor and determination of his will: "Now he has found his touch he can stand his / Ground."

In the third section of "Poet's Chair" (*Opened Ground* 426), the symmetry and precision of "My father's ploughing one, two, three, four sides" makes a framework for the child Heaney and the adult poet, who maybe returns to the same field and sits below the same tree after his father's death. The use of present tense implies that the father's guidance and moral rectitude remain with Heaney, who conflates a past, present, and future connection with the farmstead from which he grew: "here for good in every sense." He is in the center of the squarely ploughed field, and the sense of completion and fulfilment this gives him is suggested in the combination of recall and re-creation (as well as in the repetition) of composite images: he is "all-seeing," the horses are "all hoof," and the reflective poet is "all foreknowledge," as if he unconsciously sensed as a child the type of ploughing he would do as an adult, turning up the turf of language. Describing "the poem as a ploughshare that turns time / Up and over," he confirms the connection between these activities, as he had done in an earlier essay: "'Verse' comes from the Latin *versus*, which could mean a line of poetry but could also mean the turn that a ploughman made at the head of the field as he finished one furrow and faced back into another" (Heaney, *Preoccupations* 65).

In the tiny yet marvellously potent poem "The Strand" (*Opened Ground* 436), the ever-present quality of the archetypal Father in the self of the son is embodied once again in the motif of the ash plant: "The dotted line my father's ashplant made / On Sandymount Strand / Is something else the tide won't wash away." Time cannot fade nor reduce the influence of father on son; "something else" implies many other tangible records and reminiscences that continually recall this. At the same time, the son's inheritance of the father's determination, his resolution to keep sight of the invisible "dotted line," echoes the prophetic remark at the end of "Follower": the Father "will not go away." As Heaney said in commemoration of Lowell, "When a person whom we cherished dies, all that he stood for goes-a-begging, asking us somehow to occupy the space he filled, to assume into our own life values which we admired in his and thereby to conserve his unique energy" ("Robert Lowell" 26). It seems that, in the tough spareness of those few lines, Heaney is assuming the very conciseness and clarity of his father's occasional, and thus treasured, comments. He appears to suggest that the father's marks on the sand, like his own marks of words on paper, transmute the actual. The father's marks also recall the Biblical exoneration of the adulteress, once again combining the memory of the mortal father with the godlike, archetypal image of the Father as judge. In this sense, the "dotted line" could be read as Heaney's hope of his father's ultimate sanction, even approval, of the son's method of "digging," the father having spent his life "writing" his own mute, physical message in the sand.

In *The Redress of Poetry* (1995), Heaney confirms one interpretation of the book's title: "being instrumental in adjusting and correcting imbalances in the world," poetry becomes "an intended intervention into the goings-on of society," a mode of writing "involved with supreme fictions as well as actual conditions" (192). His prose and poetic works treat "poetry as an answer given in terms of . . . its need to go emotionally and artistically 'above the brim,' beyond the conventional bounds" (192). He continues, in this concluding essay, to reflect that poets of Northern Ireland "feel with a special force a need to be true to the negative nature of the evidence and at the same time to show an affirming flame, the need to be both socially responsible and creatively free" (192). This relates directly to Jung's description of an archetype as "a figure—be it daemon, a human being, or a process—that constantly recurs in the course of history and appears wherever creative fantasy is freely expressed" (*CW* 15: 81–82).

In this context, the figure of the poet becomes itself an archetype. "Creative fantasy," in Heaney's case, "is freely expressed" in the recording and mythologizing of his relationship to his father; the consequent image of his "self" creates parallels with the relationship between the individual and Irish society and history, as well as with the relationship between the poet and politics. Through this expression Heaney shows himself to have developed, in Dawson's terms, "a particular kind and degree of self-awareness" implied in "a given point of view" from which Jung's stages of withdrawal of projection can "measure adaptation" (269); in his case this "adaptation" is extensive and creative. As Heaney writes, poems can "act like their society's immune systems, going to attack whatever unhealthy or debilitating forces are at work in the body politic" (*Redress* 114): if his words act as such an immune system, the poet himself acts as one of society's guardians, a kind of father figure.

He becomes a conceiver of archetypes as well as perceiver, a re-creator of archetypes—of wise old men, society's authority figures.

Whatever voice emerges in society is both new and from the past. Its education has its roots in the past: what it chooses from its culture to express was already there. In the present, though, the poet's voice must be forged anew, resisting the cultural tradition in which any "declaration of an emotion immediately made the emotion suspect. . . . [T]he unspoken was the trustworthy and the completely trustworthy exchange was the intuitive one, and the making explicit of the intuitive somehow vitiated it" (Wilmer 78). Whatever troubles his nation politically, the poet holds on to key things, adding that which is less perceptible in prosaic reality but felt through poetic language. As Heaney has suggested, in a radio interview about *The Cure at Troy,* "political writing usually . . . blames a machinery rather than undertakes to examine a psyche. . . . [Rather than a poultice for a wound,] it's more a magic dance performed adjacent to a society in the hope that it would have palliative but not necessarily curative effects." This Jungian perspective reflects a similar literary-critical observation, made by Maud Bodkin, concerning "the nature of the ritual dance. . . . [T]his vivid sensual experience becom[es] the vehicle of a shared imaginative vision of reality. Similarly essential for communication . . . in poetry, is the sensible object created by the artist . . . the sequence of sound . . . that serves as vehicle of a vision, intuition, or emotional understanding, of certain aspects of our common reality" (323). Far from vitiating the intuitive, Heaney's expression of the Father archetype creates a powerful "sequence of sound" that serves, rather, as a vehicle of vision, intuition, and emotional understanding, at the same time enabling him to stand with his father as "a solid man / A pillar to himself and to his trade" ("Crossings," *Seeing Things* 85).

NOTES

1. Heaney is clearly conversant with Jung's psychology and its relevance to art, specifically literature; the poet's cognisance of the relevance of Jungian perspectives to his own poetry confirms the appropriateness of this use of Jungian psychological theory in exploring the meaning and purpose of his poetry. The development of his relationship to myth seems to have come through sensitivity to a numinous quality in the power of language. In his first prose collection, *Preoccupations* (1980), Heaney speaks of "The secret between the words, the binding element . . . a psychic force that is elusive, archaic and only half-apprehended by maker and audience" (186); similarly, Jung refers to "the energy underlying psychic life" and the "archetypes, which are preexistent to consciousness and condition it" (*Memories* 319).

2. "Traditional" here means especially an understanding of the archetypes as collective, transhistorical forms or potentialities within the human psyche, whose actual contents or manifestations (in dream and myth) evolve culturally and historically. The post-Jungian critique of much scholarship of the 1970s and 1980s observed the extent to which authors "essentialized" and "universalized" archetypal symbols, thereby isolating them from historical change and cultural difference. Yet Jung himself, and the best Jungian criticism of any previous decade, manages to avoid such error. In this regard (though admittedly not in others), post-Jungian theory is less a revision than it is a reminder of Jung's own initial premises regarding the origins of archetypes and their historical manifestations in symbols. To the extent that post-Jungian theory represents a more sensitive reading of Jung's texts and often a return to (rather than a divergence from) Jung's own analytic practices, the scope and method of the following analysis are actually quite compatible with post-Jungian criticism.

3. The archetypes inform the sensibilities of the individual through the common experience of human heritage, present before and throughout individual life. As Anthony Stevens has emphasized, they are present not only throughout all aspects of culture but also throughout the essential elements of the natural world, their "manifestations not only reach[ing] upwards to the spiritual heights of religion, art and metaphysics, but also down into the dark realms of organic and inorganic matter" (29).

4. Quotation of the first six lines of "Follower" may help to indicate this point more clearly:

My father worked with a horse-plough, (8)
His shoulders globed like a full sail strung (9)
Between the shafts and the furrow. (8)
The horses strained at his clicking tongue. (9)

An expert. He would set the wing (8)
And fit the bright steel-pointed sock. (8)

5. The full text of the short poem "Nerthus" is as follows:

For beauty, say an ash-fork staked in peat,
Its long grains gathering to the gouged split;
A seasoned, unsleeved taker of the weather
Where kesh and loaning finger out to heather.

WORKS CITED

Bodkin, Maud. *Archetypal Patterns in Poetry*. London: Oxford UP, 1963.

Dawson, Terence. "Jung, Literature, and Literary Criticism." Young-Eisendrath and Dawson 255–80.

English File. BBC Television 2, London. 1991.

Feder, Lillian. *Ancient Myth in Modern Poetry*. Princeton: Princeton UP, 1971.

Glob, P. V. *The Bog People: Iron-Age Man Preserved*. London: Faber, 1969.

Heaney, Seamus. "Artists on Art." *Critical Inquiry* (Spring 1982): 405–14.

———. *The Government of the Tongue*. London: Faber, 1988.

———. *Opened Ground: Poems, 1966–1996*. London: Faber, 1998.

———. *Preoccupations*. London: Faber, 1980.

———. *The Redress of Poetry*. London: Faber, 1995.

———. "Robert Lowell: A Memorial Address." *Agenda* 18.3 (1981): 23–28.

———. *Seeing Things*. London: Faber, 1991.

Jung, C. G. *The Collected Works of C.G. Jung*. Ed. Sir Herbert Read, Michael Fordham, and Gerhard Adler. Trans. R. F. C. Hull. 20 vols. Princeton: Princeton UP, 1953–1991.

———. *Memories, Dreams, Reflections*. 1961. Trans. Richard Winston and Clara Winston. Ed. Aniela Jaffe. New York: Vintage, 1989.

Kaleidoscope: The Cure at Troy. BBC Radio 4, London. 1990.

Langer, Suzanne. *Philosophy in a New Key: A Study in the Symbolism of Reason, Rite, and Art*. Cambridge: Harvard UP, 1942.

Morrison, B. "Seamus Famous: Time to Be Dazzled." *The Independent on Sunday* 19 May 1991.

Russo, Joseph. "A Jungian Analysis of Homer's Odysseus." Young-Eisendrath and Dawson 240–54.

South Bank Show. With Melvyn Bragg. ITV, London. 1991.

Stevens, Anthony. *Archetype: A Natural History of the Self*. London: Routledge, 1982.

Wilmer, C. "Poet of the Month." Interviews from BBC radio 3. Carcanet, 1991.

Young-Eisendrath, Polly, and Terence Dawson, eds. *The Cambridge Companion to Jung*. Cambridge: Cambridge UP, 1997.

"The Sun's Children"

Shadow Work in the Poetry of
LeRoi Jones/Imamu Amiri Baraka

⤸⤳

REBECCA MEACHAM

Beware the evil sun
. . .
turn you black
turn your hair
crawl your eyeballs
rot your teeth.
—LeRoi Jones,
"Hymn for Lanie Poo"

We are the suns children
Black creatures of grace—
—Imamu Amiri Baraka,
"The Nation Is Like Ourselves"

In 1961, when LeRoi Jones wrote "Hymn for Lanie Poo," his use of imagery reflected the psyche of a black man living in white-dominated America, wherein blacks embodied the "negative group projections, the collective shadow" of whites (Zweig and Abrams xx). As a member of this "collective shadow," the writer learned firsthand of its oppressive darkness: his grandfather's store was burned down twice by angry whites, and his father had to flee the South after knocking down a white usher in a movie theater (Hudson 5). Significantly, Jones's earliest published poetry identifies the shadowing power of the "evil sun" with blackness and "rot"—a recognition, in image, of something discarded or dead, as "other," as "a container of evil, [an] enemy of civilization" (Zweig and Abrams xx). Yet, like the "rotten" alchemical state of nigredo, this image of decay is also imbued with the possibility of renewal. Indeed, self-renewal was in process by 1970, when Jones embraced blackness as a force of unification and birth, his self as a cosmic creation full of "grace." Now seeing himself as a child of a life-bestowing (instead of "evil") sun, and renamed Imamu Amiri Baraka, the poet illustrates a newfound comfort in his skin. Jones/Baraka's shift in perspective—from enshadowed rot to sun-child—parallels his shifts in consciousness. In the ten years between "Hymn for Lanie Poo" and "The Nation Is Like Ourselves," Baraka's poetry also grew correspondingly tonal, rhythmic, and ritualistic as he studied mythic Africa and explored his soul. By 1973, his poetry no longer reveals a soul in decay: in a process of shadow-reversal, he urges all black people to self-reclamation, moving from the shadow imposed by whites to the light of self-illumination, to "Be conscious of your life! . . . Rise & Shine Shine Shine" (Baker, *Afrikan Revolution* 2, 5).

What follows is a study of Jones/Baraka's Beat-era and "Black Arts"-era writing through the lens of archetypal psychology. Although Jones/Baraka has written prodigiously in several genres including drama, prose, essay, and autobiography, in this analysis I will focus on the poetry he published between 1961 and 1973, during the time that the writer divorced his white wife and married a black woman. He also operated numerous magazines and presses, founded the Black Arts Repertory Theater/School, and moved from Greenwich Village to Harlem to Newark; he was arrested, tried, and acquitted for his suspected role in the Newark riots of 1967; and he established the African Free School and Spirit House. Since the writer has reinvented his self and writing style mercurially over his lifetime, an examination of his poetic quests for soul should be particularly rich.

Archetypal Analysis and Its Relevance to the African American Psyche

Certainly, the appropriateness of use of archetypal psychology to examine a writer of color is a subject for debate. The fields of psychology and psychoanalysis are sparsely populated by African American professionals and theorists (Adams 37), and there are those who view "psycho-analysis to be unsuitable in a [Black] setting and . . . in need of wide-spread overhaul before . . . [it should be] applied [to African Americans]" (Houston 155). Perhaps the "preponderance of Eurocentric theories of mental illness" has prevented more "Africentric theories" from emerging until only recently (Houston 157). Indeed, for the most part, "not only the collar but also the very skin of these professions have been white" (Adams 37).

However, do "Eurocentric theories" and "white collars" necessarily imply the exclusion of other colors or cultures? If psychical categories are universal, as Jung argued, then ethnic identity should not restrict; moreover, Jung himself wrote about the effects of culture on the psyche in two visits to North Africa. Yet Michael Vannoy Adams illustrates the social limitations of Freud and Jung, as well as the "reductive tendencies" of their theories. For example, Adams reminds us that psychiatrist John E. Lind asserted in the first psychoanalytic journal that a "Negro" was "an individual whose father was a slave and whose grandfather was a cannibal" (qtd. in Adams 125). It is not surprising, then, to read of Jung's casual use of the word "nigger" as well as his bizarre opinions about interracial sexual activity: according to Jung, "the consequence of miscegenation—'a mulatto'—will in all probability be a person of 'bad character' . . . [much as] sexual intercourse between horses and donkeys produces 'mules . . . which have particularly vicious qualities and are not fertile'" (Adams 130). This and other such discomfiting examples might tempt one to write off all applications, literary and otherwise, of Jung's theories as racist: "Farhad Dalal has argued that Jung was a racist in the white-black sense . . . and that therefore contemporary Jungian analysis has a 'racist core'" (Adams 131).

But Adams is careful to distinguish, in an interesting gesture of split-ting, "two Jungs" at work—one who categorized people biologically and another who did so historically. In fact, he credits Jung for repudi-ating "a Eurocentric, judgmental approach to other cultures" (50). And in response to Dalal, Adams writes that "Jungians are under no duress to accept uncritically everything that Jung may have said on the topic of 'race.' They *are* under a scientific and ethical obligation to scrutinize and revise Jungian theory" (131; emphasis in original). Adams concludes that "it is cultural categories, not natural categories like color—ethnic, not 'racial' categories—that provide abundant evidence of significant psychical differences" (12). Here, he is making a key distinction. If concepts of "race" are in themselves "pseudoscientific" and not "real" in a biological sense—if they are, in fact, socially constructed—then there cannot be an organic, or archetypal, foundation for racism. Since strict color categories are not accurate (since "black" and "white" encompass people of multi-hued gradations), not biologically hierarchical (pigmentation does not guarantee superior intellect or athletic prowess), nor inherently opposed (if white is the "opposite" of black, what color is "opposite" of blue?), the very logic of colorism is a "patently false premise" (Adams 17).

Rather, Adams maintains that there is a "psychical construction of reality" in which "the self continuously, projectively typifies the other" (47). This self-other archetype operates on both conscious and unconscious levels and includes "two dimensions, not just one, to the collective: an archetypal (a natural that is a transhistorical, transcultural, transethnic) dimension and a stereotypical (a historical, cultural, ethnic) dimension" (46). In other words, into the self-other archetype of the psyche, we individually place images culled from our environment—stereotypical qualities of race, color, behavior, even tastes in food, which cultures have collected throughout history:

> The unconscious purpose of projective typifications is evidently to diminish uncertainty—and attendant anxiety—in the encounter between the self and other. Such projections are a simplification by which the self . . . reduces the complexities of the other to apparently manageable, or controllable proportions. (Adams 48)

Moreover, these self-protective, simplifying, anxiety-reducing mechanisms establish a sense of self-identity in relation to an Other. In white-dominated America, African Americans have been historically characterized in opposition to, and therefore as a shadow of, the desires, abilities, freedoms, and humanity of whites.

THE ARCHETYPE OF OPPOSITES AND THE COLLECTIVE SHADOW OF WHITE AMERICA

While binaries are often understood as sets of contrasting qualities (anima/animus, flesh/soul), an Africanist paradigm might recast oppositions as a set of movements: a series of gestures between opposite poles, a performance of contrasting rhythms. Brenda Dixon Gottschild explains this dance of opposites:

> In a broad sense, the Africanist aesthetic can be understood as a precept of contrariety, or an encounter of opposites. The conflict inherent in and implied by difference, discord, and irregularity is *encompassed,*

rather than *erased or necessarily resolved.* That this principle is basic to the Africanist world view is manifested in the importance of the crossroads as a symbol of Africanist cultures worldwide. The crossroads is the locus of the coincidence of opposites. Thus, Africanist art forms deal in paradox as a matter of course, with irony following close behind. (13; emphasis added)

Paradox, the author continues, is expressed in African cacophonous or polyrhythmic music and in several dance elements. One of these elements Gottschild calls the "aesthetic of the cool," an attitude that presents "the detached, mask-like face of the drummer or dancer whose body and energy may be working fast, hard, and hot, but whose face remains cool" (16), very different from the "centeredness, control, linearity, and directness" of European aloofness during dance (17). In African dance we see juxtaposition and irony exhibited and controlled in such a way that movements "blend the impossible to create beauty" (Gottschild 15). This is quite different from theories that equate an archetype of opposition with an archetype of hierarchy and reduce all possible outcomes to one: a warlike conflict. Thus, while the archetype of opposition may guide perceptions of the Other, human *responses* aren't automatically (archetypally) driven towards division.

However, the following identities and qualities (pulled from sociology, science, alchemy, art, and popular culture) have been associated with blackness:

- Africa, jungle, ghetto, plantation; watermelon, fried chicken, cotton, razor blade; Sambo, Jim Crow, John Henry, Shine, Mandingo, Jezebel, Uncle Tom, Zip Coon, Mammy; Amos-n-Andy (Riggs)
- spontaneity, revolution, warmth, music, criminality, apelikeness, lethargy, servility, stupidity, cowardness, evil, Thanatos (Hillman, qtd. in Adams 137)
- dirty, evil, night, ugly, deadly, mysterious (Winthrop C. Jordan, qtd. in Adams 20)
- tom-toms, cannibalism, intellectual deficiency, "Sho' good eatin'"; torturer, Satan, sin, the archetype of lowest values (Fanon, qtd. in Adams 166)
- primitive (Jung, qtd. in Adams 66)
- eerie, putrid, depressing, bottomless, rotten, disconnected, lifeless, ash, dung, excrement, vermin, loss, bad luck, rats, bats, spiders, sharks, witches, nadirs, prison, chaos, sickness, divorce, graves, stench, collapse (Bosnak 68–69)

- lazy, frightened, thieving, very potent sexually, scars, generally inferior (but natural rhythms), dope peddlers, pimps, spooks, jibberjabber patme boss (Jones/Baraka, from "Poem for Willie Best" 26; *Afrikan Revolution* 2; and "It's Nation Time" 22)

It follows that the more despicable blackness appears, the more attractive whiteness becomes. Another power of the shadow archetype, then, is its ability to define through contrast: light appears more pure and brilliant when paired, bordered, or outlined by darkness. In this manner, the white American cultural constructions of blackness serve mainly to reinforce and exaggerate Anglo American ideals of whiteness. An apt metaphor for this act of shadow projection and reflection can be found in Ralph Ellison's 1952 novel, *Invisible Man*, which undoubtedly influenced the young Jones/Baraka. In Ellison's work, the young black narrator takes a job at a factory, where he's taught how to mix batches of Optic White paint. To the narrator's surprise, the American government's whitest paint is created by the addition of ten "glistening black drops" to each can of liquid—without blackness, the appearance of sheer whiteness would be impossible. Indeed, after stirring ten black drops into a bucket of white paint, the white factory foreman announces, "'That's paint . . . that'll cover just about anything! . . . White! It's the purest white that can be found'" (Ellison 202).

Yet, in Ellison's metaphor, only ten carefully measured drops of blackness are mixed into Optic White, underscoring the notion that blackness is to be contained, subsumed, and ultimately absorbed by whiteness. Despite—or perhaps because of—the controlled presence of blackness, white power structures maintain the ability to "cover just about anything." Indeed, by emphasizing the dangers of "excessive" or uncontrolled black power, Anglo American leaders have instituted social and political methods of containment—enslavement, segregation, Jim Crow laws—which consequently strengthen the fabric of the collective shadow "bag." As a result, American collective cultural shadowing "prevents the white man from ever seeing the black man as he really is. The white man can see in the black man only those aspects which confirm and justify his own projection and enable it to pass itself off as an outward and genuinely objective condition—which it is not" (Van der Post, qtd. in Adams 144). Thus African Americans have developed a paradoxical consciousness of both object and subject. Through this "double-consciousness," as W. E. B. DuBois wrote in 1903, an African American "ever feels his two-ness" and constantly measures his "soul by the tape of a world that looks on in amused contempt and pity" (38).

Throughout his art and life, Jones/Baraka worked and reworked the feelings of double-ness DuBois describes. Not surprisingly, his course of action has been self-contradictory, multiple, muted, and radical. After embracing his black-in-white cultural paradox by "going white," he separated himself from white American society through reversal, radicalism, and amplification—a process of "going black" that enshadowed and rejected all things white.

JONES/BARAKA'S "NEGRO SICKNESS": THE PATHOLOGY OF "GOING WHITE"

"For the black man there is only one destiny, and it is white," asserted Frantz Fanon in 1952 (12). Years after DuBois first wrote of "two-ness," Fanon discusses how the black psyche remains divided by oppositions:

> Every colonized people—in other words, every people in whose soul an inferiority complex has been created by the death and burial of its local cultural originality—finds itself face to face with . . . the culture of the mother country. The colonized is elevated above his jungle status in proportion to his adoption of the mother culture's standards. He becomes whiter as he renounces his blackness, his jungle. (18)

This act of self-repression Jones/Baraka calls "Negro Sickness," or "how American society convinces the Negro that he is inferior, and he starts conducting his life that way" (qtd. in Hudson 10). When Jones diagnosed this illness in others, he found himself "reacting very quickly to Negroes who talk about 'good hair'" (qtd. in Hudson 10), evident in "Hymn for Lanie Poo," dedicated to Jones's sister:

> my sister has her hair done twice a month
> my sister is a school teacher
> my sister took ballet lessons
> my sister has a fine figure: never diets
> my sister doesn't like to teach in Newark
>   because there are too many colored
> in her classes
>   my sister hates loud shades

These lines show not only "Lanie Poo's" attention to white culture (her hair) and her rejection of her own race ("colored" students and "loud shades") but also Jones's disdain for her response to white culture. His irritation is significant, as is the time in his life when the poem was published (1961). Married to Hettie Cohen (a white Jewish woman) and the father of their two daughters, as well as one of the few black artists in his Greenwich Village social circle, Jones at that time was immersed in a white lifestyle. In this poem he manifests a personal shadow—a contempt for his sister, who like himself, has "gone white."

Adams's term "going white" is used in relation to the British imperialist expression "going black," which equates to "going primitive"; in psychoanalytic terms, Adams adds, it means to regress "to an earlier and lower state" of consciousness (and therefore unconsciousness) (51). For Jones, "going" or "acting" white necessitates a denial or loss of soul or self, as well as cloaking himself in a fabric stitched from stereotypes of white collective ego and black cultural assumptions about whiteness. In "Hymn for Lanie Poo," these associations with whiteness include formal dance training, a love of Tchaikovsky, and a sort of decorum that is decidedly not loud. Of his own intellectual "whitening," Jones/Baraka notes such a dissociation from his self in the early 1960s:

> [M]y reading was, in the main, white people. Europeans, Anglo Americans. So that my ascent towards some ideal intellectual pose was at the same time a trip toward a white-out that I couldn't understand. I was learning and at the same time, unlearning. . . . But that is a tangle of nonself in that for all that. A nonself creation where you become other than you think. Where the harnesses of black life are loosened and you free-float. . . . Imbibing, gobbling, stuffing yourself with reflections of the *other*. (Jones, *Autobiography* 174)

Accordingly, his collections of poetry from 1961 to 1964 feature recurrent images of containment. Here, "Hymn for Lanie Poo" is particularly revealing. Jones opens with an epigraph from Rimbaud, which speaks of falsehood: "*Vous etes de faux Negres.*" He continues this theme in metaphor: "O / these wild trees / will make charming wicker baskets." Instead of appreciating trees (a Jungian symbol of the self) for their majesty and size, they are noted for their unruliness ("wild-assed") and seen only as fodder for more "civilized" charming wicker baskets. Processing trees into baskets requires disintegration of the natural or primitive (trees) to manufacture a decorative home object whose function, as a basket, is to hold or contain; it entails axing, stripping, making bark malleable, and finally fabricating an object that looks nothing like the original. Significantly, the imagined speaker of these lines is a "young black beautiful woman" who, even though Jones may be "putting words in her mouth," speaks with a colonialist affect, reminiscent of the pith-helmeted whites in the jungle who comment in "perfect english" how well the leopard skins and tusks will match their carpets.

The colonialist imagery, in association with themes of containment, shapes the rest of the poem as an African presence increasingly appears in the poet's daily urban life. Through juxtaposition, Jones observes the interplay of archetypal opposites—the effect of a "primitive" / jungle / black soul upon the "civilized"/city/white ego. In section 1, he warns of the "rot" produced by "evil" sun, a metaphor for the shadow projection by white culture, a signified blackness. Just as signified blackness, in a person who has adopted the white collective ego as his ego, becomes shadow, the poem's speakers and unnamed others "dropped / our shadows / onto the beach / and covered them over with sand." This shadow-burial might be read in two ways: that dropping and covering the shadow buries the black self (and its signified blackness) in the whiteness of sand—or, that shedding the white cultural shadow of containment allows the black self to connect with Africa. The speaker paradoxically sits on the "edge of the city" while "hacking open / crocodile skulls / sharpening our teeth" and prays to a female fertility god with "black boobies" and "steatopygia"—the very picture of the Hottentot Venus studied and exhibited by Victorian-era anthropologists.

This "Great Mother"/fertility icon is especially meaningful when contrasted to the poem's final image of motherhood: "Smiling & glad / in the huge and loveless / white-anglo sun / of benevolent *step* / *mother* America" (sec. 7; emphasis added). Here, two archetypal mothers conflict in archetypal opposition—"Mother Africa" who is absent, and the evil, loveless stepmother America, whose sun projects blackness on African Americans and rots them, disintegrating their psyches. In other poems, Jones imagines the stepmother archetype not only as evil with the power to rot, but also as a devouring mother who swallows black souls.

Juxtaposition—in language, in imagery, and in archetype—is the very essence of "Hymn for Lanie Poo" and reflects Jones's psyche at this time. Formally, Baraka's address to his sister echoes African Negritude poet David Diop's address to his brother in "Le Renégat," yet the arrangement of words and spaces on the page draws heavily from American poet Charles Olson's manifesto on "projective verse." At the same time, the poem's speaker is contained by an urban, "civilized" white setting that is overrun by "24 elephants" who "stomp out of the subway / with consecrated hardons." However, trapped in this setting, he must go "Way uptown for Bar B Cue"—a food stereotypically associated with African American culture that is absent from Jones's whitened landscape. A metaphor of black-white colonization is embodied in a white hunter (sec. 2) who "whizzed in at the end of a vine" at a global "coming out party"—and, in a gesture of capture, who seems to become the speaker of the poem. We see this shift in section 2, which juxtaposes the jungle and the city, as well as the adventure-fantasy of jungle hunting with the daily domestic grind:

> Monday, I spent most of the day hunting.
> Knocked off about six, gulped down a cou-
> ple of monkey foreskins, then took in a
> flick. Got to bed early.
>
> Tuesday, same thing all day. (Caught a
> mangy lioness with one tit.) Ate.
> Watched television for awhile. Read the
> paper, then hit the sack.

Here, containment imagery is underscored by Jones's style: the unpredictable drama of hunting in the wild is bounded by the speaker's idioms ("took in a flick," "hit the sack") and domesticated by a things-to-do format. In this manner, Jones's words, as well as the four-line stanzas organized like a desk-planner, enclose and tame the hunt.

This section is ambiguous as to the color or cultural orientation of the speaker: is he ironically playing the white colonial hunter, or the African tribal hunter? Is he "going" white or black? Perhaps, as he was psychologically "divided" at this time, Jones is playing both: a white hunter-adventurer who, amidst civilization, finds no passion in the hunt, *and* a "primitive" African hunter who speaks with citified ennui. Such ambiguity is consistent with Jones's use of paradox—he lives and reconciles (but does not resolve) his opposites. Regardless, common moods emerge: a sense of outsiderness—a lack of a tribe or cultural community, an isolation on the veldt—as well as humor in the situation and the voice ("Christ, I hate ape meat").

Devouring turns to personal anguish when Jones writes "It is a human love / I live inside. . . . But it has no feeling. As the metal, is hot, it is not / given to love" (Jones, "As Agony as Now," *Dead Lecturer* 15). In this image, Jones seems to recognize the increasing strains of his personal life as he prepares for an imminent split from his white wife, children, and friends. Indeed, soon after these poems were published, Jones experienced an event that further heated and forged cultural and psychological barriers:

February 21, 1965, a Sunday. [Hettie] and I and the two girls were at the Eighth Street Bookstore, at a book party. . . . Suddenly, Leroy

McLucas came in. He was weeping. "Malcolm is dead!" . . . I was stunned, shot myself. I felt stupid, ugly, useless. Downtown in my mix-matched family and my maximum leader/teacher shot dead while we bullshitted and pretended. The black core of us huddled there, my wife and family outside that circle. (Jones, *Autobiography* 293)

Cultural conflict metastasized, psychologically, in Jones. As the Civil Rights-era American landscape violently reinforced color-based opposi-tions, Jones's psyche sickened in a manner that coincides with a Jungian model of neurosis: "Psychic sickness occurs when hierarchies and oppo-sitions are rigidly maintained. Such neurotic inflexibility denies the heal-ing deconstructive forces of individuation" (Rowland 23). The death of Malcolm X polarized white and black culture and consequently cast Jones's blackness as even blacker—especially against his white family and colleagues. Such sickness was already in progress in the years before Malcolm X's assassination, when Jones's poetic imagery associates *both* "outside" (white family, white ego) and "circle" or "core" (black cul-ture, black self) with disease: "Flesh / or soul, as corrupt" (Jones, "As Agony," *Dead Lecturer* 16). In image, the poetic speaker's body—specif-ically the flesh—becomes the locus of "Negro" or psychic "sickness":

> And I am frightened
> that the flame of my sickness
> will burn off my face. And leave
> the bones, my stewed black skull,
> and empty cage of failure.
>
> ("I Substitute for the Dead
> Lecturer," *Dead Lecturer* 60)

These lines present the image of the strain of balancing opposites, the pathology of his Negro Sickness, as if through the act of writing the poet is allowing, or forcing, that disease to run its course.

Throughout the collections *The Dead Lecturer* (1964) and *Preface to a Twenty Volume Suicide Note* (1961) are recurrent images (often alchemical images) of dehumanization, disembodiment, death, and absence of soul. Jones's equation of "going white" with being consumed is analogous to a moment in *Invisible Man:* the narrator is advised by his dying grandfather to "live with your head in the lion's mouth . . . overcome [whites] with yeses, undermine 'em with grins . . . let 'em swoller you til they vomit or bust wide open" (Ellison 16). Ellison's character imagines white culture consuming blacks until *white* culture sickens and dies. In Jones's imagery, however, the speaker who lives with his head in the lion's mouth is beheaded, the lion sated. Devoured, the poetic speaker is thus "locked in with dull memories & self hate & the terrible disorder of a young man," left with only a "pitiful shadow of myself" (Jones, "The Turncoat," *Preface* 26). Even this shadow seems to evaporate: "When they say, 'It is Roi / who is dead?' I wonder / who will they mean?" ("The Liar," *Dead Lecturer* 79).

Embracing the Collective Shadow— Making Soul through Reversal

Jones's evaporation of self in the heat of a white American sun is accompanied by recurrent images of containment, rot, death, "a many starred heaven with no fixed reference points" (Bosnak 70), loss, and absence. In this way it is analogous to the alchemical state of nigredo, which, as Robert Bosnak writes, is often associated with "hated racial groups"; thus it is no surprise that the psyche of an enshadowed African American male would be influenced by this alchemical realm and perhaps even inhabit it. But according to Bosnak, "the nigredo is the initial phase of *every* process in which a transformation of form takes place. . . . In this state of nigredo, one feels as though the whole world is falling apart. . . . [D]eath is the only reality" (63). Thus, after being consumed with Negro Sickness—an attempt to repress a black self into shadow and adopt the white cultural ego—Jones dies, metaphorically. At the same time, throughout these poems of the early 1960s occur images of reversal, of movement, and of flight—images of the alchemical albedo. In this manner, it is as if Jones is illuminating his identity conflicts in imagery like "a dark night by a rising moon" (Jung qtd. in Bosnak 64), reflecting upon his life, and suffering the tension of another archetypal opposition: change versus complacency. As he had done so often before—dropping out of Rutgers for Howard, then leaving Howard for Bohemian life, then suddenly enlisting in the Air Force, then moving to the Village—Jones chose change.

Albedo themes are clear in Jones's "The Turncoat": its title not only implies a turn towards something and away from something else but also focuses attention on the poet's cloak of whiteness. The opening lines express albedo imagery of reflection and slipperiness—"The steel fibrous slant & ribboned glint / of water. The Sea. Even my secret speech is moist / with it"—and the poem reflects on the "terrible disorder of a young man." The opening stanza metaphorically examines his state of nigredo, his breakdown; from there he moves "slowly. My cape spread stiff . . . in the first night wind off the Hudson" and "glide[s] down" for

a better look at the "pitiful" self he's become. The mood of these stanzas is "pensive . . . introverted," infused with "an attitude that tolerates
the state of disintegration," and, using a "reflective patchwork-quilt
consciousness," the poet "returns to a world of darkness" (Bosnak 71).

Although similar albedo imagery threads many of Jones's poems,
the 1961 poem "The Turncoat" implies a clear progression in consciousness as the mood brightens. For example, in the third stanza, after
asking, "How can it mean anything?" and noting the "wet smells coming in," a reversal of the white-oppressive-burning-sun imagery is
offered: "The blind still / up to admit a sun that no longer exists." In a
gesture of hope in Jones's poetic world, night begins to form—a comfort
and relief after the evaporating, shadowing power of the sun. Furthermore, the approach of night allows Jones to "dream"—a relative rarity
in his poetry. In an even rarer expression of spiritual freedom, Jones
dreams of "Pure flight. Pure fantasy." Yet this psychic soaring isn't total
or complete; it is still unbalanced, as the poem ends simply, "Lean."

From leaning and flying, Jones finds a psychological "position for
myself: to move" in "The Dance" (*Dead Lecturer* 71). Here Jones
speaks of a friend's poems that are "full of what we called / so long for
you to be. A / dance," a "bright elegance / the sad meat of the body /
made." Jones yearns for "Some gesture, that / if we became, for one
blank moment, / would turn us / into creatures of rhythm," and this
compression of self and ego into pure movement, specifically dance, is
significant. As the mythic Orpheus reanimates his love through song,
Jones wishes to re-create himself—and love for himself—through dance.
This is a variation upon the Orphic therapy espoused by Hillman and
others, which encourages the de-literalizing of bodily pain and encourages creative, artistic "image work." In an Africanist twist, the body and
mind collaborate in soul making. While the speaker desires "the time of
thought," he wants to be

> sung. I want
> all my bones and meat hummed
> against thick floating
> winter sky. I want myself
> as dance. As what I am
> given love, or time, or space
> to feel myself

The speaker thus equates movement with self-creation and re-invention.
Similarly, of the transformative power of ritual Yoruban dance, an
Osugbo drummer says:

> [T]here is a belief . . . that we are reborning ourselves. . . . At every ritual, we are becoming new because we have something to reflect upon. We have something to contemplate during the journey . . . after the journey. Our brains become sharper. We become new to the world. (Drewal 37)

Thus, in an archetypal rite of passage, Jones's imagery is analogous to the ritual "reborning" of African orature. But since the poet is alienated from black culture, he must create the ritual for transformation as he must "create / myself." In the Yoruban gesture of involving the audience in performances, Jones encourages the reader to join him in soul making: "And let you, whoever / sits now breathing on my words / create a self of your own. One / that will love me." Jones's final lines are a plea for acceptance and unconditional love from an outside audience—a love undivided, which transcends oppositions.

In the mid-1960s, Jones begins his "dance" from the collective to the personal, from white-ego to black-self. To use a Jonesian metaphor, the author attempts to turn a "charming wicker basket" back into a "wild-ass tree," by—to use Ken Wilber's terms—"re-owning aspects of ourselves that we had previously alienated" (Wilber 275). The poet treated his Negro Sickness in important ways: he moved out of the Village, away from his wife and family, to Harlem; he converted to the Kewaida sect of the Muslim faith and changed his name; additionally, he embraced the teachings of Malcolm X because, as he has mentioned on numerous occasions, he was "not non-violent." Such life changes are made manifest in his 1969 collection *Black Magic,* when the poet redefines his art and his audience as "Black Art":

> We want a black poem. And a
> Black World.
> Let the world be a Black Poem
> And Let All Black People Speak This Poem
> Silently
> or LOUD
>
> (Jones, "Black Art," *LeRoi* 220)

Throughout *Black Magic,* "going black" entails erasing the line between politics and art and issuing, in verse, a call to unity and action: "Calling all black people, man woman child / Wherever you are, calling you, urgent, come in" ("SOS," *LeRoi* 218). At the same time he founded local help-houses and schools. In his poetry of 1970, he encourages all blacks to take responsibility for their selves: "you need to experience better times negro. . . . We want to see you again as ruler of your own space. . . . Dance on to freedom. . . . Sing about your pure movement / in space / Grow" (Jones, "Sermon for Our Maturity," *It's Nation Time* 15, 16); "Time to get / together / time to be one strong fast black energy space" ("It's Nation Time," *It's Nation Time* 21). The most direct appeal Jones/Baraka makes to blacks to "take responsibility" for their own shadows comes in 1973's *Afrikan Revolution,* which reads like a how-to manual of consciousness:

> Afro Americans Be
> CONSCIOUS
> You know you can run your own life.
> 　. . .
> Meet once a week. Talk about how to get
> more money, how to get educated, how
> to have scientists for children rather than
> junkies. How to kill the roaches. How to
> stop the toilet from stinking. How to get a
> better job. Once a week. Start NOW.
> How to dress better. How to read.
> How to live longer. How to be respected.
> Meet once a week. Once a week.

However, as Jones/Baraka imagines pride and respect for black audiences, he lashes out violently against whites. Wilber says this phase of shadow "reverse[s] the direction of the projection itself and gently do[es] unto others what we have heretofore been unmercifully doing to ourselves. . . . Thus, 'The world rejects me' freely translates into 'I reject, at least this moment, the whole damn world!'" (275). For Jones/Baraka, this reversal of energy resulted in a heightened sense of opposition—and instead of "embracing the opposites" in juxtaposition, he wrote and spoke intolerantly of whites: "It was a war for us. A war of liberation. . . . For me the rebellion was a cleansing fire" (Jones, *Autobiography* 375). To apply Wilber's argument, it is as if Jones began with "America rejects me as a black man" and reversed this to "STOP OBSTRUCTING US EUROPEANS! . . . America must change or be destroyed" (Baraka, *Afrikan Revolution*). And as Wilber suggests that one should start viewing life as one's shadow might view the world— "Simply assume exactly the opposite of whatever you consciously desire, like, feel, want, intend, or believe" (276)—Jones did precisely this: "I reasoned what must be consumed is all of my contradictions to revolution. My individualism and randomness, my Western, white addictions, my Negro intellectualism" (*Autobiography* 375).

Jones/Baraka's shadow-reversal phase resounds through his poetry and expresses, in image, his black self's desires for power, mayhem, and reversal of the social order—chaos to usurp the oppressive white collective ego:

> Run up and down Broad Street, niggers, take the shit you want. Take their lives if need be, but get what you want you need. . . . Our brothers are moving all over, smashing at jellywhite faces. We must make our own World man, our own world, and we can not do this unless the white man is dead. Let's get together and kill him my man, let's get to gather the fruit of the sun. (Jones, "Black People!" *LeRoi* 224)

Such violent opposition began while Jones/Baraka was still living in the Village, yet he could not express it then. In his autobiography, he writes of this irony: "I was married to a white woman; I still had many white friends. . . . But I felt justified in talking about the horrible bullshit that white people had put on the world" (285). As he began his reversal, cultural oppositions functioned in paradoxical motion within the whole of Jones/Baraka's psyche—like an African drummer, the black enshadowed part of the poet's psyche trembled with furious anti-white sentiment, while the father-husband-friend wore "the mask of the cool" (Gottschild 16).

As the reversal process progressed for Jones/Baraka, owning his self created a hostile, anti-white, even puerile identity that acted in fury, and he "could only thrash out at any white person" (*Autobiography* 285), evoking Robert Bly's shadow-bag metaphor:

> The story says that when we put a part of ourselves in the bag, it regresses. It devolves toward barbarism. Suppose a young man seals a bag at twenty and then waits fifteen or twenty years before he opens it again. What will he find? Sadly, the sexuality, the wildness, the impulsiveness, the anger, the freedom he put in have all regressed; they are not only primitive in mood, they are hostile to the person who opens the bag. (Bly 7)

When the contents of Jones/Baraka's bag were released (or forced their way out), not only did the contents rebel, they inspired the poet to call for violent retaliation: "Violence is, I think, the only way [establishing consciousness and the rediscovery of one's self] is going to come about. The European sees no need for real change. . . . There is no way in the world you can tell me the European is going to change this society voluntarily" (Clarke 11). In this climate of violence, Baraka's incorporation of politics with art invited unintended audiences: for example, though

not directly involved in the action, the writer was arrested for his proximity to a 1967 riot in Newark, the trial for which was complicated by
the concurrent publication of "Black People!" (above), cited as evidence
by the judge (Hudson 29). Jones/Baraka identified the division between
art and politics as a false binary, a false opposition: "There is no such
thing as Art and Politics, there is only life. . . . If the artist is the raised
consciousness, then all that he touches, all that impinges on his consciousness, must be raised. . . . THE LARGEST WORK OF ART IS THE
WORLD ITSELF!" (Jones, "Surviving" n.p.). Paradoxically, while committed to erasing barriers between self and community, art and world,
Jones/Baraka fiercely maintains all divisions between white and black,
enlisting that divisional energy to help smash his "whitened" ego:

> I guess during this period, I got the reputation of being a snarling,
> white-hating madman. There was some truth to it, because I was
> struggling to be born, to break out from the shell I could instinctively
> sense surrounded my own dash for freedom. I guess I was in a frenzy,
> trying to get my feet solidly on the ground of reality. (Jones, *Autobi-
> ography* 286)

Since there were few positive, human, complex images of blacks available for self-identification, Jones/Baraka amplified his soul in the image
of mythic Mother Africa to create a new self from the shreds of a negative American shadow projection.

AMPLIFICATION AND SOUL MAKING:
AFRICAN POETIC FORMS AND IMAGERY

In a 1968 interview with Austin Clarke, Jones/Baraka describes his newfound Afrocentrism as a move to "reacquaint . . . with our origin. . . .
The strongest part of us is what made us Egypt. Is what made us Ghana.
Is what made us Timbuctoo. That was the noblest part of our lives"
(Clarke 11). As Jones explored mythic and historical sources of power,
he transformed into Baraka, and his poetic imagery reflected his growing sense of the cosmos, expanding from urban and psychological landscapes to encompass the universe itself. As we see in "Sermon for Our
Maturity," Baraka has assumed a new galactic vantage point that allows
him to "bring back and feed on the new images":

> There is no connective fabric to the universe
> stronger than the atomic magnetism of
> spiritual love

> There is only the lover, as a compact
> universe, in constant motion
> The planets are in constant prayer
> The sun is the God they pray to
> We are the suns children
> Black creatures of grace—

Throughout this poem, Baraka speaks panoramically: "celestial alti-
tudes," "a star and a life sign," "Venus," "angelic definition," "clouds,"
"the serpent of unknowing," "planets in constant prayer," "atomic
magnetism," "flying planes of life," "a compact universe," "hurri-
canes," "Earth men and Earth songs," "spiritual love," and "space
lover." Consistent in all of these images is enormous scope—a sharp
contrast to the containment imagery (metal encasements, skulls, cloaks,
wicker baskets, flesh enclosures, devouring earth, serpents, and mothers)
of earlier work. Clearly, the poet's soul-work is boundless. Similarly
transcending boundaries is the white-evaporating-sun, which now creates graceful black "children." This sun no longer serves "whites-only,"
and Baraka delights in his newfound self as its child. In seeking a new
consciousness, Baraka has transcended the cultural and moved beyond
the planetary; from the tentative steps of "The Dance" and "The Turncoat," he has launched into "pure flight."

There are more literal representations of Africa in Baraka's later
work. In the same poem, for example, the speaker asks praise for
"ancestors thru whom / you came to this planet / attached to a chord
from beginning / to now" in direct reference to African origins. Then he
discusses "seven tones of the scale"; should anyone question this reference to the doctrine of Kawaida, Baraka explains (and numbers, and
underlines, and capitalizes) at the end of the poem:

> (1) *DIVINE*
>   is name We give you
> (2) *GRACE*
>   is name we give you
> (3) *MESSENGER*
>   we call you.
> ("Sermon for Our Maturity")

Abandoning metaphor and imagery, Baraka sermonizes. His new self
seems interested only in the dogmatic and the missionary, to the point of
issuing directives to his imagined "followers":

No more Poverty!
No more dirty ragged black people, cept from hard work
to beautify + energize a world we help create
Death to Backward Powers
. . .

No more Europeans in penthouses & colored people in tents
with no houses.

(*Afrikan Revolution*)

These commands become even more specific when "enemies" and victims are named: "Nixon is a sick thief why does he / remain alive? who is in charge of killing him? Why is it Cabral, Lumumba, Nkrumah, Moumie / Malcom, Dr. King, Mondlane, Mark Essex, all can / be killed by criminals & criminals are not / hung from bridges?" (*Afrikan Revolution*). In the same way that the un-bagged shadow releases stunted but powerful emotions, Baraka's poetry here is a rant, a political statement, a scream. "Interpretation" here is nearly impossible as there is no nuance, no real ambiguity, perhaps because the poet's new self has assumed a righteousness that equates to a "totality of blackness"—a singular, mythical-historical self-perspective uninterested in color gradations, hues, or variation. From this perspective, "we are all the same, all the blackness from one black allah," and as such, "Christ was black / Krishna was black shango was black" ("It's Nation Time"). In this way, Baraka mixes his own "Optic Black" paint and uses it to cover just about anything, deliberately contrasting his earlier, "whitened" work.

In an attempt to shape a self in analogy to African-oriented content, Baraka's later poetry is informed by a ritual, performative sensibility. Such departures from Anglo American culture can be seen in the poet's replacement of "perfect english" ("Hymn") with American black vernacular: "you . . . *is* the nigger . . . like James Brown *say*"; "we *waiting*," "we heard you *was* outside cairo" ("The Nation Is Like Ourselves" 10; emphasis added). But more significantly, Baraka's words evoke chant and African vocables:

Ommmmmm Mane Padme Hummmmmmmmmm
Ooshoobee dooo beee
Ashadu an la Illaha Illaha
Ooshoobee dooo beee

("Sermon")

In another departure from his earlier style, he uses rhyme and repetition:

> *We want* you to feel it *too*
> *We want* you to know its *you*
> *We in* the mountains all in the *air*
> *We want* to be all over every*where*
> ("Sermon"; emphasis added)

The use of paralanguage also dramatically contrasts his earlier work; here, lines abound with underlining and capital letters. In his Black Arts poetry, Baraka imbues each line with percussive and vocal force—an effort, perhaps, to create in text the physical energy of African performance art.

The ritual-performance qualities are further heightened through the poet's use of stage directions: "Hey aheeee (soft) / He ahhheeee (loud)" ("It's Nation Time"). Again, as in "The Dance," he situates identity and ethnic self-creation in the body, made manifest by the performance of the reader. Should the reader be someone other than Baraka, he or she is enlisted in the performance of the piece by "hearing" or reading aloud the chant of rhyme, the pitch of capitalization and the drum of underlining. Indeed, Jones/Baraka is said to read his own work with "changes in pitch and intonation, creating the effect of different speakers in different moods, and he makes his body a complement or extension of his voice" (Hudson 138). Just as Baraka refuses to delineate borders between art and activism, page and stage, he rejects an opposition of mind and body. Rather, using a modal, paradoxical, African sensibility, he analogizes sound to image, which combine with universal elements to resonate:

> Art is a high-voltage culture-reflect. Poetry the mode of thought trying to spiritualize itself. Sound-rhythm (image) in imitation of the *elementals* of the universe. So it digs deeper, goes to, beyond (the edge of "meaning," re-creates language feeling) to bring us closer to these elementals, beyond where the "intellect" reaches. (qtd. in Hudson 124)

Overall, Hillman reminds us, ritual promotes cultural and individual healing by "subduing, sublimating, supplanting raw violence" (Capen 5); thus Baraka's ritual of poetry subdues through image what would be fatal otherwise.

As the mythic-historical-cultural Africa guides the soul making of Jones/Baraka, the poet compresses his once-metaphorical formal imagery into a performative chant. Upon this Africanist period in his life, Baraka now reflects:

The solution is not to become the enemy in blackface, that's what one of the black intellectual's problems was in the first place. And even hating whites . . . might seem justifiable, but it is still a supremacy game. *The solution is revolution.* We thought that then, but didn't understand what it meant, really. We thought it meant killing white folks. But it is a system that's got to be killed and it's even twisted some blacks. It's hurt all of us. (Jones, *Autobiography* 458)

Surely, one would think, such mercurial energy would fade as Baraka matured, and, although the poet remains a shape-shifter of sorts, his archetype of opposition becomes imagined not in terms of color but in terms of class. Indeed, in his *Autobiography,* Jones/Baraka recognizes that his late 1970s image-work was knit from a "mythical blackness . . . pumped up full of the hopes and desires of a people, but also the delusions and illusions of a rather narrow sector among the people" (459). In other words, just as his Negro Sickness was a response to a white cultural projection, his reversed, new self was another type of projection—of mythic blackness, of amplification—that, in a total inversion, cast whites in shadow.

But through amplification—a journey into the mythic—Jones/Baraka has emerged with a unique and individual sense of self. Not surprisingly, he has recently written that his soul making is still in process—that there is more room for juxtaposition, for individuation, for growth, and for love between him and his wife, Amina:

Despite it all, I have already survived, living not completely quietly, in fact still full of animation and almost endless energy. Still very much on the case of the place trying to turn it around and unwilling to take no for an answer. Then that is the sharp laughter in me that you hear. . . . [Amina and I] will not be taken out easily. In fact, we are still growing, getting stronger and more knowledgeable . . . with a crowd of little ones surrounding us . . . listening for instructions. . . . Consider the rightness and strength of that, the easy effortless beauty. We are alive! Alive and conscious and in love! (*Autobiography* 465)

Works Cited

Adams, Michael Vannoy. *The Multicultural Imagination: "Race," Color and the Unconscious.* London: Routledge, 1996.

Baraka, Imamu Amiri. [LeRoi Jones]. *Afrikan Revolution.* Newark: Jihad, 1973.

Bly, Robert. "The Long Bag We Drag Behind Us." Zweig and Abrams 6–12.

Bosnak, Robert. *A Little Course in Dreams*. Boston: Shambala, 1988.

Capen, Stephen. Interview with James Hillman. *Worldmind* 25 October 1995, 13 March 1998. <http://www.worldmind.com/Cannon/Culture/Interviews/hill1x2.html>.

Clarke, Austin. "The Mind and Faith of Black Power." *Toronto Daily Star* 20 Jan 1968: 11+.

Drewal, Margaret Thompson. *Yoruba Ritual: Performers, Play, Agency*. Bloomington: Indiana UP, 1992.

DuBois, W. E. B. *The Souls of Black Folk*. 1903. Ed. and with intro. by David W. Blight and Robert Gooding-Williams. Boston: Bedford Books, 1997.

Ellison, Ralph. *Invisible Man*. 1952. New York: Vintage, 1989.

Fanon, Frantz. *Black Skin, White Masks*. New York: Grove, 1967.

Gottschild, Brenda Dixon. *Digging the Africanist Presence in American Performance*. Westport: Greenwood, 1994.

Hillman, James. *Archetypal Psychology*. Woodstock: Spring, 1983.

———. *Oedipus Variations*. With Karl Kerenyi. Woodstock: Spring, 1990.

Houston, Lawrence. *Psychological Principles and the Black Experience*. Boston: U Press of America, 1990.

Hudson, Theodore R. *From LeRoi Jones to Amiri Baraka: The Literary Works*. Durham: Duke UP, 1973.

Jones, LeRoi. *The Autobiography of LeRoi Jones*. Chicago: Lawrence Hill, 1984, 1997.

———. *The Dead Lecturer*. New York: Grove, 1964.

———. *It's Nation Time*. Chicago: Third World Press, 1970.

———. *The LeRoi Jones/Amiri Baraka Reader*. Ed. William J. Harris, with Amiri Baraka. New York: Thunder's Mouth, 2000.

———. *Preface to a Twenty Volume Suicide Note*. New York: Totem, 1961.

———. "Surviving the Reign of the Beasts." *The New York Times Sunday Ed.* 16 Nov 1969: 1+.

Lorde, Audre. "America's Outsiders." Zweig and Abrams 211–14.

Riggs, Marlon. *Ethnic Notions* (video recording). Presented by California Newsreel. Produced, written, and directed by Marlon Riggs. Edited by Deborah Hoffman. 1986.

Rowland, Susan. *C. G. Jung and Literary Theory: The Challenge from Fiction*. New York: St. Martin's, 1999.

Wilber, Ken. "Taking Responsibility for Your Shadow." Zweig and Abrams 273–79.

Zweig, Connie, and Jeremiah Abrams. "Introduction: The Shadow Side of Everyday Life." Zweig and Abrams xvi–xxv.

———. "Introduction" (Part Seven). Zweig and Abrams 164–70.

———, ed. *Meeting the Shadow*. New York: Putnam, 1991.

Sharing a Shadow

The Image of the Shrouded Stranger in the
Works of Jack Kerouac and Allen Ginsberg

༄

JAMES T. JONES

Jung conceived of the attempt to know the shadow as "a moral problem that challenges the whole ego-personality" ("Shadow" 8), and the casting of this abstract moral problem in concrete terms has historically been the province of poets, novelists, and dramatists. By examining literature as a psychic process, we gain insight into the way the "relative evil" of the personal shadow is transformed into the "absolute evil" of a verbal icon. One way to understand the relationship between the personal images of dreams and imaginative fantasies and the imagery of literary symbolism is to view literature humanistically. Its psychological function is, in part, both to reveal the connections between personal motivations and social movements and to call attention to the process by which an individual comes to recognize those connections.

To illustrate how the making of literature bears on our understanding of the shadow, I will contrast the attempts of two postmodern American authors, Allen Ginsberg and Jack Kerouac—the first a confessional poet, the second an autobiographical novelist—to know their shadows in both their personal and archetypal dimensions and to represent this knowledge in literary images. I chose these two writers in part because of their close friendship in the late 1940s and in part because of the mutual influence obvious in their works, but mainly because of the unusual circumstance that their shadows appeared to them in the same form in their dreams: that of the Shrouded Stranger.

At the end of a 1946 radio broadcast, Jung asked a (perhaps rhetorical) question that could have been posed to the entire generation of postwar writers: "The destructive power of our weapons has increased beyond all measure, and this forces a psychological question on mankind: Is the mental and moral condition of the men who decide on the use of these weapons equal to the enormity of the possible consequences?" ("Fight" 226). In a lecture delivered less than two years after this broadcast, he insisted that the contents of the shadow, unlike the other archetypes, "can in large measure be inferred from the contents of the personal unconscious" ("Shadow" 8). The moral condition of the world's leaders, therefore, lies partly in their ability to recognize the personal shadow in their weapons of mass destruction. Many artists undertook to show them the way. Both Ginsberg and Kerouac spent years trying to respond artistically to the destruction of World War II and to the threat of nuclear holocaust. Ginsberg responded in such notable works as the title poem of his 1970s collection *Plutonian Ode* and in late works such as his operatic collaboration with Philip Glass, *Hydrogen Jukebox;* Kerouac in his virtual elimination of violence from the texts of his thirteen autobiographical novels. But the road to their respective treatments began for both writers in New York City in the late 1940s with an exploration of the shadow.

Go Moan for Man, a film about Jack Kerouac released in February 2000 which one critic has dubbed "the definitive Kerouac documentary," begins and ends with the image of an old man, hooded and cloaked and carrying a staff, walking through a desert. (See figure 3.) Though most readers of Kerouac will recognize this figure as a presence (rather than an actual character) from his most famous novel, *On the Road,* they would probably not accord it the status of "the most essential image in Kerouac," the characterization given it by Doug Sharples, who wrote and directed the film. In May 2000, I interviewed Sharples at the Real Films studio in Wakonda, South Dakota. In his very first reading of *On the Road* in the late 1950s, Sharples recognized a numinous quality in the image Kerouac named "the Shrouded Stranger." Indeed, as a child growing up in Clinton, Iowa, in the early 1950s, he had had a vision of an old man in a white beard and robes. He also frequently daydreamed that he himself was a bearded prophet. Much later, when he came to make his thesis film in graduate school in the late 1960s, he found himself transforming his childhood visions into the character of a psychopath who pursues the protagonist of the story with a note. In 1992, as he studied the footage he had been shooting for the

FIGURE 3. Three images of the Shrouded Traveler from *Go Moan for Man.*

Kerouac film for a decade, the image of the Shrouded Stranger still haunted Sharples. It commended itself as the most appropriate image around which to organize the wealth of information about the Beat novelist's life and works. Sharples's wife, Judi, who produced *Go Moan for Man* and recorded its soundtrack, also found that the Shrouded Stranger somehow embodied her feelings of alienation in the late 1960s.

The scenes in the film in which the Shrouded Stranger appears were shot in 1995 in the Badlands of western South Dakota. As the Sharpleses began to shoot, Judi broke her ankle and had to be taken back to civilization. When Doug finally began to film the scenes the following day without her, a fierce storm blew in across the plains. The actor who plays the Shrouded Stranger, Steve Marsden, also plays a related character called Zacatecan Jack; he uses the same walking stick for both parts. On his way home from the location, Marsden was involved in a minor auto accident. These synchronicities confirmed in the minds of all three participants the power of Kerouac's image.

The Shrouded Stranger originally appeared in a dream Kerouac had in 1945, after his father had been diagnosed with stomach cancer. The novelist first described this dream in a 1949 letter to his Denver friend Ed White ("Letters" 127–28). Six months previous to this letter, however, he also told White that he and another friend, Neal Cassady, had created "a myth out of our dead fathers" ("Letters" 119). (Coincidentally, Jung also associated his personal shadow with his father [*Memories* 218].) This connection, as well as the timing of the occurrence of the dream, suggests that the Shrouded Stranger is at once the personification of death and a representation of Kerouac's father, who died in April 1946 with Jack in their house in Queens. In the later letter to White, Kerouac describes the image:

> This is a concept stemming from a dream I had of Jerusalem and Arabia long ago. . . . Traveling by dusty road in the white desert (where some men walk in satisfaction and drink up dust, while I stagger and look for soft trees, the Oasis), traveling from Arabia to the Protective City, I saw that I was being inexorably pursued by a Hooded Wayfarer without a Name, who carried a Stave, and slowly occupied and traversed the plain behind me, sending up a shroud of dust slowly. I don't know how I knew he was following me but I thought if I could make it to the Protective City before he caught up with me, I'd be safe. As much as I hurried and staggered and ran, he, sauntering, kept catching up slowly—or if not sauntering, it was a kind of shrouded movement on the plain he made. It was out of the question: I knew I was doomed. So I went to waylay him in a house at the side of the road, with a rifle that became a rubber toy as he drew nearer. ("Letters" 127–28)

Kerouac himself offered two explanations of the dream image. First, he speculated, "it was one's own self merely wearing a shroud" ("Letters" 128), indicating that life is an entrance of the soul into light between two periods of darkness. Further, explaining the trance-like affect of the dream, Kerouac asserted that "there is another world . . . the world which appears to us from out of our own shrouded existence which was given in darkness" ("Letters" 128). Recognizing that the details of the dream warranted further investigation, Kerouac concluded that the image of the Shrouded Stranger "is the most serious matter I can think of" ("Letters" 128).

On his first trip west, Sal Paradise, the protagonist of Kerouac's *On the Road,* attends a performance of Beethoven's *Fidelio* in Central City, Colorado. Late in the night, standing "on the roof of America" and looking out "eastward over the Plains" toward his past and place of origin, Sal imagines that "somewhere an old man with white hair was probably walking toward us with the Word, and would arrive any minute and make us silent" (*On the Road* 55). On the way home several months later, he meets "the Ghost of the Susquehanna," "a shriveled old man with a satchel," who confuses his directions and leads Sal seven miles back west along the "terrifying river" (103). But the Ghost, with his bobbing little white bag, teaches Sal that "there is a wilderness in the East," as well (105).

Just prior to his second trip west, Sal remarks that "a strange thing began to haunt me," but he can't recall whether he has forgotten "a real decision or just a thought." In any case, he associates this haunted feeling with the Shrouded Stranger. As he explains, "Carlo Marx [the Allen Ginsberg character in *On the Road*] and I once sat down together, knee to knee, in two chairs, facing, and I told him a dream I had about a strange Arabian figure that was pursuing me across the desert, that I tried to avoid; that finally overtook me just before I reached the Protective City" (*On the Road* 124). Sal rejects his own initial analysis that the Shrouded Stranger is himself, in favor of an anagogic interpretation: the Stranger is death, trying to catch him before he reaches heaven. Dean Moriarty, the antagonist in the novel, however, "instantly recognized it as the mere simple longing for pure death" (124). Dean's Freudian diagnosis is that Sal has a death wish.

On the way south, Sal and Dean and their two companions pick up Hyman Solomon, a modern wandering Jew, who "had found the real Torah where it belonged, in the wilderness" (*On the Road* 137). They drop him off in Testament, Virginia. West of New Orleans, as their journey continues, they pass "a Negro man in a white shirt walking along with his arms upspread to the inky firmament. He must have been praying or calling down a curse" (157). After they reach San Francisco, Sal has a vision of a past life in England in which his ghostly mother rejects him with these words: "'Depart! Do not haunt my soul; I have done well forgetting you. Reopen no old wounds'" (173).

On the fourth trip described in *On the Road,* just after the companions leave Denver, Sal Paradise recalls the spirit he had envisioned two years earlier from the mountainside in Central City: "Far up in the purple shades of the rock there was someone walking, walking, but we could not see; maybe that old man with the white hair I had sensed years ago up in the peaks. Zacatecan Jack. But he was coming closer to me, if only ever just behind" (*On the Road* 268). Though the Shrouded Stranger has himself receded into the distant past, he now bears a name—ironically, the novelist's first name—and is associated with Mexico, where Dean and Sal are now bound along with their young protégé, Stan Shepard. In Mexico Sal has a nighttime apparition of "a wild horse, white as a ghost . . . white as snow and immense and almost phosphorescent" (295). This pookah, or animal spirit, narrowly misses stepping on Dean's head. "What was this horse?" Sal asks himself. "What myth and ghost, what spirit?" (296).

As these related numinous images suggest, the Shrouded Stranger pervades *On the Road.* In the larger body of Kerouac's writing the presence of the shadow creates a sense that his life was haunted—first by the ghost of his brother, Gerard, who died in childhood when Jack was only four, and twenty years later by the death of his father—an archetypal quality that resonates with readers. In *Visions of Cody,* for example, the experimental sequel to *On the Road,* an unidentified narrator relating Kerouac's childhood memories says, "The shroudy stranger is my brother" (271). In *Doctor Sax,* the Gothic novel of childhood that Kerouac wrote immediately after *On the Road* and *Visions of Cody,* the young Jackie Duluoz dons a sort of shroud himself and terrorizes his playmates in the guise of the Black Thief, foreshadowing the title character. Doctor Sax, himself a version of the Shadow, a popular pulp fiction and radio superhero of the 1930s, appears mysteriously caped to lead his young charge in an assault on the evil occupants of a local castle. In the present context, *Doctor Sax,* the novel, may be seen as Kerouac's attempt to neutralize the image of the Shrouded Stranger, to make it friendly without detracting from its numinous quality. In a much later novel, *Desolation Angels,* however, even Mt. Hozomeen, a peak near where Kerouac spent a summer as a fire lookout, seems more threatening because of its shrouded aspect.

Some of the content of the Shrouded Stranger is transparently autobiographical. Kerouac, who was raised by a devout French-American

Catholic mother, conceived of life as a spiritual sojourn, so the image of a diabolical figure trying to prevent his entrance into heaven is quite traditional. In addition, at about the same time as he recorded his initial dream of the Shrouded Stranger, Kerouac began the travels around America that formed the basis for *On the Road*. Sal's interpretation of the image that it represents himself is literally true for the author. In the 1940s and 1950s Kerouac continually vacillated between the social excitement of cities such as New York, Denver, San Francisco, and Mexico City, and the solitude of the open road or the wilderness. The two figures in his dream may be taken as contrary impulses in his personality, impulses he struggled to reconcile throughout his life. In *Visions of Cody*, which was purposely written in a manner imitative of the therapeutic technique of free association in order to dredge up subconscious images and associations, the narrator offers another literal interpretation, that the Shrouded Stranger is his brother. The death of his brother, Gerard, haunted Kerouac throughout his life, to the extent that in 1956, with the thirtieth anniversary of Gerard's death approaching, he wrote an entire novel to commemorate the occasion. In *Visions of Gerard* Kerouac actually attributes his vocation as a writer to his sainted brother.

In fact, it seems to have been the death of Leo Kerouac, Jack's father, that spurred him to write his first published novel, *The Town and the City* (1950). This book concludes with a long description of the agonizing death of George Martin, the father of the large family that is the focus of the story. In the same letter to Ed White in which he described his 1945 dream of the Shrouded Stranger (which may have also been a premonition of Leo's death), Kerouac describes George Martin as "a dusty, shabby Stranger from the desert of the night," identifying him as one or both characters in the dream ("Letters" 129). The Shrouded Stranger, death, has overtaken Leo Kerouac, and now he himself—like his older son, Gerard—comes to represent death as it threatens to overtake Jack Kerouac.

In *Book of Dreams* (1961), his published dream journal, Kerouac records a dream (presumably from the 1950s, long after his father's death) in which Leo seems to take the role of the Shrouded Stranger: "He comes over to my side—I see him coming and I go blind, darkness takes the place of the entire scene, nevertheless now I feel his touch on my arm, he may have an axe . . . for my blood stop't beating when that Shroudy Stranger finally got his hand on me—He's getting closer and closer" (131). Interestingly, this Oedipal nightmare inspires Kerouac with a sense of hope, reinforced by his newfound Buddhist faith: "I know how to be beyond him now—not being concerned not believing in either life or death, if this can be possible in a humble Pratyeka at this time" (*Book of Dreams* 131). (A pratyeka is a Buddhist saint devoted to his own personal salvation rather than to the salvation of others.) This confirmation by the hand of death—his father's hand—seems to free the dreamer from his fear of death, releasing him for the time being from the feeling of being haunted, pursued by a ghost.

As Sal Paradise's description of Carlo Marx in *On the Road* indicates, the Shrouded Stranger dream had a strange appeal for Kerouac's closest literary friend, the poet Allen Ginsberg. The character modeled on him listens intently to Sal's summary. In the letter to Ed White, Kerouac introduces the longer synopsis of the dream by telling his correspondent that he had discussed the dream with Ginsberg earlier in the day ("Letters" 127). Likewise, in *Visions of Cody*, the Neal Cassady character relates his own experience on the road in Montana to the content of Kerouac's dream. Both close friends immediately recognized the numinous quality of the Shrouded Stranger and incorporated interpretations of it into their waking lives.

Indeed, Ginsberg, who first met Kerouac in 1944, only a year before Kerouac's dream occurred, subsequently devoted three early poems to the image. In a letter to Cassady dated in early 1951, he also attributed broader literary significance to it, recognizing in it a kind of symbolic lineage or historical intertextuality: "The Shroudy Stranger who reappeared to me in a dream these last years is the same man who shrieked on the heath with King Lear, the Fool (this I gathered in memory a long while back) and also Old Tom the Lunatic of late Yeats" (Ginsberg and Cassady, *As Ever* 93). It is clear from this statement not only that Ginsberg wished to connect his own image with those of Shakespeare and Yeats, but also that the Shrouded Stranger had passed from Kerouac's dream life into his own.

The image so possessed Ginsberg that he determined to write a long poem organized around it. Knowing the resonance Cassady felt for the Shrouded Stranger, he wrote to his friend to solicit "plot ideas, contributions of lines, images" for the projected work (Ginsberg and Cassady, *As Ever* 96). Ginsberg also approached the originator of the dream in conciliatory terms: "'[My] phantasies and phrases have gotten so lovingly mixed up in yours . . . I hardly knows [sic] whose is which and who's used what,' he wrote Jack. 'I'm not haggling I just want to know if it's OK to use anything that creeps in.' Much of his 'Shroudy Stranger' poem, he pointed out, could be attributed to his and Jack's conversations" (Schumacher 141). Here Ginsberg recognizes the conscious origin of the image that came to inhabit both his dreams and his poems. For at least one critic of his work, the Shrouded Stranger represents "the intense focus on death that possessed Ginsberg, not only in the few years after his visions, but . . . throughout the fifties and sixties" (Portugés 48).

Ginsberg's first use of the image comes in the playfully titled "Please Open the Window and Let Me In," dated May 1949. The poem is cast in three four-line stanzas, each of which poses a question about the identity of "the shroudy stranger of the night" (*Poems* 31). The stranger's green brow and red eye, his habit of following a scared child, and his multiple disguises all bring to mind the character of Doctor Sax, and although he had not yet completed his first published novel at the time, by 1948 Kerouac had already begun to contemplate the third volume of his Duluoz Legend, and his friend obviously recognized the connection between the dream image and the fictional character. In a brief memoir entitled "The Shrouded Stranger of the Night," Ginsberg's close friend Carl Solomon recalls the poet's "vision, or concept, of a sort of mysterious necromancer, both ugly and beautiful, who haunted River Street, in Paterson [Ginsberg's hometown], and cast spells world-wide in scope." Solomon goes on to observe that "Allen and Kerouac had this poetic mythology in common and in the character of the Shrouded Stranger lay the embryo of Kerouac's Dr. Sax" (172–73).

Perhaps the most intriguing aspect of Ginsberg's novice poem is his description of the Stranger as a "double mummer in whose hooded gaze / World has beckoned unto world once more" (*Poems* 31). Like Doctor Sax, Ginsberg's Stranger is an intermediary between dreams and waking life, between the unconscious and the conscious, between death and life. But the implication of his double mummery is that he is in disguise in both worlds, life masquerading as death and vice versa. As a kind of double agent, then, the Stranger moves easily between two apparently alien worlds, revealing their hidden connections and serving as an interpreter of their discrete languages. Ironically, his ability to communicate between radically different modes of consciousness also makes him a stranger in both worlds.

The two somewhat later poems that share the same title, "The Shrouded Stranger," are related as inside and outside, as one critic has observed (Merrill 46). The first, dated 1949 to 1951, presents the stranger speaking in his own voice, as if in answer to the questions posed by "Please Open the Window and Let Me In." The description the Stranger presents of himself is that of a homeless lunatic, who screams "at a fire on the river bank" and gives his body "to an old gas tank" (*Poems* 26). Now fifty years later, Ginsberg's depiction of the homeless and insane as the ultimate Other in postindustrial capitalist society seems prescient. Nothing could be more repulsive to bourgeois consciousness than the Stranger's invitation in the last stanza of the poem to "lie down in the dark with me / Belly to belly and knee to knee" (*Poems* 26). The sexual innuendo here serves to emphasize the utter commitment required for us to understand the emissary of our own unconscious. In order to comprehend the Other—whether it be the actual outcasts of contemporary society or the metaphorical representations of our own instinctive drives—we must look it squarely in its "hooded eye" (*Poems* 26).

The last of Ginsberg's Shrouded Stranger poems, dated 1949 to September 1950, is the longest and most complex of the three. Like *Howl* and *Kaddish,* the major long poems he wrote later in the decade, the second poem called "The Shrouded Stranger" has four parts. The first part, which consists of only four lines, concludes with the words "empty mirror," the title of Ginsberg's first published collection (*Poems* 47). The second is subtitled "A Dream," to recall the origin of the image that is the subject of the poem. In the third part, the narrator looks for and finds the Shrouded Stranger, who says to him, "I'll bet you didn't think / it was me after all" (*Poems* 48). At the culmination of the poet's long quest, the Stranger is unrecognizable. The final part of the poem, subtitled "Fragmenta Monumenti" in homage to the high modernist technique of Ezra Pound and T. S. Eliot, explains that the long poem on the subject with a title echoing Kerouac's has been abandoned (though he gives both its first and last lines), but the poet gives no reason for his change of plans.

In these four sections, all quite different in style and tone, Ginsberg traces the evolution of his brief poetic career. In effect, his mannered early verse, written during his undergraduate years at Columbia University and heavily influenced by the seventeenth-century British poetry then in vogue in academia, has been superseded by Pound's demand to "make it new." The imposing literariness of the image of the Shrouded Stranger—its relation to both Shakespeare and Yeats—crumbles at the mere touch of Ginsberg's self-deprecating humor. Henceforth, the poet seems to be saying, I will write a more straightforward poetry that reflects my own era and my own life.

According to one of his biographers, Ginsberg "had long been fascinated with the idea of a mysterious, inexplicable ghost presence, his interests dating back to the days of his youth, when he walked past the shadowy hedges along Graham Avenue in Paterson" (Schumacher 128). He was "surprised" to learn that Kerouac had had similar fantasies. Indeed, in his original plan for the long poem, Ginsberg intended that "the Shroudy Stranger would start off as an ethereal presence, not quite human and veiled in mystery, only to evolve into a tragic yet decisively human figure" (Schumacher 128), precisely the trajectory followed in Kerouac's third novel by the character Doctor Sax. Under the immediate influence of William Carlos Williams, who had befriended the young poet in the late 1940s, Ginsberg planned for the long version of the Shrouded Stranger poem to "[b]egin with symbols and end with things" (qtd. in Schumacher 128), precisely the trajectory of modern poetry in English.

For both personal and artistic reasons, then, both Kerouac and Ginsberg found the image of the Shrouded Stranger, as articulated in Kerouac's 1945 dream, of immense significance. Both men used the image in their writing (Kerouac to much greater effect than Ginsberg), and their artistic rendering seems to have neutralized the terror evoked by the image to some extent. This phenomenon of a shared fear which becomes a shared dream and then a shared image in literature makes the Shrouded Stranger especially worthy of critical attention and perfectly suited to Jungian analysis.

One of the most obvious qualities of the image, as it appears in the work of both writers, is the contrasting elements in its description, particularly the contrast between black and white. Though this contrast is lacking in Kerouac's description of the dream to Ed White, his interpretation of his own dream is full of it: "Isn't it awfully true that we come from the darkness before-birth, which for merely being dark, is therefore hell—and arrive here in life in the LIGHT of earth, which for merely being LIGHT, is heaven" ("Letters" 128). In *Visions of Cody* the title character picks up on the contrast in his restatement of it: "[Y]ou know that dream of yours about being pursued across a white desert by a shrouded stranger in a hood with a stave of shining gold, terrible feet, clouds for knees, and a black face in snow cowls . . . ?" (312). Likewise, in Ginsberg's first "Shrouded Stranger" poem, the image is elaborated in a similar way when the Stranger asserts, "My flesh is cinder and my face is snow" (*Poems* 26). Apparently, Kerouac's dream, which did not portray such contrasts, somehow gave the impression of contrast to both the dreamer and those who heard him recount the dream.

The elaboration of the dream image—in conversation or in writing—seems to have required an emphasis on contrast. The narrator of *Visions of Cody*, some version of Kerouac's own consciousness, represents the image this way: "In my dream of the Shrouded Stranger who pursued me across the desert and caught me at the gates of the Eternal City, he with his white eyes in the darkness of his rosy folds, his fire-feet in the dust, that smothered me to death in a dream, he'll never catch me if he didn't then" (383). Here the numinous fire contrasts with the dust, and even the action of the dream becomes polarized—pursuit versus escape.

In *Doctor Sax* the title character is "educated in a panel of ice and a panel of snow, taught by fires" (29), adding a tactile element to the contrast. The hero of this novel, eleven-year-old Jackie Duluoz, participates in these contrasts by masquerading as the Black Thief in his "cape and slouch hat, cape made of rubber (my sister's beach cape of the thirties, red and black like Mephistopheles)" (47). In order to be worthy of Doctor Sax's help, Jackie must first ally himself to the powers of darkness and evil. Meanwhile, Sax himself, repeatedly identified with the Shrouded Stranger (9; 77; 155; 161), is seen as "the white-haired Hawk" (69), "striding in the moonlight" (151).

In the climax of the novel, the figures of the snake and the eagle assume all the contrasting qualities that have been adopted by Jackie and Doctor Sax throughout the novel. Sax tries unsuccessfully to kill the snake with a blue ball filled with a potion he has concocted: "All the whiteness vanished when Sax jolted that vacuum ball—normal gray of the world returned" (Kerouac, *Doctor Sax* 232). After the eagle conquers the snake independently of Sax's maneuvers, he himself is transformed from a superhero and creature of the night into an ordinary citizen. After removing his costume, he remarks, "'I never knew that I would meet Judgment Day in my regular clothes without having to go around in the middle of the night with that silly cape, with that silly goddam shroudy hat, with that black face the Lord prescribed for me.'" The character's consciousness is likewise transformed: "'I see that I have to die in broad daylight where I go around in ordinary clothes'" (240).

Once Doctor Sax realizes that evil does not inhabit darkness exclusively, he dispels Jackie's childish fear of night and, by means of projection, the author's fear of death. The shades of gray that return at the end of the novel represent the "ordinary" world of the balanced, mature mind. As his supernatural protector sheds his black shroud, Jackie passes unharmed into the multi-hued world of adulthood. By projecting the dream image of the Shrouded Stranger onto the character of Doctor Sax and retrojecting him into his early adolescence, Kerouac gains some control over personal and cultural tendencies to polarize moral issues. In *Doctor Sax* the author constructs a "Myth of the Rainy Night" that may lead to equilibrium and fulfillment in adulthood for both Jackie Duluoz and his prototype, Jack Kerouac.

Allen Ginsberg's literary treatment of the Shrouded Stranger follows a similar process in the course of the three poems. At first, the Stranger is a gate-ghost who represents the land of the dead. In the second poem, spoken by the Stranger, he presents himself as the dingy lover of Apollo, a sort of apotheosized hobo. Finally, in the third poem, the Stranger, "reft of realms" (*Poems* 47), is found hiding in a corner. The poet does not even recognize him. The Shrouded Stranger turns out, as in the case of Doctor Sax, to be an ordinary human character disguised as a numinous mythic figure.

Beyond the shared significance of the image for the two writers, the contrasts associated with the Shrouded Stranger also reflect the polarization of American culture in the 1950s. It is probably not synchronicity that Kerouac's dream occurred in 1945, the year the first atomic bombs were dropped. The hooded figure in the dream may represent the new threat of nuclear holocaust, while the dreamer rushes to reach a protective shelter. Later in the 1940s, as the Cold War took shape and Russia became the primary threat to national security, the abstract threat of nuclear destruction resolved itself into a definite fear of Russian invasion, personalizing and localizing the potential cause of annihilation.

Jung's fascinating commentary on 1950s culture in *Flying Saucers: A Modern Myth of Things Seen in the Sky* (1959) is pertinent to the relationship between the image of the Shrouded Stranger and the growing anxiety about nuclear weapons in the postwar era. "Projections," Jung observed, "have what we might call different ranges, according to whether they stem from merely personal conditions or from deeper collective ones" (10). While the Shrouded Stranger arose as the shadow archetype independently in the minds of Jack Kerouac and Allen Ginsberg (though the independent occurrences were joined by the synchronicity of the meeting of the two writers in New York City in 1944), the novels and poems elaborated the archetype into a literary image that focused collective fears about the future of human society, an image not unlike that of the UFO, which spread widely in America during this same period. The Shrouded Stranger is an archetype that has passed from the collective to the personal to the social range, evidenced by its power to bond individuals (Kerouac and Ginsberg) and groups (their readers) by objectifying their instinctual reactions to the new terror of nuclear war.

The contrasting elements of the Shrouded Stranger also indicate a general quality of the human mind. As Jung says, "The psychic totality, the self, is a combination of opposites. Without a shadow even the self is not real" (*Flying Saucers* 36). His insight explains why Kerouac's initial response to his dream was to interpret the shroud as himself. But Jung, disturbed by the rising popularity of Freudian psychoanalysis in the 1950s, warned, "Whenever it is a question of archetypal formations, personalistic attempts at explanation lead us astray" (*Flying Saucers* 39). Recognizing the numinous image of the Shrouded Stranger as the shadow, Kerouac intuitively rejected his own "personalistic" interpretation not as inaccurate, but as inadequate.

By elaborating the image in their writing, both Kerouac and Ginsberg were practicing what Jung called "amplificatory interpretation"
(*Flying Saucers* 18), that is, attempting to integrate the dream image
into their conscious artistic practice (see *Flying Saucers* 38). In fact, all
art, it seems to me, is characterized by a poetics of integration of archetypal imagery with individual expression, just as careful reading—especially literary criticism—is an attempt to integrate both the archetypes
and the appeal (or numinosity) of the author's style into the reader's
consciousness in a more or less logical fashion. In analyzing his own
shadow figure, which he called Philemon, Jung once asked himself,
"'What am I really doing?' A voice within him replied, 'It is art'"
(*Memories* 185). Literary tradition, with its availing stock of numinous
images reaching back to the origins of Western culture, is the collective
unconscious writ large.

Having recognized the efforts of Kerouac and Ginsberg to integrate
the image of the Shrouded Stranger into their art, I want to give final
consideration to the spell it casts on readers some fifty years after these
novels and poems were created. A typical application of Jung's amplificatory method is to connect the archetype in question to the history of
symbols. Specifically, one might ask whether the image is related to that
of the Grim Reaper, the Wandering Jew, or, like Jung's shadow, to the
prophet Elijah (*Memories* 182). Or is it, perhaps, a postwar version of
the Hermit card of the Tarot (see figure 4), as I suspect? The Shrouded
Stranger, like the Hermit, is characterized by a mendicant's hood, cloak,
and staff, though he lacks the lantern traditionally borne by the Hermit
(and suggestive of the cynical philosopher Diogenes, who used it to
search for an honest man in broad daylight). This may suggest a modern lack of light to balance against the darkness of the night in Kerouac's
dream. In the restatement of the dream in *Visions of Cody*, the Stranger's
staff is gold, implying that self-support is extremely valuable. Kerouac
himself vacillated between a hermit-like existence and a riotous city life,
a vacillation he was never able to reconcile in a happy medium. As Jung
observed, "The city-dweller seeks artificial sensations to escape his boredom; the hermit does not seek them, but is plagued by them against his
will" (*Flying Saucers* 41). In general, and certainly in Kerouac's case, this
dichotomy presents a double bind.

Another feature of the Hermit of the Tarot that applies to both Kerouac's and Ginsberg's use of the image is that the character faces to the
left, signifying attention to the past. Both writers were deeply preoccu-
pied with resolving personal issues in their pasts. In Kerouac's case, it
was the deaths of his brother and father, for which he felt an irrational
guilt. For Ginsberg, it was the madness of his mother, for which he felt

FIGURE 4. The Hermit card of the Tarot.

partly responsible and which caused him to resent his father. Identifying the image of the Shrouded Stranger as the Hermit suggests that both writers were resisting a necessary investigation of the past. Their sense that they could not escape the Stranger served as a prelude to their acceptance of the past and their attempt to incorporate it into their art, Kerouac in the concluding chapter of *The Town and the City* and in *Visions of Gerard*, and Ginsberg in *Kaddish*, a long elegy he wrote after his mother's death. The history of this symbol also helps explain its appeal to readers, since most people are trying to integrate past experiences into their understanding of their personalities. On a cultural level, the Hermit serves to remind Americans of our responsibility for unleashing upon the world (perhaps unavoidably) the terror of nuclear holocaust.

One question remains: How is the personal version of the archetype in a dream transmuted into the literary image of a novel or a poem? The Shrouded Stranger in fiction and poetry (and even in Kerouac's letter and his dream journal) differs from its origin in the dreams of Kerouac and Ginsberg most obviously in that a sensory experience has been transformed into words. Kerouac, like Ginsberg, an inveterate recorder of his dreams, pauses in the midst of *Book of Dreams* to announce: "WRITING DREAMS, TAKE NOTE OF THE WAY DREAMING MIND CREATES" (121). The implication of this warning, which applies both to himself as an artist and to his readers, is that the dreaming mind provides both a model for artistic creation and a key to critical interpretation. Thus Kerouac's dream journal constitutes an instruction manual for his compositional practice. His focus was not so much on the images themselves as on the manner in which the mind conceived its images. His advice is difficult enough for the dreamer, let alone for the objective observer of the recorded dream image. But the critic can apply the advice to the reading of the text. Jung, in fact, observed that "Insofar as analytical treatment makes the 'shadow' conscious, it causes a cleavage and a tension of opposites which in their turn seek a compensation in unity. The adjustment is achieved through symbols" (*Memories* 335). The polarization of the image of the Shrouded Stranger is the effect of artistic intuition, a fusion of the faculties of conscious ordering and the production and retrieval of subconscious material. Both Ginsberg and Kerouac abstracted a series of contrasts from the more complex coloration of the dream image.

Ginsberg insisted in a 1987 lecture that the contrast represented their assimilation of the mind-set of the Cold War: "That's a completely polarized notion of the universe—the notion that everything is black and white" (*Deliberate Prose* 265). The Stranger, then, was made to mirror the dangerous separation of faculties that dominated the 1950s.

Presumably, like any conjunction of opposites, the image then serves to focus the psychic powers of the reader. The poles of black and white function as the terminals between which sparks of insight jump, leading beyond the literal content to the recognition that the contraries of the image are, in fact, closely related. The temporary balance created by the polarization of the image leads to the ephemeral psychic unity we call meaning. Contrast also makes the shadow appear in its proper relation to the ego—as a dark side that requires integration into the self. This resolution of contrasts mimics the artistic process itself, by which both Kerouac and Ginsberg ransacked and manipulated their dreams in order to bring the latent orderliness of the archetype from the unconscious into consciousness.

In struggling to achieve mental balance for themselves, then, Kerouac and Ginsberg abstracted the image of the Shrouded Stranger in such a way that they extended its range, first to the basic community of each other and their friends (like Ed White and Neal Cassady), where it served as a means of bonding, and then to the community of their readers, where the image mirrored not only the personal psychic tensions that gave rise to it but also social anxiety about nuclear weapons and the Cold War. But on all levels—personal, interpersonal, and social—the image resolved itself into the archetype of the Hermit, converting the shadow from an alien, objective force into a constructive feature of the self.

The potential for this conversion is implicit in Kerouac's dream in the detail of the toy gun with which he attempted to ambush the Shrouded Stranger. This childish weapon signifies the immature impulse of the ego to reject the shadow by "killing" its image. In converting the image from the dream into literature, this detail is omitted, implying that the artistic intuition recognizes the usefulness of the shadow figure. Both Ginsberg and Kerouac worked through their psychic resistance to the archetype, neutralized its threatening qualities, and humanized and personalized its radical otherness. While this process undoubtedly helped preserve their own mental stability (which in the case of both authors was often precarious), its representation in literature gave thousands of readers—including both Doug and Judi Sharples and myself—an image in which our own anxieties could be focused, made productive, and assimilated into our personalities. And this assimilation, it seems to me, is the purpose of sharing the shadow, just as the purpose of Jung's amplificatory method is to integrate the archetype into consciousness. Jack Kerouac and Allen Ginsberg succeeded, as Edmund Wilson once observed of Dostoevsky, "in restoring a moral balance to the universe which he had once felt reeling with the world of his own soul" (117–18).

In the *Poetics* Aristotle recognized not only the power of drama to conjoin historical details with philosophical abstractions but also its ability to purge the contradictory emotions of the audience. What became known as the "concrete universal" is the same principle at work in these two postmodern writers. In elaborating dream images into literary symbols, they combine personal and social numinosity, demonstrating the process by which the individual shadow can be connected to the collective archetype. Thus the process of making art stands as a model for psychic and social health. For the artist, the personal is always political, so to speak. The numinous images of literature allow the audience to experience abstract moral dilemmas in a concrete fashion. Literature, among its many services, demonstrates the obscure but intimate link between the limited evil within the individual and the seemingly limitless evil created by human society when it projects its shadow on a demagogue or a nuclear holocaust. In no other way and for no other reason can we understand why the utterances of writers—even when they are not explicitly political—are detested, punished, and suppressed by totalitarian regimes.

Reading, especially criticism, then, becomes an exercise in social responsibility. Even in this postmodern era of ironic detachment, literature continues to teach us not only how the individual shadow becomes a collective shadow but also how we may recognize that process and interpret the archetype so that it loses its dangerous mystique. In Kerouac's and Ginsberg's intuitive conversion of the Shrouded Stranger from dream image to literary image, we see not only how we ourselves convert our fears into the destructive power of local, national, and international leaders by extending the range of our own shadows. We see also how we might raise our awareness of this process, making the sharing of a shadow into a productive exploration of the relations between the individual and collective consciousness, if only we can muster the individual and collective will to learn what literature has been trying to teach us since the dawn of our culture before it is too late.

WORKS CITED

Gettings, Fred. *The Book of Tarot*. London: Triune Books, 1973.

Ginsberg, Allen. *Collected Poems 1947–1980*. New York: Harper, 1984.

———. *Deliberate Prose: Selected Essays 1952–1995*. Ed. Bill Morgan. New York: HarperCollins, 2000.

Ginsberg, Allen, and Neal Cassady. *As Ever: The Collected Correspondence of Allen Ginsberg and Neal Cassady*. Ed. with introd. by Barry Gifford. Berkeley: Creative Arts, 1977.

Jung, C. G. "The Fight with the Shadow." *Civilization in Transition*. New York: Pantheon, 1964. Vol. 10 of *The Collected Works of C. G. Jung*.

———. *Flying Saucers: A Modern Myth of Things Seen in the Sky*. London: Ark, 1977.

———. *Memories, Dreams, Reflections*. Ed. Aniela Jaffe. New York: Vintage, 1965.

———. "The Shadow." *Aion: Researches into the Phenomenology of the Self*. 2nd ed. Princeton: Princeton UP, 1968.

Kerouac, Jack. *Book of Dreams*. San Francisco: City Lights, 1981.

———. *Doctor Sax: Faust Part Three*. New York: Grove, 1959.

———. "Letters from Jack Kerouac to Ed White, 1947–68." *The Missouri Review* 17.3 (1994): 107–60.

———. *On the Road*. New York: Viking Penguin, 1991.

———. *Visions of Cody*. New York: McGraw-Hill, 1974.

———. *Visions of Gerard*. New York: McGraw-Hill, 1976.

Merrill, Thomas F. *Allen Ginsberg*. Rev. ed. Boston: Twayne, 1988.

Portugés, Paul. *The Visionary Poetics of Allen Ginsberg*. Santa Barbara: Ross-Erikson, 1978.

Schumacher, Michael. *Dharma Lion: A Critical Biography of Allen Ginsberg*. New York: St. Martin's, 1992.

Sharples, Doug, and Judi Sharples. Personal interview. May 2000.

Solomon, Carl. *Emergency Messages: An Autobiographical Miscellany*. NY: Paragon House, 1989.

Wilson, Edmund. *I Thought of Daisy*. New York: Farrar, 1953.

In the Buddha's Shadow

Jung, Zen, and the Poetry of Jane Hirshfield

cⴰⴰⴰⴰ

ANDREW ELKINS

Of all the Jungian archetypes, the shadow is probably the easiest for the modern Western reader to grasp. By now we are convinced by our experiences and world events that the human creature is a divided soul. We humans are not alone in our skin: we share our body and psyche with a dark stranger. The participants in this internal struggle are familiar to us all: in one corner, the human walking upright into the world's light, and in the other corner, the eternal adversary, the same human's shadow, walking in the penumbra of the public and conscious person. Perhaps, however, the case is not so simple.

Let us recall that the most common description of the shadow is as something dark, ominous, and evil. Jung clearly connects the shadow with evil forces: "And indeed it is a frightening thought that man also has a shadow-side to him, consisting not just of little weaknesses, but of a positively demonic dynamism" (CW 7: 29). On the same page, he refers to the shadow as "the seamy side" and elsewhere as "the dark half of the psyche," containing "all the faults which we obviously have ourselves" (CW 12: 29). The "faults" specifically are "everything that will not fit in with, and adapt to, the laws and regulations of conscious life" (CW 11: 198), making the shadow an internal rebel threatening our social standing as well as our personal sense of morality. For Jung, the shadow is volatile and dangerous, "the uncontrolled or scarcely controlled emotions" of our "primitive" self (CW 9.2: 9). In its personal manifestation, it consists of those urges or impulses that we deny as our own; in its archetypal manifestation, the dark shadow is evil itself, testimony to the fact that we are part of the evil around us from which we so want to distance ourselves.

Jung's commentators follow the master's lead. Jolande Jacobi calls the shadow "the inborn collective predisposition which we reject for ethical, aesthetic, or other reasons, and repress because it is in opposition to our conscious principles" (110). C. A. Meier describes the shadow as "the dark mirror reflex" (92) personified in the goblins and evil spirits of folklore. As June Singer phrases it, the shadow "consists of all those uncivilized desires and emotions that are incompatible with social standards and with the persona; it is all we are ashamed of" (192). Grounded in and colored by the long Western cultural tradition of thinking in dualistic terms—good/evil, higher/lower, self/other, light/dark, primitive/civilized, and more—these binaries are so basic to our understanding of the world and the way in which we articulate that understanding in language that they go largely unnoticed while carrying a tremendous amount of moral and theological freight in their wake. In the Platonic tradition, the tangible, sensual world of coarse physicality must be ignored or overcome, as much as possible, before Truth and immortality can be gained. When Christianity, still the dominant religion in the Western world, combined its tenets with the established dualistic intellectual tradition of the West and removed the sacred from the earth to hang it in the heavens, that dichotomous mode of thinking became, if anything, even more judgmental and moralistic. The internal battle between light and dark, reason and passion, morality and instinct became understood as the individual analogue for the cosmic battle being fought between God and His dark shadow, Satan. Despite the fact that we now see the struggle in secular terms more befitting our faithless age, the moral connotations of the descriptions of the shadow remain strong. The descriptions imply not only a world divided down the middle; they describe a Manichean world of good and bad—the descriptor "primitive" automatically associates the shadow with that which is inferior; the descriptors "dark," "lower," "animal," and "instinctive" automatically associate the shadow with evil to be overcome, resisted, or somehow neutralized.

In a similar fashion, Jung's prescription for integrating the shadow into the conscious psyche is loaded with Western moral and ontological assumptions. In Jung's words: "A dim premonition tells us that we cannot be whole without this negative side," for if we deny the shadow side, "we cease to be three-dimensional and become flat and without substance" (CW 7: 29). Without one's shadow, one ceases to develop and "remains a two-dimensional phantom, a more or less well brought-up child" (*CW* 7: 237). Negative/positive, round/flat, child/adult make sense as metaphors because they participate in the dichotomous intellectual tradition of the West: it is "better," for the postpubescent person at least, to be round than flat, adult than childish. Similarly, in the words of Meier, "one of the purposes of analysis is to make the person capable of coming to terms with this inferior personality . . . and to come to terms with the effects this inferior part of his person has upon him" (95–96). Add to the list superior/inferior, and compound that with the binary of rational/emotional, for the therapeutic goal is to reveal and then apprehend intellectually the shadow, because rational apprehension is assumed to be required before personal wholeness can be achieved.

Clearly, the language used to describe and explain the archetype is conditioned by the Western culture in which its roots are deeply and inextricably planted. We may go beyond that, however. The shadow, as the Other opposed to the self, is not merely phrased in Western dualistic terms; it is a perfect illustration and an inevitable product of that dualistic mind-set. The concept of "other" requires a dualistic habit of thought. The contention here is that to remain relevant to a pluralistic, multicultural, and postmodern world, Jung's concepts need to be stretched a bit beyond their Western roots: can a close but selective reading of a contemporary American poet who is also a Zen Buddhist and a reader of Jung help drag the shadow into our age? Can that poet serve as a gateway to a new reading of the shadow, a reading informed by Eastern as well as Western traditions of thought?

The poet in question is Jane Hirshfield, a resident of northern California, author of four books of poetry and one collection of essays, editor of a collection of women's spiritual poetry, and translator of a book of Japanese love poems. Hirshfield combines the best of Western and Eastern traditions. Educated at Princeton (an honors graduate in 1973 in the university's first coeducational graduating class), she then moved to San Francisco and spent eight years immersing herself in the practice of Buddhism at a Zen monastery, putting her writing career on hold until she learned, in her words, "what it meant to be a human being" (Hirshfield, "Jane Hirshfield"). In addition, she is well aware of Jung's concept of the shadow: "Part of poetry's core activity, both within an individual and within a culture, is to attend to and make visible what Jung called the shadow life. Whatever it is that isn't being attended to, poetry will be magnetically drawn toward" ("An Interview" 3). Thus examining Hirshfield with an ear for her Jungian and Buddhist connections—especially as those bear on the question of the shadow, the dark figure that in Western terminology has acquired negative moral connotations—will provide a way to understand the shadow in terms that better fit our age, and such a reading will also allow us to "save" Jung from some of the worst blunders caused by the analyst's ethnocentrism.

At the heart of Jane Hirshfield's poetry is her understanding of herself as an integrated part of the earth and universe. A consistent denier of all philosophical dualisms, the poet contends that life is a series of continuums, based ultimately upon her understanding of the continuum between herself (and, by extension, all humans) and the nonhuman world, the total contents of the place around her. Her 1997 book of essays, *Nine Gates: Entering the Mind of Poetry*, repeatedly makes this point. Responding favorably to the statement by eighteenth-century German poet Novalis that "Perceptibility is a *kind* of attentiveness," Hirshfield says, "In this radical vision of vision, there is no difference between human and nonhuman, between sentient and nonsentient. All being becomes single, alive, available, and awake" (*Nine Gates* 118). Her "vision of vision" is thus grounded in a commitment to "attentiveness" that, in the spirit of Zen, sees past division to universal connection.

Hirshfield did not reveal her eight years of Buddhist training until 1994 (in her editor's biographical note to *Women in Praise of the Sacred*), believing that her religious practice was a private matter (Hirshfield, "An Interview" 3). To its credit, her poetry is perfectly understandable to the reader who possesses no Zen background. Even so, there are clear connections to Buddhism in her works. For example, in an essay, "The Myriad Leaves of Words," Hirshfield notes, "The nonseparation of Buddhist understanding lies close to the ground of all poetry, Western as well as Eastern. Every metaphor, every description that moves its reader, every hymn-shout of praise, points to the shared existence of beings and things" (*Nine Gates* 99). This "shared existence of beings and things" is the equivalent of the continuum that eradicates all dualist categories.

She sums up the thematic grounding of her poetry in Buddhism in a passage from another essay ("Two Secrets") in the same book:

> You cannot leap beyond human consciousness without first going through it; but if you gaze deeply enough into being, eventually you will awaken into the company of everything. The thought goes back to the Buddha, who stated at the moment of his enlightenment . . . , "Now everything and I awaken." (*Nine Gates* 140)

Hirshfield's goal is to go through her personal consciousness to the shared ground of being of the world, of "everything," and thus obliterate all the dualisms so dear to Western thought. Human consciousness does not block or alienate one from non-human nature but is one of the gates through which one can pass to an understanding of that world. A quotation from the Japanese haiku master, Matsuo Basho, is appropriate here: "all who have achieved real excellence in any art possess one thing in common, that is, a mind to obey nature, to be one with nature, throughout the four seasons of the year" (71).

Such a poetry requires complete openness and attention, a state of consciousness that is, as Jung notes, difficult if not impossible to maintain twenty-four hours a day. However, in certain moments of heightened attentiveness, epiphanies similar to mini-*satori* experiences occur, the continuum becomes evident, and poetry breaks out as a collaborative effort between poet and world: "Through actively perceptive speech, outer world and inner experience collaborate in the creation of meaning" (*Nine Gates* 129). The world and poet become coauthors: "the poet becomes an intermediary, a medium through whom the world of objects and nature beyond human consciousness may speak" (*Nine Gates* 131). In those moments, the continuum of human consciousness and the world's existence is experienced, dualism is banished, and a poem emerges. The poet's chief responsibility is to embrace the world's plenitude in its entirety; her only possible sin is to refuse any part of the world, which is tantamount to self-refusal in Hirshfield's theme. From an Eastern perspective, therefore, what we call the shadow is merely dark because unacknowledged, not dark in any moral or theological sense. Judging the shadow as "demonic" is itself a form of refusal, a preference for the light over the dark and an implication that the world would be better if no dark existed, if light could always be preferred over the "inferior" darkness. Darkness and light, however, are equal participants in the universe. As Hirshfield says in "The Gift" (*Lives* 30–31): "The mercies are boundless. Every country is death's." Mercy and death are omnipresent and inseparable. Turning from the world's cruelties or one's own shadow impulses, therefore, is denying the world's and one's own demons and living inauthentically. The poet's obligation to the world is the same as her obligation to herself: live fully, be attentive, accept all, live and write from a posture of faith.

Hence the "one thing no poet does is look away" ("Letter to Hugo from Later," *Lives* 84–85), Hirschfield says, even when a friend is dying, apparently slowly and painfully—"even his wrists thinned with pain" ("Salt Heart," *Lives* 14). While Hirshfield's speaker in "Salt Heart" is understandably distraught and sympathetic with the person's suffering, she knows it is pointless to look away, curse the night, or deny the pain as evil:

> The river Suffering would take what it
> wished of him, then go. And I would stay
> and drink on, as the living do, until the rest
> would enter into that water.

From the Zen point of view, true suffering is produced only by labeling suffering as an inferior state and then attempting to avoid the inevitable. Masao Abe, perhaps the best philosophical interpreter of Zen since D. T. Suzuki, makes the point well: "The more we try to cling to pleasure and avoid suffering, the more entangled we become in the duality of pleasure and suffering. It is this whole process which constitutes Suffering" (206). Only by being true to that vision, in Hirshfield's opinion, can she write authentic poetry or live an authentic life: "I begin to believe the only sin is distance, refusal. / All others stemming from this."

If we examine Hirshfield's poetry specifically for representations of the unconscious and particularly the shadow, we can see how her Buddhist grounding enables her to attend to the "shadow life" while not denigrating it with Western moralist diction. The poet often uses animals to represent the unconscious, obviating any impulse on the reader's part to make moral judgments about traits that, in human characters, might be deemed fearsome or deplorable. Hirshfield is particularly fond of horses. In "After Work" (*Of Gravity* 2), she stops to feed corncobs to two horses. The animals emerge as if images from a dream: "They come, deepened and muscular movements / conjured out of sleep: each small noise and scent / heavy with earth, simple beyond communion." The poet comes from work, the daylight world of the mind, the conscious and purposeful world of social roles, masks, and the ego. The horses are put away each day from nine to five to allow one to function in the social world. However, they are the "earth," the primal and muscular, that resides beneath the business outfit and the tactful smile. Going to feed them, the speaker reunites herself with her own dark half, a good and gentle half that revitalizes and feeds her as she and the horses touch ("They are careful of my fingers"), rather ironically creating a variation on Hawthorne's "magnetic chain of humanity" ("Ethan Brand" 241). From the horses she receives a darkness so deep that it becomes light: "and in the night, their mares' eyes shine, reflecting stars, / the entire, outer light of the world here" (*Of Gravity* 2). Through the darkness within to the light within to the light of all: a progression through the unconscious, to self-awareness, to acknowledgment of the connection of light to dark, to knowledge of the connection of all to all, to "the entire, outer light of the world here."

If we recall two central horse images in Western intellectual tradition—Freud's and Plato's—we see that Hirshfield works with traditional imagery but stretches it to fit her Eastern-influenced orientation. In Plato, for example, when the "bad" half of the soul's two horses (the shadow side in Jung's term) comes in sight of the beloved, it "no longer responds to the whip or the goad of the charioteer; it leaps violently forward and does everything to aggravate its yokemate [the good horse or the moral, social side of the psyche] and its charioteer, trying to make them go up to the boy and suggest to him the pleasures of sex" (*Phaedrus* 254 a–b, in Plato 531). For Freud,

> The ego's relation to the id might be compared with that of a rider to his horse. The horse supplies the locomotive energy, while the rider has the privilege of deciding on the goal and of guiding the powerful animal's movement. But only too often there arises between the ego and the id the not precisely ideal situation of the rider being obliged to guide the horse along the path by which it itself wants to go. (*New Introductory Lectures* #31, "Dissection of the Personality")

In both Plato and Freud, two pillars of the tradition that gives rise to Jung's theories, the horse's "animal" passions need to be controlled, even whipped, by the ego of the rational rider. The horse in control is frightening—more vividly in Plato's version ("it leaps violently forward") than in Freud's rather bloodless prose ("the not precisely ideal situation"), but negative in both cases. The passions are a threat to rational control and to the Western thinker's morality, which dictates that humans, as the last link in the chain of being, master their "animal" passions in order to control the world. Hirshfield plays with those dualisms (horse/rider, animal/human, passionate/rational, evil/good) in order to deny them: darkness becomes light; the animal is gentle; the human receives enlightenment from the horse (who becomes much more than a means of transportation) as the horse receives nourishment from the human in a reciprocal relationship. The shadow that would be dark in Jung is still dark, but the darkness and the light are no longer opposed as opposite ends of a moral or psychological spectrum. They join hands, in fact, and show that, while physically distinct, they are essentially identical.

In "Invocation" (*Gravity* 4), raccoons fill the horse's role. The raccoons come to the back door to eat scraps. The house, again, is the well-lighted, safe world created by the ego as a stage upon which to enact its social roles. The raccoons are the dark thieves ("little mask-faced ones, / unstealthy bandits") from the psyche's night-side, feeding "on everything left out," everything tossed out as "garbage" by the respectable, daytime, house-dwelling persona. And, as is true of the horses, the raccoons and the poet are mutually nourishing in their recognition and relationship: "I'll settle with your leavings, / as you have settled for mine." We allow the poet to admire the raccoons' theft, although we would condemn such action in a human character, and, by employing animals, the poet gets us to applaud a rapaciousness that we would otherwise denounce and fear. The raccoons are even cute ("little mask-faced ones"), although a masked human would precipitate a call to 911. Surveys repeatedly show that crime is Americans' number-one fear, yet Hirshfield makes "bandits" sound affectionate, in effect demoralizing a covetousness we would recognize and renounce as an immoral human trait.

Perhaps gluttony and thievery, despite the fact that Western readers have been trained to denounce them, are too easily disguised. It is respectable, in the proper context, to admit a bit of gluttony, for example, to announce that one is hungry as a horse. However, we reserve our greatest disdain and fear for uncontrolled lust and sexual energy. To continue that simile to a horse's sexual drive would draw more than stares. However, as a poet committed to attending to all matters nonjudgmentally for the sake of identifying the continuum underlying the world's phenomena, Hirshfield unabashedly attends to and identifies with sexual desire in its most primal form. In "Heat" (*Gravity* 17), the horse, another mare, is pure, visible libido and passion (very much like Plato's bad horse) who wants nothing more than to be free from the fence behind which the poet has restrained her. The poet again enters the poem as the fence-builder, house-dweller, and worker, as representative, at least in her role as horse-owner, of the daylight world of rational control. She has the "power of bucket / and bridle," as she says. However, while Hirshfield is aligned in her role as owner with the fence-mentality and charioteer, she also metaphorically steps over the fence and identifies with the horse's desire: she "easily / recognized myself in that wide lust," without shame or judgment. In fact, she says she has to "envy her," envy the mare her single-mindedness: she is "restless sure / of heat, and need," and even food will not distract her attention for long. The bold stroke is moving from description of the horse's lust to identification with it in such an innocuous fashion, absent any glorification of the sexual urge (as we hear in Whitman or Lawrence, for example), rebellious denial of conventional morality (as in Ginsberg), or antiseptic clothing of the impulse in terms of romantic love. Hirshfield simply states lust as a fact of life.

The poet also employs foxes as symbols of the shadow life. In "Three Foxes by the Edge of the Field in Twilight" (*Lives* 32), for example, the speaker is out of the house, in the field, the realm of the Other in Western tradition, when the sun of rationality is setting. She is in danger of a shadow encounter, and, soon enough, she happens upon a trio of foxes. Psychotherapy is the process of encountering life's "foxes" consciously, of meeting them in the realm of moral choice rather than repressing the shadow images which, according to Jung, only allows them to wreak havoc, speak through our mouths, and create paranoia in us as we project our undesirable traits onto others. This meeting, however, is accidental, a Zen moment of awareness rather than an insight arrived at analytically. To seek the shadow as a therapeutic goal is to accept dualism as a premise: you only seek that which is other or lost. Hirshfield's character does not seek, for she and the fox are not truly distinct. By abandoning seeking she finds the foxes directly in her path, a paradox expressed in Buddhist terms in another poem in which a fox appears, "Inspiration" (*October Palace* 47): "'Enlightenment,' wrote one master, / 'is an accident, though certain efforts make you accident-prone.'" Walking beyond the house without fear is the "certain effort" that enables the speaker to encounter the foxes.

The poem also shows us that fears of the unruly behavior of life's primal forces are based upon our cultural tradition that associates the animal with the immoral, chaotic, and uncontrolled, rather than with any truth. The foxes simply "vanished," doing no harm. Hirshfield's poem suggests that if one adopts an ethos of openness, the unconscious will step out unbidden from the forest depths (rather than have to be wrested consciously from its lair) and when encountered will be harmless. Again, she identifies the fox in her, the dark fox-nose that pokes out of the twilight into her consciousness, and the recognition is mutual: one of the foxes "looks back from the trees, / and knows me for who I am." Not "knows who I am," but "knows me for who I am," suggesting "knows me as part-fox, as I really am, not as I appear on the outside."

Finally, the lion and the heart, perhaps the most prominent figures in Hirshfield's poetry, often represent the beauty and power we see around us, beauty and power that can be fearsome as well as inspiring. "Sometime around 1992," she says, "the lion began walking into my poems, at the same time as the recurring trope of 'the heart.' . . . I can say only the obvious—the lion is fierceness and beauty; undeniable presence; danger; power; passionate love; transformation. Perhaps, for me, as one title . . . implies, lions are the earthly answer to angels" (Hirshfield, "Jane Hirshfield"). Again, note the easy correlation of danger, power, passion, and angels. Despite the fact that in Western culture angels can be associated with danger and power—who can forget Michael's struggle or Blake's etchings—the Western mind does not, I submit, normally associate that sacred power and awesome danger with the lion's claws and teeth. "Lion and Angel Dividing the Maple Between Them" (*Lives* 102), the title to which Hirshfield refers above, is a nearly perfect "shadow-poem," beginning with the title, which vividly captures the dark, threatening, carnivorous, sensuous side of the human beast (lion) and the light, loving, peaceful, sacred side (angel), then divides the world between the two forces, and finally reunites them as one force ("one visitation") that creates the world's beauty and power.

However, knowing the necessity of offering oneself fully and faithfully to all of life in order to live well, that is, knowing the necessity of giving oneself to the lion and the angel, does not make the task any less frightening: "but how do you come / to offer your throat to either?" Perhaps humans' reluctance to seek or accept self-knowledge is due to our instinct to protect our throats. We guard ourselves from pain, keep the shadow at bay, not recognizing or not caring that doing so makes a whole, fully realized life impossible. We flinch at placing our heads on the chopping block, but the poet reminds us that the block is where life is lived most fully: "And still we go ankle deep / into that carnage, lifting first one, / then another part up to the light."

We live in the carnage, those fallen leaves that are also life itself, the process all around us of dissolution, decay, destruction, and death. We are in it up to our ankles at least, yet, like children trying to keep their feet dry while walking through an unavoidable puddle, we keep trying to carry ourselves above the blood, as if, being subject to gravity, we could ever extricate ourselves fully, and as if extricating ourselves fully would be desirable, as if the angel were not half-lion, as if the angel did not need its lion-half to be beautiful. In Hirshfield's words, we act "As if what we wanted / were not the thing that falls." Perfect fruit, as Stevens reminds us in "Sunday Morning," would never fall to the ground, would never ripen, would never be edible, would never nourish. The ripening and falling process, the life lived in the carnage, the process of death and the manifestation of our imperfection, is precisely what makes the fruit delicious, what nourishes us in the world, what we really want when we say we want fulfillment, if we would only be aware of that fact.

Such is the basic shape of Jane Hirshfield's poetry. The thematic connections to Jung's psychological theory are clear. Attend to the painful as well as the pleasurable. Seek wholeness in all its varieties, personal as well as aesthetic. Attend to the marginal and the margins where society deposits its detritus. Refuse nothing. As Hirshfield says, "The ability to keep and develop attentiveness in the face of whatever is going on—turmoil or boredom, happiness or terror—seems to me the greatest part of becoming fully human" (Moore 3). One of Hirshfield's goals in attending to the whole, as Jung would predict, in addition to awakening the world's poetry, is to live well, which she implicitly connects to writing well: "At some point I realized that you don't get a full human life if you try to cut off one end of it, that you need to agree to the entire experience, to the full spectrum of what happens" (Hirshfield, "An Interview" 3). Live a full life; write a full poetry. The contents of the psyche must be allowed to surface, where they are given symbolic form by the artist: "The openness has to do with being permeable to our own experience, in which anything and everything must be able to enter—including, of course, our experiences of chaos and despair" (Mills 3). The aesthetic and the therapeutic join hands here. Hirshfield never speaks of art as therapy but rather thinks of art as resulting from a well-lived life or being enabled by a fully aware consciousness in the artist. Art becomes the end product of awareness, as awareness becomes a necessary precondition for the production of a whole art. The two—art and awareness—emerge simultaneously.

Hirshfield reminds us that Zen also counsels attention to all aspects of the world, without discrimination: "Zen taught me how to pay attention, how to delve, how to question and enter, how to stay with—or at least want to try to stay with—whatever is going on" (Hirshfield, "An Interview" 3). Jung himself saw the connection between this attentiveness theme and Zen awareness. In his foreword to D. T. Suzuki's essential introduction to Zen, he writes: "The attainment of completeness calls for the use of the whole. Nothing less will do; hence there can be no easier conditions, no substitution, no compromise" (Suzuki 28). Hirshfield says, "Zen is a path of awareness and investigation, and poetry is also a path of awareness and investigation. Each asks of you also a full expression of what you see, what you are" (Hirshfield, "Interview: Entering" 2). And while Suzuki does not explicitly address the question of art, he does make clear that the practice of Zen requires the same attentiveness that has been talked about in connection with Hirshfield's poetry and Jung's theories. The attentiveness produces a new point of view in the seer, which is both a psychological and an aesthetic fact: "Zen wants us to acquire an entirely new point of view whereby to look into the mysteries of life and the secrets of nature" (Suzuki 59). Or, "If we want to get to the bottom of life, . . . we must acquire a new way of observation" (Suzuki 58). And further, "the discipline of Zen consists in opening the mental eye" (Suzuki 40). "Life," therefore, for Zen, "is an art" (Suzuki 64), as it is for the poet and the psychoanalyst.

However, none of the above should suggest that Zen and Jung's theories are identical systems of thought or descriptions of being-in-the-world. As noted earlier, as an inheritor of the Western allegiance to rationality and moral judgment, Jung, even while calling for the full blooming of the unconscious, grounds his approach in rational analysis. Simply using the term "analysis" to describe his method suggests the difference between Jungian theory and Zen practice. We may recall here the meeting in Hirshfield's poem between the walker and the foxes. Openness brought them together, not pursuit. Jung's therapeutic process is more like a fox hunt—with the intellect as weapon—than a fox encounter. Masao Abe makes the general point: Zen is at base "liberation from the discriminating mind itself" (115). In case the point is not clear, he continues in italics: *"emancipation must be made from thinking itself"* (Abe 117). Suzuki agrees that any analytical judgment limits the soul: "When we say 'yes,' we assert, and by asserting we limit ourselves. When we say 'no,' we deny, and to deny is exclusion. Exclusion and limitation, which after all are the same thing, murder the soul" (67). He goes on: "Zen takes us to an absolute realm wherein there are no antitheses of any sort" (Suzuki 68) between good and bad, darkness and light, sin and sacredness. For that reason, even self-consciousness, a cornerstone of the analytical process, must be transcended because "through self-consciousness we look at ourselves from the outside. We are thus separated from ourselves" (Abe 224). To analyze is to divide into parts. To divide is to create a preference for one of the members of the opposed pair. To create preference is to engender attachment. To be attached to anything in the world—to a concept as well as to an item—is to create suffering. The goal of enlightenment is to transcend suffering, which means transcending attachment, which means transcending all analysis.

As illustration, Jung's dualistic rhetoric cannot avoid implying moral judgment, preference, and attachment. A few examples from his description of the shadow suggest this clearly: "analysis liberates the animal instincts . . . to put them to higher uses" (*CW* 7: 261). A Zen writer would never use the word "higher," suggesting as it does the dualism of higher/lower, with a preference for the former. Again, Jung says that the shadow, thus liberated, is then "brought under control again through the analysis of the unconscious" (*CW* 7: 261). In other words, the "animal instincts" are "control[led]" by the "analysis" of the rational mind. The contrast to Hirshfield's work, in which animals and humans are understood as separate species but are not arranged on any hierarchy of value, is also clear. Nor would the poet suggest that "instincts" are inferior to "rational analysis."

Again, Jung writes that the shadow is to be released in order to be "expose[d] . . . to the disinfecting power of daylight" (*CW* 7: 260), employing the cleansing metaphor that echoes the moralistic position of Western philosophy and theology and implying the logical and ethical priority of light, cleanliness, and morality over darkness and dirt. To Zen, all traditional Western theological and logical distinctions are misguided. Enlightenment is transcending all dualisms and all conclusions premised in dualistic thinking, especially such thinking as it is used to give priority to one member of a logically antithetical pair of concepts. The lion and the angel are one. Pain and pleasure are the same. Shen Hui, a disciple of Hui Neng, the fifth and final Chinese successor of Bodhidharma, who left India for China where he planted the roots of the Chinese version of Indian Buddhism that eventually sprang up in Japan as Zen, employs the simile of empty space to illuminate the identity of all things, specifically good and evil:

> In itself space neither changes nor ceases to change. In daylight those are right who think it to be bright; at night those are right who think it to be dark. Yet, whether bright or dark, it is the same space. Brightness and darkness alternate while the space itself neither changes nor ceases to change. The same applies to sin and saintliness. Don't distinguish between truth and error; in reality saintliness is not different from sin. (Burtt 236)

More conventionally, Abe comments that "when positivity (or being) is ontologically prior to negativity (or non-being)," as it is in Western traditions, then negativity "is no more than something to be overcome by positivity" (130). However, in the Buddhist tradition, the two terms are logically equal: "The *negativity* of human life is felt more seriously and deeply in Buddhism than among the followers of Western intellectual traditions. This is true to such an extent that it is not considered inferior but equal to positivity" (Abe 130). Negativity, with which the shadow is associated in Western descriptions of it, is not simply something to be incorporated into the psyche until wholeness or positivity is reached. The very distinction between negativity and positivity, in Buddhism, is to be overcome. As Abe says, "in Buddhism, liberation is realized in Emptiness as the emancipation from . . . existential antinomy" (131).

Even the most horrific example of what we would term sin is only sin if seen through a particular moral point of view. "An Earthly Beauty" (*October* 83) is short:

> Others have described
> the metal bull placed over fire,

it singing while the man inside it died.
Which emperor listened, in what country,
doesn't matter, though surely
the thing itself was built by slaves.
An unearthly music, all reports agree.
We—the civilized—hearing this story,
recoil from it in horror: Not us. Not ours.
But why does my heart look back at me,
reproachful? Why does the bull? (lines 1–11)

We the civilized, we the kind, we the moral, wonder in horror how
someone, some other human supposedly like us, could listen to and
enjoy the sound of another person being parboiled inside a metal cage.
But the bull sings to us that we are identical to it, we are the anonymous
emperor. Hirshfield balances, again subtly, her description of the bull's
sound as "an unearthly music" with her title "an earthly beauty" to
reinforce her continuum theme: any distinction our Western mind would
care to make between horror and beauty, earthly and unearthly, is pointless, a prescription for "attachment" to one term as superior, and hence
a prescription for suffering.

   As difficult as this concept is for the Western mind to grasp, much
less affirm, it does not mean that Buddhism is amoral, immoral, uneth-
ical, or nihilistic, as has occasionally been claimed. Abe explains: "Eth-
ically speaking, Buddhists clearly realize that good should conquer evil";
however, that cannot be a goal, given that "good and evil are mutually
negating principles with equal power," and any "ethical effort to overcome evil with good never succeeds and results in a serious dilemma"
(132). The Zen goal is different: "In Buddhism . . . what is essential for
salvation is not to overcome evil with good and to participate in the
supreme Good, but to be emancipated from the existential antinomy of
good and evil and awaken to the Emptiness prior to the opposition
between good and evil" (Abe 132). Jung himself illustrates the difficulty
of a Western mind, even an open and educated Western mind, trying to
understand fully such Eastern concepts as Emptiness or the "equal
power" of good and evil. He chastises Westerners for writing off as mere
mysticism or nihilism such "hazy" concepts: "We are fond of putting
'Oriental wisdom' in quotation marks and banishing it to the dim region
of faith and superstition" (*CW* 13: 7). However, on the same page, he
commits the very error: "Thus he [Western man] abandons the one sure
foundation of the Western mind [i.e., Western science] and loses himself
in a *mist* of words and ideas that could never have originated in European brains and can never be profitably grafted onto them" (*CW* 13: 7;

emphasis added). Oriental ideas are like an ephemeral and obscuring "mist" covering the clear, solid foundation of Western rationality and its products, most notably science. Hirshfield's epiphanies, however, reside in Jung's land of "mist."

Again, while professing respect for the *satori* experience of intuitive illumination and the Zen perspective in general, Jung manages to denigrate the system in his foreword to Suzuki's book when he says, "I treat *satori* first of all as a psychological problem" (15). Needless to say, neither Suzuki nor any other Zen practitioner would call *satori* a problem, but Jung says that "We can of course never decide definitely whether a person is *really* 'enlightened' or 'redeemed,' or whether he merely imagines it" (Suzuki 15). Therefore, Jung's focus, as a psychologist, is not on the truth or falsity of an individual's experience of *satori,* nor on the truth or falsity of the possibility of *satori,* but on the fact that the individual imagines himself to have experienced enlightenment; therefore, to the individual the enlightenment experience is real and needs to be dealt with as such: "What others think about it can determine nothing whatever for him with regard to his experience. Even if he were to lie, his lie would be a spiritual fact" (Suzuki 15). Jung thus grounds the enlightenment experience and its importance squarely within the individual's psychological reality. This perspective almost makes *satori* a symptom of neurosis, which Jung never says but comes close to implying when he states that "a very interesting psychological treatise could still be written on the fact of such lies [i.e., religious reports of enlightenment] with the same scientific treatment with which the psychopathology of delusions is presented" (Suzuki 15).

Almost as if answering Jung, Suzuki writes that "*Satori* is not a morbid state of mind, a fit subject for the study of abnormal psychology" (97). He is much more insistent on the phenomenal truth of the experience, not merely its interest as a psychological state of an individual. While he does say that "*satori* is a sort of inner perception," which almost sounds as if Suzuki agrees that enlightenment is a purely subjective reality, he qualifies that to mean "not the perception, indeed, of a single individual object but the perception of Reality itself" (93). He later describes the experience as "the sudden flashing into consciousness of a new truth hitherto undreamed of" (95), clearly beginning from the premise that Enlightenment is enlightenment to the truth, not a simple, subjective or psychological reality but the Reality of the world itself.

While the contemporary Westerner might think of individuation as a state of being to be achieved, Zen imagines a different sort of enlightenment: "nirvana is not an objectively observable state or something which can be considered merely a goal of life, but rather an existential ground from which human life can properly begin without becoming entangled in the duality of pleasure and suffering" (Abe 207). And, far from being hazy or mystical or idealistic, Zen enlightenment constitutes what Abe calls a "radical realism" in which "everything is realized as it *is*" (211), not as our culturally conditioned moral concepts tell us it should be (e.g., that something "dark" should be "evil" or "dangerous"; that a shadow of a thing has to be inferior to the "real" thing). Surely, even a brief introduction to the poetry of Jane Hirshfield also makes it clear that a Zen perspective on the world is not in any way a rose-colored vision. In fact, one could conclude that believing in the inferiority of negativity or the logical and cosmological priority of positivity, in other words participating in the Western frame of mind, is itself wildly idealistic.

Where does this leave us with respect to the shadow? First, the shadow is not an inferior entity in the human psyche. What we are trained to think of as shameful or even sinful in ourselves is not any different from what we are trained to think of as laudatory and sacred. Second, the shadow does not have to be dragged into consciousness by rational analysis. Analysis itself splits the shadow off from the "daylight" psyche. Analysis and its attendant vocabulary of moral hierarchies, not repression, create the dualism between shadow and light. In Zen, transcending the dualistic mode of rational analysis ultimately eliminates the shadow by rendering the concept neutral. There are no pieces and parts to a soul. It is whole, and it is wholly integrated into all around it. Third, incorporating the shadow and achieving individuation may seem a wonderful boon to the Western reader. The Buddhist recognizes that the true boon is recognizing that individuation and non-individuation are not different entities or states. *Nirvana* (escape from cyclic existence, what a Westerner might call Heaven) and *samsara* (entrapment in cyclic existence and rebirth) are identical. Or, nirvana "is only samsara seen as it is" (*Fundamental Wisdom* 331). Nirvana is not a better place or a better life or a better state of being: it is seeing samsara and nirvana as the emptiness, without the delusion that the contents of the shadow are evil but can be tamed by incorporation into the fully individuated psyche. As the Buddhist saint Nagarjuna writes in *The Fundamental Wisdom of the Middle Way*, his greatest philosophical work that has inspired Buddhists of all schools,

> There is not the slightest difference
> Between cyclic existence and nirvana.
> There is not the slightest difference
> Between cyclic existence and nirvana.

Whatever is the limit of nirvana,
That is the limit of cyclic existence.
There is not even the slightest difference between them,
Or even the subtlest thing. (331)

This is realistic and even hopeful: nirvana is here and available, without wrestling and defeating any evil shadows. In our current pluralistic, multicultural, ethnically diverse world, Buddhism offers a way of seeing the world absent Western value judgments and attachment to rationality. Tolerant of all religious faiths, moral beliefs, races, and ethnicities, Buddhism offers realism without shame and guilt, freedom without the delusion of independence, fulfillment without identifying that term with conquest or acquisition (as one "conquers" and "acquires" one's shadow in much the way one would conquer an opponent and acquire a new car).

Being able to step beyond our culturally conditioned, logical categories and moral assumptions enables us to read poets like Hirschfield with an insight unavailable to us while we insisted upon seeing strictly through Western eyes:

Look: in the iron bucket,
a single nail, a single ruby—
all the heavens and hells.
They rattle in the heart and make one sound.

("Late Prayer," *Lives* 45)

All one has to do is look, open one's eyes or soul, to see that the trivial and the valuable, the constructed and the natural, all the heavens and hells ever conceived of by humankind, all reside in the same iron bucket that is life, and they all make one sound, for all, like lion and angel, are the components of life, and all are life-nourishing, the falling fruit we require to sustain us fully.

WORKS CITED

Abe, Masao. *Zen and Western Thought*. Honolulu: U of Hawaii P, 1985.

Baird, James. "Jungian Psychology in Criticism: Theoretical Problems." *Literary Criticism and Psychology*. Ed. Joseph P. Strelka. University Park: Pennsylvania State UP, 1976. 3–30.

Basho, Matsuo. *The Narrow Road to the Deep North, and Other Travel Sketches*. Trans. Nobuyuki Yuasa. New York: Penguin, 1966.

Bennet, E. A. *C. G. Jung*. New York: Dutton, 1962.

Bly, Robert. *A Little Book on the Human Shadow*. San Francisco: Harper, 1988.

Boruch, Marianne. "Comment: Blessed Knock." *American Poetry Review* (July-August, 1988): 39.

Burtt, E. A., ed. *The Teachings of the Compassionate Buddha*. New York: New American Library, 1955.

Clark, Robert A. *Six Talks on Jung's Psychology*. Pittsburgh: Boxwood, 1953.

Coward, Harold. *Jung and Eastern Thought*. Albany: State U of New York P, 1985.

Dry, Avis M. *The Psychology of Jung: A Critical Interpretation*. London: Methuen, 1961.

Freud, Sigmund. *New Introductory Lectures on Psychoanalysis*. Standard ed. Trans. and ed. James Strachey. New York: Norton & Co, 1964.

The Fundamental Wisdom of the Middle Way: Nagarjuna's Mulamadhyamakakarika. Trans. Jay L. Garfield. New York: Oxford UP, 1995.

Glotfelty, Cherell, and Harold Fromm, eds. *The Ecocriticism Reader*. Athens: U of Georgia P, 1996.

Hatcher, Ashley. "Interview with Jane Hirshfield." *University of Arizona Poetry Center Newsletter* 20.1 (Fall 1995). <http://www.coh.modlang.arizona.edu/poetry/nwsfl95.html>.

Hawthorne, Nathaniel. "Ethan Brand." *Nathaniel Hawthorne's Tales*. Ed. James McIntosh. New York: Norton, 1987.

Hirshfield, Jane. "A Conversation with Jane Hirshfield." Interview with Judith Moore. *Poetry Daily*. 1997. 2 May 2000 <http://www.poems.com/hirinter.htm>.

———. *The Lives of the Heart*. New York: HarperCollins, 1997.

———. *Nine Gates: Entering the Mind of Poetry*. New York: HarperCollins, 1997.

———. "Jane Hirshfield and the Mind of Poetry." Interview with Katherine Mary Mills. *The Montserrat Review Online*. February 1998. 3 March 2000 <http://www.themontserratreview.com/issue-02-98/interview-01.html>.

———. "Interview: Entering the Mind of Jane Hirshfield." 21 May 2000 <http://go.borders.com/features/mmk98059.xcv>.

———. "An Interview with Jane Hirshfield." *Atlantic Monthly Online*. 18 September 1997. 17 June 2001 <http://www.theatlantic.com/unbound/bookauth/jhirsh.htm>.

———. *The October Palace*. New York: HarperCollins, 1994.

———. *Of Gravity and Angels*. Hanover, NH: Wesleyan UP, 1988.

Hopcke, Robert H. *A Guided Tour of the Collected Works of C. G. Jung.* Boston: Shambhala, 1989.

Jacobi, Jolande. *The Psychology of C. G. Jung: An Introduction with Illustrations.* New Haven: Yale UP, 1942.

Jung, C. G.. *The Collected Works of C. G. Jung.* Ed. Sir Herbert Read. Trans. R. F. C. Hull. 20 vols. Princeton: Princeton UP, 1953–91.

——. *Modern Man in Search of a Soul.* New York: Harcourt, 1933.

Lauter, Estella, and Carol Schreier Rupprecht, eds. *Feminist Archetypal Theory: Interdisciplinary Re-Visions of Jungian Thought.* Knoxville: U of Tennessee P, 1985.

Mattoon, Mary Ann. *Jungian Psychology in Perspective.* New York: Free, 1981.

Meier, C. A. *Soul and Body: Essays on the Theories of C. G. Jung.* San Francisco: Lapis, 1986.

Philipson, Morris. *Outline of a Jungian Aesthetics.* Evanston: Northwestern UP, 1963.

Plato. *Complete Works.* Ed. John M. Cooper. Indianapolis: Hackett, 1997.

Rowland, Susan. *C. G. Jung and Literary Theory: The Challenge from Fiction.* London: Macmillan, 1999.

Sherwin, Elizabeth. "Poet Hirshfield Produces Private Words for Public Feast." 12 May 1996. <http://www.dcn.davis.ca.us/go/gizmo/hirshf1.html>.

Singer, June. *Boundaries of the Soul: The Practice of Jung's Psychology.* Garden City, NY: Doubleday, 1972.

Suzuki, Daisetz Teitaro. *An Introduction to Zen Buddhism.* New York: Grove, 1964.

von Franz, Marie-Louise. *C. G. Jung: His Myth in Our Time.* New York: C. G. Jung Foundation, 1975.

Zweig, Carol, and Steve Wolf. *Romancing the Shadow: Illuminating the Dark Side of the Soul.* New York: Ballantine, 1997.

A BIBLIOGRAPHY OF JUNGIAN AND POST-JUNGIAN LITERARY CRITICISM, 1980–2000

MARCIA NICHOLS

The following offers to supplement Jos van Meurs's *Jungian Literary Criticism, 1920–1980,* updating van Meurs's bibliography through the year 2000. No longer a single, unified, clearly identifiable, and delineated field (as it had remained, more or less, throughout the decades surveyed by van Meurs), recent Jungian criticism has expanded and, in many ways, blurred and dissolved its traditional boundaries, complicating and critiquing itself, metamorphosing into numerous post-Jungian strains. At the same time, literary theory generally—given its poststructuralist, hybridizing tendencies—has re-appropriated the traditional vocabulary to serve in nontraditional and often, indeed, non-Jungian contexts. The loose, popular currency of "archetype" especially makes bibliographic work a hazardous duty; understandably, readers may quarrel with individual works listed or left out. But while the following list cannot claim to be exhaustive, it does reflect the range and diversity of current Jungian and post-Jungian criticism.

Adams, Michael Vannoy. "Ahab's Jonah-and-the-Whale Complex: The Fish Archetype in *Moby Dick*." *ESQ* 28 (1982): 167–82.

———. "Deconstructive Philosophy and Imaginal Psychology: Comparative Perspectives on Jacques Derrida and James Hillman." Sugg 231–48.

———. "Madness and Right Reason, Extremes of One: The Shadow Archetype in *Moby Dick*." *Bucknell Review* 31.2 (1988): 97–109.

Adler, Thomas P. "The Pirandello in Albee: The Problem of Knowing in *The Lady from Dubuque*." *Edward Albee: An Interview and Essays*. Ed. Julian N. Wasserman, Joy L. Linsley, and Jerome A. Kramer. Houston: U of St. Thomas, 1983. 109–19.

Ameter, Brenda. "'Put Your Ear Down to Your Soul and Listen Hard': Anne Sexton's Theory and Practice of Archetypal Poetry." *Original Essays on the Poetry of Anne Sexton*. Ed. Francis Bixler. Conway: U of Central Arkansas P, 1988. 81–91.

Anastasi, Michael J. "King of Glome: Pater Rex." *Lamp Post of the Southern California C. S. Lewis Society* 19.1 (1995): 13–19.

Anderson, Mary Castiglie. "Cultural Archetype and the Female Hero: Nature and Will in Ellen Glasgow's *Barren Ground*." *Modern Fiction Studies* 28.3 (1982): 383–93.

———. "Ritual and Initiation in *The Zoo Story*." *Edward Albee: An Interview and Essays*. Ed. Julian N. Wasserman, Joy L. Linsley, and Jerome A. Kramer. Houston: U of St. Thomas, 1983. 93–108.

Andres, Sophia. "Pre-Raphaelite Paintings and Jungian Images in Wilkie Collins's *The Woman in White*." *Victorian Newsletter* 88 (1995): 26–31.

Andriano, Joseph. "Archetypal Projection in 'Ligeia': A Post-Jungian Reading." *Poe Studies* 19.2 (1986): 27–31.

———. "'Our Dual Existence': Archetypes of Love and Death in Le Fanu's 'Carmilla.'" *Contours of the Fantastic: Selected Essays from the Eighth International Conference on the Fantastic in the Arts*. Ed. Michele K. Langford. New York: Greenwood, 1994. 49–55.

Ardolino, Frank R. "Severed and Brazen Heads: Headhunting in Elizabethan Drama." *Journal of Evolutionary Psychology* 4.3/4 (1983): 169–81.

Arensberg, Mary B. "'A Curable Separation': Stevens and the Mythology of Gender." *Wallace Stevens and the Feminine*. Ed. Melita Schaum. Tuscaloosa: U of Alabama P, 1993. 23–45.

Armistead, Myra. "'Childe Roland' and Two Other Poems by Browning." *Victorian Newsletter* 66 (1984): 22–24.

Arnold, St. George Tucker, Jr. "The Dragon in the Delta: The Hero Archetype in Eudora Welty's 'The Wide Net.'" *Journal of Evolutionary Psychology* 4.3/4 (1983): 133–44.

———. "Woman's Psyche and the Archetypal Odyssey: First Voyaging in Eudora Welty's 'At the Landing.'" *Journal of Evolutionary Psychology* 8.3/4 (1987): 330–40.

Ashworth, Ann. "Durrell's Hermetic Puer and Senex in *The Alexandria Quartet*." *Critique* 26.2 (1985): 67–80.

Asper, Kathrin. "'Fitcher's Bird': Illustrations of the Negative Animus and Shadow in Persons with Narcissistic Disturbances." Trans. Elizabeth Burr. Stein and Corbett 1: 121–39.

Atfield, J. R. "Seeing Things in a Jungian Perspective." *Agenda* 33 (1996): 131–43.

Atkinson, Michael. "Robert Bly's Sleepers Joining Hands: Shadow and Self." Sugg 83–102.

——. "Type and Text in *A Study in Scarlet:* Repression and the Textual Unconscious." Sugg 328–42.

Aubrey, James R. "Jungian 'Synchronicity' and John Fowles's *The Magus.*" *Notes on Contemporary Literature* 24.2 (1994): 11–12.

——. "'Uncrucifying' the Self: John Fowles and the Motif of the Hanged Man." *Journal of Evolutionary Psychology* 14.1/2 (1993): 109–17.

Babcock, Winifred. *Jung, Hesse, Harold: The Contributions of C. G. Jung, Hermann Hesse, and Preston Harold (Author of* The Shining Stranger) *to a Spiritual Psychology.* New York: Harold Institute, 1983.

Bagg, Robert. "Merlin and Faust in Two Post-War Poems." Spivack, *Merlin vs. Faust* 189–98.

Baird, James. "'Preface' to *Ishmael:* Jungian Psychology in Criticism: Some Theoretical Problems." Sugg 38–53.

Baker, Armand F. "Self-Realization in the Leyendas of Gustavo Adolfo Becquer." *Revista Hispanica Moderna* 44.2 (1991): 191–206.

Bakker, Martin. "Magical Realism and the Archetype in Hubert Lampo's Work." *Canadian Journal of Netherlandic Studies* 12.2 (1991): 17–21.

Balaban, Avraham. *Between God and Beast: An Examination of Amos Oz's Prose.* University Park: Pennsylvania State UP, 1993.

Barker, Jill. "Does Eddie Count?: A Psychoanalytic Perspective on 'Snowed Up.'" *Literary Theories: A Case Study of Critical Performance.* Ed. Julian Wolfreys and William Baker. New York: New York UP, 1996. 75–99.

Baring, Anne. "Cinderella: An Interpretation." Stein and Corbett 1: 49–64.

Barnum, Carol M. *The Fiction of John Fowles: A Myth for Our Time.* Greenwood, FL: Penkevill, 1988.

Barrow, Craig, and Diana Barrow. "Le Guin's *Earthsea:* Voyages in Consciousness." *Extrapolation* 32.1 (1991): 20–44.

Barry, Peter. *Beginning Theory: An Introduction to Literary and Cultural Theory.* Manchester: Manchester UP, 1995.

Batten, Wayne. "Illusion and Archetype: The Curious Story of Edna Pontellier." *Southern Literary Journal* 18.1 (1985): 73–88.

Bayo, Ogunjimi. "Ritual Archetypes: Ousmane's Aesthetic Medium in *Xala.*" *Ufahamu* 14.3 (1985): 128–38.

Beck, Martha C. "Carl Jung and Plato's *Phaedrus.*" *Publications of the Arkansas Philological Association* 25.2 (1999): 1–11.

Beebe, John. "The Notorious Postwar Psyche." *Journal of Popular Film and Television* 18.1 (1990): 28–35.

———. "The Trickster in the Arts." Sugg 302–12.

Begiebing, Robert J. *Acts of Regeneration: Allegory and Archetype in the Works of Norman Mailer*. Columbia: U of Missouri P, 1980.

Benert, Annette Larson. "The Dark Sources of Love: A Jungian Reading of Two Early James Novels." *University of Hartford Studies in Literature* 12 (1980): 99–123.

Berkove, Lawrence I. "London's Developing Conceptions of Masculinity." *Jack London Journal* 3 (1996): 117–26.

Bickman, Martin. *American Romantic Psychology: Emerson, Poe, Whitman, Dickinson, Melville*. Dallas: Spring, 1988.

Birkhauser-Oeri, Sibylle. *The Mother: Archetypal Image in Fairy Tales*. Trans. Michael Mitchell. Toronto: Inner City Books, 1988.

Bishop, Paul. "Affinities between Weimar Classicism and Analytical Psychology: Goethe and Jung on the Concept of the Self." *Forum for Modern Language Studies* 36.1 (2000): 74–91.

———. "The Birth of Analytical Psychology from the Spirit of Weimar Classicism." *Journal of European Studies* 29:4 (1999): 417–40.

———. "Epistemological Problems and Aesthetic Solutions in Goethe and Jung." *Goethe Yearbook* 9 (1999): 278–317.

———. "Estrangement from the Deed and the Memory Thereof: Freud and Jung on the Pale Criminal in Nietzsche's *Zarathustra*." *Orbis Litterarum: International Review of Literary Studies* 54.6 (1999): 424–38.

———. "The Jung/Forster-Nietzsche Correspondence." *German Life and Letters* 46.4 (1993): 319–30.

———. "Jung's Annotations of Nietzsche's Works: An Analysis." *Nietzsche Studien* 24 (1995): 271–314.

———. "Paracelsus, Goethe, Jung: Reading Jung Aesthetically." *Spring* 64 (1998): 135–58.

———. "The Use of Kant in Jung's Early Psychological Works." *Journal of European Studies* 26.2 (1996): 107–40.

Blair, Rhonda L. "Archetypal Imagery in Max Frisch's *Homo Faber*: The Wise Old Man and the Shadow." *The Germanic Review* 59.3 (1984): 104–08.

———. "*Homo Faber*, Homo Ludens, and the Demeter-Kore Motif." *Germanic Review* 56.4 (1981): 140–50.

Blasingham, Mary V. "Archetypes of the Child and of Childhood in the Fiction of Flannery O'Conner." *Realist of Distances: Flannery O'Connor Revisited.* Ed. Karl Heinz Westarp and Jan Nordby Gretlund. Aarhus, Denmark: Aarhus UP, 1987. 102–12.

Blodgett, Harriet. "The Nature of *Between the Acts*." *Modern Language Studies* 13.3 (1983): 27–37.

———. "Through the Labyrinth with Daniel: The Mythic Structure of George Eliot's *Daniel Deronda*." *Journal of Evolutionary Psychology* 9.1/2 (1988): 164–79.

Boer, Charles. "Poetry and Psyche." Sugg 249–57.

Boldy, Steven. "Fathers and Sons in Fuentes' *La muerte de Artemio Cruz*." *Bulletin of Hispanic Studies* 61.1 (1984): 31–40.

Bontatibus, Donna. "Reconnecting with the Past: Personal Hauntings in Margaret Atwood's *The Robber Bride*." *Papers on Language and Literature* 34.4 (1998): 358–71.

Boss, Judith E. "The Season of Becoming: Ann Maxwell's *Change*." *Science Fiction Studies* 12 (1985): 51–65.

Branson, Clark. *Howard Hawkes: A Jungian Study*. Santa Barbara: Garland-Clarke Editions/Capra, 1987.

Brienza, Susan D. "Perilous Journeys on Beckett's Stages: Traveling through Words." *Myth and Ritual in the Plays of Samuel Beckett*. Ed. Katherine H. Burkman. Rutherford: Fairleigh Dickinson UP, 1987. 28–49.

Brinton Perera, Sylvia. *Descent to the Goddess: A Way of Initiation for Women*. Toronto: Inner City Books, 1981.

Brivic, Sheldon R. *Joyce between Freud and Jung*. Port Washington, NY: Kennikat, 1980.

Broege, Valerie. "The Journey toward Individuation of Adela Quested in E. M. Forster's and David Lean's *A Passage to India*." *Heroines of Popular Culture*. Ed. Pat Browne. Bowling Green, OH: Popular, 1987. 41–53.

Brooks, Harold F. "Blake and Jung III: Reintegration." *Aligarh Critical Miscellany* 5.1 (1992): 41–89.

Broone, F. Hal. "The Scientific Basis of George MacDonald's Dream-Frame." *The Gold Thread: Essays on George MacDonald*. Ed. William Raeper. Edinburgh: Edinburgh UP, 1990. 87–108.

Brown, Russell M., and Donna A. Bennett. "Magnus Eisengrim: The Shadow of the Trickster in the Novels of Robertson Davies." Sugg 285–301.

Brucker, Carl W. "Virtue Rewarded: The Contemporary Student and Horatio Alger." *Journal of General Education* 35.4 (1984): 270–75.

Brunauer, Dalma H., and Stephen Brunauer. "*Alexander's Bridge*: Novel and Archetype." *Journal of Evolutionary Psychology* 10.3/4 (1989): 295–99.

Brynes, Alice. *The Child: An Archetypal Symbol in Literature for Children and Adults*. New York: Peter Lang, 1995.

Buss, Helen M. *Mother and Daughter Relationships in the Manawaka Works of Margaret Laurence*. Victoria, BC: U of Victoria P, 1985.

Bzowski, Frances. "'Half-Child—Half Heroine': Emily Dickinson's Use of Traditional Female Archetypes." *ESQ* 29 (1983): 154–69.

Callan, Richard J. "Archetypes in Stories by Rafael Arevalo Martinez." *Critica Hispanica* 17.2 (1995): 293–301.

———. "Archetypal Symbolism in Two Novels of the Costa Rican, Carmen Naranjo." *Ensayos de literature europea e hispanoamericana.* Ed. Felix Menchacatorre. San Sebastian: U of del Pais Vasco P, 1990. 61–65.

———. "Cortazar's *Los premios:* A Journey of Discovery." *Revista de Estudios Hispanico* 15.3 (1981): 365–75.

———. "Cortazar's Story 'Silvia': The Hero and the Golden Hoard." *Chasqui* 20.2 (1991): 46–53.

———. "Elena Garro's *El encanto, tendajon mixto:* The Magical Woman and Maturity." *Critica Hispanica* 14.1–2 (1992): 49–57.

Campbell, Joseph. "The Fashioning of Living Myths." Sugg 75–82.

Carnell, Corbin Scott. "Ransom in C. S. Lewis's *Perelandra* as Hero in Transformation: Notes toward a Jungian Reading." *Studies in the Literary Imagination* 14.2 (1981): 67–71.

Carrabino, Victor, ed. *The Power of Myth in Literature and Film: Selected Papers from Second Annual Florida State University Conference on Literature and Film.* Tallahassee: UP of Florida, 1980.

Cederstrom, Lorelei. *Fine-Tuning the Feminine Psyche: Jungian Patterns in the Novels of Doris Lessing.* New York: Peter Lang, 1990.

———. "The 'Great Mother' in *The Grapes of Wrath.*" *Steinbeck and the Environment: Interdisciplinary Approaches.* Ed. Susan F. Beegel, Susan Shillinglaw, and Wesley Tiffney. Tuscaloosa: U of Alabama P, 1997. 76–91.

———. "A Jungian Approach to the Self in Major Whitman Poems." *Approaches to Teaching Whitman's* Leaves of Grass. Ed. Donald D. Kummings. New York: MLA, 1990. 81–89.

———. "Myth and Ceremony in Contemporary North American Native Fiction." *Canadian Journal of Native Studies* 2.2 (1982): 285–301.

———. "The Principal Archetypal Elements of *The Golden Notebook.*" *Approaches to Teaching Lessing's* The Golden Notebook. Ed. Carey Kaplan and Rose Ellen Cronan. New York: MLA, 1989. 50–57.

Cervo, Nathan. "Morris's 'Rapunzel.'" *Explicator* 51.3 (1993): 167–69.

Cech, John. *Angels and Wild Things: The Archetypal Poetics of Maurice Sendak.* University Park, PA: Penn State UP, 1995.

———. "Shadows in the Classroom: Teaching Children's Literature from a Jungian Perspective." *Teaching Children's Literature: Issues, Pedagogy, Resources.* Ed. Glenn Edward Sadler. New York: MLA, 1992. 80–88.

————. "The Triumphant Transformation of Pinocchio." *Triumphs in the Spirit in Children's Literature*. Ed. Francelia Butler and Richard Rotert. Hamden, CT: Lib. Professional, 1986. 171–77.

Clasby, Nancy Tenfelde. "Realism and the Archetypes: *Daisy Miller*." *Spring* 60 (1996): 31–44.

Clay, John. "Jung's Influence in Literature and the Arts." *Jungian Thought in the Modern World*. Ed. Elphis Christopher and Hester McFarland Solomon. London: Free Association, 2000. 233–43.

Coassin, Flavia. "Matelda: Poetic Image or Archetype?" *Visions and Revisions: Women in Italian Culture*. Ed. Mirna Cicioni and Nicole Prunster. Providence, RI: Berg, 1993. 3–12.

Cobb, Noel. *Prospero's Island: The Secret Alchemy at the Heart of* The Tempest. London: Coventure, 1984.

Collins, Alfred. "'Sunahsepa' and 'Akanandun': Eating the Son and the Indian Father's Mid-Life Initiation." Stein and Corbett 2: 123–39.

Cook, David A. "Shadows of Forgotten Ancestors: Film as Religious Art." *Post Script* 3.3 (1984): 16–23.

Cookson, Sandra. "'The Repressed Becomes the Poem': Landscape and Quest in Two Poems by Louise Bogan." *Critical Essays on Louise Bogan*. Ed. Martha Collins. Boston: Hall, 1984. 194–203.

Corbett, Lionel, and Cathy Rives. "'The Fisherman and His Wife': The Anima in the Narcissistic Character." Stein and Corbett 1: 103–20.

Costabile-Heming, Carol Anne, and Vasiliki Karandrikas. "Experimenting with Androgyny: Malina and Ingeborg Bachmann's Jungian Search for Utopia." *Mosaic* 30.3 (1997): 75–87.

Costello, Jacqueline. "When Worlds Collide: Freedom, Freud, and Jung in John Fowles's *Daniel Martin*." *University of Hartford Studies in Literature* 22.1 (1990): 31–44.

Coursen, H. R. "'Age Is Unnecessary': A Jungian Approach to *King Lear*." *The Upstart Crow* 5 (1984): 75–92.

————. *The Compensatory Psyche: A Jungian Approach to Shakespeare*. Lanham, MD: UP of America, 1986.

————. "The Death of Cordelia: A Jungian Approach." *Hebrew University Studies in Literature* 8 (1980): 1–12.

————. "A Jungian Approach to Characterization: *Macbeth*." *Shakespeare's "Rough Magic": Renaissance Essays in Honor of C. L. Barber*. Ed. Peter Erickson and Coppelia Kahn. Newark: U of Delaware P, 1985. 230–44.

Cowart, David. "Matriarchal Mythopoesis: Naylor's *Mama Day*." *Philological Quarterly* 77.4 (1998): 439–59.

Coyle, William, ed. *Aspects of Fantasy: Selected Essays from the Second International Conference on the Fantastic in Literature and Film.* Westport, CT: Greenwood, 1986.

Crapanzano, Vincent. *Hermes' Dilemma and Hamlet's Desire: On the Epistemology of Interpretation.* Cambridge, MA: Harvard UP, 1992.

———. "'Lacking Now Is Only the Leading Idea, That Is—We, the Rays, Have No Thoughts': Interlocutory Collapse in Daniel Paul Schreber's *Memoirs of My Nervous Illness.*" *Critical Inquiry* 24.3 (1998): 737–67.

Criswell, Stephen. "'Traveling into Purity and Extremity': A Jungian Reading of John Hawkes's *Travesty.*" *Publications of the Mississippi Philological Association* (1995): 32–41.

Cro, Stelio. *The Spirit and the Flesh: Manzoni and the Modern Novel.* Tallahassee: DeSoto, 1995.

Crowther, Catherine, Jane Hayres, and Kathleen Newton. "The Psychological Use of Fairy Tales." *Contemporary Jungian Analysis: Post-Jungian Perspectives from the Society of Analytical Psychology.* Ed. Ian Alister and Christopher Hauke. London: Routledge, 1998. 211–19.

Curran, Ronald T. "Complex, Archetype, and Primal Fear: King's Use of Fairy Tales in *The Shining.*" *The Dark Descent: Essays Defining Stephen King's Horrorscape.* Ed. Tony Magistrale. New York: Greenwood, 1992. 33–46.

Cusick, Edmund. "MacDonald and Jung." *The Gold Thread: Essays on George MacDonald.* Ed. William Raeper. Edinburgh: Edinburgh UP, 1990. 56–86.

Cutter, Martha J. "Philomela Speaks: Alice Walker's Revisioning of Rape Archetypes in *The Color Purple.*" *MELUS* 25.3/4 (2000): 161–80.

Daniel, Helen. "The Aborigine in Australian Fiction: Stereotype or Archetype?" *MFS* 27.1 (1981): 45–60.

David, Julian. *Interweaving Symbols of Individuation in African and European Fairy Tales: A Jungian Perspective.* Cape Town: Kaggen, 1991.

Davies, Paul. "Three Novels and Four Nouvelles: Giving Up the Ghost Be Born at Last." *The Cambridge Companion to Beckett.* Ed. John Pilling. Cambridge: Cambridge UP, 1994. 43–66.

Davis, Cynthia A. "Archetype and Structure: On Feminist Myth Criticism." *Courage and Tools: The Florence Howe Award for Feminist Scholarship.* Ed. Joanne Glasgow and Angela Ingram. New York: MLA, 1990. 109–18.

Davis, Joanne. *Mademoiselle de Scudery and the Looking-Glass Self.* New York: Peter Lang, 1993.

Davis, Marian. "Cuchulain and Women: A Jungian Perspective." *Mythlore* 76 (1994): 23–26.

Davis, Mary Kemp. "William Styron's Nat Turner as an Archetype." *Southern Literary Journal* 28.1 (1995): 67–84.

Dawson, Terence. "The Dandy in *The Picture of Dorian Gray:* Towards an Archetypal Theory of Wit." *New Comparison* 3 (1987): 133–42.

———. "Jung, Literature, and Literary Criticism." *The Cambridge Companion to Jung.* Ed. Polly Young-Eisendrath and Terence Dawson. Cambridge: Cambridge UP, 1997. 255–80.

Day, Aidan. "The Archetype That Waits: *The Lover's Tale, In Memoriam* and 'Maud.'" *Tennyson: Seven Essays.* Ed. Philip Collins. New York: St. Martin's, 1992. 76–101.

Demetrakopoulos, Stephanie. "Goddess Manifestations as Stages in Feminine Metaphysics in the Poetry and Life of Anne Sexton." *Sexton: Selected Criticism.* Ed. Diana Hume George. Urbana: U of Illinois P, 1988. 117–44.

———. "Laurence's Fiction: A Revisioning of Archetypes." *Canadian Literature* 93 (1982): 42–57.

DeMouy, Jane Krause. *Katherine Anne Porter's Women: The Eye of Her Fiction.* Austin: U of Texas P, 1983.

Denitto, Dennis. "Ingmar Bergman's *Wild Strawberries:* A Jungian Analysis." *CUNY English Forum, Vol. I.* Ed. Saul N. Brody and Harold Schechter. New York: AMS, 1985. 45–70.

Diehl, H. "Into the Maze of the Self: Protestant Transformations of the Images of the Labyrinth." *The Journal of Mediaeval and Renaissance Studies* 16.2 (1986): 281–301.

Dilworth, Thomas. "Sex and the Goddess in the Poetry of David Jones." *University of Toronto Quarterly* 54.3 (1985): 251–64.

Dobson, Joanne A. "'Oh, Susie, it is dangerous': Emily Dickinson and the Archetype." *Feminist Critics Read Emily Dickinson.* Ed. Suzanne Juhasz. Bloomington: Indiana UP, 1983. 80–97.

Doll, Mary A. *Beckett and Myth: An Archetypal Approach.* Syracuse: Syracuse UP, 1988.

———. "Rites of Story: The Old Man at Play." *Myth and Ritual in the Plays of Samuel Beckett.* Ed. Katherine H. Burkman. Rutherford: Fairleigh Dickinson UP, 1987. 73–85.

Dompkowski, Judith A. "Child-as-Artist: Bruno Schulz and the Jungian Maternal." *Bruno Schulz: New Documents and Interpretations.* Ed. Czeslaw Z. Prokopczyk. New York: Peter Lang, 1998. 123–44.

Doty, William G. "Everything You Never Wanted to Know about the Dark, Lunar Side of the Trickster." *Spring* 57 (1995): 19–38.

———. "Myth, the Archetype of All Other Fable: A Review of Recent Literature." *Soundings* 74.1/2 (1991): 243–74.

Douglas, Claire. "'Oisin's Mother': Because I Would Not Give My Love to the Druid Named Dark." Stein and Corbett 2: 33–57.

———. *The Woman in the Mirror: Analytical Psychology and the Feminine.* Boston: Sigo, 1990.

Drew, Elizabeth. "T. S. Eliot: The Mythical Vision." Sugg 9–20.

Driscoll, James P. *Identity in Shakespearean Drama.* Lewisburg: Bucknell UP, 1983.

———. *The Unfolding God of Jung and Milton.* Lexington: UP of Kentucky, 1993.

Duran, Gloria. *The Archetypes of Carlos Fuentes: From Witch to Androgyne.* Hamden, CT: Archon, 1980.

———. "*Orchids in the Moonlight:* Fuentes as Feminist and Jungian Playwright." *World Literature Today* 57.4 (1983): 595–98.

———. "Waiting for Father and Putting Up with Mother: An Iconoclastic View of Carlos Fuentes' *El tuerto es rey (The One-Eyed Man Is King).*" *Meste* 13.1 (1984): 30–39.

———. "Women and Houses—from Poe to Allende." *Confluencia* 6.2 (1991): 9–15.

Dyck, E. F. "Norman O. Brown's Body: Archetypal Metamorphosis." *Mosaic* 22.3 (1989): 31–41.

Dyer, Donald R. *Cross-Currents of Jungian Thought: An Annotated Bibliography.* Shambhala: Boston: 1991.

Eberwien, Robert T. *Film and the Dream Screen: A Sleep and a Forgetting.* Princeton: Princeton UP, 1984.

Edinger, Edward F. *Encounter with the Self: A Jungian Commentary on William Blake's Illustrations of the* Book of Job. Toronto: Inner City, 1986.

———. *Goethe's* Faust: *Notes for a Jungian Commentary.* Toronto: Inner City, 1990.

Edwards, Duane. "Erich Neumann and the Shadow Problem in *The Plumed Serpent.*" *D. H. Lawrence Review* 23.2/3 (1991): 129–41.

Egberike, J. B. "The Carrier-Scapegoat Archetype and the Cult of Altruistic Suffering: A Study in the Mythological Imagination of *Hamlet, The Flies* and *The Strong Breed.*" *Proceedings of the Eighth Congress of the International Comparative Literature Association, II.* Ed. Bela Kopeczi and Gyorgy M. Vajda. Stuttgart: Bieber, 1980. 293–301.

Elbert, Monika. "From Merlin to Faust: Emerson's Democratization of the 'Heroic Mind.'" Spivack, *Merlin vs. Faust* 113–37.

Elias, Edward. "*Tortuga:* A Novel of Archetypal Structure." *Bilingual Review* 9.1 (1982): 82–87.

Elias-Button, Karen. "Journey into an Archetype: The Dark Mother in Contemporary Women's Poetry." Sugg 355–66.

Elkins, Andrew. "'So Strangely Married': Peggy Pond Church's *The Ripened Fields:* Fifteen Sonnets of a Marriage." *Western American Literature* 30.4 (1996): 353–72.

Elsbree, Langdon. *The Rituals of Life: Patterns in Narrative.* Port Washington, NY: Kennikat, 1982.

Ennis, Stephen C. "Told as Truth: 'Wakefield' as Archetypal Experience." *Nathaniel Hawthorne Review* 14.2 (1988): 7–9.

Fairhall, James. "Hardy's 'When I Set Out for Lyonnesse.'" *Explicator* 45.1 (1986): 25–27.

Feal, Carlos. "Against the Law: Mad Lovers in *Don Quixote.*" *Quixotic Desires: Psychoanalytic Perspectives on Cervantes.* Ed. Ruth Anthony Saffar and Diana de Armas Wilson. Ithaca, NY: Cornell UP, 1993. 179–99.

Fischer, Susan L. "The Invisible Partner: A Jungian Approach to Calderon's *La dama duende.*" *Revista Canadiense de Estudios Hispanicos* 7.2 (1983): 231–47.

Fitz, Stephen S. "'You Can't Help a Hollerin' and a Shoutin'': The Unconscious World of Antebellum Slaves: A Jungian Perspective." *Worldmaking.* Ed. William Pencak. New York: Peter Lang, 1996. 139–61.

Flatto, Eli. "Emily Dickinson's 'My life closed twice': The Archetypal Import of Its Imagistic Number Two." *American Imago* 45.2 (1988): 225–27.

Fouchereaux, Jean. "Feminine Archetypes in Colette and Maire-Claire Blais." *Journal of the Midwest Modern Language Association* 19.1 (1986): 43–49.

Foust, Ronald. "The Aporia of Recent Criticism and the Contemporary Significance of Spatial Form." *Spatial Form in Narrative.* Ed. Jeffrey R. Smitten and Ann Daghistany. Ithaca: Cornell UP, 1981. 179–201.

———. "Monstrous Image: Theory of Fantasy Antagonists." *Genre* 13.4 (1980): 441–53.

François, Pierre. "Psycho-Ontological Evil in Patrick White's *The Solid Mandala.*" *Commonwealth Essays and Studies* 18.2 (1996): 104–17.

———. "Synchronicity and the Unitarian Geopsyche in Wilson Harris's *Companions of the Day and Night.*" *The Contact and the Culmination.* Ed. Marc Delrez and Benedicte Ledent. Liege, Belgium: Liege Language and Literature, 1997. 241–51.

Franklin, Rosemary F. "*The Awakening* and the Failure of Psyche." *American Literature* 56.4 (1984): 510–16.

Franz, Maire-Louise von. *Archetypal Patterns in Fairy Tales.* Toronto: Inner City, 1997.

———. *The Feminine in Fairy Tales.* Boston: Shambhala, 1993.

———. *Problems of the Feminine in Fairy Tales.* Boston: Shambhala, 1993.

———. *The Psychological Meaning of Redemption Motifs in Fairy Tales.* Toronto: Inner City, 1980.

Frentz, Thomas S., and Janice Hocker Rushing. "Integrating Ideology and Archetype in Rhetorical Criticism, Part II: A Case Study of *Jaws*." *Quarterly Journal of Speech* 79.1 (1993): 61–81.

Frey-Rohn, Liliane. *Friedrich Nietzsche: A Psychological Approach to His Life and Work.* Ed. Robert Hinshaw and Lele Fischli. Einsiedeln, Switzerland: Daimon Verlag, 1988.

Frieling, Barbara. "Blake at the Rim of the World: A Jungian Consideration of *Jerusalem*." *Journal of Evolutionary Psychology* 8.3/4 (1987): 211–18.

Frongia, Terri. "Archetypes, Stereotypes and the Female Hero: Transformations in Contemporary Perspectives." *Mythlore* 18 (1991): 15–18.

———. "Good Wizard/Bad Wizard: Merlin and Faust Archetypes in Contemporary Children's Literature." Spivack, *Merlin vs. Faust* 65–93.

Fuchs, Cynthia J. "'I Looked for You in My Closet Tonight': Voyeurs and Victims in *Blue Velvet*." *Spring* 49 (1989): 85–98.

Gad, Irene. "Beauty and the Beast and the Wonderful Sheep—The Couple in Fairy Tales: When Father's Daughter Meets Mother's Son." Stein and Corbett 1: 27–48.

Gallant, Christine. "The Archetypal Feminine in Emily Brontë's Poetry." *Women's Studies* 7.1/2 (1980): 79–94.

———. *Tabooed Jung: Marginality as Power.* New York: New York UP, 1996.

Gates, Larry. "*Angel Heart*: Descent into the Imaginal." *Journal of Evolutionary Psychology* 9.1/2 (1989): 33–40.

———. "The Reconciliation of Opposites in *The Plumed Serpent*." *Journal of Evolutionary Psychology* 15.3–4 (1994): 274–82.

Geer, Genevieve. "'The White Snake': A Servant Animus Tale." Stein and Corbett 2: 157–78.

Gelpi, Albert. "Emily Dickinson and the Deerslayer: The Dilemma of the Woman Poet in America." Sugg 103–17.

———. "The Map for the Periplum: Canto 1 as Archetypal Schema." *American Poetry* 1.2 (1984): 49–59.

———. "Two Ways of Spelling It Out: An Archetypal-Feminist Reading of H. D.'s *Trilogy* and Adrienne Rich's *Sources*." Sugg 376–94.

Gianinni, John. "The Child Archetype in Arthur: A Jungian Perspective." *Avalon to Camelot* 2.1 (1986): 19–22.

Gill, Richard. "Jung's Archetype of the Wise Old Man in Poems by Chaucer, Wordsworth, and Browning." *Journal of Evolutionary Psychology* 2.1/2 (1981): 18–32.

Gillespie, Diane Filby. "Strindberg's *To Damascus:* Archetypal Autobiography." *Modern Drama* 26.3 (1983): 290–304.

Gingell-Beckmann, Susan. "Seven Black Swans: The Symbolic Logic of Patrick White's *The Eye of the Storm.*" *World Literature Written in English* 21.2 (1982): 315–25.

Glendinning, Robert J. "The Archetypal Structure of *Hymisqvida.*" *Folklore* 91.1 (1980): 92–110.

Godard, Jerry Caris. *Eros Plays: Parts and Pieces from a Left-Handed Psychology.* Lanham: UP of America, 1990.

———. *Mental Forms Creating: William Blake Anticipates Freud, Jung and Rank.* Lanham, MD: UP of America, 1985.

Godsil, Geraldine. "Winter's Ragged Hand—Creativity in the Face of Death." *Jungian Thought in the Modern World.* Ed. Elphis Christopher and Hester McFarland Solomon. London: Free Association, 2000. 244–63.

Golden, Kenneth L. "Archetypes and 'Immoralists' in Andre Gide and Thomas Mann." *College Literature* 15.2 (1988): 189–98.

———. "Jung, Modern Dissociation, and Forster's *Howard's End.*" *College Language Association Journal* 29.2 (1985): 221–31.

———. "Self, Overmind, and the Evolution of Consciousness: Jung, Myth, and Arthur C. Clarke's *Childhood's End.*" *Publications of the Mississippi Philological Association* (1984): 134–52.

Goldenberg, Naomi R. "A Feminist Critique of Jung." *Jung and Christianity in Dialogue: Faith, Feminism and Hermeneutics.* Ed. Robert L. Moore and Daniel J. Meckel. Mahwah, NY: Paulist, 1990. 104–11.

———. "Looking at Jung Looking at Himself: A Psychoanalytic Re-Reading of *Memories, Dreams, Reflections.*" *Soundings* 73.2–3 (1990): 383–406.

Gollnick, James, ed. *Comparative Studies in Merlin from the Vedas to C. G. Jung.* Lewiston: Mellen, 1991.

———. "Merlin as Psychological Symbol: A Jungian View." Gollnick, *Comparative Studies in Merlin* 111–31.

Goode, Okey. "Acceptance and Assertion in Merlin and Faust." Spivack, *Merlin vs. Faust* 19–39.

Goodman, Ralph. "A Jungian Feminist Approach to Alexander Pope's *The Rape of the Lock.*" *Unisa English Studies* 33.1 (1995): 26–30.

Goodrich, Peter H. "The Alchemical Merlin." Gollnick, *Comparative Studies in Merlin* 91–110.

Grant, Richard B. "Victor Hugo's 'Les Deux Archers': Patterns of Disguise and Revelation." *Romance Note* 32.3 (1992): 215–20.

Gras, Vernon W. "Myth and the Reconcilliation of Opposites: Jung and Levi-Strauss." *Journal of the History of Ideas* 42.3 (1981): 471–87.

Green, Melissa. "Fleming's 'Escape' in *The Red Badge of Courage*: A Jungian Analysis." *American Literary Realism* 28.1 (1995): 80–91.

Griffin, David Ray. *Archetypal Processes: Self and Divine in Whitehead, Jung and Hillman*. Evanston, IL: Northwestern UP, 1989.

Guth, Deborah. "Archetypal Worlds Reappraised: *The French Lieutenant's Woman* and *Le Grand Meaulnes*." *Comparative Literature Studies* 22.2 (1985): 244–51.

Hagenbuchle, Helen. "Blood for the Muse: A Study of the Poetic Process in Randall Jarrell's Poetry." *Critical Essays on Randall Jarrell*. Ed. Suzanne Ferguson. Boston: Hall, 1983. 101–19.

Hallab, Mary Y. "Love and Death in *The Sacred Fount*." *Publications of the Missouri Philological Association* 11 (1986): 27–33.

Hamilton, James F. "The Gendering of Space in Chateaubriand's *Combourge*: Archetypal Architecture and Patriarchal Object." *Symposium* 50.2 (1996): 101–13.

———. "Reversed Polarities in the *Nuits*: Anatomy of a Cure." *Nineteenth Century French Studies* 20.1–2 (1991–92): 65–73.

Hansen, Terry L. "Myth-Adventure in Leigh Brackett's 'Enchantress of Venus.'" *Extrapolation* 23.1 (1982): 77–82.

Hardin, Richard F. "Archetypal Criticism." *Contemporary Literary Theory*. Ed. Douglas G. Atkins and Laura Morrow. Amherst: U of Massachusetts P, 1989. 42–59.

Harper, Anthony J. "'Mysterium Conjunctionis': On the Attraction of 'Chymical Weddings.'" *German Life and Letters* 47.4 (1994): 44–55.

Harrod, Elizabeth. "Trees in Tolkien and What Happened Under Them." *Mythlore* 11 (1984): 47–52, 58.

Hart, David L. "'The Water of Life': A Story of Healing and the Transformation of Consciousness." Stein and Corbett 2: 141–56.

Hartmann, Ellen. "*The Lady from the Sea* in a Mythologic and Psychoanalytic Perspective." *Cambridge Approaches to Literature* 9 (1997): 133–46.

Hauke, Christopher. *Jung and the Postmodern: The Interpretation of Realities*. London: Routledge, 2000.

Hayles, Nancy K., and Kathryn Dohrmann Rindskopf. "The Shadows of Violence." *Journal of Popular Film and Television* 8.2 (1980): 2–8.

Heaney, Liam F. "Freud, Jung, and Joyce: Conscious Connections." *Contemporary Review* 265 (1994): 28–31.

Held, Leonard. "Myth and Archetype in Nicolas Roeg's *Walkabout*." *Post Script* 5.3 (1986): 21–46.

Hellen, Richard A. J., and Philip M. Tucker. "The Alchemical Art of Arthur C. Clarke." *Foundation* 41 (1987): 30–41.

Henderson, Joseph L. "The Artist's Relation to the Unconscious." Sugg 54–58.

Hill, G. *Illuminating Shadows: The Mythic Power of Film.* Boston: Shambhala, 1992.

Hill, Michael Ortiz. "C. G. Jung in the Heart of Darkness." *Spring* 61 (1997): 125–33.

Hillman, James. "Healing Fiction." Sugg 129–38.

Hinton, Ladson. "'The Goose Girl': Puella and Transformation." Stein and Corbett 1: 141–53.

Hinz, Evelyn J., and John J. Teunissen. "Culture and the Humanities: The Archetypal Approach." Sugg 192–99.

———. "War, Love, and Industrialism: The Ares/Aphrodite/Hephaestus Complex in *Lady Chatterley's Lover.*" Sugg 139–52.

Hockley, Luke. *Cinematic Projections: The Analytical Psychology of C. G. Jung and Film Theory.* Luton: U of Luton P, 2001.

Hoffman, Steven K. "Sailing into the Self: Jung, Poe and 'MS. Found in a Bottle.'" *Tennessee Studies in Literature* 26 (1981): 66–74.

Hogh, Carsten. "Fairytales and Alchemy: The Psychological Functions of Folktales in the Middle Ages and Nowadays." *Arv: Nordic Yearbook of Folklore* 46 (1990): 141–56.

Holbrook, David. "George MacDonald and Dreams of the Other World." *Seven* 4 (1983): 27–37.

Holland, Mark. "Miles Coverdale: Hawthorne's Presentation of the Puer Aeternus Archetype." *Journal of Evolutionary Psychology* 9.1/2 (1989): 17–24.

Holland, Mark, and Allan L. Combs. "Synchronicity and the Myth of the Trickster: Hermes Plays the Devil." *Journal of Evolutionary Psychology* 11. 3–4 (1990): 237–46.

Hollwitz, John. "The Wonder of Passage, the Making of Gold: Alchemy and Initiation in *Out of the Silent Planet.*" *Mythlore* 11 (1985): 17–24.

House, Jeff. "Sweeny among the Archetypes: The Literary Hero in American Culture." *Journal of American Culture* 16.4 (1993): 65–71.

Hubbs, Valentine C. "German Romanticism and C. G. Jung: Selective Affinities." *Journal of Evolutionary Psychology* 4.1/2 (1983): 8–20.

Hudson, Wilson M. "Jung on Myth and the Mythic." *Psychology and Myth.* Ed. Robert A. Segal. New York: Garland, 1996. 197–213.

Hulvey, S. Yumiko. "Myths and Monsters: The Female Body as the Site for Political Agendas." *Body Politics and the Fictional Double.* Ed. Debra Walker King. Bloomington: Indiana UP, 2000. 71–88.

Iaccino, J. F. *Jungian Reflections within the Cinema: A Psychological Analysis of Sci-Fi and Fantasy Archetypes.* Westport, CT: Praeger, 1998.

Irizarry, Estelle. "The Ubiquitous Trickster Archetype in the Narrative of Francisco Ayala." *Hispania* 70.2 (1987): 222–30.

Irwin, John T. "The Triple Archetype: The Presence of *Faust* in *The Bridge*." *Arizona Quarterly* 50.1 (1994): 51–73.

Jacobson, Wendy S. "'The World within Us': Jung and Dr. Manette's Daughter." *Dickensian* 93.2 (1997): 95–104.

Jacoby, Mario. "The Analytical Psychology of C. G. Jung and the Problem of Literary Evaluation." Sugg 59–74.

Jennings, Lee B. "Meyrink's Der Golem: The Self as the Other." Coyle 55–60.

———. "Morike's Muse: An Archetypal Reflection." *Morike's Muses: Critical Essays on Eduard Morike*. Ed. Jeffrey Adams. Columbia, SC: Camden House, 1990. 88–94.

Jensen, George H. *Personality and the Teaching of Composition*. Norwood, NJ: Ablex, 1989.

———. *Writing and Personality*. Palo Alto, CA: Davies-Black, 1995.

Jensen, George H., and John K. DiTiberio. *Identities Across Texts*. Cresskill, NJ: Hampton, 2002.

Jensen, Kai. "The Drunkard and the Hag: James K. Baxter's Use of Jung." *Journal of New Zealand Literature* 13 (1995): 211–34.

Jewett, Julia. "'Allerleirauh' (All-Kinds-of-Fur): A Tale of Father Dominance, Psychological Incest, and Female Emergence." Stein and Corbett 1: 17–26.

Joh, Byunghwa. "Thomas Hardy's Love Poems: Lyrics of the Mother-Anima Conflict." *Journal of English Language and Literature* 45.4 (1999): 1101–24.

John, Brian. "Imaginative Bedrock: Kinsella's *One* and the Lebor Gabala Erenn." *Eire Ireland* 20.1 (1985): 109–32.

Johnson, David J. "Anne Sexton's 'The Awful Rowing toward God': A Jungian Perspective of the Individuation Process." *Journal of Evolutionary Psychology* 7.1/2 (1986): 117–26.

Joseph, Gerhard. "Tennyson's Parable of Soul Making: A Jungian Reading of *The Princess*." *CUNY English Forum, Vol. 1*. Ed. Saul N. Brody and Harold Schechter. New York: AMS, 1985. 231–40.

———. "Tennyson's Three Women: The Thought within the Image." *Victorian Poetry* 19.1 (1981): 1–18.

Jurkevich, Gayana. "Archetypal Motifs of the Double in Unamuno's *Able Sanchez*." *Hispania* 73.2 (1990): 345–52.

———. *The Elusive Self: Archetypal Approaches to the Novels of Miguel De Unamuno*.Columbia, MO: U of Missouri P, 1991.

Kaler, Anne K. "*Golden Girls*: Feminine Archetypal Patterns of the Complete Woman." *Journal of Popular Culture* 24.3 (1990): 49–60.

Kaltenbach, Nikki L. *Le Roman de Jaufre: A Jungian Analysis.* New York: Peter Lang, 1997.

Kapacinskas, T. J., and Judith A. Robert. "'Rapunzel': Barrenness and Bounty, Differentiation and Reconciliation." Stein and Corbett 2: 59–78.

Kaplan, Sydney Janet. "Varieties of Feminist Criticism." *Making a Difference: Feminist Literary Criticism.* Ed. Gayle Greene and Coppélia Kahn. London: Methuen, 1985. 37–58.

Karampetsos, E. D. "Ionesco and the Journey of the Shaman." *Journal of Evolutionary Psychology* 4.1/2 (1983): 64–77.

Kawai, Hayao. *The Japanese Psyche: Major Motifs in the Fairy Tales of Japan.* Dallas: Spring, 1988.

Kelley, Sean. *Individuation and the Absolute: Hegel, Jung and the Path toward Wholeness.* New York: Paulist, 1993.

Kenevan, Phyllis Berdt. *Paths of Individuation in Literature and Film: A Jungian Approach.* Lanham, MD: Lexington, 1999.

Kenny, Dorothea. "Whose Woods?" *Journal of Evolutionary Psychology* 7.3/4 (1986): 227–40.

Kerr, John. "Jung in Literary Contexts: The Devil's Elixirs, Jung's 'Theology' and the Dissolution of Freud's 'poisoning complex.'" *Jung in Contexts: A Reader.* Ed. Paul Bishop. London: Routledge, 1999. 125–53.

Kibler, W. W. "Archetypal Imagery in *Floire et Blancheflor.*" *Romance Quarterly* 35.1 (1988): 11–20.

Kimball, Jean. "Eros and Logos in *Ulysses:* A Jungian Pattern." *Gender in Joyce.* Ed. Jolanta W. Wawrzycka and Marlena G. Corcoran. Gainseville: U of Florida P, 1997. 112–32.

———. "Jung's 'Dual Mother' in Joyce's *Ulysses:* An Illustrated Psychoanalytic Intertext." *Journal of Modern Literature* 17.4 (1991): 477–90.

———. *Odyssey of the Psyche: Jungian Patterns in Joyce's* Ulysses. Carbondale: Southern Illinois UP, 1997.

Kinkead-Weakes, Mark. "The Marriage of Opposites in *The Rainbow.*" *D. H. Lawrence: Centenary Essays.* Ed. Mara Kalnins. Bristol, England: Bristol Classical, 1986. 21–39.

Kirschler, Robert. "James Dickey's 'Approaching Prayer': Ritual and the Shape of Myth." *South Atlantic Review* 61.1 (1996): 27–54.

Kitzberger, Ingrid Rosa. "Archetypal Images of Transformation and the Self in Percy Bysshe Shelley's *The Revolt of Islam.*" *Trends in English and American Studies: Literature and the Imagination.* Ed. Sabine Foisner Coelsch, et al. Lewiston, NY: Mellen, 1996. 171–87.

Klein, Lucille. "'The Goose Girl': Images of Individuation." Stein and Corbett 1: 155–66.

Kluckholm, Clyde. "Myth and Ritual: A General Theory." *Ritual and Myth: Robertson Smith, Frazer, Hooke, and Harrison.* Ed. Robert A. Segal. New York: Garland, 1996. 243–77.

Knapp, Bettina L. "Archetypal Saturn/Kronos and the Goya/Malraux Dynamis." *Romance Quarterly* 30.4 (1983): 373–87.

———. *Archetype, Architecture, and the Writer.* Bloomington: Indiana UP, 1986.

———. *Archetype, Dance, and the Writer.* New York: Bethel, 1983.

———. "Bhasa's *The Dream of Vasavadatta:* Archetypal Music—A Sacred Ritual." *Journal of Evolutionary Psychology* 9.1/2 (1989): 113–25.

———. "Baudelaire and Wagner's Archetypal Operas." *Nineteenth-Century French Studies* 17.1/2 (1988): 58–69.

———. *Critical Essays on Marguerite Duras.* New York: G. K. Hall, 1998.

———. *Exile and the Writer: Exoteric and Esoteric Experiences: A Jungian Approach.* University Park, PA: Penn State UP, 1991.

———. *Gerard de Nerval: The Mystic's Dilemma.* University, AL: U of Alabama P, 1980.

———. *A Jungian Approach to Literature.* Carbondale, IL: Southern Illinois UP, 1984.

———. *Jungian Criticism and French Literature.* Baton Rouge: Louisiana State UP, 1982.

———. "Jungian Criticism and French Literature." *L'Esprit Createur* 22.2 (1982): 5–9.

———. "A Jungian Reading of *Novalis: Hymns to the Night*—A Regressus as Uterum." *Research Studies* 49.4 (1981): 204–20.

———. "A Jungian Reading of the *Kalevala* 500–1300: Finnish Shamanism—The Patriarchal Senex Figure III: The Anima Archetype, IV: Conclusion." *Mythlore* 9 (1982): 35–36, 38, 41.

———. "A Jungian Reading of William Butler Yeats' 'At the Hawk's Well': An Unintegrated Anima Shapes a Hero's Destiny." *Etudes Irlandaises* 8 (1983): 121–38.

———. "Machine and Magus in Pirandello's *Tonight We Improvise.*" *Modern Drama* 30.3 (1987): 405–13.

———. *Machine, Metaphor and the Writer: A Jungian View.* University Park, PA: Penn State UP, 1989.

———. "Marcel Proust—Archetypal Music—An Exercise in Transcendence." *Journal of Evolutionary Psychology* 6.3/4 (1985): 250–60.

———. *Music, Archetype and the Writer.* University Park, PA: Penn State UP, 1988.

———. "Stendhal and Correggio: An Archetypal Happening." *Nineteenth-Century French Studies* 13.1 (1984): 1–21.

———. *Theatre and Alchemy.* Detroit: Wayne State UP, 1980.

———. *Women in Twentieth-Century Literature: A Jungian View.* University Park, PA: Penn State UP, 1987.

———. *Women, Myth and the Feminine Principle.* Albany: State U of New York P, 1998.

———. *Word/Image/Psyche.* University, AL: U of Alabama P, 1985.

———. "Yizhar's 'Habakuk'—Archetypal Violin Music and the Prophetic Experience. *Modern Language Studies* 17.3 (1987): 41–53.

Knipe, Rita. *The Water of Life: A Jungian Journey through Hawaiian Myth.* Honolulu: Hawaii UP, 1989.

Komar, Kathleen L. "Klytemnestra in Germany: Re-visions of a Female Archetype by Christa Reinig and Christine Bruckner." *Germanic Review* 69.1 (1994): 20–27.

Kotowski, Nathalie, and Christian Rendel. "Frodo, Sam, and Aragorn in the Light of C. G. Jung." *Inklings* 10 (1992): 145–59.

Kubitschek, Missy Dehn. "'Tuh de Horizon and Back': The Female Quest in *Their Eyes Were Watching God.*" *Black American Literature Forum* 17.3 (1983): 109–15.

Kugler, Paul. "Imagining: A Bridge to the Sublime." *Spring* 58 (1995): 103–22.

———. "Involuntary Poetics." *Spring* 15.3 (1984): 491–501.

Lambadaridou, E. A. "Patrick White's Religion of the Whole Individual." *Parousia* 7 (1991): 297–326.

Lammers, John H. "The Archetypal Molly Bloom, Joyce's Frail Wife of Bath." *James Joyce Quarterly* 25.4 (1988): 487–502.

Lauter, Estella, and Carol Schreier Rupprecht. "Feminist Archetypal Theory: A Proposal." Lauter and Rupprecht 220–37.

———, eds. *Feminist Archetypal Theory: Interdisciplinary Re-Visions of Jungian Thought.* Knoxville: U of Tennessee P, 1985.

Lee-Bonanno, Lucy. "Concha Alos' *Os habla Electra*: The Matriarchy Revisited." *Anales de la Literatura Espanola Contemporane* 12.1/2 (1987): 95–109.

Lee, M. Owen. *Death and Rebirth in Virgil's Arcadia.* Albany: The State U of New York P, 1989.

———. *Virgil as Orpheus: A Study of the Georgics.* Albany: State U of New York P, 1996.

Lemkin, Jonathan. "Archetypal Landscapes and *Jaws.*" *Planks of Reason: Essays on the Horror Film.* Ed. Garry Keith Grant. Metuchen, NJ: Scarecrow, 1984. 277–89.

Leonard, Linda Schierse. *Meeting the Madwoman: An Inner Challenge for Feminine Spirit.* New York: Bantam, 1993.

Lin, Shen fu. "Chia Pao Yu's First Visit to the Land of Illusion: An Analysis of a Literary Dream in Interdisciplinary Perspective." *Tamkang Review* 23.1–4 (1992/93): 431–79.

Lindley, Daniel A. "Dreams of Past Existence: The Archetypal Child." *The Wordsworth Circle* 20.1 (1989): 56–60.

———. "Leaving Home: A Gnostic Note in the Lives of C. G. Jung and T. S. Eliot." *The Allure of Gnosticism: The Gnostic Experience in Jungian Psychology and Contemporary Culture.* Ed. Robert A. Segal, June Singer, and Murray Stein. Chicago: Open Court, 1995. 167–72.

Livernois, Jay. "*The Last Temptation* and the Unknown God." *Spring* 49 (1989): 99–104.

Ljunggren, Magnus. *The Dream of Rebirth: A Study of Andrej Belyj's Novel* Peterburg. Stockholm, Sweden: Almqvist & Wiksell, 1982.

———. *The Russian Mephisto: A Study of the Life and Work of Emilii Medtner.* Stockholm: Almqvist & Wiksell, 1994.

Loomis, Jeffrey B. "Birth Pangs in Darkness: Hopkins's Archetypal Christian Biography." *Texas Studies in Literature and Language* 28.1 (1986): 81–106.

Loyd, D. W. "Beyond the Colonial Novel: The Last Novels of Laurens Van Der Post." *Literature and Theology* 13.4 (1999): 323–32.

Luke, Helen M. *The Inner Story: Myth and Symbol in the Bible and Literature.* New York: Crossroad, 1982.

———. *Through Defeat to Joy: The Novels of Charles Williams in the Light of Jungian Thought.* Three Rivers, MI: Apple Farms, 1980.

Maduro, Renaldo J., and Joseph B. Wheelwright. "Archetype and Archetypal Image." Sugg 181–86.

Maidenbaum, Judith. "*The Scarlet Letter:* A Contemplation of Symbol." *Psychological Perspectives* 15.2 (1984): 181–90.

Mancini, Joseph. "'Bird of Prey' or 'Dawning Day': Hilda as Anima Figure in Ibsen's *Master Builder.*" *Journal of Evolutionary Psychology* 3.1/2 (1982): 41–55.

Marcus, Jane. "A Wilderness of One's Own: Feminist Fantasy Novels of the Twenties: Rebecca West and Sylvia Townsend Warner." *Women Writers and the City: Essays in Feminist Literary Criticism.* Ed. Susan Merrill Squier. Knoxville: U of Tennessee P, 1984. 134–60.

Marks, Martha Alford. "Archetypal Symbolism in *Escuadra hacia la muerte.*" *Estreno* 11.1 (1985): 16–19.

Mathews, James W. "Peter Rugg and Cheever's Swimmer: Archetypal Missing Men." *Studies in Short Fiction* 29.1 (1992): 95–101.

Matthews, Marilyn L. "'The Snow Queen': An Interpretation." Stein and Corbett 2: 79–92.

Maud, Ralph. "Archetypal Depth Criticism and Melville." Sugg 258–68.

May, Claire B. "From Dream to Text: The Collective Unconscious in the Aesthetic Theory of Thomas De Quincey." *Journal of Evolutionary Psychology* 16.1–2 (1995): 75–83.

Mayo, Donald H. *Jung and Aesthetic Experience: The Unconscious as Source of Artistic Inspiration.* New York: Peter Lang, 1995.

McClintick, Michael. "Modern Man in Search of His Art: Jung's Theory of Man's Creative Nature." *Willamette Journal of the Liberal Arts* 4.2 (1989): 13–31.

McCurdy, Jole Cappiello. "The Structural and Archetypal Analysis of Fairy Tales." Stein and Corbett 1: 1–15.

McMaster, Juliet. "The Trinity Archetype in *The Jungle Books* and *The Wizard of Oz.*" *Children's Literature* 20 (1992): 90–110.

Meihuizen, Nicholas. "Yeats, Jung and the Integration of Archetypes." *Theoria* 80 (1993): 101–16.

Mellon, Linda Forge. "An Archetypal Analysis of Albert Camus's 'La Pierre qui pousse.' The Quest as Process of Individuation." *French Review* 64.6 (1991): 934–44.

Messer, Richard E. "Alchemy and Individuation in *The Magus.*" Sugg 343–52.

———. "A Jungian Interpretation of the Relationship of Culture: Hero and Trickster Figure within Chippewa Mythology." *Studies in Religion Sciences* 11.3 (1982): 309–20.

Metz, Christian. *The Imaginary Signifier: Psychoanalysis and Cinema.* Bloomington: Indiana UP, 1982.

Meurs, Jos van. *Jungian Literary Criticism, 1920–1980: An Annotated Critical Bibliography of Works in English.* Metuchen, NJ: Scarecrow, 1988.

Michalson, Karen. "Who Is Dagny Taggart? The Epic Hero/ine in Disguise." *Feminist Interpretations of Ayn Rand.* Ed. Mimi Reisel Gladstein and Chris Matthew Sciabarra. University Park, PA: Penn State UP, 1999. 199–219.

Michta, Natalie Cole. "'Plucked Up Out of a Mystery': Archetypal Resonance in Hawthorne's *Marble Faun.*" *ESQ* 31 (1985): 252–59.

Miller, David L. "The Death of the Clown: A Loss of Wits in the Postmodern Movement." *Spring* 58 (1995): 69–82.

———. *Hells and Holy Ghosts: A Theopoetics of Christian Beliefs.* Nashville: Abdington, 1989.

———. "Spenser's Vocation, Spenser's Career." *ELH* 50.2 (1983): 197–231.

———. "The 'Stone' Which Is Not a Stone: C. G. Jung and the Postmodern Meaning of 'Meaning.'" *Spring* 49 (1989): 110–22.

———. *Three Faces of God: Traces of the Trinity in Literature and Life.* Philadelphia: Fortress, 1986.

Miller, Kristie. "The Letters of C. G. Jung and Medill and Ruth McCormick." *Spring* 50 (1990): 1–25.

Milne, Fred L. "The Anima Archetype in Shelley's Poetry." *Journal of Evolutionary Psychology* 9.3/4 (1988): 236–47.

Mogen, David. "The Frontier Archetype and the Myth of America: Patterns That Shape the American Dream." *The Frontier Experience and the American Dream: Essays on American Literature.* Ed. David Mogen, Mark Busby, and Paul Bryant. College Station: Texas A&M UP, 1989. 15–30.

Monick, Eugene. *Phallos: Sacred Image of the Masculine.* Toronto: Inner City, 1987.

Monk, Patricia. *The Gilded Beaver: An Introduction to the Life and Works of James De Mille.* Toronto: ECW, 1991.

———. *Mud and Magic Shows: Robertson Davies Fifth Business.* Toronto: ECW, 1992.

———. *The Smaller Infinity: The Jungian Self in the Novels of Robertson Davies.* Toronto: Toronto UP, 1982.

Monsman, Gerald. "'Definite History and Dogmatic Interpretation': The 'White-Nights' of Pater's *Marius the Epicurean*." *Criticism* 26.2 (1984): 171–91.

Mootry, Maria K. "Bitches, Whores, and Woman Haters: Archetypes and Typologies in the Art of Richard Wright." *Richard Wright: A Collection of Critical Essays.* Ed. Richard Macksey and Frank E. Moorer. Englewood Cliffs, NJ: Prentice-Hall, 1984. 117–27.

Moretti, Monique Streiff. "Faust-Merlin: A Twin Metamorphosis in Louis Guilloux's *Le Sang noir*." Spivack, *Merlin vs. Faust* 161–87.

Mori, Maryellen T. "Cross-Cultural Patterns in the Quest Fiction of Okamoto Kanoko." *The Comparatist* 20 (1996): 153–78.

Morin, Gertrude. "Depression and Negative Thinking: A Cognitive Approach to *Hamlet*." *Mosaic* 25.1 (1992): 1–12.

———. "*Little More Than Kin*: Expiation and Spiritual Quest." *Journal of Evolutionary Psychology* 11.3/4 (1990): 197–209.

———. "*The Lyre of Orpheus*: A Glimpse of the Future." *Journal of Evolutionary Psychology* 13.3–4 (1992): 261–73.

Mumford, Marilyn R. "A Jungian Reading of *Sir Orfeo* and *Orpheus and Euridice*." *Scottish Studies* 4 (1984): 291–302.

Murphy, Karleen Middleton. "The Emanation: Creativity and Creation." *Sparks of Fire: Blake in a New Age.* Ed. James Bogan and Fred Goss. Richamond, CA: North Atlantic, 1982. 104–14.

Murr, Priscilla. *Shakespeare's* Antony and Cleopatra: *A Jungian Interpretation.* New York: Peter Lang, 1988.

Murray, Margaret P. "The Gothic Arsenal of Edith Wharton." *Journal of Evolutionary Psychology* 10.3/4 (1989): 315–21.

Neuer, Johanna. "Jungian Archetypes in Hermann Hesse's *Demain.*" *Germanic Review* 57.1 (1982): 9–15.

Newman, Robert D. "The Transformative Quality of the Feminine in the 'Penelope' Episode of *Ulysses.*" *Journal of Analytical Psychology* 31 (1986): 63–74.

———. "The White Goddess Restored: Affirmation in Pynchon's *V.*" *University of Mississippi Studies in English* 4 (1983): 178–86.

Noel, Daniel C. "Adios, Don Carlos, We Are the Dumbos: Castaneda's Spiritual Legacy as a Literary Trickster." *Quest* 87.1 (1999): 4–9.

———. "'Muthos Is Mouth': Myth of Shamanic Utterance in Postmodern American Poetry." *Art/Literature/Religion: Life on the Borders.* Ed. Robert Detweiler. Chico, CA: Scholars, 1983. 117–24.

Noland, Richard W. "Individuation in *2001: A Space Odyssey.*" *Journal of Evolutionary Psychology* 15.3–4 (1994): 302–09.

Noll, Richard. "Max Nordau's Degeneration, C. G. Jung's Taint." *Spring 55* (1994): 67–79.

Oakes, Elizabeth. "Polonius, the Man behind the Arras: A Jungian Study." *New Essays on Hamlet.* Ed. Mark Thornton Burnett and John Manning. New York: AMS, 1994. 103–16.

O'Brien, Timothy D. "Archetypal Encounter in 'Mending Wall.'" *American Notes and Queries* 24.9/10 (1986): 147–51.

O'Hara, J. D. "Jung and the 'Molloy' Narrative." *The Beckett Studies Reader.* Ed. S. E. Gontarski. Gainesville: UP of Florida, 1993. 129–45.

———. "Jung and the Narratives of *Molloy.*" *Journal of Beckett Studies* 7 (1982): 19–47.

O'Hara, Patricia. "Primitive Marriage, Civilized Marriage: Anthropology, Mythology and *The Egoist.*" *Victorian Literature and Culture* 20 (1992): 1–24.

Okamuro, Minako. "*Quad* and the Jungian Mandala." *Samuel Beckett Today: An Annual Bilingual Review* 6 (1997): 125–33.

Olney, James. "The Rhizome and the Flower: The Perennial Philosophy—Yeats and Jung." Sugg 118–28.

Oswald, David. "Rilke's Importance to Jungian Psychology." *Rilke Reconsidered.* Ed. Sigrid Bauschinger and Susan L. Cocalis. Tubingen: Francke, 1995. 137–47.

Parker, Alexander A. "Segismundo's Tower: A Calderonian Myth." *Bulletin of Hispanic Studies* 59.3 (1982): 247–56.

Parkin, Andrew. "Women in the Plays of W. B. Yeats." *Woman in Irish Legend, Life and Literature.* Ed. S. F. Gallagher. Totowa, NJ: Barnes & Noble, 1983. 38–57.

Parks, Frances M. "'Maid Maleen': An Image of Feminine Wholeness." Stein and Corbett 2: 1–13.

Patrick, Marietta. "The Transformation Myth in *Edgar Huntly.*" *Journal of Evolutionary Psychology* 10.3/4 (1989): 360–71.

Payne, Judith A. "Anima Rejection and Systematic Violence in *La ciudad y los perros.*" *Chasqui* 20.1 (1991): 43–49.

Perrakis, Phyllis Sternberg. "Sufism, Jung and the Myth of Kore: Revisionist Politics in Lessing's Marriages." *Mosaic* 25.3 (1995): 99–120.

Petersen, Robert C. "Type and Antitype: The Archetype of the Hero in Caroline Gordon's *The Glory of Hera.*" *Southern Literary Journal* 21.1 (1988): 31–38.

Philipson, Morris. "Outline of a Jungian Aesthetics." Sugg 214–28.

Phillips, Robert, and Branimir Rieger. "The Agony and the Ecstasy: A Jungian Analysis of Two Vampire Novels, Meredith Ann Pierce's *The Darkangel* and Bram Stoker's *Dracula.*" *West Virginia University Philological Papers* 31 (1986): 10–19.

Piehler, Paul. "Allegory without Archetype: Image and Structure in Petrarch's *Trionfi.*" *Petrarch's Triumphs: Allegory and Spectacle.* Ed. Konrad Eisenbichler. Toronto: Dovehouse, 1990. 97–112.

———. "Myth or Allegory? Archetype and Transcendence in the Fiction of C. S. Lewis." *Word and Story in C. S. Lewis.* Ed. Peter J. Schakel and Charles A. Huttar. Columbia, MO: U of Missouri P, 1991. 199–212.

Pietikainen, Petteri. *C. G. Jung and the Psychology of Symbolic Forms.* Helsinki, Finland: Academia Scientiarum Fennica, 1999.

Pollock, John J. "*Beowulf* in Jungian Perspective." *Old English Newsletter* 13.2 (1980) 25–27.

Porter, Laurence M. "'L'Amour fou' and Individuation: A Jungian Reading of Breton's *Nadja.*" *L'Esprit Createur* 22.2 (1982): 25–34.

Porterfield, Sally. *Jung's Advice to the Players.* Westport, CT: Greenwood, 1994.

Pratt, Annis V. *Archetypal Patterns in Women's Fiction.* Bloomington: Indiana UP, 1981.

———. "Archetypal Patterns in Women's Fiction." Sugg 367–76.

———. *Dancing with Goddesses: Archetypes, Poetry and Empowerment.* Bloomington: Indiana UP, 1994.

———. "Medusa in Canada." *Centennial Review* 31.1 (1987): 1–32.

———. "Spinning among Fields: Jung, Frye, Lévi-Strauss, and Feminist Archetypal Theory." Lauter and Rupprecht 93–136.

Puchek, Peter. "'Meshes of Fire, Some Great Fish Breaks at Times': Jungian Psychology in Browning's 'Caliban upon Setebos.'" *Journal of Evolutionary Psychology* 18.3–4 (1997): 258–68.

Radford, F. L., and R. R. Wulson. "Some Phases of the Jungian Moon: Jung's Influence on Modern Literature." Sugg 315–27.

Raine, Kathleen. "C. G. Jung: A Debt Acknowledged." Sugg 167–78.

———. *Golgonooza, City of Imagination: Last Studies in William Blake.* Hudson, NY: Lindisfarne, 1991.

———. *The Human Face of God: William Blake and the Book of Job.* London: Thames & Hudson, 1982.

———. *Poetry and the Frontiers of Consciousness.* London: Guild of Pastoral Psychology, 1985.

———. *W. B. Yeats and the Learning of the Imagination.* Ipswich: Golgonooza, 1999.

———. *Yeats the Initiate: Essays on Certain Themes in the Work of W. B. Yeats.* Savage, MD: Barnes & Noble, 1990.

Ramage, John. "Myth and Monomyth in Coover's *The Public Burning.*" *Critique* 23.3 (1982): 52–68.

Richards, David G. *Exploring the Divided Self: Hermann Hesse's* Steppenwolf *and Its Critics.* Columbia, SC: Camden House, 1996.

———. *The Hero's Quest for the Self: An Archetypal Approach to Hesse's* Demian *and Other Novels.* Lanham, MD: UP of America, 1987.

Richardson, Elizabeth A. "*Back to the Future:* Yang – Yin = 0, Yang + Yin = 1." *Extrapolation* 29.2 (1988): 128–39.

Rigsby, Roberta K. "Feminist Critics and Archetypal Psychology: What's in It for Us?" *Lit* 2.3 (1991): 179–200.

———. "Jungians, Archetypalists, and Fear of Feminism." *The 1994 Annual of Hermeneutics and Social Concern.* Ed. Justus George Lawler. New York: Continuum, 1994. 35–58.

Rockwood, Heide. "The Function of Pablo in Hesse's *Steppenwolf.*" *South Atlantic Review* 59.4 (1994): 47–61.

Rode, Edith P. "Blue Lake, Jung, Shiva and Waters." *Studies in Frank Waters, VI.* Ed. Charles L. Adams. Las Vegas: Frank Waters Society, 1984. 76–85.

Rosenberg, Teya. "Romanticism and Archetypes in Ruth Nichols's *Songs of the Pearl.*" *Literature and the Child: Romantic Continuations, Postmodern Contestations.* Ed. James Holt McGavran. Iowa City: U of Iowa P, 1999. 233–55.

Ross, Lena B. "Cupid and Psyche—Birth of a New Consciousness." Stein and Corbett 1: 65–90.

Roth, Lane. "Compensating Scientism through *The Black Hole.*" *Literature and Film Quarterly* 14.1 (1986): 58–63.

———. "Raiders of the Lost Archetype: The Quest and the Shadow." *Studies in the Humanities* 10 (1983): 13–21.

Rowland, Susan. "The Body's Sacred: Romance and Sacrifice in Religious and Jungian Narratives." *Literature and Theology* 10.2 (1996): 160–70.

———. *C. G. Jung and Literary Theory: The Challenge from Fiction.* New York: St. Martin's, 1999.

———. "Feminist Ethical Reading Strategies in Michele Roberts's *In the Red Kitchen:* Hysterical Reading and Making Theory Hysterical." *The Ethics in Literature.* Ed. Andre Hadfield, Dominic Rainsford, and Tim Woods. Houndmills, UK: Macmillan, 1998. 169–83.

———. *From Agatha Christie to Ruth Rendell: British Women Writers in Detective and Crime Fiction.* Basingstoke, UK: MacMillan, 2000.

———. "Imaginal Bodies and Feminine Spirits: Performing Gender in Jungian Theory and Atwood's *Alias Grace.*" *Body Matters: Feminism, Textuality, Corporeality.* Ed. Avril Horner and Angela Keane. Manchester, UK: Manchester UP, 2000. 244–54.

———. *Jung: A Feminist Revision.* Cambridge: Polity, 2001.

———. "Michele Roberts' Virgins: Contesting Gender in Fictions, Re-Writing Jungian Theory and Christian Myth." *Journal of Gender Studies* 8.1 (1999): 35–42.

———. "The Need for Alchemy in *The Dean's December.*" *Saul Bellow Journal* 13.2 (1995): 19–29.

———. "'Transformed and Translated': The Colonized Reader of Doris Lessing's Canopus in Argus Space Fiction." *British Women Writing Fiction.* Ed. H. P. Abby and Regina Barraca. Tuscaloosa: U of Alabama P, 2000. 42–55.

———. "Women, Spiritualism and Depth Psychology in Michele Roberts's Victorian Novel." *Rereading Victorian Fiction.* Ed. Alice Jenkins and John Juliet. New York: Macmillian, 2000. 201–14.

Rowley, Rebecca K. "Individuation and Religious Experience: A Jungian Approach to O'Conner's 'Revelation.'" *Southern Literary Journal* 25.2 (1993): 92–102.

Roy, Emil. "The Archetypal Unity of Eugene O'Neill's Drama." *Critical Approaches to O'Neill.* Ed. John H. Stroupe. New York: AMS, 1988. 1–15.

Rupprecht, Carol Schreier. "Divinity, Insanity, Creativity: A Renaissance Contribution to the History and Theory of Dream/Text(s)." *The Dream and the Text: Essays on Literature and Language*. Ed. Carol Schreier Rupprecht and Norman N. Holland. Albany: State U of New York P, 1993. 112–32.

———. "Enlightening Shadows: Between Feminism and Archetypalism, Literature, and Analysis." *C. G. Jung and the Humanities: Towards a Hermeneutics of Culture*. Ed. Karin Barnaby and Pelligrino D'Acierno. London: Routledge, 1990. 279–93.

Rupprecht, Carol Schreier, and Kelly Bulkly. "Reading Yourself to Sleep: Dreams in/and/as Texts." *The Dream and the Text: Essays on Literature and Language*. Ed. Carol Schreier Rupprecht and Norman N. Holland. Albany: State U of New York P, 1993. 1–12.

Rushing, Janice Hocker. "Evolution of 'The New Frontier' in *Alien* and *Aliens*: Patriarchal Co-optation of the Feminine Archetype." *Quarterly Journal of Speech* 75.1 (1989): 1–24.

Rushing, Janice Hocker, and Thomas S. Frentz. "Integrating Ideology and Archetype in Rhetorical Criticism." *Quarterly Journal of Speech* 77.4 (1991): 385–406.

———. *Projecting the Shadow: The Cyborg in American Film*. Chicago: U of Chicago P, 1995.

Russell, Keith. "Kenosis in Baxter's 'Pig Island Letters.'" *Journal of New Zealand Literature* 13 (1995): 109–20.

Russo, Joseph. " A Jungian Analysis of Homer's Odysseus." *The Cambridge Companion to Jung*. Ed. Polly Young-Eisendrath and Terence Dawson. Cambridge: Cambridge UP, 1997. 240–54.

Rybark, David. "Jedi and Jungian Forces." *Psychological Perspectives* 14.2 (1983): 238–44.

Rzepka, Charles J. "Chekhov's *The Three Sisters*, Lear's Daughters and the Weird Sisters: The Arcana of Archetypal Influence." *Modern Language Studies* 14.4 (1984): 18–27.

Saliba, David. *A Psychology of Fear: The Nightmare Formula of Edgar Allen Poe*. Lanham, MD: UP of America, 1980.

Samuels, Andrew, ed. *The Father: Contemporary Jungian Perspectives*. New York: New York UP, 1986.

———. *Jung and the Post-Jungians*. London: Routledge, 1985.

———. *The Plural Psyche: Personality, Morality, and the Father*. London: Routledge, 1989.

———. *The Political Psyche*. London: Routledge, 1993.

———. *Politics on the Couch: Citizenship and the Internal Life*. New York: Other, 2001.

Samuels, Andrew, Bani Shorter, and Fred Plaut. "Archetype, Myth, Numinosum." Sugg 187–91.

———. "'Trickster.'" Sugg 273–74.

Sarracino, Carmine. *The Scarlet Letter* and a New Ethic." *College Literature* 10.1 (1983): 50–59.

Schaffer, Susan C. "The Process of Individuation in Jose Agustin's *Cerca del fuego.*" *Mester* 21.1 (1992): 31–40.

Schectman, Jacqueline M. *The Step-Mother in Fairy Tales.* Boston: Sigo, 1990.

Scholtz, Antoine M. L. Marquart. "Africa and Creative Fantasy: Archetypes in Three of Isak Dinesen's Tales." *Isak Dinesen: Critical Views.* Ed. Olga Anastasia Pelensky. Athens: Ohio UP, 1993. 283–94.

Schuyler, William M., Jr. "Portrait of the Artist as a Jung Man: Love, Death and Art in J. G. Ballard's *Vermillion Sands, I–II.*" *New York Review of Science Fiction* 5.9 (1993): 8–11.

Sebrell, C. L. "Anais Nin and American Invention." *Spring* 62 (1997): 121–29.

Segal, Robert A., ed. *Anthropology, Folklore, and Myth.* New York: Garland, 1996.

———. *The Gnostic Jung.* London: Routledge, 1992.

———, ed. *The Myth and Ritual Theory: An Anthology.* Malden, MA: Blackwell, 1998.

———, ed. *Psychology and Myth.* New York: Garland, 1996.

———, ed. *Ritual and Myth: Robertson Smith, Frazer, Hooke, and Harrison.* New York: Garland, 1996.

———, ed. *Theories of Myth: Literary Criticism and Myth.* New York: Garland, 1996.

———. *Theorizing About Myth.* Amherst: U of Massachusetts P, 1999.

Seifert, Theodor. *Snow White: Life Almost Lost.* Trans. Boris Matthews. Wilmette, IL: Chiron, 1986.

Seybolt, Richard A. "*La casa de Bernarda Alba:* A Jungian Analysis." *Romance Quarterly* 29.2 (1982): 125–33.

Shafer, Ingrid. "*Mysterium Coniunctionis:* The Alchemical Transformation of Joseph Knecht." *Journal of Evolutionary Psychology* 9.1/2 (1988): 75–86.

Shafer, Yvonne. "Archetypal Figures in *The Caretaker:* Trickster vs. Intruder." *Literature in Performance* 6.2 (1986): 38–43.

Sharp, Daryl L. *The Secret Raven: Conflict and Transformation in the Life of Franz Kafka.* Toronto: Inner City, 1980.

Shawcross, John T. "Milton and Jung's Concepts of the Apocalyptic." *Lit* 2.4 (1991): 275–87.

Sicker, Philip. "The Belladonna: Eliot's Female Archetype in *The Waste Land*." *Twentieth-Century Literature* 30.4 (1984): 420–31.

Sigman, Joseph. "Diamond in the Ashes: A Jungian Reading of the 'Princess' Books." *For the Childlike: George MacDonald's Fantasies for Children.* Ed. Roderick McGillis. Metuchen: Scarecrow, 1992. 183–94.

Sims, Robert L. "Archetypal Approaches." *Approaches to Teaching Garcia Marquez's* One Hundred Years of Solitude. Ed. Maria Elena de Valdes and Mario J. Valdes. New York: MLA, 1990. 97–106.

Singer, June. *Blake, Jung and the Collective Unconscious: The Conflict between Reason and Imagination.* York Beach, ME: Nicolas-Hays, 2000.

Singer, Robert Lewis. "Cinematic Representations: The Merlin/Faust Archetypes in *Excalibur* and *Angel Heart*." Spivack, *Merlin vs. Faust* 95–112.

Smetak, Jacqueline. "Thomas Pynchon's Short Stories and Jung's Concepts of the Anima." *Journal of Evolutionary Psychology* 11.1–2 (1990): 178–94.

Smith, Molly. "Beckettian Symbolic Structure in Sam Shepard's *True West*: A Jungian Reading." *Journal of Evolutionary Psychology* 10.3/4 (1989): 328–34.

Snider, Clifton. "Emily Dickinson and Shamanism: 'A Druidic Difference.'" *San Francisco Jung Institute Library Journal* 14.4 (1996): 33–64.

———. *The Stuff That Dreams Are Made On: A Jungian Interpretation of Literature.* Wilmette, IL: Chiron, 1991.

———. "Victorian Trickster: A Jungian Consideration of Edward Lear's Nonsense Verse." *Psychological Perspectives* 24 (1991): 90–110.

Spignesi, Angelyn. *Lyrical-Analysis: The Unconscious through* Jane Eyre. Wilmette, IL: Chiron, 1990.

Spivack, Charlotte. "Merlin vs. Faust: An Exploration of Contending Archetypes." Spivack, *Merlin vs. Faust* 1–17.

———, ed. *Merlin versus Faust: Contending Archetypes in Western Culture.* Lewiston, NY: Mellon, 1992.

Spivey, Ted R. "Conrad Aiken's Fusion of Freud and Jung." *Studies in the Literary Imagination* 13.2 (1980): 99–112.

———. "Depth Psychology and Aiken's Vision of Consciousness." *Conrad Aiken: A Priest of Consciousness.* Ed. Ted R. Spivey and Arthur Waterman. New York: AMS, 1989. 205–18.

———. *The Journey beyond Tragedy: A Study of Myth and Modern Fiction.* Orlando, FL: UP of Florida, 1980.

Stein, Murray, and David H. Rosen. *Transformation: Emergence of Self.* College Station: Texas A&M UP, 1998.

Stein, Murray, and Lionel Corbett, eds. *Psyche's Stories: Modern Jungian Interpretations of Fairy Tales.* 2 vols. Wilmette, IL: Chiron, 1991–92.

Stevens, Caroline. "'The Old Woman in the Wood.'" Stein and Corbett 2: 15–32.

Stewart, Mary E. "The Refracted Self: Hermann Hesse, 'Der Steppenwolf.'" *The German Novel in the Twentieth Century: Beyond Realism.* Ed. David Midgley. Edinburgh: Edinburgh UP, 1993. 80–94.

Stodder, Joseph H. "Archetypal Criticism in the Teaching of Renaissance Drama." *Journal of Evolutionary Psychology* 4.3/4 (1983): 207–14.

———. "Magus and Maiden: Archetypal Roles in Greene's *Friar Bacon and Friar Bungay.*" *Journal of Evolutionary Psychology* 4.1/2 (1983): 28–37.

Stoneman, Patsy. "The Brontë Legacy: *Jane Eyre* and *Wuthering Heights* as Romance Archetypes." *Rivista di Studi Vittoriani* 3.5 (1998): 5–24.

Stratton, Florence. "The Shallow Grave: Archetypes of Female Experience in African Fiction." *Research in African Literature* 19.1 (1988): 143–69.

Strauch, Edward H. "Implications of Jung's Archetypal Approach for Literary Study." *The Aligarh Journal of English Studies* 7.1 (1982): 1–17.

Sudol, Ronald A. "Self-Representation and Personality Type in 'Letter from Birmingham Jail.'" *Understanding Literacy: Personality Preference in Rhetorical and Psycholinguistic Contexts.* Ed. Alice S. Horning and Ronald A. Sudol. Cresskill, NJ: Hampton P, 1997. 37–54.

Sugg, Richard P., ed. *Jungian Literary Criticism.* Evanston: Northwestern UP, 1993.

———. "Towards a Jungian Criticism: The Case of Fellini and Jung." *Journal of Evolutionary Psychology* 9.1/2 (1989): 41–49.

Sutton, Max Keith. "The Psychology of the Self in MacDonald's *Phantastes.*" *Seven* 5 (1984): 9–25.

Tacey, David J. "In the Lap of the Land: Misogyny and Earth-Mother Worship in *The Tree of Man*; Essays and Poems Presented to Brian Elliott, 11 April 1985." *Mapped but not Known: The Australian Landscape of the Imagination.* Ed. P. R. Eaden and F. H. Mores. Netley, S. Australia: Wakefield P, 1986. 192–209.

———. "Patrick White's *Voss:* The Teller and the Tale." *Southern Review* 18.3 (1985): 251–71.

Talbot, Lynn K. "Female Archetypes in Carmen Martin Gaite's *Entre visillos.*" *Anales de la Literatura Espanola Contemporane* 12.1/2 (1987): 74–94.

Tebbetts, Terrell L. "Dilsey and the Compsons: A Jungian Reading of Faith and Fragmentation." *Publications of the Arkansas Philological Association* 21.1 (1995): 78–98.

———. "Giving Jung a Crack at the Compsons." *Approaches to Teaching Faulkner's* The Sound and the Fury. Ed. Stephen Hahn and Arthur F. Kinney. New York: MLA, 1996. 79–83.

————. "A Jungian Reading of Othello's Fictive Self." *Publications of the Mississippi Philological Association* (1995): 106–11.

————. "Pageants for False Gaze: Jungian Perfectabilty in *Othello.*" *Publications of the Arkansas Philological Association* 23:2 (1997): 91–112.

Terrill, Robert E. "Put on a Happy Face: Batman as Schizophrenic Savior." *Quarterly Journal of Speech* 79.3 (1993): 319–35.

Theriot, Ibry G. F. "The Bitch Archetype." *Journal of Dramatic Theory and Criticism* 9.1 (1994): 119–33.

Thompson, Currie K. "The House and the Garden: The Architecture of Knowledge and *La muerte de Artemio Cruz.*" *Hispania* 77.2 (1994): 197–206.

Thompson, David. "Supinely Anticipating Red-Eyed Shadows: A Jungian Analysis of Bram Stoker's *Dracula.*" *Journal of Evolutionary Psychology* 15.3–4 (1994): 289–301.

Thompson, Raymond. "Jungian Patterns in Ursula K. Le Guin's *The Farthest Shore.*" Coyle 189–95.

Timmerman, John H. "Plath's 'Mirror.'" *Explicator* 45.2 (1987): 63–64.

Toomey, David M. "A Jungian Reading of *Light in August's* 'Christmas Sections.'" *The Southern Quarterly* 28.2 (1990): 43–57.

Tucci, Nina S. "Baudelaire's 'Les Sept Vieillards': The Archetype Seven, Symbol of Destructive Time." *Orbis Litterarum* (1989): 69–79.

Tucker, Ken. "Warring Within and Warring Without: A Psychological Nexus between Shakespeare's *Troilus and Cressida* and Tasso's *Jerusalem Delivered.*" *Journal of Evolutionary Psychology* 17.1–2 (1996): 109–24.

Tucker, Kenneth. "The Sword and the Shadow: A Jungian Reading of Malory's *Tale of Balin.*" *Journal of Evolutionary Psychology* 12.1–2 (1991): 2–16.

Turner, Dixie M. *A Jungian Psychoanalytic Interpretation of William Faulkner's* As I Lay Dying. Washington, DC: UP of America, 1981.

Turner, John. "David Elder: Between Freud and Jung." *D. H. Lawerence Review* 27 (1997–1998): 289–309.

Ulanov, Ann, and Barry Ulanov. *Cinderella and Her Sisters: The Envied and the Envying.* Philadelphia: Westminster, 1983.

Underwood, June O. "Experimental Forms and Female Archetypes: Lillian Hellman's *Pentimento.*" *Publications of the Missouri Philological Association* 5 (1980): 49–53.

Vanden-Driesen, Cynthia. "The Artist and Society: Jung and Patrick White." *Australian Literature Today.* Ed. R. K. Dhawan and David Kerr. New Delhi: Indian Society for Commonwealth Studies, 1993. 119–32.

Van Nuis, Hermine J. "'The Heart in Pilgrimage': A Jungian Reading of George Herbert's 'The Alter' and 'Iesu.'" *Readerly Writerly Texts* 4.1 (1996): 135–46.

Vazsonyi, Nicholas. "Deflated Hybris-Uncertain Telos: The Humbling of Faust and the Revival of Merlin." Spivack, *Merlin vs. Faust* 41–64.

Vieira, Nelson H. "Joao e Maria: Dalton Trevisan's Eponymous Heroes." *Hispania* 69.1 (1986): 45–52.

Waldron, Robert G. "Thomas Merton's *The Sign of Jonas:* A Jungian Commentary." *Merton Annual* 4 (1991): 59–68.

Walker, Steven F. "Magical Archetypes: Midlife Miracles in *The Satanic Verses*." *Magical Realism: Theory, History, Community*. Ed. Lois Parkinson Zamora and Wendy B. Faris. Durham: Duke UP, 1995. 347–70.

Watanabe, Nancy Ann. "Yeats's Merlin-Faust Design in *The Countess Cathleen*." Spivack, *Merlin vs. Faust* 140–59.

Weatherly, Joan. "The Death of Big Sister: Orwell's Tragic Message." *College Literature* 11.1 (1984): 22–33.

Wehr, Demaris S. *Jung and Feminism: Liberating Archetypes*. Boston: Beacon, 1987.

Welsh, Robert. "The Poet-Philosopher Confronts His Shadow: Tennyson's 'Lucretius.'" *Journal of Evolutionary Psychology* 15.3–4 (1994): 283–88.

Wesche, Ulrich. "The Spirit's Chorus in *Faust:* A Jungian Reading." *Germanic Notes* 14.4 (1983): 49–51.

West, Lon. *Deconstructing Frank Norris's Fiction: The Male-Female Dialectic*. New York: Peter Lang, 1998.

Whitlark, James. *Behind the Great Wall: A Post-Jungian Approach to Kafkaesque Literature*. Cranbury, NJ: Associated UP, 1991.

———. "A Post-Jungian Approach to Kafka." *Journal of the Kafka Society of America* 9.1/2 (1985): 145–60.

———. "Superheroes as Dream Doubles." Coyle 107–12.

Whitman, Allen. *Fairy Tales and the Kingdom of God*. Pecos, NM: Dove, 1983.

Wing, Helen. "Deviance and Legitimation: Archetypal Traps in Roig's *La hora violeta*." *Bulletin of Hispanic Studies* 72.1 (1995): 87–96.

Willeford, William. "Feeling, Imagination, and the Self." Sugg 200–13.

———. "The Fool and His Sceptre." Sugg 275–84.

———. "Myth Criticism." *Theories of Myth: Literary Criticism and Myth*. Ed. Robert A. Segal. New York: Garland, 1996. 367–70.

Williams, Anne. "Browning's 'Childe Roland,' Apprentice for Night." *Victorian Poetry* 21.1 (1983): 27–42.

Williams, Tony. "Jack London and Carl G. Jung: An Alternative Reading." *Jack London Journal* 3 (1996): 127–45.

Williamson, Eugene. "Plato's *Eidos* and the Archetypes of Jung and Frye." *Interpretations* 16.1 (1985): 94–104.

Wit, Adriaan de. "The Archetype of the Puer Aeternus in *La Valse des toreadors;* Or, the Refusal to Grow Up." *Journal of Evolutionary Psychology* 7.1/2 (1986): 2–13.

———. "*Le Neveu de Rameau:* Diderot's Doppelganger." *Journal of Evolutionary Psychology* 1.3 (1980): 192–98.

———. "Mothers and Stepmothers in Fairy Tales and Myths." *Journal of Evolutionary Psychology* 6.3/4 (1985): 315–28.

Woods, Douglas K. *Men Against Time: Nicolas Berdyaeu, T. S. Elliot, Aldous Huxley, and C. G. Jung.* Lawrence, KS: UP of Kansas, 1982.

Wright, Eleanor. "The Anacreontic Odes by Juan Melendez Valdes: Archetypes and Aesthetic Form." *Dieciocho* 10.1 (1987): 18–31.

Yarbo, Chelsea Quinn. "Cinderella's Revenge: Twists on Fairy Tale and Mythic Themes in the Work of Stephen King." *Fear Itself: The Horror Fiction of Stephen King.* Ed. Tim Underwood and Chuck Miller. San Francisco: Underwood-Miller, 1982. 45–55.

Young, Gloria L. "Quest and Discovery: Joseph Conrad's and Carl Jung's African Journeys." *Modern Fiction Studies* 28.4 (1982/83): 583–89.

Youngren, Mary Ann. "*The Journey:* An Analysis of Its Symbolic Imagery." *Willamette Journal of the Liberal Arts* 5 (1991): 45–54.

Zahner-Roloff, Lee. "'Snow White and Rose Red': Contained Oppositions." Stein and Corbett 2: 111–22.

Zimmerman, Michael. "Archetypes, Heroism and the Work of Art." *Philosophy and Archaic Experience: Essays in Honor of Edward G. Ballard.* Ed. John Sallis. Pittsburgh: Duquesne UP, 1982. 81–98.

CONTRIBUTORS

SOPHIA ANDRES is Associate Professor of English at the University of Texas, Permian Basin. A specialist in English Pre-Raphaelite and Victorian literature, her recent publications include "Elizabeth Gaskell's Re-Presentations of Pre-Raphaelite Gendered Boundaries" (*The Journal of Pre-Raphaelite Studies* 11 [2002]: 39–62). She is currently completing a book manuscript, "Reconfigurations of Pre-Raphaelite Gender Constructs in the Victorian Novel."

J. R. ATFIELD is Lecturer in English at Brunel University (UK), where she teaches linguistics, composition, and creative writing. Her publications include "Seeing Things in a Jungian Perspective" (*Agenda* 33 [1996]: 131–43) and "The Stain of Absolute Possession: The Postcolonial in the Work of Eavan Boland," a chapter (189–207) in *Contemporary Women's Poetry: Reading/Writing/Practice*, ed. Alison Mark and Deryn Rees-Jones (New York: Palgrave, 2001). Her current project, "Seamus Heaney: A Jungian Perspective," is under contract from Edwin Mellen Press.

JAMES S. BAUMLIN is Professor of English at Southwest Missouri State University, where he teaches English Renaissance literature and the history of rhetoric. His publications include *John Donne and the Rhetorics of Renaissance Discourse* (Columbia, MO: U of Missouri P, 1991) and *Rhetoric and Kairos: Essays in History, Theory, and Praxis*, co-edited with Phillip Sipiora (Albany, NY: State U of New York P, 2002).

TITA FRENCH BAUMLIN is Professor of English at Southwest Missouri State University. A specialist in Shakespeare and early modern drama, she is editor of the scholarly journal *Explorations in Renaissance Culture* and co-editor (with James S. Baumlin) of *Ethos: New Essays in Rhetorical and Critical Theory* (Dallas: Southern Methodist UP, 1994).

OLIVER DAVIS is Lecturer in French at Wadham College, Oxford. He is currently working on representations of aging in twentieth-century French autobiography and theory. Although neither a Jungian nor exactly a post-Jungian by affiliation, he is interested in the possibilities of theoretical exchange between different branches of the psychoanalytic tradition. He is collaborating as a translator on an essay collection, *French Women Philosophers: Subjectivity and Identity*, ed. Christina Howells (London: Routledge, forthcoming).

ANDREW ELKINS is Dean of the School of Arts and Sciences at Peru State College. His publications include *The Poetry of James Wright* (University, AL: U of Alabama P, 1991), which was awarded the Elizabeth Agee Prize, and *The Great Poem of the Earth: A Study of the Poetry of Thomas Hornsby Ferril* (Moscow, ID: U of Idaho P, 1997), which received the Western Literature Association's 1998 Thomas J. Lyon Award.

LUKE HOCKLEY is Head of the Department of Media Arts at the University of Luton (UK). His research interests cover film, television, and new media. Recent publications include *Cinematic Projections: The Analytical Psychology of C. G. Jung and Film Theory* (Luton: U of Luton P, 2001).

GEORGE H. JENSEN is Professor of English at Southwest Missouri State University, where he coordinates the graduate program in rhetoric. His numerous Jung-related publications include *Personality and the Teaching of Composition* (Norwood, NJ: Ablex, 1989) and *Writing and Personality* (Palo Alto, CA: Davies-Black, 1995), both coauthored with John K. DiTiberio, and *Identities Across Texts* (Cresskill, NJ: Hampton, 2002).

JAMES T. JONES is Professor of English at Southwest Missouri State University, where he teaches American literature and critical theory. A founding member of the Jung Center in Dublin, Ireland, Professor Jones's Jung-related publications include *Map of Mexico City Blues: Jack Kerouac as Poet* (Carbondale: Southern Illinois UP, 1992) and *Jack Kerouac's Duluoz Legend: The Mythic Form of an Autobiographical Fiction* (Carbondale: Southern Illinois UP, 1999).

REBECCA MEACHAM is Assistant Professor at the University of Wisconsin, Green Bay, where she teaches creative writing, twentieth-century American fiction, ethnic American literatures, and cultural theory. Her dissertation comprises a collection of her own short stories as well as a scholarly analysis of African American short fiction published between 1980 and 2000. An essay, "Teaching Nappy Hair and the Entanglements of 'Taking Things Too Personal,'" has appeared in *Race in the Classroom*, ed. Bonnie T. Smith and Maureen Reddy (New Brunswick, NJ: Rutgers UP, 2002).

MARCIA NICHOLS has recently completed her M.A. in English literature at Southwest Missouri State University. Her master's thesis features applications of post-Jungian theory and a bibliography of recent Jungian and post-Jungian literary criticism.

KEITH POLETTE is Director of the English Education program at the University of Texas at El Paso. His Jungian-inspired analyses include "Imagining Language: Shifting from Word-Processing to Arche-Typing," in *The Writer as Hero: Archetypes, Creativity and the Unconscious*, ed. Regina Foehr (Portsmouth, NH: Heinemann, forthcoming), and "Desert Voices: Southwestern Children's Literature" (*Children's Literature in Education* 28 [1997]: 163–75).

SALLY PORTERFIELD is Professor of Drama at the University of Hartford. Her *Jung's Advice to the Players* (Westport, CT: Greenwood, 1994) remains a seminal archetypal analysis of Shakespearian drama.

SUSAN ROWLAND is Senior Lecturer in English at the University of Greenwich (UK), where her teaching interests include Jung, literature, and postmodernism. She is the author of *C. G. Jung and Literary Theory: The Challenge from Fiction* (New York: St. Martin's, 1999), *From Agatha Christie to Ruth Rendell: British Women Writers in Detective and Crime Fiction* (New York: Palgrave, 2001), and *Jung: A Feminist Revision* (Cambridge: Polity, 2001).

ANDREW SAMUELS is Professor of Analytical Psychology at the University of Essex (UK), Visiting Professor of Psychoanalytic Studies at Goldsmith's College, University of London, and Training Analyst of the Society of Analytical Psychology, London. His numerous publications include *Jung and the Post-Jungians* (London: Routledge, 1985); *The Father: Contemporary Jungian Perspectives* (New York: New York UP, 1986); *The Plural Psyche: Personality, Morality, and the Father* (London: Routledge, 1989); *Psychopathology: Contemporary Jungian Perspectives* (New York: Guilford, 1990); *The Political Psyche* (London: Routledge, 1993); and *Politics on the Couch: Citizenship and the Internal Life* (New York: Other, 2001).

INDEX

Abe, Masao, 248, 254, 255
Abrams, Jeremiah, 199, 200
Adams, Michael, 3, 82, 84, 152, 201, 202, 203, 204
Aeneas, 191, 192
African Americans, 199–219; development of consciousness of object/subject by, 204; movement from white shadow, 200; "Negro sickness" and, 205–210; qualities associated with, 203–204; self-reclamation and, 200
African Free School and Spirit House, 200
African Negritude, 206
Afrikan Revolution (Jones), 217
Afrocentrism, 215
"After Work" (Hirshfield), 248
Agency: personal, 10; political, 10
Albedo themes, 210, 211
Alchemy, 2
Allen, Robert, 95, 98, 99, 113n5
Andres, Sophia, 21, 139–156
Anima, xiv, 13–15, 31–33, 177; as antitheoretical voice within, 47; characteristics of, 13, 32; characterized as unreliable women, 42; cultural construction of, 26n22; defining, 14, 31–33; falling in love and, 150–151; fantasies, 52n1; feminist criticism and, 13; gender role and, 14; irrationality of, 34; masculine reason v. feminine

unreason in, 34; occult and, 32; phallic qualities of, 45, 46, 48; as resister of theory, 35; seeking, 171; as storytelling mode, 22; as symbolic feminine, 45; theoretical development of, 22; women and, 46
Anima Mundi, 112
Animus, 13–15; awakening of female ego and, 121; characterizations of, 13; conflict with, 122; cultural construction of, 26n21; defining, 13–14; feminist criticism of, 13; gender role and, 14; partnership with, 133; patriarchy and, 14; as personal destroyer, 125; as personal ideal, 136n5; possession, 124–125; projection of, 123, 169; separation from, 130; traditional patriarchal ideals and, 125; as transpersonal ravishing penetrator, 128
Anti-Semitism, viii, ix, 3, 4, 25n13
Anti-textualism, 64–67
Appearance(s): underlying structures of, 94
Archetypes, viii; activation of, 189; androgynous, 46; collective, 185; collective unconscious and, 6–9; consciousness and, 239; constellated, 135n3; content of, 26n19; culture and, 7, 160–161; dreams and, 193; ego and, 11; evolution of, 7;

Lodge, David, 118
Logocentrism, 39, 41, 44
Lowell, Robert, 184, 185, 195
Lyotard, Jean-François, 16

MacCurdy, Marian, 5
MacLeash, Archibald, 106
Mahony, Patrick, 2
Malcolm X, 208, 212
"Man and Boy" (Heaney), 191
Marc, David, 97, 102
"Markings" (Heaney), 192
Marsden, Steve, 226
Masson, Jeffrey, 2
Materialism, 9
Maynard, John, 118, 122, 123, 130, 136n6
Meacham, Rebecca, 199–219
Meaning: assignment of, 7; conventional schemes of, 44; of culture, 42; institutionalized forms, 44; language and, 39; of psyche, 42; slippage of, 39; static image and, 67; symbolism and, 67; transparent, 7
Media: criticism and, 22; popular, 22
Meier, C.A., 244, 245
Memories, Dreams, Reflections (Jung), 17, 31, 32, 33, 34, 36, 226, 236
Memory, 2, 23n3; accuracy of, 2, 4; bodily kinds of, 5; categories of, 4; recovered, 5
Merrill, Thomas, 231
Millais, John Everett, 142, 143, 144, 145
Miller, Arthur, 161
Miller, Jacques-Alain, 64
Mitchell, Juliet, 61
Mitroff, Ian, 18
Mnemosyne, 101, 103, 112
Modernism, 16; rationality and, 25n13; unconscious foundation of, 4
Moglen, Helene, 118, 134
Moore, Thomas, viii, 253

Moral(ity): boundaries, 187; conventional, 150; polarization of issues in, 234; rectitude, 190; threats to, 243
Morrison, B., 191, 192
Moss, Anita, 109
Mother as archetype, 107–112, 117, 164, 168, 206
Musticism, viii
"Myriad Leaves of Words, The" (Hirshfield), 246
Mysterium Coniunctionis (Jung), 9, 26n22
Mysticism, x
"Myth of the Rainy Night" (Kerouac), 234
Myth(s): articulation of modern-day tensions and, 186; castration, 136n6; in collective unconscious, 67; criticism, 89; existential, 166; feminist, 134; living, 184; personal, 33–36, 37, 41, 45; priority of archetypal images over, 67; religious quality of, 183; as revelation of divine life in man, 190; triad feature, 163, 164; truth of, 134; ultimate end of, 183

Narcissism, 166; regressive, 101
Narrative(s). *See also* Literature: antifoundational, 48; extended, 67; gaps in, 5; historically contingent, 48; mythical, 185; personal, 5; postmodernism and, 47; religious, 34; space, 33
"Nation Is Like Ourselves, The" (Jones), 200
Negro Sickness, 205–210, 212
Nemerov, Howard, 113n3
"Nerthus" (Heaney), 187, 188
Neumann, Erich, 7, 8, 9, 26n19
New Criticism, 1, 11, 25n15
Nietzsche, Friedrich, 65, 72n8
Nigredo, 210
Nine Gates: Entering the Mind of Poetry (Hirshfield), 246, 247